M000119316

BEHOLD
THE
CHRIST

BEHOLD
THE
CHRIST

PROCLAIMING THE GOSPEL
OF MATTHEW

LEROY A. HUIZENGA

EMMAUS
ROAD
PUBLISHING

Steubenville, Ohio
www.emmausroad.org

Emmaus Road Publishing
1468 Parkview Circle
Steubenville, Ohio 43952

©2019 Leroy A. Huizenga
All rights reserved. Published 2019
Printed in the United States of America

Library of Congress Control Number: 2019950121

ISBN: 9781645850090

Unless otherwise noted, Scripture quotations are taken from The Revised Standard Version Second Catholic Edition (Ignatius Edition). Copyright © 2006 by the Division of Christian Education of the National Council of the Churches of Christ in the United States of America. Used by permission. All rights reserved.

Excerpts from the Catechism of the Catholic Church, second edition, copyright © 2000, Libreria Editrice Vaticana–United States Conference of Catholic Bishops, Washington, D.C. Noted as "CCC" in the text.

Nihil Obstat and Imprimatur
The Most Reverend David D. Kagan, D.D., P.A., J.C.L.,
Bishop of Bismarck
October 16, 2019

It is understood that the Nihil Obstat and Imprimatur are official declarations that a book or pamphlet is free of doctrinal or moral error. No implication is contained therein that those who have granted them agree with the content or statements expressed.

Cover image: "Jesus Christ, Crucifixion." Photo by: Alem Sánchez
Cover design and layout by Emily Demary

TABLE OF CONTENTS

PREFACE

☩

THE GOSPEL OF MATTHEW has been the Church's favorite since written accounts of Jesus began circulating in the first century. Full of stories of Jesus's doings, and records of his clear teaching, the early Church found Matthew's Gospel most useful. Indeed, the Gospel of Matthew grounds the greatest Christian doctrines—such as the Virgin Birth, Jesus's sacrificial death, and his resurrection—with simplicity and clarity, while also providing fundamental resources for devotion—such as the Lord's Prayer—and teachings like the Golden Rule.

Above all, the Gospel of Matthew is a story of fulfillment: it tells how passages, prophecies, stories, and personages from the Old Testament find their consummation in Jesus Christ. St. Matthew presents a rich picture of Jesus: a new Moses, a new Isaac, the Suffering Servant, the Christ, Israel embodied, and even the God of Israel incarnate. In showing how Jesus fulfilled the Old Testament, St. Matthew modeled the way of reading Scripture that would later be codified as the "fourfold sense."

Beyond these reasons, the early Church also put Matthew's Gospel first in the canon of Scripture because the Fathers regarded it as the work of an eyewitness to Jesus's mighty works and words—namely, St. Matthew, Matthew Levi the tax collector.

But modern scholarship in the nineteenth century came to the consensus that the Gospel of Mark was first, not the Gospel of Matthew. Attempting to solve the "synoptic problem"—how the Gospels of Matthew, Mark, and Luke, who see ("optic") Jesus's life together ("syn") in very similar ways, are related to one another—the consensus of scholars rejected St. Matthew's authorship of the gospel that bears his name for several reasons.

First, the scholarly consensus doubted the veracity of early Church traditions as an operating principle, including what the Church Fathers believed about authorship of New Testament documents. Second, the consensus regarded the Gospel of Mark as primitive, with bad Greek, a human Jesus, deficient content, and haphazard organization. Third, as the consensus arose in the nineteenth century, scholars assumed evolutionary processes happened in literature like they do in Darwinian biology. Thus, the Gospel of Mark being worst, it must have been first; things go from lower to higher. That meant that the Gospel of Matthew, in which scholars found a divine Jesus, decent Greek, important content, and good organization, must have come later, and thus used Mark as a source.

But that made problems for St. Matthew's authorship of the Gospel of Matthew. Why, scholars asked, would an eyewitness like St. Matthew copy and edit wide swaths of the Gospel of Mark if he really witnessed what Jesus said and did? If the Gospel of Matthew was dependent on the Gospel of Mark, it made the historical St. Matthew's authorship of the Gospel that bears his name highly unlikely.

Further, the belief that the Gospel of Matthew came later than the Gospel of Mark fit scholars's worldview and prejudices most conveniently. The academic consensus was developed largely by liberal Protestant scholars. While brilliant and gifted, they were enamored with Enlightenment philosophy and were anti-Catholic in a genteel sort of way, and so they rejected out-of-hand miracles, the fulfillment of prophecy, sacrificial understandings of Jesus's death and the Eucharist, and the idea that Jesus would have founded a church. The Gospel of Mark does not have the story of the Virgin Birth, appearances of the risen Jesus, or Jesus founding the Church on Peter and giving him the keys to the kingdom of heaven; the Gospel of Matthew has all three. The consensus thus holds that many things traditional Christianity and Catholicism especially hold most dear did not come from Jesus himself but were later developments invented by the early Church. Things like the Virgin Birth and Jesus's resurrection appearances were mythology borrowed from paganism and the Old Testament, and the hierarchical offices were a later concoction invented in the second century after Christianity went decadent, becoming a Church concerned with the twin evils of structure and dogma.

Moreover, believing the Gospel of Matthew to be dependent on the Gospel of Mark, later scholars accepting the liberal Protestant consensus developed a method of interpretation called "redaction criticism." "Redaction" comes from a German word meaning "editing," and redaction critics thus compare similar passages in the Gospels of Mark and Matthew and ask how the anonymous author of the latter would edit the text of the former, and find meaning there, in the changes, passage by passage.

In doing so, they lost the plot. Reading the Gospel of Matthew with Enlightenment convictions reduced Jesus to a teacher of mere morals, the only thing remaining once prophecy, miracles, sacrifice, and Church are stripped away. Further, because redaction criticism simply compares common passages between Gospels, it ignores the story form of the Gospel of Matthew as the author actually wrote it—it takes passages out of their contexts in the Gospel's storyline to compare them to the similar passage in the Gospel of Mark. Thus, they lost the fundamental story of St. Matthew's Gospel and so missed its real message.

This modest work, written for those with serious interest in what the Gospel of Matthew is all about, is an attempt at recovering St. Matthew's story as he composed it. When we read St. Matthew's Gospel as a story with the convictions of St. Matthew's Christian worldview, we will find it to be a compelling drama narrating how Jesus the Christ came to save Jews and Gentiles by means of the Faith and sacraments that the Church he founded delivers to the world.

The Gospel of Matthew is massive in terms of its import and substance; treating every detail in each passage is not possible in an efficient work like the present volume. Therefore, I will focus more on how the contours of the story affect our reading of the Gospel than on the explication of every detail; I will emphasize the whole more than the parts. In doing so, I hope to fill the void, as few narrative treatments of the Gospel of Matthew exist. For more details and consideration of technical issues, readers can turn to critical commentaries.

This book is divided into two parts. In the first part, we'll look at the basics of Matthew's Gospel and how its emphasis on religious discipline and ritual confronts and challenges our contemporary Gnostic age of Moral Therapeutic Deism (I explain these concepts in depth in the first part of this book). While I discuss interpretation and preaching, I do not simply represent what I discussed in my prior book on Mark's Gospel, *Loosing the Lion: Proclaiming the Gospel of Mark*,[1]

---

[1]   Dr. Leroy A. Huizenga, *Loosing the Lion: Proclaiming the Gospel of Mark* (Steubenville, OH: Emmaus Road, 2017).

though readers may want to consult that work for its reflections on the task of preaching. In the second part, we'll read through St. Matthew's story as it is keyed to the lectionary in an attempt to help homilists and Mass-goers make ever better sense of the Gospel of Matthew.

A note on the language of "Christ" and "Messiah": Both words mean "anointed one," the former coming from Greek (*christos*) and the latter from Hebrew (*mashiach*). By the time of Jesus most Jews were expecting an end-time Christ/Messiah in the mold of the original Christ/Messiah, David, anointed by Samuel to be king (1 Sam 16:1–13), who, like King David, would establish a kingdom, this time forever and ever. It has become fashionable in scholarship to use "Messiah" in English instead of "Christ" to recover and reinforce for modern readers the fact that Jesus was Jewish. In this way of thinking, the use of "Christ" supposedly sounds too Gentile and too Christian and thus obscures Jesus's Jewish religious and ethnic identity. While I regard it as absolutely crucial to remember Jesus's Jewish identity as a matter of both history and theology, I question this line of thinking, and so use "Christ" in most places (except on occasion where style commends the use of "messianic" as a ready adjective; "Christological" would work but is associated with later dogmatics concerning Jesus's person and natures; and "Christianic" would be a most barbarous neologism). St. Matthew wrote his Gospel in Greek as a Greek-speaking Jew, as were the majority of Jews in the Roman Empire, and so uses the Greek *christos* throughout his Gospel. In my judgment, then, "Christ" captures the Jewish nature of Jesus, as *christos* was a fully Jewish term and concept with the widest currency.

My thanks to Bishop Paul J. Swain and Mr. Matthew Althoff of the Diocese of Sioux Falls, South Dakota, for inviting me to give the talks on the Gospel of Matthew out of which this book grew. Thanks also to the staff at Emmaus Road for their hard work. Finally, thanks are due to my wife and children, whose love and support make my vocation as teacher and scholar possible.

Feast of Saints Peter and Paul
June 29, 2019

I. The Challenge of St. Matthew's Gospel to the Spirit of the Age

CHAPTER 1

✝

PREACHING MATTHEW'S GOSPEL IN A POSTMODERN AGE

FROM THE COMING OF SIN IN GENESIS 3 TO TODAY, the World has been hostile to God and his people. Israel is at the mercy of the nations, often oppressed from without while suffering from iniquity, infidelity, and idolatry within. Existing among the nations, the Church, too, is a martyr Church, often at odds with the powers of the World even in those ages in which Christendom supposedly reigned. The World is not heaven, and the World is not the Church. We shouldn't expect, then, any of our Scriptures to fit comfortably with the spirit of any given age. The Scriptures always challenge the World.

In our postmodern times, the spirit of the age runs counter to the spirit of the Gospel of Matthew at every turn. For our moment finds itself spiritual, and not religious, hostile to ritual, rules, and righteousness. It rejects any constraints and all boundaries. It seeks affirmation, not salvation. It even attempts to recruit Jesus himself as a mascot for its views and desires instead of submitting to Jesus as Master.

The Gospel of Matthew, on the other hand, presents a Jesus who teaches the disciplines that make for righteousness and institutes a decisive ritual, the Eucharist, for his Church, over which the Apostles rule, with Peter at their head, holding the power of the keys. And Matthew's Jesus is no mere rabbi; he's the Christ, the Son of God, even God himself come to be with his people (Matt 1:23) and perfect them (Matt 5:48), accompanying them even until the end of the age (Matt 28:20). As such, St. Matthew's Gospel provides the perfect message for confronting the spirit of our times. Against our libertine, creation-denying, body-hating regime of Gnostic ideology, the Gospel of Matthew proclaims a religion rooted in creation, transforming it into the new creation. It completes nature with grace, through embodied discipleship and material sacraments.

CONFRONTING OUR GNOSTIC EMPIRE OF DESIRE

We live now in the West under a Gnostic empire of desire. But what is Gnosticism? It's basically a radical reading of Plato as regards matter and the body. In Plato's dialogues, the senses deceive and the visible realm is illusory and in constant flux, whereas the invisible realm of the spirit is stable, unchanging, and ultimately Real. We have knowledge of it through the spiritual soul's contemplation of it. And so, in Plato's dialogues, the body is a problem. Indeed, it's described even as a tomb and a prison,[1] neither of which are nice places.

Gnosticism, then, as radical Platonism, is a worldview which sees matter, and thus bodies, not just as a problem but as fundamentally evil, something that imprisons and entombs

---

[1] Plato, *Phaedo* 66b–67b; *Phaedrus* 250c; *Cratylus* 400b–c.

spirits. And so the true essence of a person is the spirit. And seeing the body as a prison or tomb, Gnosticism strains for spiritual liberation from the body's constraints.

Gnosticism was the greatest heretical challenge to the early Church prior to Nicaea. Christian Gnostics basically interpreted Christian beliefs through the lens of their radical Platonism. And so they necessarily believed in at least two gods, with the creator-god of the material, visible world as presented in the Old Testament being an evil deity responsible for imprisoning spirits in bodies. But the kind, loving father-god of Jesus as presented in the New Testament worked to liberate spirits from bodies.

With regard to humanity, Gnosticism was, and is, also elitist, holding that there is a hierarchy within humanity. The highest rank comprises the pneumatics, the "spirituals" (as *pneuma* in Greek means "spirit"). These people have spirits that can be liberated from their bodies. The next rank comprises the psychics, "soulish" people (*psyche* meaning "soul") who may not be able to be saved, as they lack spirits, but who, having souls, can achieve some degree of illumination. And the final rank comprises the vast mass of humanity, the *hylics* (*hule* meaning "matter"), who are only bodies, lacking spirits and souls. They're cattle, and cannot be illuminated or saved.

Salvation for Gnosticism is a matter of knowledge. Indeed, that's where "Gnostic" comes from, as the Greek word for knowledge is *gnōsis*, as in the English words *prognosis* (knowledge of how a disease will progress), *diagnosis* (knowledge of a disease through its symptoms), and *agnostic* (someone who doesn't know if there's a god). One must know that reality is really how Gnostics understand it, know that one belongs to the elite who can be saved, and know the secret code that will liberate spirit from body.

Secrecy: Gnosticism trades in it. The elites simply know

the very structure of the universe and the secret code of salvation. They also have claimed to know secret sayings of Jesus. Gnostic Gospels composed long after Jesus lived concoct secret sayings of Jesus and conversations with him in which he happens to support their ideology. For instance, the *Gospel of Thomas*, a collection of supposed sayings of Jesus created by a Gnostic school around the middle of the second century, begins, "These are the secret sayings which the living Jesus spoke and which Didymos Judas Thomas wrote down." The *Gospel of Judas*, composed around the middle of the third century, begins, "The secret account of the revelation that Jesus spoke in conversation with Judas Iscariot during a week three days before he celebrated Passover." Of course, the Church Fathers would also point out that the claim of secrecy was a necessary device for those making up teachings Jesus himself never uttered.[2]

The Gnostic ideology meant three major things in the realm of faith and morals, all flowing from the idea that matter, and thus bodies, is intrinsically evil. In terms of the Faith, it meant sacraments were senseless. Sacraments are essentially God working through matter, but Gnostics regard matter as intrinsically evil. In terms of morality, it meant that babies were bad; what else is a newborn but seven pounds of

---

[2] See St. Irenaeus, *Adversus haereses* 2.2.1–2.4.1. In 3.3.1 he writes, "We are in a position to reckon up those who were by the apostles instituted bishops in the Churches, and [to demonstrate] the succession of these men to our own times; those who neither taught nor knew of anything like what these heretics rave about. For if the apostles had known hidden mysteries [*recondita mysteria*], which they were in the habit of imparting to 'the perfect' apart and privily from the rest, they would have delivered them especially to those to whom they were also committing to the Churches themselves" (*Ante-Nicene Fathers: The Writings of the Fathers Down to A.D. 325*, 10 vols., eds. Alexander Roberts and James Donaldson [repr., Peabody, MA: Hendrickson, 2004], 1:415; hereafter abbreviated as ANF).

inherently evil matter? And so Gnostics advocated and practiced contraception and abortion, both of which existed in the ancient world. And again as regards morals, Gnostics were often antinomian, meaning that they rejected any rules or laws (Greek, *nomos*) disciplining the body, and so felt free to engage in licentious behavior; if the body doesn't matter, why not use it as we please?[3]

At every point, then, Christian Gnosticism understood the Christian story in a way diametrically opposed to the Church's understanding of her own story. Catholics, such as St. Irenaeus, fought Gnosticism by emphasizing the ancient rule of faith (*regula fidei*) going back to Jesus. The rule of faith as found in the Church Fathers looks much like what we know today as the Apostles's Creed. It's monotheist, affirming there is one God, the Creator, who made everything, including matter and bodies: "I believe in God the Father Almighty, Creator of heaven and earth." It's Trinitarian: "I believe in Jesus Christ, his only Son, our Lord"—and so

---

3 Carpocrates was an ancient Christian Gnostic whose heresies, especially the communal sharing of wives, came under especial fire from certain Church Fathers. Theodoret says that the members of his sect regard licentiousness as law (*Compendium Haereticarum Fabularum* 1.5). St. Clement of Alexandria says, "They purify themselves for this licentiousness. Their baptism is out of responsible self-control into sexual immorality. Their philosophy is the gratification of their pleasures and passions. They teach a change from self-discipline to indiscipline. The hope they offer is the titillation of their genitals" (*Stromateis* 3.2.9, in *Stromateis, Books 1–3*, trans. and ed. John Ferguson, Fathers of the Church Patristic Series 85 [Washington, DC: Catholic University of America Press, 2005], 325; see the wider section at 3.2.5–10). St. Irenaeus says, "They lead a licentious life" (*Adversus haereses* 1.25.3 [ANF 1:351]) and "the 'most perfect' among them addict themselves without fear to all those kinds of forbidden deeds of which the Scriptures assure us that 'they who do such things shall not inherit the kingdom of God'" (*Adversus haereses* 1.6.3 [ANF 1:324]). But the logic can cut the other way, too, leading some Gnostics to extreme asceticism: if the body is evil, best not to feed its passions for food, drink, or sex in any way.

the Creator God is the Father of Jesus, not a different God. And of course the third person of the Trinity is affirmed, and that Spirit guides and empowers the visible Church. For that reason, Church follows Spirit in the rule of our Faith and in our Apostles's Creed: "I believe in the Holy Spirit, the holy Catholic Church."

And as regards supposedly secret traditions known to the elite leaders of the Gnostic antichurch, St. Irenaeus affirmed apostolic succession (he himself traces his lineage back to Jesus through his mentor Polycarp and Polycarp's mentor, St. John the Apostle[4]) in the visible Church established by Jesus and declared that anyone could walk into any Catholic church and find true Christian teaching being proclaimed publicly there.[5] And not only teaching but sacraments were there as well. The Creator God, Father of the Lord Jesus Christ, made matter and he works through matter, giving his people sacramental nourishment for body and soul. And on that point, the Catholic Church was for everyone, for there is no fundamental division of humanity. Every single person has a spiritual soul, not just a body, from the Emperor and the sage to the lowest slave. As regards morality, the early Church rejected contraception and abortion.

GNOSTICISM AND AMERICAN CULTURE

Gnosticism is not merely ancient. As a perennial ideology, it has proven itself a powerful cultural current through the centuries. In the middle ages it resurfaced in the heresy of Albigensianism (or Catharism), which denied the necessity of the Church and its sacraments for salvation, as sacraments are

---

[4] St. Irenaeus, *Adversus haereses* 3.3.4; and *Fragments* 2.

[5] Irenaeus, *Adversus haereses* 3.3.1.

material. And many in our own day have found America to be fundamentally Gnostic.[6] Americans flee the constraints of the visible world, particularly the limitations of the body. White Americans fled Europe, a product of history with all the constraints historical legacy imposes, and founded a republic based on an idea. While the Founders attempted to establish a republic founded on what the Declaration of Independence termed the "Laws of Nature, and Nature's God," Americans today are at heart revolutionaries for revolution's sake alone, rebelling now not against oppressive monarchies for the sake of ordered liberty but rebelling against the very truths of Nature and Nature's God.

Americans today are like Gnostics, then, in rejecting any and all constraints. For us, freedom is antinomian license. During his visit to the United States in 1998, Pope St. John Paul II reminded Americans of the true nature of freedom:

> Surely it is important for America that the moral truths which make freedom possible should be passed on to each new generation. Every generation of Americans needs to know that freedom consists not in doing what we like, but in having the right to do what we ought.[7]

With these words, John Paul was attempting to correct our warped understanding of freedom. For Americans today see freedom as freedom from any and all constraints, any and

---

[6] See Harold Bloom, *The American Religion* (New York: Simon & Schuster, 1992); and Cyril O'Regan, *Gnostic Return in Modernity* (Albany: State University of New York Press, 2001).

[7] Pope St. John Paul II, Homily of His Holiness John Paul II, Oriole Park at Camden Yards, Baltimore (October 8, 1995), https://w2.vatican.va/content/john-paul-ii/en/homilies/1995/documents/hf_jp-ii_hom_19951008_baltimore.html.

all rules, any and all laws, while true freedom is having the freedom to live virtuous lives ordered to the Good.

Alongside the throwing off of constraints comes the rejection of the body as a gift given by God. In recent years extreme body piercing and tattooing have become common, while disorders like anorexia and bulimia are on the rise, all of which at the least reflect confusion regarding the goodness of the body as given, and even its rejection. So too with the more obvious examples of elective cosmetic surgery, body modification, and sex change operations (or "gender reassignment surgery," as it's now often called). Some people have even used surgery to make themselves resemble zombies or dragons.

Gnosticism is also seen in America's ready acceptance of contraception and our abortion regime. Progressives now see contraception as an absolute right that must be provided by private employers, government entities, and even religious organizations, while under our abortion administration, over fifty million have died before seeing the light of day. Robert George, a Catholic who serves as the McCormick Professor of Jurisprudence at Princeton University, writes:

> The moral implications [of contemporary Gnosticism] are clear. It is personal life that we have reason to hold inviolate and protect against harm; by contrast, we can legitimately use other creatures for our purposes. So someone who buys into a Gnostic anthropology that separates person and body in the way I have described will find it easier to speak of those with undeveloped, defective, or diminished mental capacities as non-persons. They will find it easier to justify abortion; infanticide; euthanasia for the cognitively impaired; and the production, use, and destruction of human embryos for biomedical research.

By the same token, such an anthropology under-writes social liberalism's rejection of traditional marital and sexual ethics and its vision of marriage as a male-female union. That vision makes no sense if the body is a mere instrument of the person, to be used to satisfy subjective goals or produce desirable feelings in the person-as-conscious-subject. If we are not our bodies, marriage cannot essentially involve the one-flesh union of man and woman, as Jewish, Christian, and classical ethics hold. For if the body is not part of the personal reality of the human being, there can be nothing morally or humanly important about "merely biological" union, apart from its contingent psychological effects.[8]

GNOSTICISM AND THE LAW

Gnosticism, particularly in the form of the licentiousness of the sexual revolution, has come to infect American jurisprudence as well. The legal regime legitimizing contraception and abortion (and indeed the broader sexual revolution) is not found in the text of the Constitution but rather in its shadows, the "penumbras" and "emanations." In his opinion in Griswold vs. Connecticut (1965), which struck down state laws banning contraception, Justice William O. Douglas wrote, "The foregoing cases suggest that specific guarantees in the Bill of Rights have penumbras, formed by emanations from those guarantees that help give them life and substance. Various guarantees create zones of privacy." Ancient Gnostics used the same terms—"penumbras" and "emanations"—and

---

[8] Robert P. George, "Gnostic Liberalism," *First Things* 268 (December 2016): 33–38, at 34–35, https://www.firstthings.com/article/2016/12/gnostic-liberalism.

their elites simply knew what was found in those shadowy domains by virtue of being the elite, much like our justices simply know that a right to privacy undergirding the ideology of the sexual revolution is somehow there not in the words but in the shadows of the Constitution. Quoting the late Supreme Court Justice Antonin Scalia, the late jurist and one-time Supreme Court nominee Robert Bork writes:

> Most members of the Court seem to be Gnostics, firmly believing they have access to wisdom denied the rest of us. "What secret knowledge, one must wonder, is breathed into lawyers when they become Justices of this Court?" Scalia has asked. "Day by day, case by case, [the Court] is busy designing a Constitution for a country I do not recognize."[9]

Jurisprudential Gnosticism is found in Justice Anthony Kennedy's decision in *Planned Parenthood vs. Casey* (1992), which upheld and strengthened the abortion regime of *Roe vs. Wade* (1973). Writing for the majority, Kennedy asserted:

> These matters, involving the most intimate and personal choices a person may make in a lifetime, choices central to personal dignity and autonomy, are central to the liberty protected by the Fourteenth Amendment. At the heart of liberty is the right to define one's own concept of existence, of meaning, of the universe, and of the mystery of human life. Beliefs about these

---

[9]   Robert Bork, "The End of Democracy? Our Judicial Oligarchy," *First Things* 67 (November 1996): 21–24, at 21, https://www.firstthings.com/article/1996/11/the-end-of-democracy-our-judicial-oligarchy.

matters could not define the attributes of personhood were they formed under compulsion of the State.[10]

If Gnosticism is radical Platonism, this is radical Gnosticism. Kennedy does not argue for his claim that liberty has at its heart "the right to define one's own concept of existence, of meaning, of the universe, and of the mystery of human life," he just asserts it. He simply *knows* it, as the most elite of an elite, the functional swing vote of the Supreme Court of the United States. He has secret knowledge, somehow.

Our Gnosticism is more relativistic than ancient Gnosticism, however. The ancient Gnostics, at least, believed that the invisible was an objective, stable realm, ultimate Reality, the same for everyone, even if the visible realm was inconstant illusory flux. For Americans today, however, invisible, ultimate Reality is also up for grabs, defined as whatever any individual wants it to be. Gnostics had the principle of universal doctrine, true for everybody. Kennedy's quote encapsulates the total relativism of our age: we now believe Reality is whatever someone wishes it to be.

This is why we may speak of a Gnostic empire of desire. The Gnostic empire involves the imperious tendency to promote the sexual revolution by force of the majesty of the law, a revolution which has desire at the center of its conception of the self.

Classical Judeo-Christian anthropology saw man as a body–soul composite, with the soul as the seat of the intellect and will ruling the passions. In the Enlightenment's "Age of Reason," man was seen chiefly as a mind, and reason was regarded as universal and supreme. But the postmodern age, inaugurated in philosophy and culture by Friedrich

---

[10] Planned Parenthood v. Casey, 505 U.S. at 852 (1992).

Nietzsche, saw desire as primary. Nietzsche counterposed Dionysian passion against Apollonian reason, predicting the essence of our postmodern age. The desires of the self now define individuals.

As Orthodox writer and social critic Rod Dreher points out, this means we are operating with a new cosmology at odds with historic Western, Judeo-Christian cosmology, which put the procreative union of man and woman as the image of God at the center of its cosmology. Dreher writes:

> Gay marriage signifies the final triumph of the Sexual Revolution and the dethroning of Christianity because it denies the core concept of Christian anthropology. In classical Christian teaching, the divinely sanctioned union of male and female is an icon of the relationship of Christ to His church and ultimately of God to His creation. This is why gay marriage negates Christian cosmology, from which we derive our modern concept of human rights and other fundamental goods of modernity. Whether we can keep them in the post-Christian epoch remains to be seen.[11]

And so identity is now bound up with desire, and our Gnostic jurisprudence sees its task as defending and promoting the expression of the self's desires against any and all would-be legal and cultural constraints. In explaining the "New Gnosticism" undergirding the Supreme Court's finding of a right to gay marriage in *Obergefell vs. Hodges*, Sherif Girgis writes:

---

[11] Rod Dreher, "Sex After Christianity," *The American Conservative* (April 11, 2013), https://www.theamericanconservative.com/articles/sex-after-christianity/.

The Court did not simply allow new relationships; it required their recognition as marriages, as similar to opposite-sex bonds in every important way. In other words, it didn't simply free people to live by the New Gnosticism. It required us, "the People," to endorse this dogma, by forbidding us to enact distinctions that cut against it. It held that your dignity demands more than the freedom to lead your life as a purely spiritual subject. It requires us all to treat you as a purely spiritual subject. Anything else is demeaning; it implies that you are essentially bound by a body.

It's not that the New Gnostics are an especially vindictive bunch. It's that a certain kind of coercion is built into their view from the start. If your most valuable, defining core just is the self that you choose to express, there can be no real difference between you as a person, and your acts of self-expression; I can't affirm you and oppose those acts. Not to embrace self-expressive acts is to despise the self those acts express. I don't simply err by gainsaying your sense of self. I deny your existence, and do you an injustice. For the New Gnostic, then, a just society cannot live and let live, when it comes to sex. Sooner or later, the common good—respect for people as self-defining subjects—will require social approval of their self-definition and -expression.[12]

In short, people are what they feel they desire to be, in spite of their bodies, and for anyone to deny their felt identity is a fundamental injustice, which the Law cannot tolerate.

---

[12] Sherif Girgis, "Obergefell and the New Gnosticism," *First Things* "Web Exclusives" (June 28, 2016), https://www.firstthings.com/web-exclusives/2016/06/obergefell-and-the-new-gnosticism.

GNOSTICISM AND RELIGION

Contemporary Gnosticism is a totalizing ideology that brooks no opposition and tolerates no dissent. Now ideologies pretend to be philosophies, but they're not. A philosophy, in principle, is flexible; it reacts to Truth. It can adjust itself as its adherents use their reason to wrestle with the ultimate Reality it attempts to approach.[13] A philosophy is not doctrinaire. An ideology, by contrast, is inflexible, believing it has the ultimate Truth of Reality. Its adherents do not engage in deep, rational reflection, for their ideology is a projection of their deepest desires. They simply think they know with absolute certainty that they're right because their feelings about their identity and their picture of the universe is so strong. Philosophies involve convictions, but one of those convictions is the freedom to explore Reality and adjust one's philosophy as needed. Ideology, by contrast, believes the answers are already known, that there's nothing left to explore, and so it coerces others to belief.[14]

Contemporary Gnosticism therefore employs all sorts of techniques in service of compulsion, from mass media to law. It wants to separate humans from all tradition and social locations (family, community, and so on) that serve as natural points of opposition. Separated from tradition, family,

---

[13] Eric Voegelin is the premier theorist of contemporary Gnosticism in the West. He writes: "Its aim is knowledge of the order of being, of the levels of hierarchy of being and their interrelationships, of the essential structure of the realms of being, and especially of human nature and its place in the totality of being. Analysis, therefore, is scientific and leads to a science of order through the fact that, and insofar as, it is ontologically oriented" (*Science, Politics and Gnosticism* [Wilmington, DE: Intercollegiate Studies Institute, 2005], 13).

[14] Voegelin believes that a defining characteristic of contemporary Gnosticism is the "prohibition of questions" (*Science, Politics and Gnosticism*, 17).

culture, and nature, the individual becomes a subject of the State facing the stick of coercion. But there's also a carrot. Like all ideologies, contemporary Gnosticism entices postmodern men and women with promises of a perfect utopia, a heaven on earth in the here and now, if only we trust elites to run with their plans for us. Gnostic ideologues promise to rip heaven down to earth, to force the eschaton now, but quite apart from Jesus. As such, ideology is idolatry: the State replaces Jesus, forcing a false heaven for the true one, the kingdom of heaven his Second Coming will bring.[15] In short, elite sophisticates replace God.

Gnostic ideologies therefore deceive. The result is that the individual is set against nature. The order of the cosmos that philosophy seeks and finds is replaced by the false order asserted by the ideologue. Disorientation results; on a practical level, subjects of totalitarian societies, such as ours is becoming, are pulled between what they perceive to be the truths of nature and what the State asserts must be the truth. In totalitarian societies, such as the former communist eastern Europe, people either become true believers in the ideological system or they come to realize that they are living under an enforced lie. Those who take the red pill either suffer under the lie or join the resistance.

That's the totalizing way of the sexual revolution: most people believe in men and women, but that's fast becoming a belief that will get one written out of polite society and penalized by the law. Those of us who recognize the lie either keep

---

[15] The Catechism finds in this "secular messianism" the Antichrist: "The Antichrist's deception already begins to take shape in the world every time the claim is made to realize within history that messianic hope which can only be realized beyond history through the eschatological judgment. The Church has rejected even modified forms of this falsification of the kingdom to come under the name of millenarianism, especially the 'intrinsically perverse' political form of a secular messianism" (CCC 676).

our heads down (which for some may be a justified, advisable, prudential path) or engage in acts of subtle or overt resistance.

Gnosticism is our root worldview, and it issues forth today on a more practical level as "Moral Therapeutic Deism," a phrase coined by sociologists Christian Smith and Melissa Lundquist Denton in *Soul Searching: The Religious and Spiritual Lives of American Teenagers*.[16] They summarize Moral Therapeutic Deism (MTD) in five points:

1. A God exists who created and orders the world and watches over human life on earth.
2. God wants people to be good, nice, and fair to each other, as taught in the Bible and by most world religions.
3. The central goal of life is to be happy and to feel good about oneself.
4. God does not need to be particularly involved in one's life except when God is needed to resolve a problem.
5. Good people go to heaven when they die.[17]

"Deism" is the idea that God made the world and then stepped away from it. God's not intimately involved; there is no Providence. "Moral" comes from the concern to be a generally good person. "Therapeutic" concerns feelings and brings us closest to Gnosticism: we live in a therapeutic age, in which feelings dominate and now determine much in religion, culture, politics, and law.[18]

---

[16] Christian Smith and Melissa Lundquist Denton, *Soul Searching: The Religious and Spiritual Lives of American Teenagers* (New York: Oxford University Press, 2005).

[17] Smith and Lundquist Denten, *Soul Searching*, 162–163.

[18] See Phillip Rieff, *The Triumph of the Therapeutic: Uses of Faith after Freud* (Wilmington, DE: Intercollegiate Studies Institute, 2006).

Finally, like ancient Gnosticism, our contemporary age of Moral Therapeutic Deism seeks to reimagine Jesus as a mascot for its ideology. Modernist Christianity, rooted in the Enlightenment, sought to adapt its understanding of Christian faith to the latest knowledge in secular domains—the sciences, hard and soft, as well as philosophy and ethics. It therefore was, and is, embarrassed by the miraculous and the sacrificial, both of which belonged to an unscientific premodern age. And so modernist Christians sought to save the faith for modernity by purifying it of all that modernity rejects. What is left over is ethics; Jesus is preserved as a great moral teacher of enduring relevance through demythologization— that is, through stripping away the miraculous and sacrificial myths around his legend and going "behind the Gospels" to find a historical Jesus congenial to the spirit of the age. Even here, however, with regard to ethics, Jesus is understood to teach what the Enlightenment believed anyway, and so Jesus was remade in the image of (say) the German Philosopher Immanuel Kant.

So too now in our postmodern age. We make a malleable Messiah in our image, a tolerant, inclusive Jesus, a breaker of all boundaries who does so purely for the sake of transgression, and all those who would insist on maintaining religion's traditional rules and rituals are written off as rigid, pilloried as Pharisees. Far from seeing him as our Master, the postmodern age makes Jesus our mascot, the one who affirms our favored causes and affirms us in our deepest selves, where we find ourselves defined by our severest desires.

But that means we're trapped; in our desire to escape from all constraints, we're constrained by desire. We're imprisoned by our very selves, slaves to our passions, even making them the determiners of our very identity. Trying to find an escape from our bodies, we find ourselves ensnared even more deeply by the passions that define ourselves. And as St. Augustine famously prayed to God, "Without you, what am I to myself but a guide to my own self-destruction?"[19]

St. Augustine's solution to self-entrapment in one's own passions is the gospel: God, both the Creator outside of us creatures and yet also inside us, is closer to us than we are to ourselves: "You were more inward than my most inward part and higher than the highest element within me."[20] And this Creator God comes to us in Jesus Christ to reorder our disordered passions and restore us to our true selves found only in Christ.

This, I think, is the way of St. Matthew, who in his Gospel tells how the God of Israel came to us in Jesus to be Emmanuel, God with us (Matt 1:23), to give us back our truest selves, to rightly order our passions, to form us body and soul to be like Christ himself through Christ's own power. He gives us the gifts of his New Messianic Law and indeed himself in the sacraments, in and through the Church he founded. Following the broad way that leads to destruction, we can remain slaves to the self, or following the narrow way that leads to life, we can become servants of Christ.

THE APPEAL OF GNOSTICISM

If Gnosticism is so bad, why have so many people through the ages found it so appealing? Gnosticism tells a captivating counterstory to the Christian story of salvation history, a story that allows one to reject traditional Christianity while still claiming the name. In the time of the early Church, as we have seen, the Gnostics proclaimed that a wicked creator

---

[19] St. Augustine, *Confessions* 4.1.1, in *Saint Augustine: Confessions*, trans. Henry Chadwick (Oxford: Oxford University Press, 2008), 52.

[20] St. Augustine, *Confessions* 3.6.11 (p. 43).

god trapped divine spirits in the evil of material bodies, and so for them salvation consisted of the escape from the body and indeed all of material creation, an opportunity provided by the higher, kind, and loving god, the father of Jesus Christ. That god sends the divine son to appear like a man to teach the spiritual elite, the pneumatics, the secret to spiritual liberation.

The Gnostic story is compelling then and now because it squares with historic human experience and promises an easy way out, the way of knowledge (as opposed to faith). For most people, life is hard and often miserable. Thomas Hobbes, an English philosopher of the 1600s, described the fundamental essence of human existence in the hypothetical state of nature as "solitary, poore [sic], nasty, brutish, and short."[21] For most of human history, this has been the case. Ancient skeletal remains reveal that over ninety percent of humans suffered from malnutrition. Famine and plague were regular threats. Many children, perhaps more than half, died in infancy, and many women died in childbirth.[22] And this is not merely the situation in the ancient or medieval world. In Florence at the height of the Renaissance, sixty-one percent of children died before their first birthday.[23] And we need say little about

---

[21] Thomas Hobbes, *Leviathan*, Penguin Classics (1651; repr., New York: Penguin, 1985), 186.

[22] A poignant epitaph from Pannonia Inferior (dated to the second century AD) reveals the realities of life and death in the ancient world: "Here do I lie at rest, a married woman, Veturia by name and descent, the wife of Fortunatus, the daughter of Veturius. I lived for thrice nine years, poor me, and I was married for twice eight. I slept with one man, I was married to one man. After having borne six children, one of whom survives me, I died. Titus Julius Fortunatus, centurion of the Second Legion *Adiutrix Pia Fidelis*, set this up for his wife: she was incomparable and notably respectful to him" (*Corpus Inscriptionum Latinarum* 3.3572, in *Roman Social History: A Sourcebook* [New York: Routledge, 2007], 52).

[23] James M. Kittelson, *Luther the Reformer: The Story of the Man and His Career* (Minneapolis: Fortress, 2003), 34.

twentieth-century disasters, as they are well known. The year 1918 saw over one hundred million people die of influenza; five hundred million people were infected out of a world population of 1.8 billion. The two World Wars saw about seventy million dead, and Communism is blamed for another seventy million deaths. Stable food supplies and radically decreased mortality and morbidity resulted only recently from the postwar boom in the United States and western Europe.

And so Gnosticism is appealing to the degree that one finds the world horrible, for *it explains extreme pain and suffering in a coherent but extreme way, and promises a way out.* Suffering is not our fault but rather the creator-god's, and salvation is not found *through* suffering but is defined as *escape* from suffering and all that causes suffering.

The desire to explain and escape suffering is why various flavors of Gnosticism are so appealing today. Think of modern people, often affluent and pampered members of the upper classes, uttering statements like, "I wouldn't want to bring a child into this horrible world." That's Gnosticism speaking, and that Gnostic attitude undergirds our contraception and abortion regime. Or think of popular televangelists who present a heretical Christianity promising health, wealth, and freedom from suffering in the here and now. That, too, is fundamentally Gnostic.

CHAPTER 2

✝

THE CATHOLIC STORY

So MUCH, THEN, FOR GNOSTICISM, its implications, and its appeal. What we are dealing with is a clash of narratives, two competing stories, one original and the other a parasitic twisting of the original. Now our Christian story is the original. It came before the Gnostic story, which deformed the Christian story by reading it through radical Platonism. The Christian story claims that there is one Creator God, good and loving. Pain and suffering result from Original Sin, bequeathed to the human race by Adam and Eve. Salvation was achieved by the real suffering in soul and body of Jesus Christ, and our salvation depends on sharing in his suffering: "If any man would come after me, let him deny himself and take up his cross and follow me" (Matt 16:24). And ultimate salvation consists in the redemption of the entire creation (Rom 8:18–23), with our bodies transformed and glorified (1 Cor 15:20–28, 35–58).

In the Christian story, then, suffering is the fault of the human race abusing the gift of free will, but it is now also the means to our salvation, whether Christ's suffering or our own united to his. With and in Christ, we're not saved *from* suffering; we're saved *by* suffering, Christ's, as well as ours when united to Christ's. No wonder, then, many today either reject or twist true Christianity. We moderns are simply allergic to suffering.

Let's take a deeper look at the Christian drama of redemption, then, which the Gospel of Matthew assumes and retells. It's a story in four basic acts: Creation, Fall, Redemption, and Glory.

1. *Creation.* Creation is really the fundamental Christian doctrine, perhaps the only Christian doctrine. That he is Creator is the most important fact about God, making him different from all other conceptions of God, and all Christian doctrines flow from the doctrine of creation. The doctrine of sin (hamartiology) addresses how creation is fallen. The doctrines about salvation, grace, Jesus (Christology), and the Church (ecclesiology) concern how God redeems creation. The doctrine of the end times (eschatology) concerns how God will bring redemption to its ultimate completion. All Christian theology is fundamentally about the Creator and the making, fall, and redemption of his creation.

In creation, the one God makes all things visible and invisible out of absolutely nothing (the Latin theological term is *ex nihilo*). Creation is the "beginning"; even time and space are created. Creation is not God sticking stuff into empty time and space but rather the making of time and space itself, as well as things visible and invisible.

Pagans thought otherwise: whether dealing with crude myths or the highest reflections of Aristotle, the pagan notion is that everything existed in the past and will exist eternally into the future. There is no beginning and no end. Even myths that look like creation stories—whether in ancient Babylonian texts such as the *Enuma Elish* or in Plato's dialogue

Timaeus—have divine agents fashioning the order of the cosmos out of preexisting stuff.

But Genesis teaches (and so Jews and Christians believe) that God made all out of nothing, *ex nihilo*. But why does it matter? What's the significance? The Christian doctrine of creation *ex nihilo* means this: God is totally Lord over everything because he made it. Conversely, everything owes its very existence to God the Creator; nothing can exist apart from him at any moment. The pagan notion implies that God (or the gods) isn't fully in control: stuff, or matter, or the primordial soup, has always existed, and so any god is not supreme; stuff has a somewhat independent existence from the divine. (Because of this, it's improper to speak of pagan stories of "creation.") But in Judaism and Christianity, God the Creator is the reason why everything exists, and so He's truly and totally Lord over all his creation.

Further, Genesis affirms that God made everything good, seven times over (Gen 1:4, 10, 12, 18, 21, 25, 31). In spite of what we now see in the world, in defiance of Gnostic claims to the contrary, God the Creator made everything fundamentally good, and even after the Fall, creation remains good.

The highest expression of that goodness is found in marriage and procreation. In Genesis 1 the human race is made in the image of God (1:26) as male and female (1:27) and commanded, "Be fruitful and multiply, and fill the earth and subdue it" (1:28). At the end of Genesis 2, God takes the one human and cleaves him in two, making a woman from his side, so that in marriage the two, male and female, become one, a man now leaving mother and father to cleave to his wife (Gen 2:18–25). Human love now becomes not just a possibility but a reality.

Finally, human love points to the answer of the question of why does God create anything. The answer is simply love. God created out of love, and human love reveals something about divine love. Here we must be careful. We throw around the phrase "God is love" carelessly, and most people assume that means that our notion of love is God. But when Christians, following the Bible, say God is love, they mean two things: First, God's very essential nature is *agapē, caritas*, those strong, Greek and Latin words we translate as "love." Second, God is the Holy Trinity of Father, Son, and Holy Spirit, and to say God is love is then to declare the truth that Father, Son, and Holy Spirit love each other perfectly; God is a Trinitarian communion of love, each of the divine persons loving the others.

The human race is made in the image of God (Gen 1:26), and since God is a Trinity of love, the image of God is found in fruitful human love, in marriage. In Trinitarian theology, the Father and Son love each other, and their love generates a third, the Holy Spirit, who in turn is the bond of love between Father and Son.[1] In marriage, husband and wife love each other, and their love generates children. The human family is the image of the Holy Trinity. And just as the persons of the Trinity cannot be separated, nothing should separate the persons of the family. That's the deep reason why Christians historically (and, sadly, Catholics alone today) reject divorce, contraception, and abortion. Those unloving things divide the persons of the family from each other, while the persons of the human family are to have the same sort of indivisible relationships the persons of the Holy Trinity have.

In creation, God makes a world into which the divine love of the Father, Son, and Holy Spirit may flow outside of himself. And so God commands procreation so that human love may flow outside of itself in children and into the world.

---

[1] St. Augustine, *On the Trinity* 15.17.24.

Procreation is a furthering of creation.

2. *Fall.* If creation is good, why does life look so bad? The Christian answer is that Adam and Eve abused their free will; they chose poorly. Instead of loving the God who loved them into existence and gave them everything they should have, they chose disobedience, wanting to be like God in the wrong way, taking the shortcut of the forbidden fruit. As a result, the whole cosmos got corrupted; both moral and natural evils resulted.

Moral evils pertain to persons; when they sinned, Adam and Eve corrupted the human nature we all inherit. Original Sin isn't simply their first sin in Genesis 3, but the sin at the origins of the human race, which is now a congenital condition for us. But what about natural evils, which pertain to impersonal things? How does the sin of Adam and Eve introduce chaos into the entire cosmos?

The answer is that Adam and Eve are made of the stuff of earth. The man was fashioned from the dust of the ground (Gen 2:7), and the woman from his side (2:21-22). As man and woman were made from the stuff of earth, when they sinned, they corrupted not only their souls but also their bodies and indeed the very stuff of earth from which they were made. Thus all creation is tarnished, not just the human race, and so all creation, not just people, will be redeemed.[2]

It is often asked why God would allow humans free will and risk the Fall, especially when he, being all-knowing, must have known full well what would happen. The short answer is that love requires freedom; true love must be truly free. On this point we can do no better than C. S. Lewis:

---

[2] That's why St. Paul will speak of the redemption of the entire creation in Romans 8:20-23. Redemption involves not just people, but everything.

God created things which had free will. That means
creatures which can go wrong or right. Some people
think they can imagine a creature which was free but
had no possibility of going wrong, but I can't. If a thing
is free to be good it's also free to be bad. And free will
is what has made evil possible. Why, then, did God
give them free will? Because free will, though it makes
evil possible, is also the only thing that makes possible
any love or goodness or joy worth having. A world of
automata—of creatures that worked like machines—
would hardly be worth creating. The happiness which
God designs for His higher creatures is the happiness
of being freely, voluntarily united to Him and to each
other in an ecstasy of love and delight compared with
which the most rapturous love between a man and a
woman on this earth is mere milk and water. And for
that they've got to be free.

Of course God knew what would happen if they
used their freedom the wrong way: apparently, He
thought it worth the risk. . . . If God thinks this state
of war in the universe a price worth paying for free
will—that is, for making a real world in which creatures can do real good or harm and something of real
importance can happen, instead of a toy world which
only moves when He pulls the strings—then we may
take it it is worth paying.[3]

And so instead of ordering their love to God, Adam and Eve
engaged in disordered love of self and threw the entire cosmos
into chaos.

---

[3] C. S. Lewis, *Mere Christianity* (1952; repr., New York: HarperCollins, 2001), 47–48.

Yet creation remains good. It's damaged, and now, after the Fall, the perfectly intimate, loving relationships once shared among God, man and woman, and nature are impaired. In Genesis 3 this is signified by Adam and Eve sewing fig leaves after realizing they're naked, hiding from God in the garden, and receiving the judgment of discipline in regard to farming and childbearing. Creation is broken, relationships fractured.

3. *Redemption.* God the Creator will redeem his broken creation. God does so by instituting a sacred, covenantal line, the people of God as a family running from Adam and Eve through Seth, Noah, Shem, and Abraham to Jacob, who, having defeated God in a wrestling match (Gen 32:22–32), receives the new name of "Israel" and becomes the father of twelve sons who in their turn become the fathers of the twelve tribes of Israel. God continues the line in making covenants with Moses, David and the kingdom of Israel, and ultimately Jesus and the Church. From beginning to end, salvation history flows in covenantal continuity.[4]

Redemption, the third act of the Christian story, thus falls into three scenes: (1) Israel, (2) Jesus, and (3) the Church. The Old Testament story of Israel's sacred covenantal line culminates in Jesus, the ideal Israelite, even the incarnation of Israel. Jesus then founds a church that will continue Israel's mission to be a "light to the nations" (Isa 49:6). His Church proclaims Jesus as Savior and Lord and provides his followers with the sacraments so that they might share in Jesus himself and indeed, Jesus being Emmanuel ("God with us," Matt 1:23), the very life of God himself. The grace lost to the human race in the Fall is given to us bite by precious bite, sip by precious

---

[4] This vision is as ancient as the Evangelists, particularly St. Matthew and St. Luke, and St. Irenaeus was its most powerful patristic explicator. For a modern casting of classical salvation history, see Scott Hahn, *A Father Who Keeps His Promises* (Cincinnati, OH: Servant, 1998).

sip, as we journey in the Church on the way to glory.

4. *Glory*. Glory is the fourth and final act, when the end comes, when heaven and earth are finally transformed forever. The Church looks forward to this end, calling it "Judgment Day" and the "Second Coming," as Jesus's return to judge the living and the dead ushers it in. Thinking in terms of "heaven" as most understand it doesn't catch the full Christian eschatological vision, for it suggests an ethereal place somewhere else far away from creation (at least the visible, material aspects) where our souls go when we die. St. Augustine's term of "glory" better captures what the New Testament and the Church teach: God's glory, his very Reality, like the *shekinah* or cloud of glory that filled the ancient tabernacle (Exod 34:34–35), will come to fill and transform all of creation, all of heaven and earth. And so St. Paul can write in Romans about this future glory:

> I consider that the sufferings of this present time are not worth comparing with the glory that is to be revealed to us. For the creation waits with eager longing for the revealing of the sons of God; for the creation was subjected to futility, not of its own will but by the will of him who subjected it in hope; because the creation itself will be set free from its bondage to decay and obtain the glorious liberty of the children of God. We know that the whole creation has been groaning in travail together until now; and not only the creation, but we ourselves, who have the first fruits of the Spirit, groan inwardly as we wait for adoption as sons, the redemption of our bodies. For in this hope we were saved. (Rom 8:18–24a)

St. Matthew for his part also presents the end in similar substance; indeed, in the very first verse of his Gospel he suggests Jesus the Christ brings a new Genesis, a new creation (see below on Matt 1:1). And so, in the Gospel of Matthew, Jesus speaks of eschatological glory:

> For the Son of man is to come with his angels in the glory of his Father, and then he will repay every man for what he has done. (16:27)

> [T]hen will appear the sign of the Son of man in heaven, and then all the tribes of the earth will mourn, and they will see the Son of man coming on the clouds of heaven with power and great glory. (24:30)

> When the Son of man comes in his glory, and all the angels with him, then he will sit on his glorious throne. (25:31)

> But I tell you, hereafter you will see the Son of man seated at the right hand of Power, and coming on the clouds of heaven. (26:64b)

The language of "the kingdom of heaven/God" that St. Matthew regularly employs should also be thought of in terms of something that advances to reclaim a wayward cosmos, heaven and earth, things visible and invisible, rather than the realm apart from most of creation where disembodied souls go to find final rest. In the explanation of the Parable of the Weeds among the Wheat (Matt 13:36–43; the parable itself is prior in 13:24–30), Jesus says that at the close of the age, "[t]he Son of man will send his angels, and they will gather out of his kingdom all causes of sin and all evildoers" (13:41).

Causes of sin and evildoers belong to the realm of earth, and so the idea here is that the angels will come and purify earth as heaven is pure, and thus reestablish God's reign—the kingdom of heaven—over earth. Indeed, this is precisely what we pray for in the Lord's Prayer: "Thy kingdom come, Thy will be done, On earth as it is in heaven" (6:10). When the kingdom comes, then God's divine glory fills all and transforms all.

INTERPRETING THE BIBLE IN LIGHT OF THE STORY

The Structure of the Testaments

This four-act drama, this Christian story of salvation history, explains the Bible's very structure and also determines how the Bible is to be interpreted. The Christian Old Testament presents Creation, Fall, and the first scene of Redemption, Israel. In its fourfold structure, it begins with Genesis for a reason, continues with histories like Joshua, then presents Wisdom literature, and ends with the prophets because they ultimately prophesy Jesus and the Church.

The New Testament also follows a fourfold arrangement. It tells of Jesus and the Church (the second and third scene of Redemption), and the Church in all times and places looks forward to that glory of which the prophets and Jesus himself spoke. And so it begins with the Gospels, which come first because they tell directly of Jesus, the fulfillment of the Old Testament, and the Gospel of Matthew comes first among them because (among other things) it is a Gospel of fulfill-ment. The New Testament continues with Acts, which tells of the early Church, founded by Jesus, as it expands into the ancient Roman world to embrace the nations. Next the New Testament presents Paul's letters and the general letters, written by Apostles during the beginning of the Church. Revelation forms a fitting conclusion to the New Testament, as the Church founded by Jesus whose story is told in Acts anticipates the return of the Lord and the consummation of creation in glory. So each Testament falls into four parts, and those parts are ordered on the basis of the four-act story, with the third act (Redemption) consisting of Israel's story culminating in Jesus, who founds the Church, which persists until glory transforms heaven and earth.

Standing in the Continuity of the Story

Now the Christian drama assumes continuity, which is absolutely crucial to understand for the proper interpretation of the Scriptures. Jesus and the Church do not make doctrine and practice up out of "whole cloth." Even those elements which may seem new have Old Testament antecedents, and the New Testament simply swims in the waters of the Old. The Old Testament, as well as its reception in Judaism (traditions of interpretations and practices), is the matrix for the New, and every word of the New presumes in some way the Old, before one even gets to the myriad of specific allusions to and quotations of the Old.

Most Christians struggle with the Old Testament because they read the Bible as a jigsaw puzzle, a collection of Bible verses containing individual units of absolute truth to be arranged conceptually. It's how we train young people: we have them memorize individual verses. It's like a person is sitting in front of the Bible, every page open, with every verse coming at her all at once. And so a Bible verse from Leviticus, then one from 1 John, and another from Haggai, and one from Luke, and one from Proverbs, and yet another from Revelation all present themselves and beg to be reconciled. And that's a tall order that most Christians can't fill. They can't fill it because the Bible wasn't meant to be read that way. How did we get to this point?

Christian Scripture presumes and presents a coherent story, the story of salvation history, from creation and fall through redemption to the eschaton, the end of the world. Indeed, that story is the Bible's organizing principle, from Genesis to Revelation. But the Bible's unity has largely been lost among modern Christians, because most moderns believe the competence and authority to interpret the Bible lies in the individual who is free to interpret biblical texts however he or she wills.

These are rooted not only in intellectual currents flowing from the Reformation and its child the Enlightenment but also in the situation made by the introduction of the printing press. It made Bibles inexpensive and drove literacy, making for the possibility of personal and private interpretation. Further, our modern system of numbering Bible verses was first used in the 1560 Geneva Bible (printed in Geneva in English for Protestants), and that above all else made the Bible a jigsaw puzzle. The result is that the verses are often interpreted apart from their contexts. That we all have Bibles we can read is a good thing, but we also have to rededicate ourselves to reading the Bible in accord with the Christian story, perceiving the sweep of the forest and not just the trees.

Rather than standing outside the Bible, with its individual verses coming to us like a jigsaw puzzle, we actually stand inside the Bible. Indeed, we stand *in* the New Testament. The Book of Acts is really open ended: it closes with Paul under a gentle house arrest preaching the kingdom of God, with no real resolution to the drama. It's as if it is inviting us to see ourselves as standing in the story of the Church it begins to tell. And the letters written to various churches and individuals are also addressed to us, because we're part of the same Church that (say) the Corinthians belonged to, that Timothy belonged to.

Thus we stand in the time of the Church (the third scene of act two, Redemption). We look back from our position in the Church, accepting its Tradition and teachings, through the lens of Jesus and the Apostles to the Old Testament, and forward to the eschaton, the end of the world, as the Nicene Creed makes clear: "We look for the resurrection of the dead, and the life of the world to come."

So we read the Old Testament through the lens of the New, as Jesus and the Apostles interpreted it. And as we stand within the Church, the New Testament as read through the Church's Tradition is directly applicable to us today. It's not as if there is a great metaphysical or moral gap between our time and the ancient world. The New Testament addresses us directly: Acts is open-ended; Pentecost never terminated.

Embodying the Scriptures in the Church

So how, then, do we read, interpret, and embody the Scriptures? That last word—"embody"—is deliberate. For biblical interpretation isn't simply a matter of running biblical texts through some intellectual method and getting a result on the other side, as if interpretation were merely a matter of generating content. That's how computers work, and the reason most people think that's the way biblical interpretation should work is because religion got reduced to ethics during the Enlightenment, which thought truth was a mere matter of simple verbal statements and which, having done away with Aristotle, Natural Law, and good metaphysics, needed to reestablish ethics on some other basis. And so having ditched historic Christian tradition, people began to ask the Bible whether basic things were right or wrong.

But in historic Christianity, and especially Catholicism, biblical interpretation was a matter of embodying the biblical story in the contemporary Church for the sake of witness in the world. My doctoral mentor at Duke, Richard Hays, a faithful Methodist, writes that biblical interpretation is not finished until we take up the task of

> embodying Scripture's imperatives in the life of the Christian community. Without this living embodiment of the Word, none of the above deliberation [about history, exegesis, and hermeneutics] matters. . . . The value of our exegesis and hermeneutics will be tested by their capacity to produce persons and communities whose character is commensurate with Jesus Christ and thereby pleasing to God.[5]

Embodying the Scriptures in the Liturgy

For Catholics, Scripture is embodied not merely in our lives but also in liturgy. Indeed, it's embodied first in liturgy, from the Mass to private devotions, and that's where we find our formation.

Reading Scripture, then, isn't simply a matter of seeing how the New Testament fulfills the Old. For much of Protestantism, the New Testament fulfills the Old, and then, the meaning of the Bible having been determined, the preacher delivers it as content. But for Catholicism, the New Testament fulfills the Old; then Jesus Christ, who is the fulfillment of the Old, delivers himself in the Eucharist. Just as the Israelites and Jews

---

[5] Richard B. Hays, *The Moral Vision of the New Testament: Community, Cross, New Creation: A Contemporary Introduction to New Testament Ethics* (New York: HarperCollins, 1996), 7.

performed liturgies that Jesus himself performed, fulfilled, and transformed, the Church, in imitation of and obedience to Jesus, performs the liturgy of the Eucharist, the Mass.

A liturgical approach to the realization of Scripture is no Catholic imposition left over from the middle ages but is consonant with the canon itself. For from Genesis to Revelation, liturgy dominates Scripture. Consider the following:

The Garden of Eden is a temple—because the presence of a god or God makes a temple in the ancient world—with Adam as priest; thus the later Israelite temples were designed to reflect Eden, with the priesthood fulfilling the role of Adam (and of course Jesus Christ, the new Adam, is the great high priest). And as evangelical scholar Gordon J. Wenham observes:

> Genesis is much more interested in the cult than is normally realized. It begins by describing the creation of the world in a way that foreshadows the building of the tabernacle. The garden of Eden is portrayed as a sanctuary decorated with features that subsequently adorned the tabernacle and temple, gold, precious stones, cherubim, and trees. Eden was where God walked . . . and Adam served as priest.[6]

Genesis then later presents other significant figures offering sacrifices at significant moments, among them Abel, Noah, and Abraham. Moses commanded Pharaoh to let the Hebrew people go so that they might worship: "Thus says the

---

[6] See Gordon J. Wenham, "The Aqedah: A Paradigm of Sacrifice," in *Pomegranates and Golden Bells: Studies in Biblical, Jewish, and Near Eastern Ritual, Law, and Literature in Honor of Jacob Milgrom*, ed. David P. Wright, David Noel Freedman, and Avi Hurvitz (Winona Lake, IN: Eisenbrauns, 1995), 93.

LORD, the God of Israel, 'Let my people go, that they may hold a feast to me in the wilderness'" (Exod 5:1b). Much of the Pentateuch, the five books of Moses, concern liturgy and sacrifices, especially from the last third of Exodus through Deuteronomy. The books of history are marked with sacrifices. The Psalms were sung in sacrificial liturgy. And the prophets weren't opposed to sacrificial liturgy as such, but wanted the people to live righteous lives, lest their sacrifices be hypocritical (the idea that the prophets were resistant to the sacrificial priesthood comes from Protestant scholars of the nineteenth century reading their own opposition to the Catholic priesthood back into the texts). Ezekiel himself was a priest, and Isaiah foresaw the Gentiles bringing their sacrifices to Zion at the end of time (Isa 56:6–8).

In the New Testament, Jesus institutes the sacrificial ritual of the Eucharist. In Acts, the early Christians attend services in the temple while they also devote themselves to "the apostles' teaching and fellowship, to the breaking of bread and the prayers" (Acts 2:42). In 1 Corinthians 11, St. Paul spills a good amount of ink dealing with propriety in the Eucharistic liturgy. Hebrews is a long argument for the superiority of the Mass to Jewish sacrifices. And the Book of Revelation is less about the horrors of the end times and much more about the eternal liturgy of heaven; as such, it's primarily been used as a pattern for liturgies on earth.[7]

Further, believers throughout history have encountered Scripture primarily in liturgy. From the ancient world until perhaps the sixteen hundreds, five or maybe ten percent of the population could read. And so Israelites, Jews, and Christians would hear the Bible read in worship, in the temples, syna-

---

[7] See Scott Hahn, *The Lamb's Supper: The Mass as Heaven on Earth* (New York: Doubleday, 1999), 61–113.

gogues, and churches. In fact, the driving question that led to the formation of the New Testament canon was not "Which of these documents were inspired?" As the early Church sorted through writings, from the Gospel of Mark to Third Corinthians, from 2 John to the Acts of Paul and Thecla, from Hebrews to the Gospel of Peter, the question was "Which of these documents may be read in the Church's liturgy?" The early Church did so by asking which documents came from the Apostles and reflected the apostolic Faith, which they did to determine what could be read and preached in the Mass.

So what does that look like? It's a three-stage process, involving the Old Testament, the New Testament, and the Church's liturgy. The Old Testament foreshadows and prefigures the events of the New, and so the New in turn fulfills the events of the Old. Unlike Gnosticism, which splits the Old Testament from the New and sees different gods superintending each, Catholics operate with the conviction that the same God superintends both Testaments, which together tell the salvific story from creation to consummation.

Allegory and Mystagogy

The conviction that the Old Testament, the New Testament, and the Liturgy stood in an organic relationship required, in turn, the appropriation of allegory as the tool for understanding the Old Testament rightly (in the West this looked much like what today is called typology, although the word was not in use until the mid-nineteenth century). Thus certain words of St. Augustine become the celebrated phrase: *Novum Testamentum in Vetere latet, Vetus in Novo patet* ("The New Testament is latent in the Old, the Old is made patent in the New").[8]

---

[8] St. Augustine, *Quaestiones in Heptateuchum* 2, 73 (20, 19). The full Latin

So the relationship of the New Testament to the Old Testament is *allegorical*. And then the relationship of the Church's liturgy to the New Testament is *mystagogical*. Allegory culminates in mystagogy, as the events foreshadowed in the Old Testament are fulfilled in the New Testament and then made real in the present through the Church's sacramental mysteries—think of how often one hears the language of "mystery" in the Mass, such as "as we prepare to celebrate these sacred mysteries."

The supreme example of allegory and mystagogy? The Passover becomes a type of Christ's sacrifice and the Last Supper, which are in turn celebrated in the Church's celebration of the Eucharist. In Exodus the blood of the lambs preserved the enslaved Israelites from the avenging Angel of Death, and this thus instituted the annual festivals of Passover and Unleavened Bread, with the slaughter of the Passover lambs. Jesus then institutes his ongoing sacrificial meal, transforming the Passover meal into his Church's Eucharist, the ritual that perpetually re-presents his cruciform sacrifice in the Mass. And so we have the threefold movement: (1) Exodus and Passover in the Old Testament and Israelite and Jewish tradition point to (2) the crucifixion and Last Supper in the New Testament, and (3) the Church, still living in the time of the New Testament, celebrates the Eucharistic liturgy, the Mass, heaven on earth in time, to the end of time.

Biblical interpretation, then, is ultimately not academic but liturgical. For the Catholic, the Bible is realized in the Mass, where elements of creation (such as water, wheat, and wine) that Israelites and Jews employed in their own liturgies

---

is: *Loquere tu nobis, et non loquatur ad nos Deus, ne quando moriamur* [Exod 20:19]. Multum et solide significatur, ad Vetus Testamentum timorem potius pertinere, sicut ad Novum dilectionem: quamquam et in Vetere Novum lateat, et in Novo Vetus pateat.

and rituals become the agents of our redemption, which was necessitated by the Fall, while with them we anticipate the consummation. Creation, Fall, Redemption, and Glory are all found there.

For interpretation, then, we stand in the time of the Church, we stand in the New Testament. We look back through the New Testament documents, through Jesus and the Apostles, through Tradition, and read the Old Testament. It addresses us truly, but through those lenses. We read the New Testament through the Church's Tradition, which made the New Testament (Tradition determined its contents and its interpretation) but which the New Testament also helped birth. Tradition and Scripture are reciprocal; the New Testament is written Tradition, and Tradition squares with the New Testament. We then look forward to the eschaton, the end of the world, from our position in the time of the Church. We stand *in* the story, not outside it.

Interpreting Old Testament Law and Ritual

Here, then, we need to address how Christians interpret the Old Testament from our position in the Church, particularly the legal and ritual elements, which have caused so much consternation for many Christians. Again, much of the Law in the Old Testament concerns worship as a sacrificial ceremony. Many of the laws Moses gave the people concern eating, sex, and death. Why? Because eating, sex, and death are all bodily things, and God does not have a body. To approach God in the tabernacle, temples, or synagogues (which didn't have sacrifices but which were treated as temples as concerns their sanctity), one needed to be as much like God as possible. And bodily functions make one unlike God. So the Law provided rituals dealing with menstruation, emissions, childbirth, eating, and contact with corpses (none of which are sinful and, in fact, are often required by the same Mosaic Law) to restore people to a godlike state of ritual purity so that they might again enter a sacred edifice to offer worship to God.[9]

Now we may divide the Mosaic Law into three categories: (1) the sacrificial, (2) the moral, and (3) the "ethnic." Each were transformed by Jesus in delivering the Catholic Faith to the Church. First, the sacrificial laws are fulfilled in Jesus's crucifixion and Eucharist, and so Christians do not slaughter animals in their liturgies. Second, the moral law, if anything, is maintained and intensified in the Church. Jesus makes morality a matter not merely of the body but the heart in the Sermon on the Mount, moving from literal murder and adultery to hatred and lust (Matt 5:21–30), and Jesus forbids divorce and remarriage (Matt 5:31–32, 19:3–9), unlike Moses, who permitted it (Deut 24:1–4). The early Church discerned that Gentiles who wished to become Christians had to refrain from four fundamental pagan sins: idolatry, the meat of strangled animals, blood, and sexual immorality (Acts 15:20, 29). "Sexual immorality" probably means the early Church was maintaining the sexual morality found throughout Leviticus 18–20, and Jewish sexual customs more broadly.

Third, the laws that appear absurd to moderns might be deemed "ethnic," in that they were meant to keep the nation of Israel separate from the pagan nations surrounding them. Customs of diet and dress served to distinguish Israelites and Jews from pagans, to keep Israel "weird" in the eyes of her pagan neighbors. This is similar to how the customs of contemporary Christians of the radical Reformation—Amish, Mennonites, and Hutterites—aren't simply a brute rejection

---

[9] We find echoes of these Mosaic rituals in Catholicism, such as in priestly celibacy and the venerable ritual of the "churching of women" who have delivered a child.

of modernity but rather function to keep them separate from all others.

These laws of Moses are abolished for Christians, because God intended them for the time of Israel, when Israel needed to be kept separate from the pagan nations. But in the time of the Church, Jews and Gentiles are meant to be one, in Christ, through Baptism, with each other in Eucharistic communion. Thus St. Paul can write, "There is neither Jew nor Greek . . . you are all one in Christ Jesus" (Gal 3:28). Or consider his grandiloquent, moving words in Ephesians 2:11–22:

> Therefore remember that at one time you Gentiles in the flesh, called the uncircumcision by what is called the circumcision [Jews], which is made in the flesh by hands—remember that you were at that time separated from Christ, alienated from the commonwealth of Israel, and strangers to the covenants of promise, having no hope and without God in the world. But now in Christ Jesus you who once were far off [Gentiles] have been brought near in the blood of Christ. For he is our peace, who has made us both [Jews and Gentiles] one, and has broken down the dividing wall of hostility [the Mosaic Law], by abolishing in his flesh the law of commandments and ordinances, that he might create in himself one new man [the Christian] in place of the two [Jews and Gentiles], so making peace, and might reconcile us both [Jews and Gentiles] to God in one body [the Church] through the cross, thereby bringing the hostility [between Jews and Gentiles] to an end. And he came and preached peace to you who were far off [Gentiles] and peace to those who were near [Jews]; for through him we both [Jews and Gentiles] have access in one Spirit to the

Father. So then you [Gentiles] are no longer strangers and sojourners, but you are fellow citizens with the saints and members of the household of God [the Church], built upon the foundation of the apostles and prophets, Christ Jesus himself being the cornerstone, in whom the whole structure is joined together and grows into a holy temple in the Lord; in whom you also are built into it for a dwelling place of God in the Spirit.

I hope you will have pardoned the interpolations, but most modern Christians are not accustomed to reading St. Paul's letters with attention to his concerns for the unity of Jews and Gentiles in the Church as Christians.

Indeed, for St. Paul and the early Church, Christians were a third race, neither Jew nor Gentile but Christian. In the Church, gone are the tribal and national identities of Egyptian, Numidian, Teuton, Briton, Arab, and even Roman and Jew. For, as St. Paul writes, "For our citizenship subsists in heaven, and we long for a Savior from there, the Lord Jesus Christ" (Phil 3:20; my translation). We might say we belong to a tribe called "Christian."

Indeed, the later *Letter to Diognetus* quotes and amplifies St. Paul's words to the Philippians on Christians's heavenly citizenship:

For the Christians are distinguished from other men neither by country, nor language, nor the customs which they observe. For they neither inhabit cities of their own, nor employ a peculiar form of speech, nor lead a life which is marked out by any singularity. . . . But, inhabiting Greek as well as barbarian cities, according as the lot of each of them has been determined, and following the customs of the natives in respect to clothing, food, and the rest of their ordinary conduct, they display to us their wonderful and confessedly striking method of life. They dwell in their own countries, but simply as sojourners. As citizens, they share in all things with others, and yet endure all things as if foreigners. Every foreign land is to them as their native country, and every land of their birth as a land of strangers. They marry, as do all [others]; they beget children; but they do not destroy their offspring. They have a common table, but not a common bed. They are in the flesh, but do not live after the flesh. They pass their days on earth, but they are citizens of heaven. They obey the prescribed laws, and at the same time surpass the laws by their lives. They love all men, and are persecuted by all. They are unknown and condemned; they are put to death, and restored to life. They are poor, yet make many rich; they are in lack of all things, and yet abound in all; they are dishonoured, and yet in their very dishonour are glorified. They are evil spoken of, and yet are justified; they are reviled, and bless; they are insulted, and repay the insult with honor; they do good, yet are punished as evil-doers. When punished, they rejoice as if quickened into life; they are assailed by the Jews as foreigners, and are persecuted by the Greeks; yet those who hate them are unable to assign any reason for their hatred. To sum up all in one word—what the soul is in the body, that are Christians in the world. The soul is dispersed through all the members of the body, and Christians are scattered through all the cities of the world. The soul dwells in the body, yet is not of the body; and Christians dwell in the world, yet are not of the world.[10]

The upshot is this: if Christian Jews continued to observe the "ethnic" parts of the Mosaic Law, the Church would be divided between Jew and Gentile as a practical matter. As a theological matter, St. Paul insists that that one's allegiance to Christ replaces all prior allegiances, and one's identity in Christ replaces all prior identities. It cannot be otherwise, for we are in Christ and Christ is in us to the point that we are Christ and Christ is us. "I have been crucified with Christ; it is no longer I who live, but Christ who lives in me" (Gal 2:20a). And what's more, the Church is Christ and Christ is the Church. When the ascended Jesus blinds Saul (later, St. Paul) on the road to Damascus, he asks, "Saul, Saul, why do you persecute me?" (Acts 9:4). In response to Saul's question, "Who are you, Lord?" Jesus responds, "I am Jesus, whom you are persecuting" (Acts 9:5). Jesus does not ask, "Why do you persecute my followers?" but rather, "Why do you persecute me?" Nor does he respond, "I am Jesus, whose followers you are persecuting," but rather, "I am Jesus, whom you are persecuting." It's subtle, but here Jesus identifies directly with his followers and identifies his followers directly with him. And so the Catechism of the Catholic Church in section 795 teaches this ancient, biblical idea: "Christ and his Church thus together make up the 'whole Christ' (*Christus totus*). The Church is one with Christ. The saints are acutely aware of this unity." Expounding upon this, the Catechism goes on to quote some saints:

---

[10] Mathetes, *Letter to Diognetus* 5–6a (ANF 1:26–27).

Let us rejoice then and give thanks that we have become not only Christians, but Christ himself. Do you understand and grasp, brethren, God's grace toward us? Marvel and rejoice: we have become Christ. For if he is the head, we are the members; he and we together are the whole man . . . . the fullness of Christ then is the head and the members. But what does "head and members" mean? Christ and the Church. [St. Augustine, *In Jo. ev.* 21,8:PL 35, 1568.]

Our redeemer has shown himself to be one person with the holy Church whom he has taken to himself. [Pope St. Gregory the Great, *Moralia in Job, præf.,* 14:PL 75,525A.]

Head and members form as it were one and the same mystical person. [St. Thomas Aquinas, *STh* III,48,2.]

A reply of St. Joan of Arc to her judges sums up the faith of the holy doctors and the good sense of the believer: "About Jesus Christ and the Church, I simply know they're just one thing, and we shouldn't complicate the matter." [Acts of the Trial of Joan of Arc.]

Christ fulfilled the Law, and in doing so transformed it. He fulfilled the sacrifices, and gave his Church the sacraments. He maintained the best of Jewish morality and raised it. And he made Jew and Gentile one in him, the Church.

All of what I have written prior is not simply a general reflection on Catholic interpretation but is particularly crucial for interpreting the Gospel of Matthew rightly. Indeed Catholic interpretation is born in large part from St. Matthew's written witness to Jesus Christ; the Gospel of Matthew is the First Gospel, and as such it stands at the very center of the canon of Scripture.

MATTHEW AMONG THE GOSPELS

The Gospels are the theological center of the canon of Scripture, and the Gospel of Matthew stands first among the Gospels. Now the Bible and the Gospels within do not stand alone as mere documents to be read, believed, and acted upon. Rather, the Bible finds its true home in the liturgy, for the biblical texts were written for and used in worship from the first, both in ancient Israel and in the earliest Church. And as the Gospels are central to the canon of Scripture, the Gospels are fundamental to the liturgy of the Word: Catholics (and other liturgical Christians) sit for the Old Testament reading, the Psalm, and the Epistle, but stand for the reading of the Gospel. The Gospels are central to the liturgy of the Word because they are central to Scripture, and they are central to Scripture because they tell directly of the coming of Jesus Christ, the Son of God, who by the Incarnation is the unmediated and ultimate revelation of God himself to humanity, in the very flesh.

If the Gospels are the theological center of the canon, then the Gospel of Matthew stands at the forefront of the four Gospels as the most important Gospel. Calling the Gospel of Matthew the "First Gospel" need not be merely a clever way to duck questions of authorship (many modern scholars deny Matthew wrote it) but a way of recognizing its preeminence, for it has been regarded not only as the first among equals but even more as that Gospel which regulates readings of the others.

To distinguish among the contents of the canon of Scripture in this way is not to affirm some sort of "canon within a canon," determined by prior confessional commitments with the effect of tossing wide swaths of Sacred Scripture overboard, but rather to recognize Scripture as a coherent story in which every word plays its role, a mosaic in which every piece matters and contributes to the picture of the whole. And for the historic Church, all roads lead to and from the Gospel of Matthew.[11]

The Priority of the Gospel of Matthew

Why has the Gospel of Matthew achieved such preeminence in Christian history, not only among Catholics but also among Christians of the radical Reformation, such as the Amish and Mennonites?

First, the Gospel of Matthew has proven itself in liturgy and life. It is accessible. It has been found practical and relatively easy to read, preach, teach, and apply. The reason for this concerns, in turn, the breadth, depth, and clarity of its comprehensive content: stories teaching what became fundamental Christian doctrine are found in it, such as the Virgin

---

[11] Protestants, however, have generally turned to St. Paul, and especially his letter to the Romans, to find their center of theological gravity. In 1522 in his "Preface to the Epistle of St. Paul to the Romans," Martin Luther wrote, "This epistle is in truth the most important document in the New Testament, the gospel in its purest expression . . . in essence, it is a brilliant light, almost enough to illumine the whole Bible" (*Martin Luther: Selections from His Writings*, ed. John Dillenberger [Garden City, NY: Doubleday, 1961], 19). John Calvin wrote similarly: "If we understand this Epistle [Romans], we have a passage opened to us to the understanding of the whole of Scripture" (*Calvin's New Testament Commentaries*, vol. 8 [Grand Rapids, MI: Eerdmans, 1995], 2). In our own day, evangelical Calvinist J. I. Packer has written, "All roads in the Bible lead to Romans, and all views afforded by the Bible are seen most clearly from Romans, and when the message of Romans gets into a person's heart there is no telling what may happen" (*Knowing God* [Downers Grove, IL: InterVarsity Press, 1993], 237).

Birth, the sacrificial crucifixion and Eucharist, and the resurrection and ascension of Our Lord, while Jesus himself issues plenty of direct and applicable teachings in his five great discourses (especially the beloved Sermon on the Mount) and instructs by example in the narrative sections.

Second, until relatively recently in Christian and academic history, the Gospel of Matthew was thought to be not only the first written but also an eyewitness account. The Gospel of Mark was thought to be a summary of the Gospel of Matthew; the prologue of the Gospel of Luke admits its account is derivative of Matthew's (see Luke 1:1–4); and John was thought to have written a spiritual, theological Gospel complementing the three prior Gospels.[12] And thus the

---

[12] Eusebius (*Ecclesiastical History* 6.14) records that Clement of Alexandria writes, "But John, the last [evangelist] of all, seeing that what was corporeal was set forth in the [first three] Gospels, on the entreaty of his intimate friends, and inspired by the Spirit, composed a spiritual Gospel" (ANF 1:580). St. Augustine, so important for Western Catholic Christianity, expressed similar sentiments at some length in his *Harmony of the Gospels* 1.4.7:

These three evangelists, however, were for the most part engaged with those things which Christ did through the vehicle of the flesh of man, and after the temporal fashion. But John, on the other hand, had in view that true divinity of the Lord in which He is the Father's equal, and directed his efforts above all to the setting forth of the divine nature in his Gospel in such a way as he believed to be adequate to men's needs and notions. Therefore he is borne to loftier heights, in which he leaves the other three far behind him; so that, while in them you see men who have their conversation in a certain manner with the man Christ on earth, in him you perceive one who has passed beyond the cloud in which the whole earth is wrapped, and who has reached the liquid heaven from which, with clearest and steadiest mental eye, he is able to look upon God the Word, who was in the beginning with God, and by whom all things were made. And there, too, he can recognise Him who was made flesh in order that He might dwell amongst us; [that Word of whom we say] that He assumed the flesh, not that He was changed into the flesh. For had not this assumption of the flesh been effected in such a manner as at the

Gospels received their canonical order for deep theological and historical reasons. In the canonical order, one also sees movement from the particularity of the Gospel of Matthew, situated as it is within the orbit of conservative normative and Pharisaic Judaism, to the universality of the Gospels of Luke and John, in which Gentile inclusion in the people of God is clear throughout.

A third, if subtle, reason for the Gospel of Matthew's preeminence and position in the canon and Christian history as the first Gospel concerns its very particular nature. Salvation history in Israel and Judaism culminates in Jesus the Jew, as salvation is from the Jews (see John 4:22); the gospel is for the Jew first, then the Gentile (Rom 1:16). The Gospel of Matthew is concerned with fulfillment. All is fulfilled in the Matthean Jesus—the Scriptures, righteousness, obedience, the various Old Testament types Jesus completes. And so the Gospel of Matthew shows most clearly the culmination of sal-

---

same time to conserve the unchangeable Divinity, such a word as this could never have been spoken,—namely, "I and the Father are one." For surely the Father and the flesh are not one. And the same John is also the only one who has recorded that witness which the Lord gave concerning Himself, when He said: "He that has seen me, has seen the Father also"; and, "I am in the Father, and the Father is in me"; "that they may be one, even as we are one"; and, "Whatsoever the Father does, these same things does the Son likewise." And whatever other statements there may be to the same effect, calculated to betoken, to those who are possessed of right understanding, that divinity of Christ in which He is the Father's equal, of all these we might almost say that we are indebted for their introduction into the Gospel narrative to John alone. For he is like one who has drunk in the secret of His divinity more richly and somehow more familiarly than others, as if he drew it from the very bosom of his Lord on which it was his wont to recline when He sat at meat. (St. Augustine, *Harmony of the Gospels*, in *A Select Library of Nicene and Post-Nicene Fathers of the Christian Church*, 1st series, 14 vols., ed. Philip Schaff [repr., Peabody, MA: Hendrickson, 1994], 6:79–80.)

vation history in Jesus the Jew who was sent to Israel (Matt 10:5–6, 15:24) and then who commands his disciples to take him and his teaching to the nations (28:16–20).

The story of salvation history begins with the parents of the universal human race, but narrows as it goes on, running through the southern tribes of Judah and Benjamin, the Jews. But with the coming of Jesus Christ it begins to open up again, as it were, as the promises to Abraham concerning not just Israel or the Jews but indeed the whole human race are fulfilled. Part of God's original promises to Abraham was that in him "all the families of the earth shall bless themselves" (Gen 12:3b)—not just Israelite families; it was a promise with universal import that the prophets reaffirmed in their own oracles (see, for instance, Isa 56:6–8).

A "Jewish" Gospel

Nowadays the Gospel of Matthew is sometimes colloquially called a "Jewish" Gospel. This is misleading because all the New Testament documents are fundamentally Jewish, since early Christianity was a Jewish phenomenon, firmly rooted in the practice and belief of common Judaism (this was so even as it expanded beyond the bounds of the Holy Land and incorporated Gentiles). Basic Christian beliefs like monotheism, election, God as lawgiver, and the eschaton are Jewish and in no way pagan. The pagan gods neither choose a people nor give them a way to live out of love, nor judge the world at the end of time. But the misnomer is meant to convey a truth: The Gospel of Matthew attends to the concerns of conservative, common Judaism, such as how to interpret the Mosaic Law, what makes for righteousness, what it means to be a child of Abraham, and how Scripture is fulfilled.

And so the Jesus of the Gospel of Matthew looks very

much like his Pharisaic opponents—a conservative Jew of the Holy Land concerned with the right interpretation of the Law while affirming the Law's enduring relevance (see Matt 5:17–18 and 23:23)—and a large part of the reason for their mutual hostility (see Matt 23) lies in their common convictions. As it is said, the bitterest wars are fought between brothers. In any event, one observes that the Matthean genealogy begins not with Adam (as in the Gospel of Luke, which does so to signal the universal relevance of the gospel message) but Abraham (thus signaling concern for intra-Jewish issues). Moreover, the Matthean Jesus himself evinces little interest in Gentiles until his resurrection (see Matt 28:16–20), going so far as to declare his mission restricted to Israel on two occasions (Matt 10:5–6 and 15:24).

Given this ethos, it makes canonical sense for the Gospel of Matthew to be situated at the beginning of the fourfold Gospel canon, for salvation history has not yet widened out again, as it were, to the universal embrace of the nations, something which happens at the very end of the Gospel of Matthew. This book (which is the Gospel most concerned with fulfillment) marks the shift from particular to universal in its own narrative, as it shows in the unfolding of its story that God's purposes and prophecies are being fulfilled not only for Jews but also for Gentiles.

THE MATTHEAN STORY

The Gospel of Matthew is the first and foremost Gospel of the Church, then, because of its particular character, its particular story. This Gospel understands itself as a universal, authoritative document persisting for all time, and its community as the universal Church enduring to the end. It understands itself and the Church in this way because it affirms that Jesus

Christ the Jew, the Christ and divine Son of God in whom resides all authority, is the final fulfillment of God's promises, not only for Jews but also Gentiles. It also affirms that Jesus Christ inaugurates the final period of God's plan of salvation history, and that he has commanded what he teaches in the Gospel of Matthew to be taught to converts in the age of the Church until the end.

How (Not) to Read a Gospel

This First Gospel presents itself as a universal, authoritative document persisting for all time for the Church enduring for all time through its narrative, through the form of a story. Reading the Gospel of Matthew, then, requires significant attention to its narrative dynamics. Again, redaction criticism—comparing passages in the Gospel of Matthew with similar or near-identical passages in the Gospels of Mark and Luke apart from their narrative contexts in the Gospels in an attempt to get at what the Gospel writers thought—fails to take account of the storyline of each of the Gospels and ironically goes beyond and behind a Gospel writer's intention. The evangelists did not intend their Gospels to be read in the way redaction critics peruse, with scrupulous attention to presumed prior sources (in the case of the Gospel of Mark) and utterly hypothetical, not-extant sources (in the case of what scholars call "Q," a pure reconstruction made from similar passages in Matthew and Luke that supposedly lies behind them). The Gospels draw attention to the Old Testament through the rhetorical devices of allusion and quotation, but they do not quote material from other Gospels directly.

Above all, the Gospels read well as stories, as narratives, for that is what they are; the evangelists composed wholes and intended them to be read as such. Moreover, when one

reads the Gospels using redaction criticism, they become sur-
reptitious stories about crises in their anonymous author's
hypothetical communities when they in fact present themselves openly as stories about Jesus. To read as redaction critics
do is to read against the grain of the texts. Finally, in canonical perspective, the Gospel of Matthew's primary position in
the fourfold Gospel canon suggests it is to be read before the
other three.

For these reasons we will read the Gospel of Matthew as
the story it purports to be, and ask what St. Matthew would
have an ideal reader make of the story he tells. Human beings
are narrative by nature; we're hardwired to hear and tell stories,
to appreciate and interpret them. We tell each other the little
tales that make up our lives and sometimes the big story that
is our life, and read and watch stories all the time. And so
this narrative-approach isn't some esoteric science but simply
a matter of paying attention to the basics we all know from
experience and often from school. A story-approach permits
the entirety of the text of the Gospel of Matthew to be taken
into account (unlike redaction criticism, which focuses on
that small percentage of a Gospel's text that constitutes addi-
tions, omissions, and changes) and its narrative dynamics.

A Story of Fulfillment, Reversal, and Triumph

When we read the story of the Gospel of Matthew, we find the
Gospel pointing not only backward—as it interprets the Old
Testament and Judaism through Jesus's words and deeds—but
also forward. Its final words, the Great Commission, wherein
Jesus commands his disciples to "make disciples of all nations"
(Matt 28:16–20), are not oriented to its own long-lost origi-
nal community reconstructed through redaction criticism but
to the future, to the Church's time of mission. True, it draws

deeply on the past; it is a Gospel of radical continuity with the tradition of the Old Testament and their community of Israel and the later Jews. Yet that continuity is neither repristination nor nostalgia. It draws on that tradition as a resource for mission in the Church's perpetual present, as the tips of leaves draw on roots.

Above all, the Gospel of Matthew is a story of fulfillment, telling (1) how God has come to earth in Jesus the Christ, the Son of God, to fulfill the promises God made to Israel and the entire human race; (2) how Jesus's followers can attain true righteousness and salvation; and (3) how Jesus founded a Church to bring God's promises and sacraments to the ends of the earth.

The Gospel of Matthew tells an ironic story of reversal that is both tragedy and triumph. Ironic because the initial expectations the Gospel raises for us readers are ultimately reversed; tragic, for Israel loses its status as the privileged agent of God's mission in the world; but also a triumph, in that God's purposes for the world are not thwarted in spite of the human race's rejection of Jesus the Christ. Indeed, as the Jesus of Matthew is the embodiment of Israel and the fulfillment of its promises and mission, in Jesus's vindication at the resurrection and exaltation into heaven Israel herself is vindicated and exalted; Israel's mission to be a "light to the nations" (Isa 49:6) commences anew as the Church goes into all the world to make "disciples of all nations" (Matt 28:16–20).

The Conflict at the Coming of the Christ Child

The first chapter of the Gospel sets us deeply in the world of traditional, conservative first-century Palestinian Judaism. The initial verse—"The book of the genealogy of Jesus Christ, the son of David, the son of Abraham"—suggests that

Jesus Christ is to be understood in terms of two fundamental Christological categories. First, the phrase "son of David" means "Christ," as Jews of Jesus's day understood the Christ to be David's ultimate descendent. Second, "son of Abraham" implies he will be a sacrifice like Isaac (see Gen 22). The genealogy then begins with Abraham (Matt 1:2–17), whom Jews regarded as the first Jew. Following this, St. Matthew presents the story of the Virgin Birth, identifying Jesus Christ with God ("Emmanuel," which means "God with us," 1:23) and thus investing him with divine personhood and authority (see also 28:18: "All authority in heaven and on earth has been given to me"). Most interesting is the explanation of Jesus's very name: "[Y]ou shall call his name Jesus, for he will save his people from their sins" (1:21). The explanation raises two implicit questions for the readers: Who are Jesus's people, and how will Jesus save them from their sins?

In general while reading, the human mind confronts and answers such implicit questions automatically again and again in a subconscious fashion. But here it is helpful to engage in some conscious guessing: the text here raises these questions, and drawing on the knowledge of ancient Judaism, which St. Matthew expects an ideal reader to know, we would first hazard that "his people" are the Jews and that Jesus will save them from their sins by killing for them. That is what the Davidic Messiah was generally expected to do: save the Jews from the penalty of their sins—namely, Roman domination—by leading a decisive, end-time war against the Romans. Because of their sins the people are under the oppression of Roman rule (albeit indirectly; there was not a true Italian centurion on every street corner in Jerusalem), and forgiveness of sins means violent liberation from oppression so that the Jews once more might have something greater than the Maccabees. They might have a new, eschatological, united monarchy (like that over which David had ruled) with a new, end-time, Messianic David as eternal King.

So far, then, the ideal reader would expect a story of violent conquest in which Israel's liberation will be achieved in the end times, beginning now with Jesus's advent. But those initial assumptions are immediately thrown into question with the story of the Magi in the second chapter of Matthew. The Magi (pagan astrologers from the East[13]) arrive searching for the "king of the Jews" (Matt 2:2), a title already given to Herod the Great by the Roman Senate roughly forty years prior, a fact a model reader should know. Herod and "all Jerusalem" are "troubled" (2:3)—not pleased, not overjoyed—by news that some are seeking a new king. Unless one is in Narnia, there can be only one king or queen.

And so Herod tries to kill baby Jesus. Herod wants to destroy him (Matt 2:13; see also 12:14 and 27:20). Being warned about this in a dream, Joseph takes mother and child and flees to Egypt. Then follows a formula citation of Hosea 11:1b in Matthew 2:15: "Out of Egypt have I called my son"; this presents Jesus as the embodiment of Israel, as Israel/Jacob is expressly named as God's son in Hosea 11. Further, the quotation occurs immediately after the Holy Family travels to Egypt, but they do not return from Egypt to Galilee until Matthew 2:19–21. The Gospel of Matthew thus subtly describes the infant Jesus's contemporary Israel as Egypt and therefore inverts the two. Israel is now the house of bondage, the land of slavery, and Egypt the promised land of refuge. Moreover, it is Herod, the king of Israel, who seeks to destroy

---

[13] See Fr. Dwight Longenecker, *Mystery of the Magi: The Quest to Identify the Three Wise Men* (Washington, DC: Regnery History, 2017), for an overview of possible ethnic identities of the Magi and his own thesis that they were Nabatean Arabs who served in the court of the king at ancient Petra.

Jesus, whereas the Magi, Gentile foreigners, are paying Jesus the homage he deserves. Finally, Hosea provides no heroic recollection of the exodus. Rather, God's love for Israel is contrasted with Israel's abject failure, detailed in Hosea 11:2: "The more I called them, the more they went from me; they kept sacrificing to the Ba'als, and burning incense to idols." The episode is thus an early instance of the significant Matthean theme of Jesus's conflict with Jewish leadership leading to Gentile inclusion.

The Mission of the Christ: First to the Jew . . .

Jesus, however, does not seem to know that his mission extends to the Gentiles. He sends his disciples only to the lost sheep of the house of Israel (Matt 10:5-6) and refuses, at first, to aid a pagan, a Canaanite woman with a demonized daughter, because Jesus believes himself to have been sent only to the lost sheep of the house of Israel (15:21-28). In the instance of the healing of the centurion's servant, Jesus does voice the conviction that "many will come from east and west and sit at table with Abraham, Isaac, and Jacob in the kingdom of heaven, while the sons of the kingdom will be thrown into the outer darkness; there men will weep and gnash their teeth" (8:11-12); otherwise, Jesus seeks out no Gentiles and says nothing positive about them until after the resurrection (28:16-20). Given that the healing of the centurion's servant appears before Jesus's declaration of the restriction of his mission to the house of Israel, it is likely that the Matthean Jesus is thinking not of a mission to the Gentiles in history, the time of Israel, or the time of the Church, but the eschatological coming of the Gentiles to Zion (see, for instance, Isa 2:2, 5:26, and 49:6b). The centurion comes to him; Jesus does not go to the centurion.

. . . *Then to the Gentile*

The ultimate perspective is fuller, however. St. Matthew as narrator shows in the story of the Magi and through explicit prophecy that God's promises to the Gentiles will be realized in Jesus. To do so, he quotes Isaiah 9 in Matthew 4 and, above all, Isaiah 42 in Matthew 12: "[H]e shall proclaim justice to the Gentiles . . . and in his name will the Gentiles hope" (12:18, 21). Jesus's declared mission to Israel expands to include Gentiles after the resurrection, after the Jews's decisive rejection of him at the crucifixion.

But if the God of Israel who prophesied through Isaiah knew all along that Gentiles would receive their promised blessings through Jesus, their inclusion involves Jewish rejection of Jesus on a human level, a pattern seen throughout the New Testament (see Acts 28:28 and Rom 9–11). Herod, the King of the Jews, has tried to kill little baby Jesus, and John the Baptist excoriates those who will become Jesus's foremost opponents even before his baptism of the latter. Indeed, in an oft-overlooked instance of Matthean parallelism, the Gospel presents both John and Jesus facing mortal threats that lead to Jesus's withdrawal and then a quotation from Isaiah promising Gentile inclusion. In Matthew 4:12 Jesus hears John is arrested and "withdrew" (*anechōrēsen*) from there to Capernaum, near Zebulun and Naphtali, according to St. Matthew, occasioning a quote from Isaiah 9:1–2, promising good things to pagans:

> The land of Zeb'ulun and the land of Naph'tali, toward the sea, across the Jordan, Galilee of the Gentiles—the people who sat in darkness have seen a great light, and for those who sat in the region and shadow of death light has dawned. (Matt 4:15–16)

In Matthew 12:14–21, Jesus encounters the threat of the Pharisees's murderous conspiracy and, aware of it, "withdrew" (*anechōrēsen*) from there, upon which St. Matthew supplies another quote from Isaiah promising good things to pagans, this time from Isaiah 42: "[My servant] shall proclaim justice to the Gentiles. . . . [I]n his name will the Gentiles hope" (Matt 12:18, 21).

The Church as Remnant and New Israel

After rising opposition from the Jewish leadership, Jesus founds a Church, a remnant community formed to continue Israel's mission of the redemption of the world, as Israel's leadership refuses to let Jesus lead (Matt 16). But here Gentiles are not yet in view. In the prior chapter Jesus had ignored the Canaanite woman (15:21–28) and refused her request for a remote exorcism of her daughter, claiming again that he was sent only to the lost sheep of the house of Israel (15:24). Too often popular piety protects Jesus in this passage, claiming that Jesus is trying to tease faith out of the woman but really wanting to help her all along. A better reading more faithful to the cultural and literary context of the passage sees the Matthean Jesus here as a conservative male Jew who has little time for either women or pagans, even though he will later expand the Church's mission to the Gentiles.

So the Church in Matthew 16 should not yet be envisioned to include Gentiles. The Church appears implicitly in the Parable of the Wicked Tenants (Matt 21:33–46). Jesus tells the parable against "the chief priests and the elders of the people" (21:23), telling them fatefully, "Therefore I tell you, the kingdom of God will be taken away from you and given to a nation producing the fruits of it" (21:43). Crucial is the fact that "nation" here is singular, not plural; we do not have here—nor do we find elsewhere in Matthew—ethnic Israel replaced by a Gentile Church. Rather, given the flow of the story, at this point the singular "nation" is likely the Church, but the Church is as of yet regarded as exclusively Jewish, a remnant body from within Israel continuing Israel's redeeming work in the world.

Salvation by Eucharistic Ritual Sacrifice

However, the Church will continue Israel's redeeming work apart from the mainstream body of Israel's institutions, such as the rabbinate ("rabbi" is never a positive word in the Gospel of Matthew; see 23:7, 26:25, and 26:49) and the temple (as Jesus predicts its destruction; see 24:2). By this point in the narrative, an ideal reader is considering a different answer to the question "Who are his people?" The initial and justified assumption is that his people is Israel, the Jews. But now the reader is starting to see that "his people" is actually the Church. And as that body of the Church begins to break from the parent body of Jewish Israel, the reader finds Jesus erecting himself and his sacrifice as replacements for the rabbinate and the temple. In Matthew 23:8, Jesus says, "But you are not to be called rabbi, for you have one teacher"—presumably Jesus himself—"and you are all brethren." In Matthew 21:12–13 Jesus prophesies the temple's destruction, not only by the prophetic act of turning over tables but also by quoting from Jeremiah 7 in Matthew 21:13b, a prophecy of destruction made explicit to his disciples and readers in Matthew 24:2. And most notably, in Matthew 26:26–29, Jesus institutes the Eucharist in the context of the Passover meal.

Here Jesus sets himself up as a new Passover, something well understood in early Christianity (see 1 Cor 5:7: "For Christ, our paschal lamb, has been sacrificed"). Jesus takes the

Passover ritual and transforms it into his own Catholic rite. In particular, Jesus claims the chalice is "my blood of the [new] covenant, which is poured out for many for the forgiveness of sins" (Matt 26:28). Jesus's blood is "poured out," or "shed" (*ekchunnomenon*, from the word *ekchunnō*), a word with sacrificial meaning in the Greek Old Testament, in Exodus 29:12 and Leviticus 4:7, 12, 25, 30, 8:15, and 9:9. The answer to the second question—"How will he save his people from their sins?"—then, is unexpected, the total reverse of what an ideal reader would have initially suspected: Jesus will save his people not by killing for them but by dying for them.

The Church and Israel

What of the relationship of Israel and Jews, on one hand, and the Church, on the other? After the horrors of the Holocaust, it's a fraught question. Many American Christians are deeply invested in modern Israel, spiritually and emotionally. They see the establishment of the State of Israel in 1948 as the fulfillment of biblical prophecy and a sign of God's enduring fidelity to the Jews. (It's interesting to note, however, that many Orthodox Jews do not see the establishment of the State of Israel as the fulfillment of prophecy, as they find the modern State of Israel sorely deficient, matching in no way God's promises and prophecies in the Bible.)

As regards St. Matthew's vision for the relationship of the Church to Israel, it's best to say that the Church continues Israel's mission to be a "light to the nations" (Isa 49:6b). We do not have a Gentile Church replacing the Jewish Israel of Jesus's day. Rather, the Church in Matthew is originally Jewish (Jesus and the Twelve Apostles are all Jewish) but also ultimately open to Gentiles (as in Matt 28:19, "[M]ake disciples of all nations"). But the Gospel of Matthew is clear that the

Church, including all willing Jews and Gentiles baptized in Jesus's name, bears the burden of God's mission in the world going forward.

In His Name the Nations Will Hope

By this point in the story, then, Jesus the Christ has fulfilled God's promises to Israel, ushering in the inbreaking of the kingdom, but after encountering opposition, Jesus has formed the Church as a remnant community to carry forth Israel's work of redemption in the world, a community with its teacher in Jesus, its leaders in the Twelve, and its sacrifice in the Eucharist.

When, then, do the Gentiles enter Jesus's plans? After the Israel contemporary with Jesus rejects him utterly. In Matthew 27 Jesus Christ is before Pilate, along with a man named Jesus Barabbas,[14] and "Barabbas" means "son of the father." Pilate attempts to release Jesus Christ, whom the reader knows is the true Son of the Father (see especially Jesus's words in Matt 11:27: "All things have been delivered to me by my Father; and no one knows the Son except the Father, and no one knows the Father except the Son and any one to whom the Son chooses to reveal him"). But the crowd demands Jesus's crucifixion and the release of the imposter son of the Father, Jesus Barabbas. The craven Pilate washes his hands of the matter and declares he is innocent of Jesus's blood (27:24). And then "all the people" cry out some of the most horrifying and consequential words in human history: "His blood

---

[14] Matthew 27:16 has many ancient manuscripts naming him "Jesus Barabbas." It's likely that this name is in fact what St. Matthew wrote, but a later pious scribe omitted it in the copy of St. Matthew's Gospel he was making because he couldn't bear to associate the sacred Name of Jesus with a criminal.

be on us and on our children!" (27:25). The phrase "all the people" recalls for the ideal reader "all Jerusalem" being troubled along with Herod at the rumors of the birth of a new king of the Jews (2:3). Here what is hinted at in chapter two is fulfilled: the ultimate rejection of Jesus not just by Jewish leadership, parties, and sects but, indeed, "all the people."

It is crucial at this point to understand several things: First, Gentiles are not yet in Jesus's picture; ethnic Israel is not being replaced by a Church of Gentiles. Second, Jesus remains Jewish, and his original disciples remain Jewish and remain so past the time of the Gospel into the period of the Church and indeed the eschaton. Third, "His blood be on us and on our children" need not imply a perpetual curse upon ethnic Jews. Rather, in the world of the Matthean story, any "curse" here lasts two generations: first upon the generation calling for Jesus's crucifixion, and then their children, the generation which endures the horrors of the siege and destruction of Jerusalem and its temple at the hands of the Roman legions, predicted by Jesus himself.

But again, on a human level, this Jewish rejection of Jesus precipitates Gentile inclusion. Only after, but soon after, "all the people" utter these terrifying words does Jesus give definitive, positive mention of a Gentile mission: "Go therefore and make disciples of all nations, baptizing them in the name of the Father and of the Son and of the Holy Spirit, teaching them to observe all that I have commanded you" (Matt 28:19–20a). Here, now, for the first time, Jesus clearly and directly encourages mission to Gentiles. The direction is important: Jesus sends the Church to them. In the story of the Gospel of Matthew itself, Jesus never approaches Gentiles; they come to him, whether the Magi (2:1–12), the centurion in Capernaum (8:5–13; though Jesus is willing to go with him, the centurion comes first to him, and Jesus ultimately does not go with him), or the Canaanite woman (15:21–28). Here, then, at the end of the Gospel, is something new: deliberate mission to the Gentiles.

Re-Reading Matthew's Gospel in Light of the Resurrection

Now many interpreters of Scripture operate with a hermeneutics of the gap, thinking that the idea is to bridge a chasm between the Bible in the ancient world and their situation in the modern world. But reading with a sense of continuity in which we stand in the time of the Church anticipating the end of time helps us read the Gospel of Matthew as Christian Scripture. For in the Gospel of Matthew's perspective, it is always the time of the Church, from resurrection to end.

The last line from Matthew—"teaching them to observe all that I have commanded you" (28:20a)—functions to make the Gospel of Matthew more than a mere Jewish document from antiquity, a textual artifact bearing witness to a long-dead apocalyptic sect within Judaism; it makes it a Christian document of perpetual relevance, Sacred Scripture. For as many Matthean scholars have recognized, the phrase invites a rereading of the Gospel of Matthew; and one should do so with the knowledge that the ideal reader has acquired along the way, as all that Jesus has commanded and now commands (to teach others among the nations) is contained in the prior material of the Gospel itself.

Thus is enabled a reading of Matthew that is allegorical (as St. Augustine and St. Thomas Aquinas, as representatives of the West, would understand it, in a limited sense, rooted in the letter). For instance, in light of Jesus's institution of the Eucharist, references to the altar throughout the Gospel of Matthew may now be understood to refer to the Christian altar of the Eucharist and not only the altar of the temple, as in Matthew 5:23–24: "So if you are offering your gift at the altar, and there remember that your brother has something against you, leave your gift there before the altar and go; first be reconciled to your brother, and then come and offer your gift." In this way, Jesus's predictions of the destruction of the temple, which would seem to be rendered more or less pointless after the fact, find perpetual relevance. Why would St. Matthew waste papyrus and ink having Jesus talk about the high altar in the Jewish temple when that same Jesus predicts its destruction? If on a first reading the Gospel of Matthew presents a Jesus who would lead *Israel* into and in the new age, on subsequent readings the Gospel of Matthew presents a Jesus who would lead the *Church* into and in the new age as her Christ and Savior.

One might say that there are thus two Gospels of Matthew an ideal reader encounters, as "teaching them to observe all that I have commanded you" puts the reader on a cyclical loop into that future "to the close of the age" (Matt 28:20), making the Gospel of Matthew a document of perpetual relevance for the Church. And in either of these Gospels—the one the model reader encounters on a first reading, or the one the model reader encounters on a second reading—it is a time of fulfillment.

The Church's Time of Eucharistic Mission

The theme of "fulfillment" in the Gospel of Matthew has occasioned much discussion, particularly in light of the "lure" of the formula quotations, in which St. Matthew uses a common formula to introduce quotations from the Old Testament, such as "All this took place to fulfil what the Lord had spoken by the prophet" (Matt 1:22).[15] But the phenomenon of "fulfillment" permeates the entirety of the Gospel of Matthew; it is not found only in the formula quotations. They "lure" us away from all the other ways the Gospel of Matthew presents fulfillment. Every word of the Gospel of Matthew is geared toward fulfillment, showing how Jesus and the Church fulfill stories and figures from the Old Testament and Jewish tradition. Indeed, Jesus's very life takes the very shape of Israel's story.[16]

This makes sense of the structure of the Christian Scriptures, which situates the Gospel of Matthew in the canonical center as the First Gospel, as well as making sense of the Gospel of Matthew itself. The Gospel of Matthew comes first precisely because it is a Gospel of fulfillment, the canon suggesting to Christians that Jesus is indeed the fulfillment of the prophets's words, which come last in the Christian Old Testament.

The Gospel of Matthew presents Jesus as a new Israel, as the embodiment of Israel. The formula quotation of Hosea 11:1b in Matthew 2:15 ("Out of Egypt have I called my son") presents Jesus as the embodiment of Israel. So too does the story of Jesus's Temptation in the wilderness (Matt 4:1–11) concern the testing of Jesus as the embodiment of Israel. The ideal reader raises the question, however, as to whether Jesus as the embodiment of Israel will be faithful, for Israel's history contains instances of gross failure and disobedience by corporate Israel and otherwise heroic individuals therein. Hosea

---

[15] See Donald Senior, "The Lure of the Formula Quotations: Re-Assessing Matthew's Use of the Old Testament with the Passion Narrative as a Test Case," in *The Scriptures in the Gospels*, ed. Christopher M. Tuckett (Leuven: Leuven University Press, 1997), 89–115.

[16] J. R. Daniel Kirk, "Conceptualizing Fulfillment in Matthew," *Tyndale Bulletin* 59 (2008): 77–98.

11 itself recounts the disobedience of Israel. The Temptation Narrative answers this question affirmatively and definitively: Jesus is tested (4:1); Israel was tested in the wilderness (Deut 8:2). Jesus is in the desert forty days and nights (Matt 4:1); Israel was in the wilderness forty years (Deut 8:2). Jesus is hungry (Matt 4:1); Israel was hungry (Deut 8:3). In this brief story there are three quotations from Deuteronomy (Deut 8:3 in Matt 4:4; Deut 6:16 in Matt 4:7; Deut 6:13 in Matt 4:10). In this section of Deuteronomy, Israel is adjured repeatedly to be faithful to the Lord in light of the Exodus and the giving of the Commandments (Deut 5). As such, "we have before us a haggadic tale which has issued forth from reflection on Deut[eronomy] 6–8. Jesus, the Son of God, is repeating the experience of Israel in the desert."[17] Jesus obeys perfectly, unlike Israel in the wilderness. If one has an incarnational reading of Matthew 1:23, then, God himself (who is not the God of the philosophers but the God of Abraham, Isaac, and Jacob, the God of Israel) who has come to his people in Jesus fulfills Israel's story himself. All other Christological typologies and titles ought to be subordinated to this one. Jesus fulfills not only particular biblical personalities in a typological way but indeed the entirety of the "law and the prophets" (Matt 5:17).

If God fulfills Israel's story in Jesus, then an ideal reader sees more clearly the Matthean emphasis on continuity. It is easy to emphasize discontinuity in the Gospel of Matthew, given the history of Christian anti-Judaism, the Gospel's own historical role in generating that history as it suffers misreading, and the radical claims of newness in the Gospel, rooted in the uniqueness of the divine authority of Jesus's own person

---

[17] W. D. Davies and Dale C. Allison, Jr., *A Critical and Exegetical Commentary on the Gospel According to Saint Matthew*, 3 vols., International Critical Commentary (Edinburgh: T&T Clark, 1988–1997), 1:352.

(see, for instance, Matt 7:29: "for he taught them as one who had authority, and not as their scribes"); Jesus is the one who is so bold as to issue his own commandments (see 5:19–20, in which the near demonstrative pronoun qualifying "these" commandments and the repeated references to the kingdom of God Jesus inaugurates [see 4:17] indicate not the Law and Prophets as such are in view, but Jesus's own commandments which follow in the Sermon on the Mount and the Gospel as a whole). But there is continuity: Jesus fulfills the line of Israel as son of Abraham (a new Isaac, and thus a sacrifice) and son of David (Christ) (1:1–17), as God himself come to earth (1:18–25) who is with us always (1:23; 28:20).

Jesus is and remains Jewish. Jesus assumes a Jewish worldview, whatever his particular mindset within Judaism. Jesus does not start from scratch, as docetic and moralistic Enlightenment theology would have it. And an ideal reader perceives that continuity. The story of Israel culminates in Jesus the Jew, but—as a result both of the divine plan as indicated in the story of the Magi and the quotations of Isaiah 9 and 12 and also human hostility—Jesus founds the Church not to replace Israel in a brute substitution but to continue her work to be the servant proclaiming "justice to the Gentiles," Jesus himself leading those Jews (and also Gentiles, post-resurrection) who would join him as his disciples as he, God with them (Matt 1:23), present in their midst when gathered (18:20), promises to be with them to the end of the age (28:20). The time of the Gospel of Matthew, then, is the now: the time of the Eucharistic mission of the Church to all the nations, as the Church is to do what Jesus commands, which chief above all other things is to celebrate the Eucharist (26:26–29), which he commanded by his example in its institution. The Gospel of Matthew makes clear that Jesus Christ stands at the center of salvation history and that his presence in the Eucharist stands at the center of the Church's mission and thus our salvation today. Commanded to make disciples of all nations, the Church stands in the time of Eucharistic mission.

Interpretive Implications: The True Faith in the True Church

I would offer, then, some interpretive reflections on reading the Scriptures in terms of salvation history with the Gospel of Matthew at their theological center. First, and above all, this interpretive stance helps us see that Jesus Christ remains Jewish and thus that the Faith remains Jewish in character, since the Matthean Christ is situated deeply in the world of conservative first-century common Judaism. Too often the noble desire for the gospel message's enculturation results in the creation of a Christ in one's own racial, social, or cultural image, abstracted from the written Gospels and removed from the one very real story of salvation history, which Jesus Christ himself as the Incarnation of the second person of the Trinity superintends. One winds up with an ideal and thus unreal Christ, not the real resurrected and ascended Christ who now sits "at the right hand of the Father." Enculturation risks making particular cultures normative and thus determinative of the gospel message. But Christ is more than a teacher and Christianity more than a doctrinal system. Christ himself is the Church, and thus the universal Church is prior to any particular Church in any given time and place. The universal Church is one, not a collection of churches, and is indeed its own nation (Matt 21:43) with its own practices and beliefs, its own culture. Even as the Church permeates particular human cultures, it is its own culture rooted in the cultus of the Eucharistic liturgy.

Second, recognizing continuity in salvation history means

we read Scripture from within the story itself, as part of that ecclesial culture Scripture itself has generated and nurtured. We do not stand outside and above Scripture's story, as if the Bible were a discrete object with its constituent verses crashing upon us all at once, requiring us to sift and sort them with some interpretive principle as if there were a hermeneutical gap between Now and Then. Rather, we stand in the time of the Church, and hear Jesus's words directly as the Apostles did, who were part of the same Church he founded.

OUTLINE, THEMES, AND THEOLOGICAL EMPHASES OF MATTHEW'S GOSPEL

That, then is the basic story of St. Matthew's Gospel. In terms of a formal outline, it must first be observed that generating them for biblical books is notoriously difficult. If one scans study Bibles and commentaries of a single biblical book, one will find radically different outlines. This is true of the Gospel of Matthew. On one hand, a simple structure is apparent. The first four chapters tell of Jesus's origins and the beginning of his public ministry. Then follow five great blocks of teaching given mainly to his disciples, beginning with the Sermon on the Mount (chs. 5–7) and concluding with Jesus's teaching about the destruction of the temple and the end of the world (chs. 24–25). The five blocks are interspersed with four narrative sections in which Jesus heals, exorcises, works miracles, teaches publicly and privately, and endures conflict with Jewish authorities. The Gospel concludes with the Passion Narrative telling of Jesus's death and resurrection (chs. 26–28). And so a rudimentary outline looks like this:

1–4	Origins and beginnings of ministry
5–7	Teaching: Sermon on the Mount
8–9	Narrative: Largely healings
10	Teaching: Missionary Discourse
11–12	Narrative: Public teaching and dialogue, conflict
13	Teaching: Parables of the Kingdom
14–17	Narrative: Miracles, public teaching and dialogue, conflict, founding of the Church, predictions of his Passion
18	Teaching: Church Discipline Discourse
19–23	Narrative: Public teaching and dialogue, healing, Triumphal Entry into Jerusalem, teaching and conflict in the temple
24–25	Destruction of the Temple and End Times Discourse
26–28	Passion Narrative

As my wordy summaries for the narrative sections reveal, however, pressing beyond the simple outline of alternating teaching and narrative sections is not easy; there is no obvious structure to the narrative sections, and commentators regularly observe that the outline of the Sermon on the Mount—especially the second half—is not clear.

Biblical scholars of earlier generations were fascinated with "chiasms," concentric patterns in which a passage or even entire document is like a mirror or a folded piece of paper, in which beginning and ending reflect and inform each other, and then the next and next-to last material, and so forth. ("Chiasm" comes from the Greek letter *chi*, X, as if the outline moved from the top of the left side of the letter to the middle and back out as it moved down again.) Some have seen the

Gospel of Matthew as one large chiasm with the pattern A-B-C-D-E-F-E-D-C-B-A. The first four chapters go with the last three so that Jesus's beginning and end reflect and inform each other, with the first and fifth teaching sections reflecting and informing each other, and so forth. Those who see chiasms often insist the middle is key, and right in the middle of Matthew stands chapter 13, Parables of the Kingdom.

But there are real problems with this. First, it's not obvious that St. Matthew had this in mind. Second, there's little interpretive payoff—it doesn't help us interpret the Gospel to say that the Parables of the Kingdom in chapter 13 are the most important part. That brings us to the third problem: the other parts matter too, and chiastic approaches neglect them.

Above all, chiastic interpretation ignores the story structure of texts, such as the Gospel of Matthew, that have all the characteristics of complex narratives. However, one outline proposed by J. D. Kingsbury takes the story structure of Matthew fully into account.[18] Kingsbury sees 1:1–4:16 as a section introducing Jesus the Christ, 4:17–16:20 as a section concerning Jesus's ministry to Israel, and 16:21–28:20 as a section concerning Jesus's journey to Jerusalem to endure his Passion. In both 4:17 and 16:21 we find the phrase "From that time Jesus began" (*apo tote ērxeto ho Iēsous*). In the former, Jesus begins to preach repentance in light of the coming kingdom, and in the latter, Jesus begins to teach his disciples he must suffer, die, and be raised. Both 4:17 and 16:21, then, introduce the material that follows in the broader section.

While critics have noted that Kingsbury's outline doesn't fit well with the five-discourse structure of Matthew that seems so obvious (Kingsbury's second section would have

---

[18] Jack Dean Kingsbury, *Matthew: Structure, Christology, Kingdom* (repr., Minneapolis: Augsburg, 1991), 1–39.

three discourses while the third would have two), the blocks of teaching discourse fit well in terms of content in Kingsbury's divisions and, more importantly, make deep sense of the story-structure of Matthew's Gospel. As such I assume Kingsbury's outline in this book.

Again, Matthew's Gospel is a story of *fulfillment*. It shows how Jesus and the Church realize the Old Testament promises made to Israel and through Israel to the Gentiles. Jesus Christ is presented as the new presentation of most every important personage from the Old Testament (e.g., Moses, Isaac, Joseph, and as the Christ, King David) and as the one who completes the Mosaic Law perfectly in all righteousness (see Matt 3:17 and 5:17). Not only are the Law and righteousness consummated in the coming of Jesus, but also Scripture as a whole, as Matthew's Gospel presents numerous instances where some event fulfills some prophet's prophecy, often using the "formula quotations," discussed above. But the fulfillment of Scripture in Matthew's Gospel is broader than the explicit formula quotations. St. Matthew also shows this by subtle allusions, using phrases from the Old Testament to draw the alert reader's attention to an Old Testament passage where the allusion evokes a paradigm, wherein a story in the Gospel recapitulates a story from the Old Testament (e.g., Jesus's forty days in the wilderness recapitulates Israel's forty years in the wilderness). Further, these mechanisms of drawing on the Old Testament are not exclusive; we often find quotation, allusion, and paradigm functioning together in the same Matthean passage.

The emphasis on fulfillment raises the issues of the relationship of "old" and "new" in Matthew's Gospel. At the end of Jesus's delivery of a chapter of parables, Jesus tells his disciples, "Therefore every scribe who has been trained for the kingdom of heaven is like a householder who brings out of his treasure what is new and what is old" (Matt 13:52). Much that is old in the Old Testament and Judaism abides in the new time of the Church, but much is done away with (such as the dietary laws, as Jesus declares them irrelevant, 15:10–20), and what is kept of the old is kept by being fulfilled and transformed. Thus, the emphasis in Matthew's Gospel really falls on newness. The sacrifices of the old covenant are fulfilled in the sacrifice of the Eucharist. The Ten Commandments and their interpretation in Judaism are fulfilled, interpreted, and transformed in the Sermon on the Mount. Inward righteousness now complements outward righteousness and fulfills it (e.g., literal adultery and murder remain sins, but Jesus moves to lust, anger, and invective in the heart and on the lips, 5:21–30). The Church is now God's agent of mission in the world, the new Israel continuing the mission of Israel to be a light to the Gentile nations.

In Matthew's Gospel the identity of Jesus is determined largely by how the Gospel draws on the Old Testament. Who, then, is Jesus in Matthew's Gospel? Above all, he is God come to earth in the Incarnation ("'his name shall be called Emmanuel' [which means, God with us]," Matt 1:23). He is thus Son of God, which implies not just his divinity but also makes him a new Adam, the original son of God, and Christ, as the anointed one in the Old Testament is presented as the son of God the Father (2 Sam 7:14). He is also "son of David," which means Christ, for by the time of Jesus most Jews believed that the Christ would be David's ultimate descendant. He is Son of man, which refers not simply to Jesus's humanity but again to Adam and to the divine, end-time deliverer of Daniel 7:13. After that, he is presented as the embodiment of Israel, the faithful Israelite where Israel failed—the Temptation over forty days in the wilderness (Matt 4:1–11) is the recapitulation of Israel's forty years in the wilderness. And he fulfills other Old Testament personages, like Isaac, as Jesus is a new sacrifice; like Moses, as Jesus brings the New Law in five major blocks of teaching, imagining the five books of Moses; like Joseph, as Jesus was handed over to pagans by those who were his ethnic brothers; and like the righteous sufferer of the Psalms, Isaiah, and Wisdom.

Jesus, being all these things, especially the divine Christ, brings the New Law in proclaiming himself the ultimate, authoritative interpreter of what now becomes the Old Law. In chapter 5, Jesus six times says, "You have heard it said . . . but I say to you . . ." Matthew does not present him as another smart interpreter among many but as the One with the authority to declare the ultimate truth. And so the disciples and crowds marvel, because "he taught them as one who had authority, and not as their scribes" (Matt 7:29).

It is absolutely crucial—not just for Matthew's Gospel but for Christianity in general—to rightly understand the relationship of the Old Law and the New, the Old Testament and the New, the Law and the gospel. Many today think that Jesus came to do away with all laws and rules whatsoever. Judaism then becomes a decadent, burdensome religion of righteousness by works, while Christianity is not even a religion but a movement characterized by faith, grace, and love. That's actually an ancient heresy called Marcionism, after the second-century shipbuilder Marcion, who thought the god of the Old Testament was cruel and wicked, while the God of the New Testament was the kind and loving Father of Jesus Christ. Marcion thus made a Bible consisting only of the Gospel of Luke and ten letters of Paul, all expurgated of what Marcion thought were Jewish elements wicked scribes had introduced.

The watchword for Christians, and especially Catholics, is *continuity*. There is continuity between old and new, and the Old Testament remains enduring Scripture for Christians, read through the lens of the crucified and risen Christ and, for Catholics, in accord with the Tradition of the Church. And it will not do at all to think that Jesus (or Paul, for that matter) did away with all rules in the name of some sort of freedom from the Law. Rather, both Judaism and Christianity have rules. The real issue is whether one accepts Jesus and the rules he brings in his divine authority.

For instance, in Matthew's Gospel Jesus simply teaches that one's works matter for salvation. "Enter by the narrow gate; for the gate is wide and the way is easy, that leads to destruction, and those who enter by it are many. For the gate is narrow and the way is hard, that leads to life, and those who find it are few" (7:13–14). For those who might suggest that the narrow way is simply justifying faith in Christ, Jesus follows up a few verses later: "Not every one who says to me, 'Lord, Lord,' shall enter the kingdom of heaven, but he who does the will of my Father who is in heaven" (7:21). And shortly thereafter comes the Parable of the Wise and Foolish builders:

> Every one then who hears these words of mine and does them will be like a wise man who built his house upon the rock; and the rain fell, and the floods came, and the winds blew and beat upon that house, but it did not fall, because it had been founded on the rock. And every one who hears these words of mine and does not do them will be like a foolish man who built his house upon the sand; and the rain fell, and the floods came, and the winds blew and beat against that house, and it fell; and great was the fall of it. (7:24–27)

"Every one then who hears these words of mine and does them"—good deeds matter in Matthew's Gospel. In fact, Jesus will later teach his disciples that his heavenly Father will treat them as the unforgiving servant, unless they forgive their brother from their heart (Matt 18:23–35).

What, then, of the scribes and Pharisees, Jesus's chief antagonists in Matthew's Gospel? The problem isn't that they had laws and rules; the problem is that they misinterpreted what they had, in the first place, and rejected Jesus and his New Law, in the second place. In doing so, they spurned the God of Israel to whom they thought they were the paragons of allegiance. That's why Jesus taught, "For I tell you, unless your righteousness exceeds that of the scribes and Pharisees, you will never enter the kingdom of heaven" (5:20).

The secret, as it were, is to get the heart right. One's righteousness will exceed that of the scribes and Pharisees when one's heart is rightly ordered to love of God and love of neighbor. For instance, Jesus teaches, "For out of the abundance of the heart the mouth speaks" (12:34), and, "But what comes out of the mouth proceeds from the heart, and this defiles a man" (15:18).

That's how one can begin to make a start on becoming perfect, as Jesus commands: "You, therefore, must be perfect, as your heavenly Father is perfect" (Matt 5:48). And yet, even if one focuses on the heart, the radical things that Jesus demands in Matthew's Gospel—forgiveness, remaining married, perfection—would be impossible in our own fallen power. But Matthew's Gospel presents grace as God's presence (Jesus) in his Church, empowering disciples to do what Jesus commands.

In short, Matthew's Gospel operates with what Catholics call "cooperative grace." It is a Gospel of "withness." Jesus is Emmanuel, God with us (Matt 1:23). He is present with disciples where two or three of them are gathered in his name (18:20). And the risen Christ promises to be "with" his disciples, even to the very end of the age (28:20). In Jesus Christ, God is with us, enabling us to do what Jesus Christ commands. And so is fulfilled what is written in the Catechism: "What God commands, He makes possible by His grace" (2082).

One crucial thing Jesus commands is to eat his body and drink his blood (Matt 26:26–29). Christianity is a religion not only of rules but also of ritual—although those who think it has nothing to do with rules also deny it has much to do with ritual. And yet, in Matthew's Gospel, Jesus is there, affirming ritual. He teaches that those making an offering at the altar who remember someone has something against them should go and be reconciled, and then come and offer the gift (5:23–24). He tells the scribes and Pharisees that while they've practiced the tithing of their herbs to the neglect of the weightier matters of the Law (namely, justice, mercy, and faith), they should have kept the former without neglecting the latter (23:23). That is, Jesus does not deny the legal ritual of tithing but affirms it while subordinating it to the weightier matters of the Law.

Again and above all, as the story of Matthew's Gospel comes to its climax, we find the institution of the Eucharist. Jesus institutes a definitive, enduring ritual for the Church. Why? Jesus intends his sacrificial Eucharist to be the Church's ritual replacing the sacrifices of the temple. The Jewish leadership has opposed Jesus, and will have him killed, so Jesus founds the Church (Matt 16:13–20) to be a remnant community within Israel. He will soon predict the destruction of the temple by the prophetic deed of overturning the tables (21:12–17) and by his prophetic words to his disciples (23:1–4, and 5–28). Jesus's Eucharist will endure in the Church after Israel's sacrifices desist with the annihilation of the temple.

In sum, then, as a Gospel of ritual (Eucharist), rules (the New Law), discipline (discipleship), and community (Church), Matthew presents a challenge to and remedy for contemporary Gnosticism and Moral Therapeutic Deism, which disdains creation, libertinism, superficial morality, and individuality. To Matthew's Gospel we now turn.

II. The Gosepl of Matthew in the Lectionary

PART I

THE GENESIS OF JESUS THE CHRIST

IN THE FIRST MAJOR SECTION of St. Matthew's Gospel, the origins of Jesus the Christ are presented as are the roots of his public ministry as John the Baptist's successor and as the one who marks the advent of the new age, the inbreaking of the new creation, the new Genesis.

CHAPTER 3

THE ORIGINS OF JESUS THE CHRIST

MATTHEW 1

THE LECTIONARY DRAWS on the first chapter of the Gospel of Matthew frequently:

> Matthew 1:1–25: Nativity of the Lord Vigil Mass (Long Form; Short Form: 1:18–25)
>
> Nativity of the Blessed Virgin Mary (September 8, Long Form: 1:1–16, 18–23; Short Form: 1:18–23)
>
> December 17 in Advent (1:1–17)
>
> Solemnity for Saint Joseph, Spouse of the Blessed Virgin Mary (March 19, first option: 1:16, 18–21, 24a)
>
> Fourth Sunday of Advent (1:18–24)
>
> December 18 in Advent (1:18–25)

We will thus deal with Matthew 1 according to the three parts it naturally falls into: 1:1, 1:2–17, and 1:18–25.

MATTHEW 1:1: CHRIST AND SACRIFICE

Translation is interpretation. In the Revised Standard Version (Catholic Second Edition), the very first verse of the Gospel of Matthew reads, "The book of the genealogy of Jesus Christ, the son of David, the son of Abraham." The translation suggests that the first verse is introducing the genealogy that follows in verses 2–18. It makes some sense, since David and Abraham are mentioned, and they function as turning points in the genealogy to follow (Matt 1:2, 6b).

But the genealogy has three parts, not two—one would think if the first verse was introducing only the genealogy that it would also have three parts. Further, the figures suggested by "son of David" and "son of Abraham"—namely the Christ, who Jews understood to be the "son of David," and Isaac, the "son of Abraham"—play major roles in the Gospel of Matthew.

Therefore I'm convinced that the first verse introduces the entire Gospel of Matthew, and so there's another way to translate the Greek (which is *biblos geneseōs Iēsou Christou huiou David huiou Abraam*): "The book of the new creation Jesus Christ brings, who is son of David and son of Abraham." *Geneseōs* recalls the very Book of Genesis, which tells of the creation of the heaven and the earth, of all things visible and invisible. Reading the Gospel of Matthew, we will find that Jesus Christ brings the new creation: the renewal, redemption, and transformation of creation. It's a fitting verse to begin the New Testament, which in its entirety proclaims the new creation brought by Jesus Christ.

"Son of David" and "son of Abraham," then, suggest the figure of the Christ and the figure of Isaac to the reader. St. Matthew is setting up two main categories with which to understand Jesus. He will be the Christ, the deliverer of Israel, and he will be a sacrifice like Isaac. Stanley Hauerwas, a Protestant theologian friendly to Catholicism, writes:

> It is interesting to ask why Matthew names Jesus the son of David prior to being the son of Abraham. The answer may be simply that Matthew thinks naming Abraham second provides a useful transition to the list of descendants beginning with Isaac. Yet no words or ordering of words in scripture is without significance. Matthew knows he is telling the story of one that was born a king, yet a king to be sacrificed. God had tested Abraham by commanding him to sacrifice Isaac. By beginning with "Son of David" Matthew prepares us to recognize that this is a king who will end up on the cross.[1]

As Isaac was the son of Abraham his father, so Jesus is the Son of God his Father. As Abraham offered his only son Isaac in sacrifice (Gen 22), God the Father offers Jesus, his only Son, in sacrifice. For St. Matthew, this also solves the embarrassing problem of a crucified Christ. Nowhere in Jewish tradition do we find a Christ killed by his enemies; the Christ is supposed to kill his enemies and deliver Israel thereby.[2] The Isaac typology supplies the concept of the atoning death of a martyr. How can it be that Jesus is the Christ, but also that he ends up crucified? Because he is not only the Christ, the deliverer, but also Isaac, the sacrifice. And of course St. Matthew

---

[1] Stanley Hauerwas, *Matthew*, Brazos Theological Commentary on the Bible (Grand Rapids, MI: Brazos, 2006), 17.

[2] St. Paul's words in 1 Corinthians 1:23 are important here: "we preach Christ crucified, a stumbling block to Jews." One of the chief obstacles to Jewish belief in Jesus in the earliest Church's mission was precisely this, that the Christ was not supposed to suffer.

will tie these two together ironically: Jesus the Christ delivers his people not by killing for them but by dying for them. Christ and Isaac become one in Jesus.[3]

MATTHEW 1:2–17: THE MATTHEAN GENEALOGY

Genealogies are hard for moderns because we're dislocated. In our age we define ourselves by our career and lifestyle choices, getting educated and going where we will. The average American family moves once every five years, and few people from the middle or upper classes spend their adult lives in the city or county in which they grew up. Further, we also have much smaller families than people in St. Matthew's day. And so what few relatives we have often live far away.

In the biblical world, however, people generally stayed put, living out their days among their large extended families. In that situation, a genealogy defines who you are. You are the son or daughter of someone, and your identity is determined by family, clan, tribe, and ancestors.

And so our modern eyes glaze over when we encounter a genealogy, because we're mobile, dislocated from home and estranged from family.

Every name in a biblical genealogy is an allusion to a story, an ancestral milestone of who someone is. In a distinctively Jewish way, the genealogy in Matthew 1:2–17 also

---

[3] The Jewish scholar Jon Levenson observes, "Within the overall structures of the Gospels . . . the two vocabularies of sonship, that of the beloved son and that of the Davidic king as the son of God, reinforce each other powerfully. They yield a story in which the rejection, suffering, and death of the putatively Davidic figure is made to confirm rather than contradict [Jesus's] status as God's only begotten Son" (*The Death and Resurrection of the Beloved Son: The Transformation of Child Sacrifice in Judaism and Christianity* [New Haven: Yale University Press, 1993], 206).

reinforces Jesus's identity as son of David, or Christ, and son of Abraham, or Isaac. Its very structure includes *gematria*, which involves finding meanings in numbers.[4] The genealogy has three divisions of fourteen names, to which St. Matthew draws explicit attention in Matthew 1:17. David's name in Hebrew, *DWD*, has three consonants whose value totals fourteen. Jews used their letters for numerals, and *D* is worth four while *W* is worth 6. This sort of math even a biblical scholar can do: four plus six plus four is fourteen.

This is "meaning by number." Moderns may not like it, but it's got a long pedigree. The ancient Pythagoreans and Plato (for a time) believed the universe to be composed of numbers, and patristic and medieval Christians like St. Augustine got much mileage out of Wisdom 11:20: "But you have arranged all things by measure and number and weight." In our own day, the idea is captured in the movie *The Matrix*. Binary code rolls down several computer monitors, and Cypher, a programmer, declares he can see the universe of the Matrix through the code: "You get used to it. I don't even see the code. All I see is a blonde, brunette, redhead." In short, the reality of the matrix in the movie is fundamentally numbers. It's the filmmakers bringing the ancient idea into modern film.

The genealogy also suggests Isaac. If one does St. Matthew's math, Jesus came at the beginning of the forty-second generation after Abraham. The ancient *Book of Jubilees* situates the sacrifice of Isaac right before the beginning of the forty-second "jubilee" after creation.[5] Not only do the three consonants of David's name total fourteen, but also the three divisions of fourteen names add up to forty-two. The very

---

[4] The most well-known example is the number of the beast, 666, in Revelation 13:18.

[5] See Roy Rosenberg, "Jesus, Isaac, and the Suffering Servant," *Journal of Biblical Literature* 84 (1965): 387.

structure of the genealogy reveals that in Jesus, the son of David (the Christ) and the son of Abraham (Isaac) are one.

MATTHEW 1:18–25: THE EXTRAORDINARY CONCEPTIONS OF TWO PROMISED CHILDREN

We find a third allusion to Isaac and a fulfillment of prophecy in the angel's message to Joseph in Matthew 1:18–25. The allusion and the quotation of Isaiah 7:14 LXX make for a rhetorical one-two punch, functioning together to reinforce the reader's acceptance of the Virgin Birth.

In Matthew 1:20–21, the angel's words allude to Gen 17:19 LXX, which contains the first mention of Isaac in the Old Testament:

Matthew 1:20–21:

But as he considered this, behold, an angel of the Lord appeared to him in a dream, saying, "Joseph, son of David, do not fear to take Mary your wife, for that which is conceived in her is of the Holy Spirit; she will bear a son, and you shall call his name Jesus, for he will save his people from their sins."

Genesis 17:19 LXX:

God said, "No, but Sarah your wife shall bear you a son, and you shall call his name Isaac. I will establish my covenant with him as an everlasting covenant for his descendants after him."

We discover the passages sharing several Greek words as St. Matthew alludes with all deliberation to Isaac's birth in his story of the annunciation of the Virgin Birth: *Marian tēn gunaika sou . . . texetai de huion, kai kaleseis to onoma autou Iēsoun* ("Mary your wife . . . will bear a son, and you shall call his name Jesus") alludes to *Sarra hē gunē sou texetai soi huion kai kaleseis to onoma autou Isaak* ("Sarah your wife shall bear you a son, and you shall call his name Isaac").

In this passage, then, St. Matthew sets up a fourfold typology between the angel, Joseph, Mary, and Jesus, on the one hand, and God, Abraham, Sarah, and Isaac on the other. In both stories a heavenly person (the angel and God) announces to the fathers (Joseph and Abraham) that their respective wives (Mary and Sarah) will conceive promised children (Jesus and Isaac) through a miracle.

Of course in Scripture God's angel is as good as God himself, with Old Testament texts often switching between "the angel of the LORD" and "God" in the same passage as if they're the same person, because they are (as in Gen 22:9–19; see verses 11, 12, 15, 16). And both Joseph and Abraham are righteous; St. Matthew describes the former as a righteous (or "just") man (Matt 1:19), while Abraham's faith in God was "reckoned . . . to him as righteousness" (Gen 15:6). And both Jesus and Isaac are promised children, conceived miraculously, on whom depend the promises of God, and both will grow up to be sacrifices.

What of Sarah and Mary? The weight of the allusive typology lies here. St. Matthew is encouraging belief in the Virgin Birth by reminding the reader that God opened the womb of the mother of the original holy family, Sarah, and thus suggesting that he can do it again with the virginal womb of the mother of the ultimate Holy Family, Mary. If the conception of Isaac by a barren woman was possible, so too the conception of Jesus by a virgin.

The allusion is subtle, and so St. Matthew reinforces the

point bluntly through the formula quotation of Isaiah 7:14 LXX in Matthew 1:22–23: "All this took place to fulfil what the Lord had spoken by the prophet: 'Behold, a virgin shall conceive and bear a son, and his name shall be called Emmanuel' (which means, God with us)." The Gospel of Matthew presents the reader with two complementary rhetorical devices encouraging belief in Mary's virginal conception of Jesus, an obvious quotation following up the subtle allusion. Mary's virginal conception of Jesus was not only prophesied by Scripture (the quotation of Isa 7:14 LXX) but indeed had precedent in Israel's sacred matriarchal history (the allusion to Gen 17:19 LXX).

Church Fathers saw in Sarah a typological prefiguration of the Virgin Mary. St. Ambrose connects Sarah and Mary, asserting that the birth of Jesus was foreshadowed in Isaac: "An aged woman who was sterile brought him to birth according to God's promise, so that we might believe that God has power to bring it about that even a virgin may give birth."[6] St. John Chrysostom does likewise in his forty-ninth homily on Genesis. He asserts that the stories of the barren matriarchs Rebecca, Sarah, and Rachel were "told for our benefit," foreshadowing the situation of the Virgin Mary:

> What, then, is the reason? So that when you see the Virgin giving birth to our common Lord you may not be incredulous. Exercise your mind, it [i.e., the biblical text] is saying, on the womb of these sterile women so that when you see an infertile and sealed womb opened for childbearing by God's grace, you may not be surprised to hear that a maiden gave birth.

---

6 St. Ambrose, *Isaac* 1.1, in *Saint Ambrose: Seven Exegetical Works*, trans. M. P. McHugh, Fathers of the Church 65 (Washington, DC: Catholic University of America Press, 1972), 10–65.

Or rather, feel surprise and amazement, but don't refuse faith in the marvel. So when the Jew says, How did the Virgin give birth? say to him, How did the sterile old woman give birth? In that case, you see, there were two impediments, her advanced age and the imperfect condition of nature, whereas with the Virgin there was one impediment, her not having experienced marriage. Consequently, the barren woman prepares the way for the Virgin.[7]

Chrysostom also observes that the archangel Gabriel made a similar argument to Mary herself, who, after hearing the archangel's shocking annunciation that she would conceive the Davidic Christ and Son of the Most High God, asks, "How can this be, since I have no husband?" (Luke 1:34). Gabriel uses Mary's barren relative Elizabeth to depict to Mary the very possibility of his startling prophecy. Chrysostom writes:

For your part, dearly beloved, consider, I ask you, how the barren woman led her [i.e., Mary] to faith in the birth. You see, since the first demonstration was beyond the maiden's imagining, listen to how he [i.e., Gabriel] brought his words down to a lower level and gave her guidance through visible realities. "Behold," he said, "your kinswoman Elizabeth has herself conceived a son in her old age, and this is actually the sixth month for her, despite her being called barren" [Luke 1:36]. It is solely for the Virgin's sake that he

---

7 St. John Chrysostom, *Homilies on Genesis* 49.6–7, in *Saint John Chrysostom: Homilies on Genesis 46–67*, trans. Robert C. Hill, Fathers of the Church 74 (Washington, DC: Catholic University of America Press, 1992), 42–49.

made mention of the barren woman; otherwise, why did he mention her kinswoman's birth to her and why say "despite her being called barren"?[8]

Just as Gabriel employed barren Elizabeth to explain to Mary that her virginal conception of a Son was possible, Chrysostom himself employs the barren matriarchs to illustrate the same to his audience. Both Gabriel's and Chrysostom's rhetoric deploys the principle of *nihil sub sole novum*: there is nothing new under the sun.

A Greek homily once attributed to St. Ephrem the Syrian, the "*Sermo in Abraham et Isaac*," also plays on the parallels between Sarah and Mary. Both Sarah's and Abraham's bodies were "bowed under nature's law now that their youth had wasted away" (strophe 7). But "the hope in God which flourished" in both Abraham and Sarah "was not only unageing but invincible" (strophe 8). The homilist then sets Isaac and Christ in parallel: "Therefore beyond hope she gave birth to Isaac who bore in every way the type of the Master" (strophe 9). Strophes 10–14 then extend the typology to Sarah and Mary:

> It was not nature's work / that a dead womb conceived
> and breasts that were dry / gave Isaac milk.
> It was not nature's work / that the Virgin Mary conceived without a man / and without corruption gave birth.
> He made Sara / a mother in old age;
> revealed Mary / a virgin after child-birth.
> An Angel in the tent / said to the patriarch,

---

[8]   Chrysostom, *Homilies on Genesis* 49.10–11 (*Saint John Chrysostom*, 47).

"At this time / Sara will have a son" [Gen 18:10, 14].

An Angel in Nazareth / said to Mary,
 "Behold, you will bear a son / O highly
 favoured" [Luke 1:31, 28].[9]

The homilist equates the situations of the Virgin Mary and barren Sarah: both women conceived with divine assistance, contrary to the course of nature.

The above quotations from the Fathers are general and deal mostly with the Gospel of Luke, but seeing Scripture as a whole, they would not think their insights invalid when applied to the Gospel of Matthew. One anonymous patristic text, however, finds the Sarah-Mary and Isaac-Jesus typologies directly in the Gospel of Matthew. The *Opus imperfectum in Matthaeum* (the "Unfinished Work on Matthew") compares Sarah and Mary as well as Isaac and Jesus in its commentary on the genealogy. The anonymous Father writes:

> For in this way Isaac was bestowed to parents who had long given up hope as a joy in their extreme old age. Isaac was not understood as a son of nature but as a son of grace. In this way Isaac was born by a Judean mother at the very end of her life as a joy for all to behold. In this same way the angel spoke to the shepherds: "Lo, I announce to you a great joy which will be for all people" [Luke 2:10]. And in this same way the apostle said, "When the time came, God sent his Son born of a woman, born under law" [Gal 4:4]. Although God's Son was born from a virgin and Isaac

---

[9] The translation here employed is from Archimandrite Ephrem (at https://web.archive.org/web/20160319215955/http://anastasis.org.uk/AbrIsaac.htm).

from an old woman, both were born wholly beyond the expectations of nature. The former [Isaac] had delayed until after his mother was able to give birth; the latter [Jesus] would arrive before his mother was able to give birth. The former was born from an old woman who was already failing to some extent; the latter was born from a chaste virgin.[10]

The Fathers, then, interpret Sarah and Mary consistently: the women resemble each other in that both conceived their promised children, in the words of the *Opus*, "wholly beyond the expectations of nature."

A theological word about literary typology is in order. St. Matthew and the Fathers, following in his footsteps, are able to employ typological resonances between barren Sarah and the Virgin Mary to great rhetorical and apologetic effect, because unlike the Gnostics, they knew that the one triune Creator God superintends both Testaments and indeed the whole story of salvation history they tell. For orthodox Christian faith, the God of the Old and New Testaments is the same, and he is constant. He works in the same ways in every age, whether the age of Israel or the age of the Church.

Finally, beginnings of stories, from fairy tales to television procedurals, are crucial in that they set up everything, from characters to plot. Implicit, subconscious questions are raised for the reader: What is this story about? What conflicts will happen? How will the protagonist face them? Who's the guilty party? This final section of the first chapter of the Gospel of Matthew raises two fundamental questions for the

---

[10] *Opus imperfectum in Matthaeum*, in *Matthew 1–13*, trans. Manlio Simonetti, Ancient Christian Commentary on Scripture Ia (Downers Grove, IL: InterVarsity Press, 2001), 5. The work likely dates from the early fifth century and was once wrongly attributed to Chrysostom.

reader. In Matthew 1:20–21, we read, "[Y]ou shall call his name Jesus, for he will save his people from their sins." Again, as mentioned above in the first part, the questions raised are Who are his people? and How will he save them from their sins?

Matthew's Gospel has asserted that Jesus is the Jewish Christ, the ultimate son of David, who was the first king of Israel. Indeed, "Christ" (*christos* in Greek), means "anointed one," and David was the original *christos*, anointed as a boy by Samuel as eventual king of Israel (1 Sam 16:1–13). David delivered his Israelite people by uniting the tribes (2 Sam 5:1–5), conquering their enemies, and establishing a kingdom largely at peace.

The Israelites of Jesus's day, the Jews—the descendants of the two southern tribes who returned from the Babylonian Exile, Judah (from which derives the word "Jew") and Benjamin—were paying for their sins by suffering under Roman domination. The Maccabees, facing the extermination of their religion and race, had liberated Israel from Syrian oppression in 164 BC and established the Hasmonean dynasty, which lasted a hundred years. On one hand, it was a golden age of independence, but on the other hand, it was marked by conflict, intrigue, and violence. Intrigue spelled the dynasty's end when rivalry for the high priesthood and throne enabled the Roman general Pompey to invade and conquer Jerusalem in 63 BC, and the ancient kingdom of Judah was reduced to the Roman province of Judea.

So at this early point in the story of the Gospel of Matthew, the ideal reader should assume that Jesus's people are the Jews, and that he will save them from Roman domination by killing for them, as Jesus is the Christ, the new David, who will establish the final kingdom, just as King David of old conquered Israel's enemies and established his kingdom.

Jesus's very name brings yet another warrior of old into the mix, Joshua, for Joshua and Jesus have the exact same names in both Hebrew (the language of the Old Testament; *Y'shua*), and Greek (the language of the New Testament; *Iēsous*). So the reader here hears echoes of Joshua, and of course Joshua, like David, also saved the Israelite people from their enemies by killing for them. In short, the informed reader of Matthew 1:20–21 assumes Jesus the Christ will save his Jewish people by killing for them.

But those who have read the Gospel of Matthew know that the story takes a radically different turn. By the end of the Gospel, Jesus's people is the Church (open to both Jews and also Gentiles, thanks to Jewish rejection of Jesus), and he saves his people not by killing for them but by dying for them. The Gospel of Matthew, then, is a story of reversal and tragedy, its surprising twists making way for the triumph of the Cross.

And the triumph of the Cross isn't some victory won by Jesus in the abstract apart from us. Rather, our way to salvation runs right through the Cross in our own lives of discipleship. The name of Jesus given in Matthew 1:23, Emmanuel, matters much here, for God has promised to be with us in Jesus, providing us with his enduring divine presence as power for discipleship. God doesn't just show up for a while so that Jesus can deliver definitive doctrines and then abscond again into heaven, as many assume, but being God with us, he stays with us in Jesus, in his Church, to the very end of the age: "[A]nd behold, I am with you always, to the close of the age" (28:20).

CHAPTER 4

✝

WORSHIP AND REJECTION OF THE CHRIST CHILD

MATTHEW 2:1–12: THE EPIPHANY OF THE LORD

IN THE PRIOR CHAPTER, the Gospel of Matthew set up the story, introducing its protagonist, Jesus, as Christ and new Isaac, deliverer and sacrifice. The fundamental plot concerns Jesus saving his people from their sins, and the reader assumes that means Jesus the Christ will deliver his Jewish people from Roman oppression by killing for them.

Yet even in the first chapter, the suggestion that Jesus is also a new Isaac and thus a sacrifice complicates the assumption that Jesus's mission involves nothing but triumphant conquest. And now in the second chapter, St. Matthew's story of the Magi begins to tear those initial assumptions down. For in the story, we see reversal through rejection: those who should welcome their Christ in little baby Jesus—Herod, the King of the Jews, the chief priests and scribes, and all Jerusalem—reject him, while pagan astrologers from the East, the Magi, travel afar to worship him. Indeed, St. Matthew will even engage in literary jujitsu, inverting Jesus's contemporary Israel and Egypt, having the Holy Family execute a reverse exodus, escaping the wrath of a new murderous Pharaoh, Herod, by fleeing Israel, the new house of bondage, to escape to Egypt, the new land of refuge.

Herod the Great was given the formal title "King of the Jews" by the Roman Senate in 40 BC when he began pacifying the Holy Land, which was finished with the conquest of Jerusalem in 37 BC. He was "Great" in that he accomplished much during his long reign. Above all, he refurbished the temple complex, while also building great fortresses at Masada and the Herodian as well a Mediterranean port for Jerusalem, Caesarea Maritima. He was also brutal, meriting comparison with the later English tyrant Henry VIII. Like Henry, he was ruthless, executing those he suspected of disloyalty, including many family members, such as several wives (among them Mariamne, a Hasmonean princess) and three of his sons. As a client king of Rome, he needed permission to execute family members, as they were nobility. So Emperor Augustus, upon signing a death warrant, remarked, "It's better to be Herod's pig (*hus*) than his son (*huios*),"[1] the joke involving the play on words in Greek, implying that Jews like Herod may not eat pork but do execute their offspring. Finally, approaching his demise, Herod knew that there wouldn't be mourning for his death, so he attempted to ensure there would be mourning at his death. The Jewish historian Josephus records that Herod arranged a mass execution upon his demise:

---

[1] Macrobius, *Saturnalia* 2.4.11: "Melius est Herodis porcum esse quam filium." Macrobius writes in Latin, but the play on words that Augustus would have uttered was in Greek (*hus* for pig, *huios* for son).

He started on his return journey and reached Jericho in an atrabilious condition, in which, hurling defiance as it were at death itself, he proceeded to devise an outrageous scheme. Having assembled the distinguished men from every village from one end of Judaea to the other, he ordered them to be locked into the hippodrome [a Greco-Roman racetrack for horses and chariots]. He then summoned his sister Salome and her husband Alexas and said: "I know that the Jews will celebrate my death by a festival; yet I can obtain a vicarious mourning and a magnificent funeral, if you consent to follow my instructions. You know these men here in custody; the moment I expire have them surrounded by the soldiers and massacred; so shall all Judaea and every household weep for me, whether they will or no."[2]

Herod died, but his daughter Salome had the mass execution canceled.

St. Matthew expects the reader to know of Herod's kingship and brutality, and yet reminds his readers that Herod was indeed king, calling him "Herod the King" twice (Matt 2:1 and 3) and "king" once (2:9). When the Magi arrive, then, asking about "he who has been born king of the Jews" (2:2), the reader sees the obvious problem. There can be only one sovereign in a domain, one king in a kingdom (unless one is in Narnia).

And so Herod is "troubled," because rumors of a new king mean a challenge to his reign. St. Matthew then states that "all

---

[2] Josephus, *War* 1.659–660, in *The Jewish War*, trans. H. St. J. Thackeray, vols. 1–3, Loeb Classical Library (Cambridge: Harvard University Press, 1927–1928) [Loeb Classical Library is hereafter abbreviated as LCL]; here citing LCL 203, at 1:313, 315.

Jerusalem" was troubled along with Herod, here suggesting to the reader that the Jews will reject the one sent to them as their rightful divine King. Herod calls upon the chief priests and scribes (Matt 2:4), which implies they're Herod's men and thus will also reject Jesus. They consult the Scriptures, which prophesy that the Christ will be born in Bethlehem (5:6, quoting Mic 5:2).

Herod then calls upon the Magi—again, pagan astrologers—instructing them to find the child and report back to him "that I too may come and worship him" (Matt 2:7–8). Herod has no intention of doing so; again, the reader is to know how brutal Herod is and that he will permit no challenge to his sovereign reign as king of the Jews.

The star leads the Magi to baby Jesus and his mother Mary. The star is actually an angel, as the biblical world sees stars and angels as equivalent. That's how it can come to "rest over the place where the child was" (Matt 2:9). The Magi rejoice, fall down, and worship the Christ child (2:9–10a), and they do so with the symbolic gifts of gold, frankincense, and myrrh.

Symbolic? Yes; traditionally, the gifts indicate Jesus's kingly status (gold), his nature as God (frankincense, incense being used in worship), and his sacrificial death (myrrh being used to anoint corpses).

They depart to their own country after "being warned in a dream not to return to Herod" (Matt 2:12). Dreams in the Gospel of Matthew come from God, and so St. Matthew here indicates that God knows how hostile Herod is, showing Herod to be God's enemy. Further, St. Matthew declines to call Herod "king" here, because in the baby Jesus, the Christ has been revealed to the entire world, as if the days of Herod's kingship were now over. His death will very soon follow, as the Christ child has begun his rightful reign.

In the passage, then, St. Matthew gives the reader clues that all Israel will reject the one sent to them by God to be her rightful King. What is more, St. Matthew has suggested that the Christ child is indeed God incarnate through the Magi's worship and their presentation of the royal gift of gold.

Finally, the passage has political implications. Religion cannot be a matter of mere piety, simply having Jesus in our hearts, for God Almighty is sovereign over his whole cosmos, and the Church is its own nation, a tribe called Christian. Herod rules at Rome's pleasure, and his murderous intentions reveal the hostility not only of the Jews but also the Romans (and thus the Gentiles) to God. They all resist and reject God's rightful reign over them. God, however, intends to smash the diabolical powers and assert his reign over the world, invading it in Jesus to establish his kingdom once and for all. And so we pray, "Thy Kingdom come."

MATTHEW 2:13–18: THE HOLY INNOCENTS, MARTYRS (DECEMBER 28) / THE HOLY FAMILY OF JESUS, MARY, AND JOSEPH (SUNDAY WITHIN THE OCTAVE OF THE NATIVITY OF THE LORD, OR IF THERE IS NO SUNDAY, DECEMBER 30; 2:13–15, 19–23)

From beginning to read the second chapter of Matthew, the reader has had initial assumptions about Jesus's people and mission thrown into question as St. Matthew engages in an ironic literary reversal, telling how Israel's king and religious leadership—both Church and State, as we might put it today—oppose God come to earth in the newborn Christ, while pagan astrologers from far away come to worship the child. Now St. Matthew will take it a step further, inverting Israel and Egypt as the Holy Family engages in a reverse

WORSHIP AND REJECTION OF THE CHRIST CHILD

exodus, with Herod as the new Pharaoh.

In Exodus 1, four centuries after Joseph (the Israelite lord of all Egypt, second only to the Pharaoh of his day), a new Pharaoh has risen "who did not know Joseph" (Exod 1:8). The Israelites having grown numerous, this later Pharaoh fears their strength and reduces them to slavery before commencing a program of slow genocide, decreeing that newborn Hebrew (Israelite) boys are to be killed (1:16, 22). Most people overlook the genocide—because movies about the exodus have plenty of Hebrew men—but Pharaoh's plan is to bleed the men out and breed the women out so that Israel would be no more. Egypt, then, in biblical memory, is the worst place possible, the first of many attempts to erase the Hebrews from the earth.

It's shocking, then, that St. Matthew tells of an angel of the Lord appearing to Joseph in a dream and instructing him to flee with child and mother to Egypt, "for Herod is about to search for the child, to destroy him" (Matt 2:13). Joseph does so immediately, "by night" (2:14), just as the Hebrews fled Egypt "by night" in the immediate wake of the slaughter of the Egyptian firstborn: Pharaoh "summoned Moses and Aaron by night, and said, 'Rise up, go forth from among my people, both you and the people of Israel'" (Exod 12:31a).

According to St. Matthew, the Holy Family's flight to Egypt fulfilled Hosea 11:1: "Out of Egypt have I called my son" (Matt 2:15). Now, older scholarship often asserted that St. Matthew blundered here, for the Holy Family is yet in Egypt; they do not in fact return to Israel until Matthew 2:21, after Herod's death. But it's better to give biblical authors the benefit of the doubt and ask if they're doing something along literary lines that historical-critical scholars, typically lacking literary-critical sensibilities, would miss. And in fact, this is what St. Matthew is doing. He is directly equating

Jesus's Israel with Egypt of old. And so he also equates Herod with Pharaoh of old. Herod flies into fury and has all boys in the region of Bethlehem under two years old murdered, as Pharaoh of old ordered Hebrew boys murdered.

We must not gloss over the import of the quotation of Hosea 11:1. Of course Christian readers of the Gospel of Matthew know that Jesus is God's Son, but St. Matthew does not often quote piecemeal. Rather, the wider background context of a shorter quotation is often in view. The "son" of Hosea 11:1 is originally the nation of Israel: "When Israel was a child, I loved him, and out of Egypt I called my son." Here St. Matthew is presenting Jesus not just as the Son of God but as the embodiment of all Israel, the ideal Israelite.

He will do likewise in the linked scenes of the Baptism (Matt 3:13–17) and Temptation (4:1–11). Jesus is baptized in the Jordan River; the Israelites crossed the Jordan River. Jesus next combats Satan; the Israelites then combatted the inhabitants of the land. Jesus, the embodiment of Israel, is recapitulating Israel's entry into the land not long after (in literary terms in the Gospel of Matthew) the child Jesus escaped in the new exodus to Egypt. And the reader will see in the Temptation Narrative that Jesus, the new Israel, proves faithful, whereas the old Israel did not.

Upon the Holy Family's return to Israel, Joseph learns Archelaeus, Herod's son, is ruling Judea. Archelaeus was about as brutal as his father but half as smart and a third as competent; in AD 6 Rome would remove him for his maladministration and begin ruling Judea with Roman prefects (such as Pontius Pilate) and, later, procurators. And so the Holy Family relocates to Nazareth in Galilee, in which St. Matthew finds the fulfillment of prophecies: "He shall be called a Nazarene" (*Nazōraios*, Matthew 2:23b).

Prophecies, plural; the quotation isn't found anywhere

directly in the Old Testament, nor is the word St. Matthew uses for "Nazarene," *Nazōraios*. We observe that St. Matthew introduces the quote by stating that the Holy Family's settling in Nazareth fulfills "what was spoken" not by some individual prophet but expressly "by the prophets" (Matt 2:23), in the plural. Elsewhere in the Gospel of Matthew, we find St. Matthew doing something similar, finding in an event a general fulfillment of plural prophecies. At his own arrest, Jesus says, "But how then should the scriptures be fulfilled, that it must be so?" (Matt 26:54), and two verses later Jesus will state, "But all this has taken place, that the scriptures of the prophets might be fulfilled" (26:56). Earlier in the Gospel, Jesus also claimed that the Golden Rule sums up the Scriptures: "So whatever you wish that men would do to you, do so to them; for this is the law and the prophets" (7:12). It's as if St. Matthew sees the wide swaths and indeed the totality of the Old Testament fulfilled in Jesus the Christ and his teaching.

In Matthew 2:23, then, it's most likely that St. Matthew is playing on words to point to Jesus as the Christ. In Jesus's Aramaic dialect of Hebrew, Nazareth would be *Naṣrat*. The word "branch," *nēṣer*, appears in the Christological prophecy of Isaiah 11:1: "There shall come forth a shoot from the stump of Jesse, and a branch shall grow out of his roots."[3] The

---

[3] Jerome, "Letter 57—To Pammachius on the Best Method of Translating": "Once more it is written in the pages of the same evangelist, 'And he came and dwelt in a city called Nazareth: that it might be fulfilled which was spoken by the prophets, He shall be called a Nazarene.' Let these word fanciers and nice critics of all composition tell us where they have read the words; and if they cannot, let me tell them that they are in Isaiah. For in the place where we read and translate, 'There shall come forth a rod out of the stem of Jesse, and a branch shall grow out of his roots' [Isaiah 11:1], in the Hebrew idiom it is written thus, 'There shall come forth a rod out of the root of Jesse and a Nazarene shall grow from his root'" (*A Select Library of Nicene and Post-Nicene Fathers*, trans. W. H. Fremantle,

play on words between *Naṣrat* and *nēṣer* implies the Christ comes from Nazareth.

Other Old Testament prophecies are similar, but they lack the precise word *nēṣer*, employing instead the very similar words *shoresh* or *tzemach*:

> In that day the root (*shōresh*) of Jesse shall stand as an ensign to the peoples; him shall the nations seek, and his dwellings shall be glorious. (Isa 11:10)

> Behold, the days are coming, says the LORD, when I will raise up for David a righteous Branch (*tzemach*), and he shall reign as king and deal wisely, and shall execute justice and righteousness in the land. (Jer 23:5)

> In those days and at that time I will cause a righteous Branch (*tzemach*) to spring forth for David; and he shall execute justice and righteousness in the land. (Jer 33:15)

> [B]ehold, I will bring my servant the Branch (*tzemach*). (Zech 3:8b)

> Thus says the LORD of hosts, "Behold, the man whose name is the Branch (*tzemach*): for he shall grow up in his place, and he shall build the temple of the LORD." (Zech 6:12)

Given how strongly St. Matthew has already endeavored to present Jesus as the Christ, it's most likely that the reader is

G. Lewis, and W. G. Martley, 2nd series, 14 vols., ed. Philip Schaff and Henry Wace [repr., Peabody, MA: Hendrickson, 1994], 6:115–116).

meant to perceive messianic references here in Matthew 2:23.

And in the Gospel of Matthew, Jesus, the Christ of Israel, endures rejection, from birth to crucifixion. Another avenue of interpretation opens up, then, seeing in the description of Jesus as "Nazarene" the figures of rejected righteous sufferers in the Old Testament. Nazareth had a negative reputation in Jesus's day. In the Gospel of John, Philip tells Nathanael of "Jesus of Nazareth" as the one prophesied by Moses and the prophets (John 1:45), and Nathanael replies, "Can anything good come out of Nazareth?" (1:46). It's probable that Galilee had a good amount of Gentiles living in it, and Nazareth of Galilee was a smaller town (fewer than 2,000 people) that likely also housed a Roman military outpost with a sizable garrison. Hence Nathanael's question.

The prophetic Psalms also saw the Christ's rejection. Jesus, St. Matthew, and the early Church in general believed the Psalms to be prophetic.[4] Written mainly by David, they thought it stood to reason that the Psalms would ultimately concern the Christ, David's ultimate descendant. Psalm 22 reads like a subtle map of the Passion of Jesus Christ, and Jesus even quotes its opening line as his last words: "My God, my God, why have you forsaken me?" (Ps 22:1 in Matt 27:46). Elsewhere the Psalm reads:

> But I am a worm, and no man;
>> scorned by men, and despised by
>> the people.
> All who see me mock at me,
>> they make mouths at me, they wag their heads.
> (Ps 22:6–7)

---

[4] In Acts 2:30, St. Peter identifies David as a "prophet" whose Psalms therefore pointed to his ultimate descendant, the Christ.

Similarly, the Servant Songs of Isaiah famously present a righteous sufferer, deplored and derided:

> He was despised and rejected by men;
> a man of sorrows, and acquainted
> with grief;
> and as one from whom men hide their faces
> he was despised, and we esteemed him not.
> (Isa 53:3)

Given the hostility the Christ child Jesus has faced in Matthew 2, then, St. Matthew finds in the Holy Family's settling in Nazareth an indication that Jesus will be as despised as the town he hails from.

CHAPTER 5

✝

THE ADVENT OF THE KINGDOM

MATTHEW 3:1–12: SUNDAY OF THE SECOND WEEK OF ADVENT

THE FIRST CHAPTER of the Gospel of Matthew established Jesus as Christ and new Isaac, deliverer by sacrifice, and also God himself with us, his people (Matt 1:23), while raising plot possibilities for the reader. The second chapter began reversing the reader's original expectations as those who should welcome the Christ child recoil at his advent, even to the point of bloody mass murder.

The opening two chapters are absolutely foundational for the story of the Gospel of Matthew, as they take place roughly thirty years before Jesus begins his public ministry in chapter 3. The separation in time between chapters 1 and 2 and chapter 3 suggests all that Jesus is and will do is sketched in the opening two chapters; they are the Gospel of Matthew in a nutshell. When the reader arrives at chapter 3, then, it's no surprise to find more Christological and sacrificial references, as well as opposition to Jesus.

John the Baptist appears in the wilderness (Matt 3:1), preaching, "Repent, for the kingdom of heaven is at hand" (3:2). The entire passage seems to scream "apocalyptic eschatology"—for our purposes, the announcement of the violent, imminent end of the world—but the reader's assumptions about that will be challenged and changed through the course of the further narrative.

The very concept of the "kingdom of God" (or "kingdom of heaven") makes one think of the end, as Jews believed the Christ would establish an everlasting, eternal kingdom transcending the earthly, temporal kingdom David established centuries before. And so many people, especially historical-critical scholars, think Jesus and the early Christians believed the world was going to end very soon, that Jesus would return and bring history to a close by ushering in the final, eternal kingdom. And not without reason. In Matthew 16:28, for instance, Jesus says, "Truly, I say to you, there are some standing here who will not taste death before they see the Son of man coming in his kingdom." This scholarly conception holds that both John the Baptist (3:2) and Jesus (4:17) proclaimed the kingdom of God as the end of the world coming violently at a particular point in time, soon.

John may have thought that, and certainly the Gospel of Matthew frames his appearing that way. St. Matthew provides a formula quotation of Isaiah 40:3 in Matthew 3:3 that suggests the arrival of the Lord God of Israel at the end of time: "Prepare the way of the Lord, make his paths straight." Further, John looks like Elijah come again. St. Matthew records John wearing "a garment of camel's hair, and a leather girdle around his waist" (Matt 3:4), while in 2 Kings 1:8 the messengers of King Ahaziah describe Elijah as wearing "a garment of haircloth, with a girdle of leather about his loins."

Elijah, of course, didn't die but was assumed into heaven

(2 Kgs 2:1–12), and so it was part and parcel of Jewish belief that Elijah would return at the end of time. Indeed, Malachi the prophet expressly prophesies Elijah's return at the end of time: "Behold, I will send you Eli'jah the prophet before the great and terrible day of the LORD comes" (Mal 4:5a). And John's words seem to suggest the end of the world is indeed at hand: Addressing the Pharisees and Sadducees, John screams, "You brood of vipers! Who warned you to flee from the wrath to come?" (Matt 3:7). That wrath is fiery: "Even now the axe is laid to the root of the trees; every tree therefore that does not bear good fruit is cut down and thrown into the fire" (3:10). The one John declares is coming after him has a "winnowing fork . . . in his hand, and he will clear his threshing floor and gather his wheat into the granary, but the chaff he will burn with unquenchable fire" (3:12).

So the reader of the Gospel of Matthew might assume that Jesus's coming means the end of the world. And yet reading further will reveal to the reader that in Jesus's teaching and St. Matthew's understanding, the kingdom of God isn't so much a matter of time but a matter of place; it's not temporal but spatial.

Jesus does not do what John expects. Instead of raining down fiery judgment, Jesus's first public acts after his Baptism and Temptation involve preaching good news, healing, and exorcism:

> And he went about all Galilee, teaching in their synagogues and preaching the gospel of the kingdom and healing every disease and every infirmity among the people. So his fame spread throughout all Syria, and they brought him all the sick, those afflicted with various diseases and pains, demoniacs, epileptics, and paralytics, and he healed them. (Matt 4:23–24)

Of course in Matthew 5–7 Jesus will continue the theme of these deeds in his famous Sermon on the Mount. It closes with dire apocalyptic warnings, to be sure (see Matt 7:13–27), but Jesus hasn't done yet what John expects. In chapters 8–10 Jesus will engage in healing and exorcism, and even raise a dead girl to life, and send the Twelve on a mission and give them robust teaching on their missionary discipleship.

And so in Matthew 11 John the Baptist, languishing in prison, shows himself confused. He sends messengers to Jesus: "Now when John heard in prison about the deeds of the Christ, he sent word by his disciples and said to him, 'Are you he who is to come, or shall we look for another?'" (Matt 11:2–3). Back in Matthew 3:11–12, John had prophesied that "he who is coming after me" would baptize "with the Holy Spirit and with fire" and separate the wheat and the chaff for all time, burning the latter "with unquenchable fire." Jesus hasn't done any of that, and so John sends the messengers, indicating John's doubts about Jesus: "Should we look for someone else?"

Jesus responds, "Go and tell John what you hear and see: the blind receive their sight and the lame walk, lepers are cleansed and the deaf hear, and the dead are raised up, and the poor have good news preached to them. And blessed is he who takes no offense at me" (Matt 11:4–6). Jesus responds in a way that informs John that he, Jesus, is indeed the one who is to come, but that John shouldn't be offended—scandalized— by the way Jesus exercises his ministry as Christ.

The point is that the very story of the Gospel of Matthew indicates Jesus didn't endeavor to bring the end of the world suddenly. John's apocalyptic expectations are upset, and so he doubts.

Another indication that the announcement of the kingdom of God does not mean the imminent end of the world is Jesus's telling the "parables of growth," which in the Gospel of Matthew include the Parable of the Sower (Matt 13:1–9), the Parable of the Weeds among the Wheat (13:24–30), and the Parable of the Mustard Seed (13:31–32). These agricultural parables suggest that the kingdom of God is something that grows slowly, steadily, over a sustained period of time. The import of the brief Parable of the Yeast (13:33) is the same, as it takes time for yeast to be well-worked throughout dough. These parables do not square with the idea that the kingdom is coming suddenly.

It's better, then, to see the kingdom of God in the Gospel of Matthew (and in all the Gospels) more as a matter of location: the kingdom is present in Jesus. Indeed, in Jesus, king and kingdom are one. Where he is, there is healing, exorcism, life, liberation from sin, and the renewal of creation. It's also helpful to see the Church and the kingdom tied tightly together, as classical theology before the nineteenth century observed, for Jesus in the Gospel of Matthew founds a Church to carry on his kingdom-work in the world till the true end of time.[1]

Indeed, the Catechism, following the Second Vatican Council, teaches, "The kingdom of heaven was inaugurated on earth by Christ. 'This kingdom shone out before men in the word, in the works and in the presence of Christ' [*Lumen Gentium* 5]. The Church is the seed and beginning of this kingdom" (567).[2]

---

[1] It's important to note that the modern scholarship that separated Church and kingdom was driven largely by Protestants, who in the nineteenth and twentieth centuries let their Enlightenment commitments to individualism move them beyond Luther's belief in a visible church.

[2] See *Lumen Gentium* 5a more fully: "The mystery of the holy Church is manifest in its very foundation. The Lord Jesus set it on its course by preaching the Good News, that is, the coming of the Kingdom of God, which, for centuries, had been promised in the Scriptures: 'The time is fulfilled, and the kingdom of God is at hand.'"

The kingdom, then, progresses in history with the Church. The apocalyptic scenario that John and Jesus preach will come to pass, but not until the mustard seed achieves maturity.

Finally, the note of opposition in Matthew 3:1–12 is strong. Before they've done anything else in St. Matthew's story, the Pharisees and Sadducees find themselves the recipients of a most severe tongue-lashing, as John the Baptist excoriates them: "You brood of vipers! Who warned you to flee from the wrath to come?" (Matt 3:7b). The story here indicates bluntly to the reader that these groups will give Jesus no end of grief in the Gospel. And then John makes another crucial point. Literal descent from Abraham, first father of the Jews, is meaningless: "[D]o not presume to say to yourselves, 'We have Abraham as our father'; for I tell you, God is able from these stones to raise up children to Abraham" (3:9). This is a theme common in the earliest Christianity: to access the promises made originally to Abraham, one needs to be in Christ, Abraham's ultimate heir. As St. Paul says in Galatians, "Now the promises were made to Abraham and to his offspring. . . . which is Christ" (Gal 3:16); "And if you are Christ's, then you are Abraham's offspring, heirs according to promise" (3:29). As St. Matthew sees Jesus as a new Isaac, it is fitting that the line of promise must run through Jesus.

MATTHEW 3:13–17: FIRST SUNDAY IN ORDINARY TIME / SUNDAY AFTER THE EPIPHANY OF THE LORD (OR FOLLOWING MONDAY WHERE EPIPHANY IS TRANSFERRED TO SUNDAY) / BAPTISM OF THE LORD (JANUARY 9)

John the Baptist has been baptizing the crowds coming to him for repentance, and now Jesus presents himself for John's baptism (Matt 3:13). John hesitates, for it would seem that the greater should baptize the lesser (Matt 3:14). But Jesus commands John to baptize him, saying, "Let it be so now; for thus it is fitting for us to fulfil all righteousness" (3:15).

In the Gospel of Matthew, Jesus is always in control. St. Matthew will sketch scenes in such a way as to show that nothing happens apart from Jesus's permission. The great example is Jesus's arrest (Matt 26:47–56). Judas had told the mob to seize Jesus once he, Judas, kissed him: "The one I shall kiss is the man; seize him" (26:48b). But when Judas brings the mob to Jesus, Jesus interrupts. Judas greets Jesus and kisses him (26:49), but Jesus halts the action to declare, "Friend, now do that for which you've come" (26:50a).[3] "Then"—and only then—do they lay hands on Jesus and seize him (26:50b). Jesus interrupts Judas's proposed two-step plan of kissing and seizing; only after Jesus gives permission can the crowd seize him. So too here, at the baptism. John objects, Jesus commands and explains, and "then"—and only then—does John consent.

Jesus explains that it's "fitting" for them "to fulfil all righteousness" (Matt 3:15). "Fitting" is an important word. Some things are theologically necessary or unnecessary, but there's another category many forget, the category of "fitting" (one finds it used frequently in St. Thomas Aquinas's works, and indeed in medieval theology more broadly). For instance, it's not strictly necessary for the Blessed Virgin Mary to have remained a virgin after delivering the Christ child, but it's certainly fitting—things used for sacred purposes are seldom, if ever, returned to common use. Chalices that hold the Precious Blood aren't later used as common wine goblets, and old flags generally aren't turned into quilts.

So too here. Jesus does not need John's baptism of repent-

---

3 My translation of *hetaire eph' ho parei.*

ance, but it's fitting nonetheless. Why? Jesus's answer is "to fulfil all righteousness." But what does that mean? Why does Jesus insist on submitting to John's baptism? Several reasons: First, "repentance" means "turning" at root, to turn from sin and turn toward God, to follow the path God has marked out for the righteous. Sinners make a 180-degree turn; Jesus makes a 90. Jesus need not turn from sin, since he has none, but now in the baptism he turns to his public ministry. He now begins to follow the specific path to which his Father calls him. Thus his obedience is his righteousness, and he fulfills it here.

Second, salvation is a matter of sharing in Christ, of being in Christ, as the New Testament emphasizes throughout. In particular, the discipleship that leads to salvation involves sharing in Christ's sufferings: "If any man would come after me, let him deny himself and take up his cross and follow me" (Matt 16:24; see also 10:38). Some contemporary evangelical and Pentecostal theologies affirm vicarious, substitutionary atonement: Jesus suffers for us, in our place, instead of us suffering. From here it's a short step to claiming Christians shouldn't suffer, won't suffer, and if they do, God's punishing them for something. (One encounters this all too often in churches committed to the "prosperity gospel.") But traditional Christianity, including good Protestant theology, affirms the reality and necessity of suffering with and in Christ. Here, then, in the Baptism of Our Lord, Tradition and good theology makes clear that Jesus gets baptized to show his identification with sinners, indeed, to incorporate them into him through the waters of sacramental baptism.

This brings us to a third major point: John's baptism is not Christian baptism. In Acts we find some who were only baptized by John and who never received Christian baptism, such as Apollos, a missionary for Jesus (Acts 18:25b: "he knew only the baptism of John"). In Acts 19:1–3, Paul encounters some believers in Ephesus who know nothing of the Holy Spirit, who had only been baptized by John. Paul explains to them, "John baptized with the baptism of repentance, telling the people to believe in the one who was to come after him, that is, Jesus" (19:4). Thereupon they are baptized into Jesus and receive the Holy Spirit (19:5–7).

In his baptism by John, then, Jesus institutes Christian baptism. Now, we see in the Bible that people are affected by what nature and super-nature throw at them. They're subject to winds, to storms, to famine, to disease, to demons, to ritual impurity. They're vulnerable. But with Jesus, the direction is reversed. He stills winds, calms storms, multiplies bread and loaves, heals, exorcises, and cleanses, because he brings the kingdom in himself. And so here, too, in the Baptism. In receiving baptism from John, he actually gives: he supercharges the waters, as it were, making Christian baptism possible. From now on, Christian baptism will bind the believer to the Trinity, giving one an initial measure of the Holy Spirit.

And thus it's no accident that the scene of Jesus's Baptism is the first revelation of the Holy Trinity in Scripture, and that Jesus receives the Holy Spirit. The Son is there as Jesus, of course; the Father is present, revealed by the heavenly voice declaring Jesus his Son; and the Holy Spirit lights upon Jesus in the form of a dove. The Holy Trinity is here made manifest, and so Christian baptism involves the Name of the Holy Trinity (see Matt 28:19).

Finally, the heavenly voice contains a shocking allusion. When God the Father speaks from heaven, he says, "This is my beloved Son" (Matt 3:17). It's an allusion to Genesis 22:2, 12, and 16 LXX, wherein Isaac is thrice named the beloved son. In Scripture, in Christian theology, baptism means the death of the old man and the rising of the new in Christ; baptism effects the death of the old self and constitutes a continual call to cooperation in that work of death. And in the heavenly voice, Jesus finds himself called to particular obedience unto sacrificial death, like Isaac. Here Jesus receives his sacrificial commission.

MATTHEW 4:1–11: FIRST SUNDAY OF LENT

By this point, the Gospel of Matthew has presented Jesus as the Christ, indeed both King of Israel and the embodiment of Israel (see Matt 2:15), as well as a new Isaac, with the mission to be a sacrifice. The Temptation Narrative in Matthew 4 addresses the implicit question of whether Jesus the Christ will be faithful like Isaac and unlike Israel of old.

Israel and Cross cast their shadows upon St. Matthew's story of the Temptation of Our Lord. Jesus is tested in the wilderness (Matt 4:1), just as Israel was tested in the wilderness (Deut 8:2). Jesus endures forty days and nights there (Matt 4:1), just as Israel was in the wilderness forty years (Deut 8:2). Jesus is hungry (Matt 4:1), just as Israel was hungry (Deut 8:3). And in the Temptation story, the reader encounters three quotations from Deuteronomy (Deut 8:3 in Matt 4:4; Deut 6:16 in Matt 4:7; Deut 6:13 in Matt 4:10). In these passages of Deuteronomy, the Israelites are admonished again and again to remain faithful to the Lord God and are reminded repeatedly of their deliverance at the exodus and their receiving of the Commandments (Deut 5). St. Matthew is writing Jesus into the story of Deuteronomy 6–8. Jesus, the new Israel, is recapitulating the story of Israel in the desert. But Jesus obeys perfectly, unlike Israel.

The reader notes also that in Deuteronomy it's God who tests the Israelites, whereas in the Gospel of Matthew it is the Devil who tests Jesus. St. Matthew's Gospel is apocalyptic, and thus dualistic, reflecting the enduring battle between

God and Satan, and therefore the Gospel of Matthew operates with a *"Christus Victor"* (Christ the conqueror, or victor)
soteriology. What this means is that Jesus saves us not simply
by inspiring us to a better life or pacifying God's wrath toward
us, but by conquering, through his cruciform death and resurrection, those implacable, infernal forces arrayed against us:
Sin, Death, Hell, and the Devil.

And so the Temptation Narrative is rightly understood as
a story of testing, like a contest between two opponents, Jesus
our champion in one corner, Satan in the other. (In emulation
of Jesus's struggle against Satan, the monks and martyrs of the
early Church, especially the Desert Fathers, were often called
the *athletae Dei,* the athletes of God.) And here the Cross
casts its shadow. Showing that Jesus is obedient as the new
Israel, the Temptation story now shows also that Jesus is faithful to the sacrificial commission given him in his Baptism as
the new Isaac.

Each of the three particular tests in the story concern
Jesus's obedience as Son to his Father and contain hints of the
Passion. And each test involves the theme of the power and
authority that rightly belong to Jesus as Son of God, implied
in the concept of divine Sonship itself and confirmed later for
the reader throughout the Gospel of Matthew (see 7:29; 8–9,
esp. 8:5–13 and 9:1–8; 10:1; 21:23–27; 24:30; 24:64; and
above all 26:16–20, to which the third test in 4:8–10 is tied).

The first test concerns not so much Jesus's *ability* to
turn stones to bread (that'd be easy for him, of course), but
rather *whether he will use his power to do so.* And so the Devil
in essence asks, "Since" (a better translation than "if," as the
Devil knows Jesus is the Son of God) "you are the Son of God,
why not simply turn these stones to bread?" The suggestion
seems innocent; Jesus has already fasted forty days and nights
and was naturally hungry (Matt 4:2). Why not eat now? Old

Testament scholar Walter Moberly writes:

> If Jesus is Son to God, then he is in a position to be a channel for divine power; and indeed in his ministry Jesus will exercise this power for others, both to feed and to heal. The question is whether he should exercise this power for himself, even to meet a legitimate need of hunger. The danger in this is that as soon as the divine power is used for himself, then it may become a means to his own ends. A relationship of mutuality and trust could be reduced, albeit subtly, to a means of self-gratification.[4]

Later in the Gospel the Passion Narrative will allude back to this test, showing that Sonship concerns active self-sacrifice. In Matthew 27:40b, those who mock Jesus use the same words of the Devil in 4:3: "If you are the Son of God, come down from the cross." Jesus's biblical response stresses his absolute devotion to his Father and the sacrificial mission given him: "Man shall not live by bread alone, but by every word that proceeds from the mouth of God" (Deut 8:3 in Matt 4:4). Moreover, his refusal to eat is an instance of supererogation, of doing more than he really needs to do, in the same way that he submitted to baptism. Jesus is hungry after fasting forty days and nights, but he refuses any suggestion of the Devil, even though in itself it's permissible for him to eat.

The first test concerns Jesus's own power; the second concerns God's. The Devil's challenge is skillful. He cites Psalm 90:11–12: "'He will give his angels charge of you,' and 'On their hands they will bear you up, lest you strike your foot

---

[4] R. W. L. Moberly, *The Bible, Theology, and Faith: A Study of Abraham and Jesus*, Cambridge Studies in Christian Doctrine (Cambridge: Cambridge University Press, 2000), 201.

against a stone'" (Matt 4:6). Jesus quoted Scripture, so now the Devil does likewise to trip him up, demanding diabolic consistency from him. The Devil is telling the truth here, as he's quoting Scripture: the Psalm promises God's angelic protection to the Christ. Jesus's response from Deuteronomy 6:16, that one should not put the Lord God to the test, emphasizes Jesus's total obedience. Indeed, the Devil is testing Jesus by trying to get Jesus to test God the Father himself, to force God's hand by God's own promise.

And here, too, will the reader find the Passion Narrative referring back to this second test. Jesus refuses the angelic protection promised in the Psalm, and he will refuse it again at his arrest: "Do you think that I cannot appeal to my Father, and he will at once send me more than twelve legions of angels?" (Matt 26:53). Jesus refuses divinely guaranteed angelic aid for the sake of the Cross.

In the third test, Jesus refuses the dominion over the world to which he is absolutely entitled. Swiss scholar Ulrich Luz observes, "He who, on the mountain, rejected the devil's offer of world domination (4:8–10) and chose the path of obedience, will for this very reason, again on a mountain, be granted all the power in heaven and on earth at the end of his chosen path of obedience (28:16–20). And so again a passage much later in the Gospel sheds light on what's happening here in the Temptation Narrative.

The Devil is offering that which Jesus is truly entitled to as God's Son by means of the shortcut of Devil worship, which would mean breaking fidelity to his Father. Jesus's response, "Begone, Satan! For it is written, 'You shall worship the Lord your God and him only shall you serve'" (Matt 4:10, quoting Deut 6:13) therefore stresses Jesus's obedience to God his Father. And again, a later passage in the Gospel sheds light on this one. The reader will later discover that Jesus's obedience here is unto death: Jesus's words *hupage satana* ("Begone, Satan!") in Matthew 4:10a are precisely those he speaks to rebuke Peter following Peter's rejection of Jesus's Passion prediction in 16:23a: "Get behind me, Satan!" (*hupage satana*).

In sum, the Temptation Narrative stands under the shadow of the Cross, and Jesus refuses to do the three otherwise-legitimate things the Devil suggests he do, precisely because he is committed to the way of the Cross announced allusively in the Baptism: "This is my beloved Son." Alluding to Isaac, Jesus's filial obedience as Son of God must run its course through the Cross.

It is here we see that the Cross works according to the logic of *Christus Victor*: Christ conquers the Devil, and thus also Sin, Death, and the possibility of Hell that the Devil brought to the world. Jesus's victory in the Temptation Narrative is defensive, in that he survived, his fidelity intact. But Jesus's victory is also offensive, as his conquest of Satan here in the wilderness is like the Israelites's initial conquest of the Canaanites in the Promised Land. In Deuteronomy 6:18–19, Moses relates that the Israelites would have conquered their enemies in the land if they had only remained faithful and not succumbed to their temptations. Jesus, the new Israel, the new Isaac, and indeed the new Joshua, conquers through his obedience, leading the way to the Cross set out for him by his Father.

PART II

THE MINISTRY OF JESUS THE CHRIST

IN THIS SECOND MAJOR SECTION of St. Matthew's Gospel, Jesus begins his public ministry, imparting words of truth, as well as teaching by deeds of miracles, healings, and exorcisms. He will encounter rising opposition from Jewish elites even while the crowds marvel.

CHAPTER 6

✝

THE LAUNCH OF JESUS'S
PUBLIC MINISTRY

MATTHEW 4:12–23 (OR 4:12–17): THIRD
SUNDAY IN ORDINARY TIME / MONDAY
AFTER EPIPHANY (OR JANUARY 7; 4:12–17,
23–25) / ST. ANDREW, APOSTLE (NOVEMBER
30; 4:18–22)

CONFLICT AND THREAT are constant themes in the Gospel
of Matthew. The Christ child is under threat in Matthew
2; John the Baptist savages the Pharisees and Sadducees in
Matthew 3; and Jesus bests Satan in Matthew 4. Now in the
present passage the themes of threat and conflict continue as
John's arrest launches Jesus's public ministry, with Jesus proclaiming the exact same message John proclaimed: "Repent,
for the kingdom of heaven is at hand" (Matt 4:17; see 3:2).

St. Matthew mentions John's arrest almost in passing:
"Now when he heard that John had been arrested . . ." (Matt
4:12). The details of John's arrest and death will be provided

later, in Matthew 14:1–12, as a flashback. Here, since John is Jesus's forerunner, the reader perceives a threat to Jesus. And so does Jesus: hearing John had been arrested, Jesus "withdrew into Galilee" (4:12b) to Capernaum. A quotation from Isaiah follows, promising good things to the Gentiles: "The land of Zeb'ulun and the land of Naph'tali, toward the sea, across the Jordan, Galilee of the Gentiles—the people who sat in darkness have seen a great light, and for those who sat in the region and shadow of death light has dawned" (4:15–16, quoting a version of Isa 9:1–2).

There's a pattern here: (1) threat (John's arrest); (2) then Jesus "withdrew" (*anachōreō*); and (3) a quotation from Isaiah that (4) promises good things to the Gentiles. We see the same pattern later in Matthew 12:9–21. Jesus heals the man with a withered hand in the synagogue on the Sabbath, and as a result "the Pharisees went out and took counsel against him, how to destroy him" (12:14). Thereupon Jesus "withdrew" (*anachōreō*, v. 15), and St. Matthew provides a quotation from Isaiah promising good things to the Gentiles: "Behold, my servant whom I have chosen, my beloved with whom my soul is well pleased. I will put my Spirit upon him, and he shall proclaim justice to the Gentiles. . . . [I]n his name will the Gentiles hope" (12:18–21, quoting a version of Isa 42:1–4). The pattern is the same in chapter 12 as in chapter 4: threat, withdrawal, Isaiah, and Gentiles.

Here, in story form, with quotations from Isaiah, St. Matthew is presenting a theme that runs throughout the New Testament. On a human level, Jewish rejection of Jesus leads to Gentile inclusion in the Church. St. Paul wrestles marvelously with the theme in Romans 9–11 (see 11:11 and 25 in particular), and we find the theme also throughout Acts (see especially 13:46 and 18:6). On a divine level, however, Gentile inclusion in the people of God, the Church, was always the divine plan, as the quotations of Isaiah make plain, for Isaiah the prophet speaks God's very words. In St. Matthew's Gospel, then, we see the mystery of providence at work: Jesus's mission will eventually extend to Gentiles, as God always intended, but it will happen through the unfortunate mechanism of Jewish rejection of Jesus.

For now, Jesus begins preaching the kingdom of heaven to his fellow Jews. Matthew 4:17 marks a major turning point in the Gospel of Matthew. We find a phrase found only in one other place: "From that time Jesus began . . ." (*apo tote ērxato ho Iēsous . . .*). Here in 4:17, with Jesus beginning to preach the kingdom, the phrase marks a literary break with what came before: Matthew 1:1–4:16 has served to introduce Jesus through stories of his lineage, birth, and baptism. Now he turns to his public ministry, which in 4:17–16:20 will be marked by Jesus's preaching, healings, exorcisms, and miracles, as well as increasing conflict with Jewish experts and authorities.

Then later, in 16:21, we find the phrase the second time: "From that time Jesus began . . ." (*apo tote ērxato ho Iēsous . . .*); but now instead of preaching the kingdom to the public, Jesus begins "to show his disciples that he must go to Jerusalem and suffer many things from the elders and chief priests and scribes, and be killed, and on the third day be raised." Matthew 16:21 thus marks a new, third, and final section of the Gospel in which Jesus focuses not on preaching to the public as such but, in the wake of opposition to him, teaching his disciples as an inside group, the apostolic band of the Twelve, who are the bishops and priests of the Church he just founded (16:13–20), as a remnant community to carry on Israel's mission of redemption. And as just quoted, he teaches them mainly about the necessity of his Passion and their necessity to take up their own crosses in discipleship after him. Here again, then, as in the Temptation Narrative, the Gospel of Matthew is prospective, looking forward, and this earlier scene thus foreshadows later scenes.

The events of Matthew 4:17–16:20, then, disclose the nature of the kingdom: it involves preaching truth, the healing of disease, the exorcism of evil spirits, and miracles. It will also involve conflict on earth. And with the later founding of the Church, we see that the Church will carry on the mission and works of the kingdom, and also endure opposition.

St. Matthew models the proper response to the kingdom in the stories of the calling of the two pairs of brothers, Simon Peter and Andrew, on one hand, and James and John, on the other. Perhaps they had heard of Jesus, but the way the stories are told, Jesus simply shows up, calls them, and they immediately respond: "Immediately they left their nets and followed him" (Matt 4:20); "Immediately they left the boat and their father, and followed him" (4:22). In real life no one simply leaves his livelihood behind to follow some random rabbi. And in ancient Israel especially one does not simply leave one's father in the boat to depart forever. The point? The presence of the kingdom in Jesus demands a decisive response.

Having begun to assemble his team, Jesus now launches. His preaching, healings, and exorcisms throughout Galilee make him incredibly popular, as if he's Jesus Christ Superstar. St. Matthew emphasizes the total dominance of Jesus, as he so often does: Jesus healed "every disease" and "every infirmity" (Matt 4:23); he healed "all the sick" (4:24). As a result "his fame spread throughout all Syria" (4:24)—the large region of the Roman province of Syria extending well north of Galilee—and Matthew 4:25 informs us that "great crowds followed him" not only from Galilee but also from "the Decapolis"—the region of the league of ten cities, east of the northern Jordan River—as well as from "Jerusalem and

Judea and from beyond the Jordan"—the last likely being the area extending well east of the southern Jordan River.

First, Jesus's popularity here sets the stage for dramatic tension, as literary plot revolves around conflict. In the Gospels, Jesus is initially popular, but then encounters suspicion, then opposition, then hostility. The same pattern obtains in Acts: the early Church is esteemed, "having favor with all the people" (Acts 2:47), but then encounters opposition with the jailing and beating of Peter and John and the other Apostles in Acts 3–5, and then enters a perpetual season of persecution with the martyrdom of St. Stephen in Acts 7.

Second, the mention of so many regions relatively distant from Galilee in an age of travel by foot, horse, and camel signifies the extension of the Church's mission beyond the borders of Israel to the nations. Just as Jesus's fame spreads abroad from Galilee and people come to him from far away, so too at the end of the Gospel of Matthew will the risen Jesus send the Church abroad to the nations: "Now the eleven disciples went to Galilee . . ." (Matt 28:16), from where Jesus sends them to "[g]o . . . and make disciples of all nations" (28:19). And so once again we have a scene early in the Gospel that is prospective, looking forward, its full significance revealed only in the future.

CHAPTER 7

☩

THE SERMON ON THE MOUNT

IN MATTHEW 5–7 we come to the Sermon on the Mount. On one hand, it's Jesus's most famous sermon, and for good reason. Christians and others have recognized its greatness, as it's provided the Church and world with the richest teaching and most memorable sayings. The Beatitudes and the Lord's Prayer are found there, as well as the carefree wisdom of trusting in one's heavenly Father unburdened by the cares of the world. On the other hand, the Sermon on the Mount is the first of five great discourses. Much of the Sermon's popularity actually results from its misinterpretation as a mere code of ethics, as if Jesus were simply telling people in general a good way to live, which just happened to concern the universal Fatherhood of God, brotherhood of man, and (as an old jibe had it) the neighborhood of Boston.

Religion has been reduced to mere ethics for centuries now, as modern thinkers wanted to preserve what they regarded as the kernel of Christianity while separating it from the husk of miracle, Church, and dogma. In doing so they merely made Jesus a mascot for their convictions, already arrived at on other grounds. The Sermon on the Mount was thus read apart from its context in the Gospel of Matthew and apart from its status as Christian Scripture for the Church of the Triune God.

And so we need to read the Sermon on the Mount with care, seeing clearly its situation in the storyline of St. Matthew's Gospel, its apocalyptic character, and its ecclesial nature. For in the Sermon on the Mount we have Jesus the Christ bringing the new messianic Torah for the kingdom of God, now present in and with Jesus. As such, the Sermon on the Mount is not generic ethical teaching, universally valid in and of itself, but rather depends for its influence on Jesus's own person and authority, and thus is intelligible only in connection with Jesus. Further, that same Jesus will found a Church to carry on his kingdom mission, and so the Sermon on the Mount becomes the Church's kingdom charter. Finally, the Sermon on the Mount is apocalyptic; its kingdom message is oriented to that future Day when Jesus will return and God will judge every one according to his or her deeds.

One major debate has concerned whether the Sermon on the Mount is intended for everyone, or just for Jesus's followers. The older approach that saw in the Sermon a universal ethic thought it was good advice for everyone, whereas serious, traditional Christians emphasized its particular nature. The answer, as with so many debates, is both–and. The Sermon on the Mount is from Jesus, for the Church; it's to be practiced by Jesus's followers. Yet the Gospel of Matthew does not envision the Church as a closed community cut off from the world, but rather sees the Church as a missionary enterprise, open to all (see, of course, the Great Commission in Matthew 28:16–20).

The beginning and end of the Sermon on the Mount make this clear. In Matthew 5:1 Jesus sees the *crowds* and ascends the mountain, and then after he sits, "his *disciples* came to him." Matthew 5:2 then relates that "he . . . taught *them*," without specifying the antecedent—that is, did Jesus teach the *crowds* or the *disciples*?

I think St. Matthew here is deliberately ambiguous. The disciples are closest to Jesus, and so they certainly receive Jesus's teaching, but the crowds are mentioned, as if they, too, are invited not only to hear but to come closer and make themselves disciples. In fact, at the very end of the Sermon, St. Matthew informs us, "And when Jesus finished these sayings, the *crowds* were astonished at his teaching" (Matt 7:28).

A final interpretive issue that's less bedeviling than certain interpreters have made it: Are the contents of the Sermon on the Mount commands, or promises? When Jesus says, "Blessed are the meek" (Matt 5:5), are those who are already meek simply blessed, or is Jesus telling all his hearers to endeavor to become meek?

Both. For commands are promises in the Gospel of Matthew, thanks to the Catholic concept of cooperative grace, which has its very roots in the Gospel of Matthew. On one hand, Jesus commands his followers to do hard things: to stay married (Matt 19:3–9), to accept celibacy if possible (19:10–12), to forgive one's brother from the heart (18:35), to be perfect as our heavenly Father is perfect (5:48). On the other hand, what makes Jesus's expectations possible, instead of just an impossible ideal or something only religious and clergy can achieve, is the fact that he is God with his people, empowering them to do what he commands. He is Emmanuel, God with us (1:23), and promises to be with us always (28:20). One can do no better here than quote C. S. Lewis:

> I find a good many people have been bothered by what
> I said in the previous chapter about Our Lord's words,

"Be ye perfect." . . . I think He meant "The only help I will give is help to become perfect. You may want something less: but I will give you nothing less."

Let me explain. When I was a child I often had toothache, and I knew that if I went to my mother she would give me something which would deaden the pain for that night and let me get to sleep. But I did not go to my mother—at least, not till the pain became very bad. And the reason I did not go was this. I did not doubt she would give me the aspirin; but I knew she would also do something else. I knew she would take me to the dentist next morning. I could not get what I wanted out of her without getting something more, which I did not want. I wanted immediate relief from pain: but I could not get it without having my teeth set permanently right. And I knew those dentists: I knew they started fiddling about with all sorts of other teeth which had not yet begun to ache. They would not let sleeping dogs lie, if you gave them an inch they took an ell.

Now, if I may put it that way, Our Lord is like the dentists. If you give Him an inch, He will take an ell. Dozens of people go to Him to be cured of some one particular sin which they are ashamed of (like mastur-bation or physical cowardice) or which is obviously spoiling daily life (like bad temper or drunkenness). Well, He will cure it all right: but He will not stop there. That may be all you asked; but if once you call Him in, He will give you the full treatment.

That is why He warned people to "count the cost" before becoming Christians. "Make no mistake," He says, "if you let me, I will make you perfect. The moment you put yourself in My hands, that is what

you are in for. Nothing less, or other, than that. You
have free will, and if you choose, you can push Me
away. But if you do not push Me away, understand
that I am going to see this job through. Whatever suffering it may cost you in your earthly life, whatever
inconceivable purification it may cost you after death,
whatever it costs Me, I will never rest, nor let you rest,
until you are literally perfect—until my Father can
say without reservation that He is well pleased with
you, as He said He was well pleased with me. This I
can do and will do. But I will not do anything less."[1]

That's how one solves the riddle of Jesus laying high
demands on his followers while he also at the same time claims
his yoke is easy and his burden light (11:30). All attempts at
righteousness done in one's own power by one's own efforts—
from the efforts of Pharisees of his day to the harangues of
the sanctimonious moralists of ours—involve the denial of
the abiding power of Christ in one's life to do what he says.
Compared to that, an approach destined to fail, or at best
to produce rigid, grudging people—Jesus's yoke is easy and
burden light because we're yoked to him and he helps us carry
the very burden he himself bids us bear. With Christ, yoked to
him, we're free to excel in human and Christian virtue.

MATTHEW 5:1–12: FOURTH SUNDAY IN ORDINARY TIME / MONDAY WEEK 10

In the Gospel of Matthew, Jesus and his Church are both
the new Israel and thus fulfill the Old Testament. The new
covenant Jesus brings fulfills and transforms the covenant

---

[1] Lewis, *Mere Christianity*, 201–202.

made of old with Israel. And so one major personage from the Old Testament Jesus fulfills is that of Moses. The Gospel of Matthew itself has Jesus present five great blocks of teaching, just as Moses had five books. Moses gave the Torah to the people of Israel, while Jesus gives the new messianic Torah to the Church, the new Israel. And so the Sermon on the Mount presents Jesus as a new Moses.

Just as Moses went up the mountain to receive and deliver the Ten Commandments, Jesus "went up on the mountain" (Matt 5:1), traditionally Mount Eremos on the northern side of the Sea of Galilee, slightly west, between Capernaum and Tabgha, themselves a bit more than a mile apart. Jesus "sat down" (5:1), and Jewish tradition records Moses sitting to teach.[2] Jesus then "open[s] his mouth" (5:2), a phrase which prophets and wise men use in the Old Testament to declare they are uttering God's words by his power (see Job 33:2, Ps 78:2, Ezek 33:22, and Dan 10:16). St. Matthew will use Psalm 78:2 in a fulfillment quotation in Matthew 13:35 to indicate Jesus's parables are matters of divine, prophetic wisdom: "This was to fulfil what was spoken by the prophet: 'I will open my mouth in parables, I will utter what has been hidden since the foundation of the world.'" St. Matthew therefore indicates that what follows isn't simply sound advice but God's own truth, prophetic wisdom from on high.

And so with his disciples around him and the crowds listening on, Jesus opens his Sermon with the famous Beatitudes (from the Latin word for "blessed," *beatitudo*).

Many are so familiar with the Beatitudes that they miss

---

[2] Dale Allison, *The New Moses: A Matthean Typology* (Minneapolis: Fortress, 1993), 172–180. Allison discusses *b. Megillah* 21a; Philo, *On the Sacrifices of Cain and Abel* 8; and *4 Ezra* 14, among others. Sitting was regarded as the common posture for teaching in the ancient world, and so it was thought Moses sat when teaching.

the shock they should feel. All the Beatitudes undermine the world's wisdom, and many subvert common Jewish assumptions of the day. For the world's wisdom centers on power, and many Jews (reading Deuteronomy well, with its promises of blessings for obedience) assumed health and wealth were marks of divine favor. Jesus, on the other hand, declares that those the world regards as sad and week and those many Jews would regard as cursed are those who are actually blessed.

The world does not esteem the poor in spirit, those in mourning, the meek, those pursuing righteousness, the merciful, or peacemakers. It glories in war and hails victors; it promotes indulgence, and mocks virtue. And for many Jews, many of those whom Jesus lists would be regarded as sinners because of their apparent misfortune.

But Jesus declares them fortunate, indeed blessed, truly happy. Against all expectations it's precisely those sorts of people who possess the kingdom, receive divine comfort, inherit the earth, have their pursuit of righteousness satisfied, receive mercy, and see God as sons of God.

For illustration, a couple particular Beatitudes merit specific mention. Consider first Matthew 5:5, "Blessed are the meek, for they shall inherit the earth." The word "earth" (*hē gē* in Greek) can also be translated "land." In Jesus's day, many Jews, especially the revolutionary Zealots, wanted to drive the Romans from the Holy Land (and Jesus had one of the Zealots, Simon, among his twelve disciples). Jesus's first hearers would likely have heard "land" here, and so what Jesus says opposes expectations diametrically: it is not the violent, the warriors, the rebels, says Jesus, who will inherit the land, but rather the meek, those who eschew violence. No Jew—neither Zealot revolutionary nor collaborator with Rome—would have thought that.

Some, then, have seen in Jesus's Sermon on the Mount a call to absolute pacifism. The meek inherit the earth, and the peacemakers (not the warriors) are the sons of God. Quoting the Sermon on the Mount, the Church teaches, "In the Sermon on the Mount, the Lord recalls the commandment, 'You shall not kill,' and adds to it the proscription of anger, hatred, and vengeance. Going further, Christ asks his disciples to turn the other cheek, to love their enemies. He did not defend himself and told Peter to leave his sword in its sheath" (CCC 2262).

But immediately following, the Church draws on Natural Law and Tradition to teach: "The legitimate defense of persons and societies is not an exception to the prohibition against the murder of the innocent that constitutes intentional killing" (CCC 2263a), and so one may defend oneself: "Love toward oneself remains a fundamental principle of morality. Therefore it is legitimate to insist on respect for one's own right to life. Someone who defends his life is not guilty of murder even if he is forced to deal his aggressor a lethal blow" (CCC 2264a). Similarly, one can defend others: "Legitimate defense can be not only a right but a grave duty for one who is responsible for the lives of others" (CCC 2265a).

The Church understands Jesus, its founder, and indeed the Creator and divine reason incarnate (see John 1:1–3), then, to be teaching that one should not use violence to defend oneself from minor slights or from martyrdom, but that in other cases, where life or serious bodily violation is at issue, defending oneself with minimal requisite force is permitted.

That the meek will inherit the land here, however, has a second meaning, commensurate with the rereading that the Gospel of Matthew itself invites.[3] Again, in Matthew 28:20 Jesus commands his disciples to teach those they convert to obey all Jesus has commanded, and that teaching is found in the very Gospel of Matthew the reader is finishing reading.

---

3 See what follows on Matthew 28:16–20.

And so the reader returns to the beginning, having been through the story once, but now reads it with Christian eyes, with the teaching in word and deed Jesus has given throughout. In doing so, now the literal "land" (*hē gē*) of Matthew 5:5 is understood spiritually, not simply as the Holy Land of Israel but indeed the entire earth given to Christians to rule at the end of time.

Mercy merits mention as well. In the Gospel of Matthew, the merciful obtain mercy. In Matthew 7:2, Jesus says, "For with the judgment you pronounce you will be judged, and the measure you give will be the measure you get." In the Parable of the Unmerciful Servant in Matthew 18:23–35, Jesus tells a story in which a king forgives a man ten thousand talents—an astronomical, absurd sum, perhaps as much as fifteen years's worth of wages—instead of selling all his possessions and his family into slavery. But the man then turned around and refused to forgive a debtor one hundred denarii, about one hundred days's wages. And so the king finds him and declares, "[S]hould not you have had mercy on your fellow servant, as I had mercy on you?" (18:33), and has him tossed into prison. Or again in the Lord's Prayer: "And forgive us our debts, as we also have forgiven our debtors" (6:12). Those truly forgiven can, and must, turn around and forgive others. But mercy in the Gospel of Matthew is real forgiveness, not license, not downplaying the gravity of sin.

The Beatitudes close with chilling words about persecution (Matt 5:10–12). On one hand, this is not surprising, given Herod's attempt to kill the Christ child in Matthew 2, John the Baptist's hostility to the Pharisees and Sadducees in Matthew 3, and John's arrest in Matthew 4. From the beginning, Jesus and those with him face hostility. And now Jesus effectively promises persecution to the righteous, to those who suffer opposition for Jesus's sake. On the other hand, as with many of the other categories of persons Jesus describes in the Sermon on the Mount, few would regard those persecuted as blessed. We have enough scenes of the persecuted in our own day to know the miseries of their existence, such as religious or ethnic minorities in totalitarian regimes as many of our Christian brothers and sisters are. Yet Our Lord calls them blessed; why? Because the kingdom of heaven belongs to them (5:10), in which they'll have a great reward (5:12).

St. Matthew then brings up the example of the prophets; the persecuted are to rejoice in their persecution, "for so men persecuted the prophets who were before you" (Matt 5:12b). Now the New Testament repeatedly reminds its readers that Christianity is the way of the Cross, that Christians belong to a martyr faith. In the Gospel of Matthew, Jesus says, "If any man would come after me, let him deny himself and take up his cross and follow me" (16:24; see also 10:38). Discipleship embraces the Cross. And here with the reference to the persecution of the prophets, Jesus reminds his hearers that the crosses they assume are no novelty; God's faithful people suffer as a rule. The suffering of the righteous in the Old Testament points to the suffering of the Righteous One and his followers in the New.

But Jesus mentions prophets in particular. According to tradition, the prophet Isaiah was sawed in half upside down—a chilling episode which finds oblique mention in Hebrews 11:37. Elijah was hunted by Jezebel (1 Kgs 19:1–3). Jeremiah was tossed to the bottom of a muddy well (Jer 38:1–13). Later in the Gospel of Matthew, Jesus will conclude a speech damning the scribes and Pharisees with these words:

> Woe to you, scribes and Pharisees, hypocrites! for you build the tombs of the prophets and adorn the monuments of the righteous, saying, "If we had lived in the days of our fathers, we would not have taken

part with them in shedding the blood of the prophets." Thus you witness against yourselves, that you
are sons of those who murdered the prophets. Fill up,
then, the measure of your fathers. (Matt 23:29–32)

Jesus sees both himself and his Apostles standing in the
line of the prophets as inheritors of the prophetic mantle.
And so Jesus draws the parallel moral: just as the scribes and
Pharisees descended from those who murdered the prophets,
they, too, will murder the heirs of the prophets, Jesus and his
apostolic missionaries:

Therefore I send you prophets and wise men and
scribes, some of whom you will kill and crucify, and
some you will scourge in your synagogues and persecute from town to town, that upon you may come all
the righteous blood shed on earth, from the blood of
innocent Abel to the blood of Zechari'ah the son of
Barachi'ah, whom you murdered between the sanctuary and the altar. (Matt 23:34–35)

Here one also ought to consider the Parable of the Wicked
Tenants (Matt 21:33–46), in which the servants and then son
sent to collect the harvest, who were beaten and killed by the
wicked tenants, stand for the prophets and finally the Son,
Jesus, sent by God to Israel over the centuries.

The Gospel of Matthew, then, presents a particular view
of salvation history, in which the dominant, powerful rulers
of Israel oppress, persecute, and kill the righteous and the
prophets in particular. There is continuity between Old and
New Testaments, then, as Jesus and his missionary disciples
stand in the line of the persecuted righteous and prophets and
will suffer and die like the righteous and prophets of old.

MATTHEW 5:13-16: FIFTH SUNDAY IN ORDINARY TIME / TUESDAY WEEK 10

In the Beatitudes Jesus has defined the character and lot of those who would follow him in and into the kingdom of heaven according to his new messianic Torah. They are oppressed, marginalized, suffering, persecuted, but blessed nonetheless. Now he teaches his hearers that in spite of their marginal social situation, they actually hold a lofty position, that God works through them, in their lowly status, to redeem the world. They are the world's salvation, even though the world regards them as cursed, as enemies.

Salt was crucial in the ancient world. A preservative, it kept food from spoiling, and had medicinal properties; Galen the physician observed warm salt baths soothed his manic patients. Even today salt is therapeutic, from Epsom salts to saline solution to psychoactive lithium. And so it was valuable and functioned as a commodity and currency. Legionaries were sometimes paid in salt, from which we get the metaphorical use of salt as wages in the word "salary." And so Jesus calls his followers "the salt of the earth" (Matt 5:13a), suggesting their very existence sustains the world.

But there's also a word of warning: "[B]ut if salt has lost its taste, how shall its saltness be restored? It is no longer good for anything except to be thrown out and trodden under foot by men" (Matt 5:13b). Now it's true that salt can't really degrade, that it can't go bland. As he so often does, Jesus here stretches language to make the obvious point: discipleship doesn't endure automatically. Disciples can fail and fall away. And so Jesus warns them not to let that happen, or they will meet a bad end.

So too with Jesus's teaching that his followers are "the light of the world" (Matt 5:14). He is essentially telling them that they now, as his followers, have inherited Israel's mission to be a "light to the nations" (Isa 42:6, 49:6). And he reminds them that hiding light is absurd: "A city set on a hill cannot be hid. Nor do men light a lamp and put it under a bushel, but on a stand, and it gives light to all in the house" (Matt 5:14b–15).

Thus Jesus tells them, "Let your light so shine before men, that they may see your good works and give glory to your Father who is in heaven" (Matt 5:16). The disciple isn't supposed to receive praise for his own sake. Rather, disciples are to live in such a way that those watching them perceive that Christians are powered by God, living for God, bearing witness to God. The beauty of our witness redounds to the glory of God the Father. "Not to us, O LORD, not to us, but to your name give glory" (Ps 115:1a).

And finally, we have here in the Gospel of Matthew the first mention of God as Father, indeed "your Father" (Matt 5:16). The Fatherhood of God is a major theme in the Sermon on the Mount and in the wider Gospel of Matthew. It's no mere metaphor, and it's not meant to be simply sentimental. Rather, "Father" is God's very name ("Our Father, who art in heaven, Hallowed be thy name," 6:9), and thus it is God's very identity. God has the nature of the ideal father, and as such he determines the nature of human fatherhood. As sons and daughters of the Father, we the Church are family, princes and princesses in the kingdom.

MATTHEW 5:17–37: SIXTH SUNDAY IN ORDI-
NARY TIME (LONG FORM: 5:17–37; SHORT
FORM: 5:20–22A, 27–28, 33–34A, 37) /
WEDNESDAY OF THE THIRD WEEK OF LENT
(5:17–19) / WEDNESDAY WEEK 10 (5:17–19)

Chief among St. Matthew's concerns is how the new age brought by the advent of Jesus Christ and all that entails—

gospel, kingdom, and Church—relates to the old age. There is much continuity: the gospel is the fulfillment of God's promises to Israel and the world in the Old Testament; the Church continues Israel's work of redemption in the world; the Eucharist is the Church's sacrificial rite fulfilling the sacrificial rites of Israel. And yet many things change in Jesus's coming as Christ and the fulfillment of all things old.

And so here in Matthew 5:17–20 (the lectionary separates verses 19 and 20, but 20 properly concludes the unit), St. Matthew's Jesus explains in detail what his new messianic Torah, his Christian Law, means for the old Torah, Moses's Law, in the pursuit of kingdom-righteousness.

In Matthew 5:17, Jesus says, "Think not that I have come to abolish the law and the prophets; I have come not to abolish them but to fulfil them." So on one hand, Jesus here claims continuity. He does not simply dismiss what is old but fulfills it. On the other hand, Jesus will effectively abolish much of the Old Mosaic Law, as well as longstanding traditions of interpretation in what follows in the Sermon on the Mount and in the wider Gospel. In Matthew 15:10–20, Jesus effectively does away with Jewish dietary laws: "Hear and understand: not what goes into the mouth defiles a man, but what comes out of the mouth, this defiles a man. . . . Do you not see that whatever goes into the mouth passes into the stomach and so passes on? But what comes out of the mouth proceeds from the heart, and this defiles a man. . . . [T]o eat with unwashed hands does not defile a man" (15:10b–11, 17–18, 20).

A simple threefold division of the Mosaic Law is helpful here. First, much of the Old Law concerns worship and thus sacrifice, as in the ancient world there was no worship without sacrifice. And so Jesus in his sacrificial crucifixion and Eucharist fulfills the sacrifices of the Old Testament. Second, the moral dimensions of the Mosaic Law are maintained and even generally made more rigorous by Jesus and the early Church. Jesus forbids divorce (Matt 19:3–9) whereas Moses permitted it (Deut 24:1–4); but the early Church, following Jesus's lead, did away with almost everything in the Mosaic Law for Gentiles who wished to become Christians, requiring them only to abstain from idolatry, meat of strangled animals (which was sacrificed to pagan idols), consumption of blood, and sexual immorality. The early Church thus maintained the substance of the Levitical laws for sex and marriage.

Third are those parts of the Mosaic Law we might deem "ethnic," in that (in Christian understanding) they were intended to apply only to ethnic Israel and only for a time. These are the laws pertaining to diet and dress and such that served to keep Israel separate from the nations for a time and thus free of the nations's idolatrous practices. In the Church these rules needed to go away, however, for they had served to separate Christian Jews and Gentiles, and the Church needs to be one. And so Jesus abolishes this dimension of the Old Law.

In Matthew 5:18, Jesus explains the rationale for his claim in the prior verse: "For truly, I say to you, till heaven and earth pass away, not an iota, not a dot, will pass from the law until all is accomplished." At first glance, it sounds as if Jesus is saying the Mosaic Law will endure to the end of time. And yet again in the Sermon on the Mount and in the wider Gospel of Matthew, Jesus will declare that aspects of the Law have indeed passed.

On the subsequent rereadings of the Gospel of Matthew the Gospel itself invites (Matt 28:20: "teaching them to obey all I have commanded you," which refers the reader back to reread the Gospel with fresh Christian eyes), the reader will more clearly perceive what Jesus is subtly teaching here, now that the reader knows the end of the story. Jesus will have abolished aspects of the Law, and the Gospel will assert that the destruction of the temple forty years later, which Jesus predicts (Matt 24), is divine punishment for the murder of God's Son. When the curtain of the temple is torn in two at Jesus's death (Matt 27:51), it's not so much symbolizing that Jesus's death gives us total access to God the Father, but that God is fleeing the Holy of Holies, leaving the temple undefended, and forty years later the Romans will level it.

So Jesus is teaching that aspects of the Law will pass with his crucifixion and the resulting destruction of the temple. His crucifixion is the fulfillment of his obedience to his Father's sacrificial commission, which means the sacrificial aspects of the Law are replaced by the Eucharist. But his crucifixion being a murder, God departs from the temple in recompense for the murder of his Son. This explains the cryptic phrase "till heaven and earth pass away" (Matt 5:18): it refers not to the totality of the cosmos *but to the temple*, which Jews believed was the center of the cosmos, and thus used "heaven and earth" *as a circumlocution, a phrase for the temple.*[4] As it contained the Holy of Holies, the very dwelling place of God, the temple was where heaven and earth met. And so when Jesus speaks of "heaven and earth" passing away, he's speaking of the temple's destruction.

Jesus then speaks of relaxing and keeping commandments in Matthew 5:19: "Whoever then relaxes one of the least of these commandments and teaches men so, shall be called least in the kingdom of heaven; but he who does them and

---

[4] See Crispin H. T. Fletcher-Louis, "The Destruction of the Temple and the Relativization of the Old Covenant: Mark 13:31 and Matthew 5:18," in *Eschatology in Bible & Theology: Evangelical Essays at the Dawn of a New Millennium*, ed. K. Brower and M. Elliot (Downers Grove, IL: InterVarsity, 1997), 145–169.

teaches them shall be called great in the kingdom of heaven." A superficial reading again suggests that Jesus is merely teaching the abiding endurance of the Mosaic Law. And yet there are indications that Jesus's own teaching is in view. Again, the rereading of the Gospel that Matthew 28:19 invites is crucial. For at the end of the Gospel of Matthew, Jesus instructs his eleven disciples to teach their converts "to observe all that I have commanded you"—all that Jesus, *not Moses*, has commanded. And in what immediately follows (in Matthew 5:21–48), Jesus will six times use a form of the formula "You have heard that it was said . . . But I say to you . . ." Jesus contrasts what Moses said with what he, Jesus, says, in a way that asserts Jesus's authority in a given case either interprets, transforms, or dispenses with what Moses taught.

So "these commandments" in Matthew 5:19 are in all likelihood Jesus's own commandments. Further confirmation is found in the very word "these," the near demonstrative pronoun, which suggests the referent is what Jesus is about to teach in Matthew 5:21 through the end of the Sermon on the Mount. Were he thinking of Moses's teaching, Jesus might have said "those commandments," using the far demonstrative pronoun. Moreover, the relaxing or keeping of the commandments at issue bears on one's position as least or great *in the kingdom of heaven*, which Jesus brings and proclaims. And so it stands to reason that his commandments, which concern life in the kingdom, are in view here.

In short, final judgment involves how well one keeps and teaches Jesus's teaching. But it's interesting to observe that the judgment here doesn't involve the binary options of the reward of heaven or the pains of hell but rather one's relative position in heaven. The perfection Jesus will demand (Matt 5:48) is more a matter of process toward the goal of love than it is flawless sinlessness, and so those deficient in keeping and teaching Jesus's commandments still may achieve salvation. Further, though it offends contemporary egalitarian sensibilities, here Jesus teaches there is hierarchy in heaven. St. Paul taught similarly, as those who build poorly on the foundation of Christ may themselves be saved "but only as through fire" (1 Cor 3:15). And so Christian tradition has affirmed the idea that heaven itself has rankings.

Matthew 5:20 completes this unit in the Gospel. The lectionary places it with the following passage through 5:26, seemingly doing so because it is assuming, rightly, that what follows in 5:21–26 will clarify what that "righteousness" that Jesus mentions in 5:20 means.

Jesus asserts, in Matthew 5:20, "For I tell you, unless your righteousness exceeds that of the scribes and Pharisees, you will never enter the kingdom of heaven." "Exceeds" is a quantitative word, as if Jesus were saying one needs to be more righteous than the Pharisees, but the reader will find that being more righteous than the Pharisees means being righteous in a qualitatively different way than they.

The Gospel of Matthew presents the Pharisees as being concerned with externals alone, keeping the outward rules and rituals, with no attention to internals, the attitude of the heart. Much scholarship, rooted in the liberal and anti-semitic Protestantism of the nineteenth century, has made a mistake here, thinking that Jesus advocates a religion of the heart alone in opposition to the Pharisees's focus on externals. For the Jesus of the Gospel of Matthew, however, the problem isn't the Pharisees concern for externals but their neglect of internals. Their hearts are out of line with their behavior. And so Jesus will later say to them, "Woe to you, scribes and Pharisees, hypocrites! for you tithe mint and dill and cummin, and have neglected the weightier matters of the law, justice and mercy and faith; *these you ought to have done*, without neglecting the others" Matthew 23:23, emphasis mine). And so Jesus thinks externals matter; what he demands is that one's heart, the internal, line up with one's actions, the external. And indeed as we have seen above with reference to Matthew 15:10–20, the heart has priority.

Thinking religion is a matter of the heart alone is a particularly modern conceit and leads to absurdities. In what follows, Jesus will talk about anger and insulting speech when discussing the Fifth Commandment and lust when discussing the Sixth. He moves to the interior, to the attitudes of the heart underlying murder and adultery. But he does not then say the external, bodily matters of literal murder and literal adultery do not matter. Obviously the external dimensions of the Fifth and Sixth Commandments are kept. For Jesus, then, the internal (not hating or insulting, not lusting) must line up with the external (not murdering, not committing adultery).

MATTHEW 5:20–26: FRIDAY OF THE FIRST WEEK OF LENT / THURSDAY WEEK 10

In the remainder of Matthew 5, Jesus delivers six sets of pairings, contrasting in various ways Moses and Jewish traditions of interpretation with his own authoritative pronouncements: "You have heard it said . . . but I say unto you." These pairings have traditionally been called "antitheses," but that's misleading, for not all of the pairings are truly antithetical, that is, set in diametric opposition to each other. Each pairing, though, does present its own precise relationship between what is old with Moses and what is new with Jesus.

Matthew 5:20 functions as a fulcrum between Jesus's general principles in 5:17–19, about how his mission and teaching relate to what has come before, and six particular cases of teaching in 5:21–47, which illustrate the general principles.

But the six paired cases are not random; they're significant, even foundational, in that they deal with major matters of life for most people and the fundamental character of discipleship in the kingdom. In short, the six pairings delineate what the true righteousness that permits entry into the kingdom of heaven (5:20) looks like on the ground. Ultimately, that righteousness involves being perfect as the heavenly Father is perfect (5:48). Jesus's words there in 5:48 do not simply close the sixth subsection on love of enemies, but rather close what 5:20 opened. To have a kingdom-gaining righteousness that exceeds that of the scribes and Pharisees means to cultivate the perfect *imitatio Dei*, the imitation of God, the heavenly Father, who loves all whether they be just or unjust, whether they love him or not, who speaks truly though every man be a liar, who keeps his commitments though men break theirs.

In Matthew 5:21–26, Jesus delivers his teaching about killing, and in 5:27–30, his teaching on adultery. Here (as discussed above) he does not abolish the old; certainly the prohibitions against literal murder and adultery stand. But in accord with his thematic insistence in the Gospel of Matthew that one's interior, one's heart, must be as righteous as one's external actions, Jesus goes to the root of murder (anger and insulting speech) and the root of adultery (lust).

Keeping the outward Commandment is not hard in these two cases: very few people conceive to commit literal murder and fewer carry it out, and while adultery is much more common than murder, here, too, fulfilling the Commandment is within reach; fundamental fidelity is not impossible even in human terms quite apart from grace. But Jesus goes to the substance of the matter, to the root, deeper, and in doing so, it seems his new way is indeed harder than the old. Very few men murder, but many murmur, mock, slander, and slight. Some men adulterate, but very many lust. And so fundamental Christian discipleship involves controlling one's tongue and custody of the eyes—much harder tasks than keeping the outward Commandments. Yet with grace all is possible; Jesus's burden is light because his easy yoke is his presence with us, helping us do that which he commands.

Jesus's teaching here on these two Commandments is radical and illustrates the radicalism of his teaching in the Sermon on the Mount and the Gospel of Matthew more broadly. Radical doesn't really mean "extreme," as in common usage. Rather, it has to do with the "root" of things, coming from the Latin *radix* (like "radish," as it happens). So Jesus's teaching isn't extreme in the sense that it's pushing beyond the bounds, but it's radical in that it goes to the most basic root of what the reality of the kingdom is—which is reality itself, the only reality that matters. As such, it seems extreme because it contradicts supposed common sense and common experience, but that's because we live in a world wracked by sin. What's really extreme is the degree to which the world is estranged from God. And so here in the apocalyptic Sermon on the Mount, Jesus the Christ, God on earth, reveals the true nature of sin and righteousness, and their ends.

And so Jesus's teaching is radical, but not extreme, because it's true. Those who are angry, who insult their brothers, are at risk of serious judgment, including hell (Matt 5:22). Similarly, lust leads to hell (5:29b, 30b). Given the reality of that risk, Jesus advises radical action: gouge the eye and sever the hand lest the entire body be cast into hell (5:29–30). Better to lose parts than the whole. Even though hyperbole, Jesus's language here is shocking. Similarly, those who have wronged one's brother need drop everything, even a sacrifice, and seek reconciliation (5:23–24), while those accused, rightly or wrongly, ought to sue for peace as soon as possible (5:25–26).

Second meanings abound here, as the Gospel of Matthew

is spiritual, allegorical (and hyperbolic language is a form of spiritual, allegorical speech). It appropriates the Old Testament in every verse, and it points to heavenly realities. And so in Matthew 5:25–26, Jesus's words about seeking reconciliation with one's accuser isn't simply the sort of pragmatic legal advice a Saul Goodman might dispense. Rather, Jesus's words suggest final judgment: those indicted, as are we all, should do all in one's power to escape a final verdict of guilty. Note, too, that we should do so not by defending ourselves but by making friends with our accuser (5:25a): those who will not have God as friend will have him as judge alone.

The reference to leaving one's gift at the altar and seeking reconciliation with one's brother in Mathew 5:23–24 is also allegorical. On a first reading, Jesus speaks these words roughly around AD 30, and they refer to the altar in the Jewish temple of Jerusalem, which is still standing. But the second and subsequent readings that the Gospel of Matthew invites (28:19) mean understanding with Christian eyes, and so the "altar" mentioned here becomes every Christian altar of the sacrifice of the Eucharist. For the sake of argument, let's say that the Gospel of Matthew was written after AD 70, as critical scholarship claims. If Jesus's words referred only to the altar of the Jewish temple, they'd be irrelevant, for the Romans destroyed the temple in AD 70. If we affirm St. Matthew wrote the Gospel that bears his name in (perhaps) the 50s, the same situation obtains: since Jesus in the very Gospel of Matthew predicts the destruction of the temple in Matthew 24, it wouldn't make sense for Jesus's words about the altar in Matthew 5 to refer to the Jewish altar alone, as it's going to disappear in forty years. It'd be like his teaching here has a short shelf-life relative to history.

And so in the Gospel of Matthew, the Eucharist, offered on the Christian altar of sacrifice, is no mere individual thing but is the sacrament of unity in brotherhood. Indeed, "brother" in the Gospel of Matthew is no generic term but refers ultimately to Christians, to followers of Jesus, members of his community, the Church.

In the prior two pairings, Jesus does not overturn the literal meaning of what is said by Moses but moves to the interior roots of external behavior. In the next two pairings, however, Jesus's teaching becomes more radical, as he does overturn what Moses said.

MATTHEW 5:27–32: FRIDAY WEEK 10

We will deal with Jesus's teaching on marriage and divorce more fully in our discussion of Matthew 19:3–9, in which Jesus delivers his instruction on divorce, in conflict with the Pharisees. In the passage before us now, however, the reader first observes that Jesus simply declares Moses over on this point, forbidding divorce and remarriage.

In Matthew 5:31, without quoting anything verbatim, Jesus refers to Deuteronomy 24:1–4, in which Moses permits and regulates divorce. Now in the Pentateuch, we may determine a shift in the function and nature of the Old Law after the Israelites's idolatrous worship of Ba′al at Pe′or in Numbers 25. Prior to that, with the giving of the Ten Commandments (Exod 20) and the subsequent rules and rituals for worship and other laws in Exodus and Numbers, the Law was positive, meant to make people good, to show them the way to righteousness, which involved love of God and love of neighbor. But it seems after Numbers 25, after the people show themselves incapable and unwilling to keep the Law of righteousness, God through Moses then gives them negative Law: the Law now functions as a restraint to keep them from falling further into sin. That means Deuteronomy—which in fact means "second Law," as it's Moses's reinterpretation of the Law for the Israelites going forward—is a lesser law for a sinful people.[5]

And so the regulation of Deuteronomy 24:1–4 is not the ideal, not what God ultimately wanted for a righteous people. Jesus can then overturn it with ease because of its very nature as lesser Law, as concession, not merely because he has the raw authority to do so. The Christian God, and so also his Son, Jesus, is not arbitrary, not random. There's a logic to his teaching, new though it be, reason for his radicalism.

Moses, then, regulates divorce because under sin it's a sad reality, and better to have a regular mechanism for the protection of women being divorced than having them killed or tossed into the street. Jesus, however, forbids divorce ("everyone who divorces his wife . . . makes her an adulteress"), as well as marrying a divorced woman ("whoever marries a divorced woman commits adultery") (Matt 5:32). He also teaches the permanent indissolubility of marriage subtly by the latter teaching, "whoever marries a divorced woman commits adultery"; the teaching presumes such a woman remains in God's sight in the first, true, and only marriage. The eternal truth of the indissoluble marriage bond here triumphs over the temporal particulars of any situation on earth.

Is Jesus's teaching really radical, however? Jesus does provide an "exception" clause—"except on the ground of unchastity" (*porneia*, Matt 5:32). Now Moses gave as the ground for divorce the finding of some "indecency" in a wife (Deut 24:1). Jesus must be saying something different here than Moses, so it cannot be that Jesus is permitting divorce for reasons similar to Moses. Given what Jesus will

---

[5] See Scott Hahn and John Bergsma, "What Laws Were Not Good: A Canonical Approach to the Theological Problem of Ezekiel 20:25–26," *Journal of Biblical Literature* 123 (2004): 201–218.

do later in Matthew 19—draw on both Genesis 1 and 2 to teach that marriage is indissoluble—the exception clause in all likelihood refers to the forbidden degrees of consanguinity found in Leviticus 18, which forbids sex (and thus marriage) between close relatives. Given that such marriages happened among pagans, *porneia*, "unchastity," likely refers to marriages between very close relatives. And so the exception clause means pagans in such marriages who would convert to Christianity can "divorce" their spouses because they couldn't have been real marriages in the first place. It's very much like modern "annulments" or (better) declarations of nullity.

MATTHEW 5:33–37: SATURDAY WEEK 10

In Matthew 5:33–37, Jesus seems to overturn Moses again. What Jesus quotes in Matthew 5:33—"You shall not swear falsely, but shall perform to the Lord what you have sworn"—is not found directly in the Old Testament. Closest is Leviticus 19:12: "And you shall not swear by my name falsely, and so profane the name of your God: I am the LORD." Deuteronomy 23:23 might also be in mind: "You shall be careful to perform what has passed your lips, for you have voluntarily vowed to the LORD your God what you have promised with your mouth." Deuteronomy 6:13 speaks of "swearing": "You shall fear the LORD your God; you shall serve him, and swear by his name." The prohibition of taking the Lord's name in vain in the Second Commandment (Exod 10:7 and Deut 5:11) might also be in view.

In any event, Jesus forbids oaths here, prohibiting swearing on anything. What's interesting is the reason, the rationale. Here we have hints of Matthew 5:48—"[B]e perfect, as your heavenly Father is perfect"—for Jesus roots his teaching in God. Sovereign over all things, God is God, and heaven and Jerusalem are his, not yours, and even the hairs of your head belong to him, so it's pointless to swear by what is not yours; it'd be a bit like offering your neighbor's house as collateral on a loan. Further, God does not lie; he is Truth itself. And so to be perfect like one's heavenly Father means simply telling the truth, which can stand on its own. Those who are perfect, like God, do not need to buttress their claims by making oaths. The disciple is transparently truthful, like God.

MATTHEW 5:38–48: SEVENTH SUNDAY IN ORDINARY TIME / MONDAY WEEK 11 (5:38–42) / SATURDAY OF THE FIRST WEEK OF LENT (5:43–48) / TUESDAY WEEK 11 (5:43–48)

In the final two pairings in Matthew 5:38–48, Jesus becomes even more radical. Moses is again overturned. "An eye for an eye and a tooth for a tooth" (Matt 5:38, quoting Exod 21:24 and Lev 24:20), like the regulation of divorce, served to limit sin by preventing escalating spirals of violence. Jesus, however, teaches that the disciple is simply to suffer personal wrongs and impositions rather than striking back.

Notice, however, that what Jesus mentions doesn't rise to the level of mortal threat. As the Catechism teaches, if it comes to it, one can defend one's life and the lives of others.[6] It is often the better part of valor to walk away from a lower-level confrontation lest one become involved in an escalating spiral of violence, and to let others impose on one for the sake of peace, to let goods go, and to go the extra mile when asked

---

[6] "Love toward oneself remains a fundamental principle of morality" (CCC 2264a); "Legitimate defense can be not only a right but a grave duty for one who is responsible for the lives of others" (2265a).

or forced to do a relatively minor thing, as it makes for better witness and peace.

Jesus's words regarding love of one's enemies continues these ideas and is in fact his most radical teaching yet. It's also the perfect fulfillment of imitation of the perfection of God. In Mathew 5:43, Jesus quotes from Leviticus 19:18: "You shall not take vengeance or bear any grudge against the sons of your own people, but you shall love your neighbor as yourself: I am the LORD." Now Leviticus itself seems to restrict the scope of "neighbor" to "the sons of your own people." And so later Jewish interpreters clarified the meaning of neighbor as one's fellow Jew and defined enemies as pagans, so what Jesus also quotes logically seems to follow: ". . . and hate your enemy."

But Jesus says that won't do in the kingdom: "But I say to you, Love your enemies and pray for those who persecute you" (Matt 5:44). The rationale is the imitation of God's divine perfection: "so that you may be sons of your Father who is in heaven; for he makes his sun rise on the evil and on the good, and sends rain on the just and on the unjust" (5:45). Even if the world is fundamentally hostile to God, even if most men and women neglect, deny, or hate him, God returns the world's rejection with love and nurture. Honor is found even among thieves, we say, and Jesus notes even tax collectors and Gentiles love their own (5:46b–47), but the disciple must imitate God, loving and caring for even those who persecute us (for what is love lacking action?). No saintly Christian martyr condemns his executioner, but like St. Stephen or St. Thomas More, forgives them and wishes them well.

Perfection: Jesus closes these pairings by teaching, "You, therefore, must be perfect, as your heavenly Father is perfect" (Matt 5:48). The saying doesn't simply close the teaching on love of enemies, but in fact forms an *inclusio*, a bookend, with Matthew 5:20, in which Jesus teaches that the disciple's righteousness must exceed that of the scribes and Pharisees. The six pairings then illustrate what that sort of righteousness and perfection look like.

Our society struggles with perfection, as young women's struggles with body image bear witness, and men have their own struggles. Thus this verse can weigh heavily on those who would follow Jesus. Isn't this sort of perfection impossible? Isn't being perfect *like God is perfect* an impossible, soul- and psyche-crushing demand?

I would suggest that religious and cultural understandings of "perfection" lead many of us astray here. For in Protestantism and in Anglo-Saxon law (both of which made America what it is, particularly Puritanism), excellence is an absolute standard which permits no shortcomings or deviations whatsoever. One must score one hundred percent; one must fulfill one's duties totally; one may not fail in any way whatsoever. Protestantism, of course, rightly saw that as impossible, and so decided that the point not just of Mosaic Law but any religious rules whatsoever—including those of the Sermon on the Mount—was to make us realize we are sinners. God sets up impossible demands to break us so that we turn to his Son in faith and receive grace apart from any works of the Law or good works in general. This leads to antinomianism, the idea that rules don't matter, so we can do what we want. And Anglo-Saxon law is not forgiving (unlike Roman law). The lawgiver may not relax the law, and the law must be followed precisely.

The influences, then, of both Protestantism and Anglo-Saxon law have led to our situation in American culture, which (in the words of the late archbishop of Chicago, Francis Cardinal George) tolerates everything but forgives nothing. We have become antinomians, finding any constraint an oppression of our God-given freedom, but then (human nature being what it is) we lapsed Puritans derive other rules from the *Zeitgeist,* the spirit of the age, concerning "tolerance" and inclusive of "diversity." And so anyone appearing intolerant or exclusive is punished with social ostracization and sometimes with the force of real law.

A follower of the Jesus of the Gospel of Matthew, however, shouldn't fear Our Lord's call to perfection. Not only is Jesus God on earth, standing by his disciples to the end of time (Matt 1:23, 28:20), empowering them to do what he commands, but perfection in 5:28 means something other than our Puritan, Anglo-Saxon assumptions would lead us to assume.

To be perfect is to be *teleios* in Greek, which is the adjective St. Matthew employs here. It's from the noun *telos*, which means "purpose, goal, end." So something is *teleios* when it's being used for its purpose; a screwdriver is *teleios* when it's driving screws, doing what it's supposed to do. So perfection isn't meeting God's own standard of flawlessness, but it does mean acting fundamentally in the way we should, doing as followers of Jesus's kingdom are supposed to do. And so, fundamentally we should act as our heavenly Father acts: suffering and forgiving like he does, operating out of a stance of love and mercy toward those who oppress and persecute us.

So perfection is a fundamental stance, and from that stance, a process. And that tracks nicely with Catholic understandings of cooperative grace. Now those who have walked the way of cooperative grace best before us are the saints, and in seeking perfection, the saints were not yet perfect. They went to confession, frequently. Bishop Robert Barron writes:

> G. K. Chesterton once remarked, 'There are saints in my religion, but that just means men who know they are sinners.' For the great English apologist,

the relevant distinction is not between sinners and non-sinners, but between those sinners who know their sin and those who, for whatever reason, don't. The heroes of the faith—the saints—are precisely those who are ordered toward God and who therefore have a keener appreciation of how far they fall short of the ideal. St. John of the Cross compared the soul to a pane of glass. When it is facing away from the light, its smudges and imperfections are barely noticeable, but when it is directed at the light, every mark, even the smallest, becomes visible. This explains the paradox that the saints are most keenly aware of their sins, even to the point of describing themselves as the worst of sinners. We might mistake this for false modesty, but it is in fact a function of a truly saintly psychology.[7]

Perfection is a way, the way of Jesus, who helps us along it with his gracious power. Jesus will answer St. Augustine's famous prayer for every cooperative Christian: "Grant what you command, and command what you will."[8]

MATTHEW 6:1–6, 16–18: ASH WEDNESDAY / WEDNESDAY WEEK 11

Having established the character of kingdom-righteousness in Matthew 5, Jesus now turns to the traditional, foundational Jewish practices of righteousness: almsgiving, prayer, and fasting. These naturally became foundational and traditional also for Catholics, especially during the penitential season of

---

[7] Bishop Robert Barron, *Catholicism: A Journey to the Heart of the Faith* (New York: Image, 2011), 176.

[8] St. Augustine, *Confessions* 10.29.40 (*St. Augustine*, 202).

Lent, during which rather than simply giving some one thing up (a form of fasting), it's best to intensify one's giving, one's prayer, one's fasting.

Turning to these three practices, Jesus takes pain to warn against pride: "Beware of practicing your piety before men in order to be seen by them; for then you will have no reward from your Father who is in heaven" (Matt 6:1). Here again Jesus is emphasizing purity of heart. Do we do these things to appear pious, or for their own sake and thus God's? Even today in a supposed post-religious age, our nonreligious friends will often declare their admiration for our religious faith and practice, and so pride remains a real risk. Jesus, however, wants the internal, the heart, to line up with the external practice, and if we're doing what we do from the heart, we'll have no desire to seek the approval of others. Purity of purpose in pious practices is paramount.

"Hypocrites" do what they do to be "praised by men" (Matt 6:2) and "seen by men" (6:5, 16). Their purpose is pride, and the esteem of men their sole reward (6:2b, 5b, 16b). Jesus's words teach that we should instead seek the secret praise of God, our Father, who will then "reward" us (6:4, 6, 18). Three times then, in parallel, Jesus condemns hypocrites for doing what they do for honor in men's eyes, and commends pure, secret righteousness, which receives reward from God.

Hypocrisy in Jesus's teaching is different from how it functions for us today. For us, hypocrisy is failing to live up to one's convictions, for not walking the talk. For Jesus, hypocrisy is doing things for exterior motives only, for having impure, hard hearts.

Reward for good deeds is simply part and parcel of Jewish and Christian tradition. Protestant theology is uncomfortable with it for obvious reasons: it seems to encourage justification by works, not by faith alone. The best solution here is simply to go with St. Augustine in one of his most Catholic moments: we are indeed rewarded for our works, but (in accord with his midcareer understanding of cooperative grace) our good works are only made possible by God's grace working in us prior. Thus we return to God what he's already given us.

Finally, though it may be obvious to pious, practicing Catholics, it should be said that these practices of almsgiving, prayer, and fasting are neither optional nor seasonal but rather required, expected. Friday is a traditional day of at least partial fasting and abstinence for Christians of the Latin West, while Easterners customarily fast on both Wednesdays and Fridays, as the *Didache* from the late first century teaches: "But let not your fasts be with the hypocrites; for they fast on the second and fifth day of the week; but do ye fast on the fourth day [Wednesday] and the Preparation [Friday]."[9] However it is done, Jesus assumes fasting: "When you fast . . ." (Matt 6:16).

MATTHEW 6:7–15: TUESDAY OF THE FIRST WEEK OF LENT / THURSDAY WEEK 11

In the center of Jesus's teaching on almsgiving, prayer, and fasting, and indeed in the very heart of the Sermon on the Mount, stands the Lord's Prayer. The placing is suggestive: prayer as Jesus taught it stands at the center of the three traditional pious practices of righteousness and powers them, and indeed kindles kingdom discipleship in the wider Sermon as Jesus taught it. Most people in the West learn the Lord's Prayer by heart, even if they haven't set foot in a church in years, and can recite it at holiday gatherings or funerals.

---

[9] *Didache* 8:1 (ANF 7:379).

Yet that very familiarity means it's often understood out of context, and the context reveals fascinating dimensions to the Lord's Prayer many will never know. The immediate introductory context finds Jesus contrasting his way of prayer with pagan prayer: "And in praying do not heap up empty phrases as the Gentiles do; for they think that they will be heard for their many words. Do not be like them, for your Father knows what you need before you ask him" (Matt 6:7–8).

Pagan religion is transactional; the gods don't love their devotees. Rather, it's a situation in which gods and worshippers use each other according to the ancient principle of *do ut des*: "I give so that you give back." That is, the worshipper provides a sacrifice to a god that pleases and empowers the god, who then turns around and does the worshipper favors. Because the gods are often indifferent to humans, worshippers engage in repeated ritual to reach out and get a god's attention.

Through teaching the Lord's Prayer, I have found that the encounter of Elijah with the prophets of Ba'al on Mount Carmel in 1 Kings 18 is most helpful, although one could never prove that Jesus or St. Matthew had it in mind when teaching or writing down the Lord's Prayer. Elijah challenges the prophets of Ba'al to a contest: each will build an altar and offer a sacrifice to their divinity, and the god (God) who answers by fire will have proven himself the true god (God) (18:20–24). The prophets of Ba'al limp around their altar for hours, crying out "O Ba'al, answer us!" (18:26). The result? "But there was no voice, and no one answered. And they limped about the altar which they had made" (18:26).

Elijah, emboldened, starts talking smack (as young people say): "Cry aloud, for he is a god; either he is musing, or he has gone aside,[10] or he is on a journey, or perhaps he is asleep and must be awakened" (18:27). And so the prophets of Ba'al continue, now cutting themselves "until the blood gushed out upon them" (18:28) in their vain attempt to get their unreal god to answer: "but there was no voice; no one answered, no one heeded" (18:29).

Now it's Elijah's turn: he builds an altar of twelve stones for the twelve tribes in the Name of the Lord, slaughters the bull, and has the offering on the altar doused three times with water (1 Kgs 18:30–35). No trickery here, just the power of the living God. Then, in contrast to the many prophets of Ba'al, who cried out all day and cut themselves in a futile attempt to get their god to answer, Elijah, the one true remaining prophet of the Lord, offers a simple prayer, once:

O LORD, God of Abraham, Isaac, and Israel, let it be known this day that you are God in Israel, and that I am your servant, and that I have done all these things at your word. Answer me, O LORD, answer me, that this people may know that you, O LORD, are God, and that you have turned their hearts back. (18:36b–37)

Fire falls from heaven, devouring offering, wood, stones, dust, and even the water (18:38). The Lord God has answered. Because that God lives, and loves, he hears and answers simple prayer.

Thus Jesus teaches his prayer according to similar principles. Our heavenly Father knows what we need before we ask him (Matt 6:8), the same God who cares for sparrows

---

[10] The Hebrew is much more vulgar, amounting to "Maybe he's out back in the alley taking a piss."

and lilies, so that we need have no anxiety (6:25–34). To the prayer, then:

"Our Father who art in heaven, Hallowed be thy name" (Matt 6:9). We address the Father, with all that implies about God's love and solicitude for us. And yet we do not pray "hallowed be thy metaphor." We pray "hallowed be thy name." "Father" is then the very Name of God for Christians (the fuller Trinitarian Name of God being Father, Son, and Holy Spirit) and may not be dispensed with. In the Bible, and in traditional societies, names are not random but reveal the essence of things. Even the Anglo-Saxon names with which we are familiar have deep meanings in the antecedent Hebrew, Greek, and Latin.

And so God reveals himself in his very Name, and we are not at liberty to rename him in accord with the spirit of the age, which is not a fan of fatherhood. Of course many women, and men, as it happens, have had bad experiences of their earthly fathers, and the Fatherhood of God is tainted thereby. The remedy, challenging a process it may be, is to find in God the true nature of Fatherhood.

Our Father is "in heaven." Heaven is always prior in Christian faith and practice. God exists prior to creation; time, space, and all things that inhabit space-time are dependent on him. Heaven is the unchanging realm where God has always reigned perfectly. And so praying "in heaven" means we rely on the unchanging God, recognizing there's a stable realm untouched by sin and flux.

Keeping God's Name of Father holy means the obvious, no cursing, but it also means no frivolous swearing using God's Name, as Jesus has forbidden oaths just above in Mathew 5:33–37. For us today, it also means cultivating reverence for the divine Name. Our casual age regards familiarity as a virtue, and we toss around "God" and "Jesus" carelessly.

In the ancient world and the Bible, names were important. The Bible records name changes at pivotal points in salvation history. Abram becomes Abraham, Sarai becomes Sarah, Jacob becomes Israel, and Simon becomes Peter. And names are powerful. Romulus never named "Rome" by that word. He gave it a secret name so that no one could use its name against it—there's power in a name. "Rome" is simply the first syllable of Romulus's name. Or consider exorcism. Names have power because they are bound to the very substance they name, and so Jesus adjures demons to silence when they declare his divine identity, and he demands the demons's names.

Israelites and Jews regarded God's Name as revealed to Moses in Exodus 3:14 so sacred that they refused to pronounce it, saying "Lord" (*Adonai*) in its place—that's why English translations of the Old Testament read "LORD," in all caps, when the sacred Name of God is found in the Hebrew (YHWH). And ancient manuscripts would even use the scribal device of *nomina sacra* ("sacred names"), wherein scribes would write two letters of God or Jesus with a line over them, so *Iēsous*, "Jesus," would appear as IΣ, which in English would be IS for J(esu)S.[11]

Indeed, prior generations of Catholics wouldn't utter the sacred Name of "Jesus." They would simply say, "Our Lord"— for instance, "As Our Lord taught in the Sermon on the Mount," or, "In Our Lord's Parable of the Sower," and so on. Today, Our Lord's Prayer invites us to rediscover reverence for the Sacred Names of God: Father, Son, Holy Spirit, Jesus.

"Thy kingdom come, Thy will be done, On earth as it is in heaven" (Matt 6:10). In a cooperative way, the kingdom

---

[11] Similarly, the "IHS" that we see on some chasubles and in some works of Catholic art is the first three letters of Jesus's name in Greek.

doesn't advance on its own, nor does it advance by our own power exclusively. Rather, God advances it in cooperation with our own prayer and action. Note here again that heaven is prior: God's will is always done in heaven, and we pray then that God's reign would extend on earth to reflect ever more the situation in heaven. And for Catholics, the Church that Jesus founds in Matthew 16 is the instrument that advances the kingdom.

"Give us this day our daily bread; And forgive us our debts, As we also have forgiven our debtors" (Matt 6:11–12). Forgiveness is a key theme in the Gospel of Matthew. Jesus, using hyperbole, tells Peter in effect to forgive a brother who sins against him an infinite number of times (18:22) and reinforces the point with the Parable of the Unforgiving Servant (18:23–35). Severe punishment awaits those who do not forgive their brothers from the heart.

Sometimes in the New Testament, forgiveness should be given apart from any request for it, as Jesus forgave those torturing and crucifying him (Luke 24:34), and as Stephen forgave his murderers at his martyrdom (Acts 7:60). Other times, though, a request and repentance is requisite: "[I]f your brother sins, rebuke him, and if he repents, forgive him" (Luke 17:3). Forgiveness is often good for us, releasing us from grudges we would otherwise hold on to that continue to injure us deep inside. St. Matthew would have us forgive others outright for that reason, I suspect, but also because it reflects the Father's gracious stance toward humanity.

That's why Jesus will shortly teach that our forgiveness depends on our forgiving others: "For if you forgive men their trespasses, your heavenly Father also will forgive you; but if you do not forgive men their trespasses, neither will your Father forgive your trespasses" (6:14–15). And again, that sort of forgiveness on which ours depends isn't achieved by our own emotional grit, but by the grace of the God who is with us always in Jesus Christ, empowering us to do what he commands. And forgiving is not forgetting. We cannot easily forget the real hurts done unto us by others, but we need not hold them against others. Instead, our wounds, like the wounds of the resurrected Christ, are places where the light of God illumines us.

Jesus here speaks literally of "debts," and for a reason. We love money, because money is power—from the ability to pay our bills, to buy our favorite toys, and (if we have sufficient money) to effectively if not literally buy and sell others in our current world. Releasing others from the monetary debts they owe is therefore concrete, and it is difficult. If we love others, we will forgive their debts.

Jesus then extends his literal teaching regarding debts in Matthew 6:12 in a figurative direction in Matthew 6:14–15, in which he requires us to forgive men their "trespasses" against us. (This is why most memorize the Lord's Prayer at Matthew 6:12 as "Forgive us our trespasses, as we forgive those who trespass against us.") Whether we're talking about literal debts or the more figurative trespassers, the stance of the kingdom disciple is forgiveness toward all. And all means all: Jesus says we should forgive "men"—all men, not just Christians.

"And lead us not into temptation, But deliver us from evil" (Matt 6:13). The sense of the Greek, in keeping with the apocalyptic, dualist nature of the Sermon on the Mount and the wider Gospel of Matthew, is more like "May we not be put to the Satanic time of trial, but rather deliver us from the designs of the Evil One." For "evil" is actually a substantive adjective in the Greek here; it is not "evil" as some sort of nebulous force but the root of all we call evil, Satan, the Devil, the Evil One himself. God would not tempt us to any sin minor or major, from stealing a candy bar to committing adultery, but Satan wants to sift us like wheat (Luke 22:31), and so we pray God's protection from him.

MATTHEW 6:19–23: FRIDAY WEEK 11

In these verses Jesus builds on what he has taught in Matthew 6:1–18 about the traditional Jewish triad of righteous deeds: almsgiving, prayer, and fasting. One who performs the deeds of this righteous triad is precisely the one who does not "lay up . . . treasures on earth" but rather "treasures in heaven" (6:19–20a). Heaven is stable, secure, certain, eternal, enduring, while earth is the opposite: unstable, insecure, uncertain, transient. And so in the earthly realm things pass away, they decay, they break, they wear down.

Now Matthew's Gospel is "Jewish" (with all the caveats about that claim mentioned in the introduction) and a document of the first century AD, not a heavy philosophical treatise of the sort other ancient Jews (like, say, Philo of Alexandria) and Christians (like, say, St. Augustine) produced. And yet, like the developed Christian tradition, Matthew's Gospel here tracks with the basic Christian philosophical conviction that reality is a matter of two levels: the eternal realm and the temporal realm, the heavenly and the earthly. For Plato, for Philo, for St. Augustine, for St. Thomas, the eternal, the heavenly realm of stability and perfection, though invisible, is most real, while the temporal, earthly level is the realm of flux, change, decay—indeed the "vale of tears" God's pilgrim people pass through on the way to eternal, heavenly glory. And in substance, even if he's not quoting Plato or Aristotle, St. Matthew is operating with the same two-level view of reality. Even when St. Augustine uses Plato as a theological resource, or St. Thomas uses Aristotle, they're not importing

Greek concepts alien to the biblical spirit. Rather, these lumi-naries are building on what's already there in St. Matthew's Gospel, as gritty and Jewish and practical as it seems on the surface.

The "heart" merits reflection here, as it's crucial for Mat-thew's Gospel. In the Bible, the heart is like the soul, the seat of what the philosophical and Christian traditions will deline-ate as the intellect, the will, and the passions. Those traditions will teach that a life of sanity involves the intellect's knowl-edge of the Good, the True, and the Beautiful guiding the will to act rightly and to ride herd on the passions when they want the Bad, the False, and the Ugly. And that is accomplished through virtue—the habitual choosing of the Good so that it becomes an ingrained habit. The Christian life, then, is like athletics, or music, where one practices a move, drill, or a scale until it becomes automatic. Matthew's Gospel operates with these very concepts. Here the passage is telling us to practice orienting our hearts (our intellect, will, and passions) toward heaven.

Now in Matthew's Gospel, the heart is foundational. All flows from the heart, whether good or bad deeds, speech, or attitudes. The question, then, is how does one engage in a ren-ovation of the heart? If the heart is so important, what do we do if our hearts are weak, divided, disordered? Fortunately, in Matthew's Gospel matters of the heart are a two-way street. Everything flows from the heart, but the heart itself can be changed. By doing Christian things—acts of charity like almsgiving, prayer, fasting, and participating in the sac-raments—God works with and in us to renovate our hearts so that they may be focused on heaven. That's why Jesus says, "For where your treasure is, there will your heart be also" (Matt 6:21). Do you see the pattern? Storing up your treas-ures in heaven will lead your heart to find its rest there.

Next St. Matthew switches organs and begins speaking of the eye as the "lamp of the body" (Matt 6:22–23). Not only do eyes take in light that our brains interpret as visual scenes, but eyes also show forth much about what's going on inside us. Indeed, they might be the most expressive component of our countenance, which is why, I suppose, they've been called the "windows of the soul." And so Jesus is teaching here that what we focus on—what we take into our minds or, in his language, our hearts—will affect our bodies, which means everything we do. (One should also remember here Jesus's teaching in the prior chapter about plucking out one's eye if it leads one to lust.) Darkening the eye with sin—in the immediate context, like the sin of envy of another's possessions—will lead to sinful actions with the body. Focusing the eye on righteousness will lead to righteous actions with the body.

MATTHEW 6:24–34: EIGHTH SUNDAY IN ORDINARY TIME

Here Jesus introduces another dualism—namely, God and mammon, which track with heaven and earth. And he does so using the subtle suggestion of slavery by employing the word "master." In the ancient world slavery was simply an accepted reality, although historians would inform us that ancient slavery differed from chattel slavery in the American south. In the ancient world, slavery was not directly racial, slaves earned wages, and slaves were often freed (either through the generosity of their masters or by purchasing their freedom). That said, they were slaves and often suffered indignities, torture, and execution for the flimsiest of reasons.

In any event, Jesus here evokes slavery by speaking of God and mammon as potential masters. It might be unpalatable for us moderns to imagine ourselves as slaves of God, but it's a theme that shows up in the New Testament more than one might think, especially in St. Paul.[12] For instance, in Romans 6:22 he writes, "But now that you have been set free from sin and have become slaves of God, the return you get is sanctification and its end, eternal life." Of course, the believer is enslaved not to a human master but to God, who is all loving and a kind Master. It's also important to note that when the New Testament employs slave language for Christians, the emphasis falls on the believer's duty, obedience, and loyalty to God, not on God's authority and power to treat us as slaves. More germane to the present passage is slavery to mammon, a most cruel master. Jesus here is warning that the very impersonal things we desire to acquire—for "mammon" comes from an Aramaic word meaning wealth and possessions—will become bondage for us.

Jesus then moves to anxiety. In our anxiety about the vicissitudes of life, we seek security on earth by seeking wealth, for money can purchase good medical care and great legal representation. It can pay for good schools and move others to do for us what we want them to do. But Jesus, having taught that we should be slaves to God, not mammon, now teaches us that our slavery to that kind, loving Master means he will take care of us; we do not need to be anxious.

Jesus here uses an argument called *qal wahomer* (the Jewish, Aramaic term) or *a fortiori* (the Greco-Roman Latin term), which means "from the lesser to the greater." If something is true in a lesser case, it ought to hold in a greater case. And so Jesus points to nature, superintended by the Author of nature, to remind his hearers that God in his providence pro-

---

[12] See Dale B. Martin, *Slavery as Salvation: The Metaphor of Slavery in Pauline Christianity* (New Haven: Yale University Press, 1990).

vides all that is truly necessary. The lilies flourish, surpassing Solomon in beauty, while the birds feed and feast; and we are of more value to God than they.

Anxiety for the things of this world, therefore, does us no good. Indeed, the disquiet of striving for the things of this world—the unholy anti-Trinity of money, sex, and power—is the mark of the pagan, who seeks such things in what St. Augustine would later call the City of Man, marked by strife and striving. But God our heavenly Father knows what we need already and wants to provide for us, so we ought to trust him.

The mention of pagans (i.e., Gentiles) recalls Jesus's words prefacing the Lord's Prayer in Matthew 6:7, where he says that the pagans think the gods will hear them because they utter many words. They do not know the One God as their heavenly Father, and so cannot pray simply. Neither, then, can they trust simply for the provision of their needs, even their daily bread, but they instead live in anxiety and striving, trying to compensate for the earthly goods their gods fail to deliver.

Jesus then tells his hearers to "seek first his kingdom and his righteousness, and all these things shall be yours as well" (Matt 6:33). Precisely because God is our heavenly Father and we are his blessed children enslaved to him, we put him first by such seeking. In doing so, all falls into place as he provides us with the basics we really need.

In this chapter, the theme of simplicity dominates. Mammon makes for complexity and drags our eyes and hearts down into the things of the world, with all the anxiety that entails. Think of all the time we spend maintaining our possessions—automobiles, appliances, entertainment devices, sporting goods, homes. Some are useful for navigating modern life, but most of us do not live simply. Simple living means having just enough for sustenance and to fulfill one's vocation, whatever it may be. Simplicity is the way of the Lord, and shedding possessions and sumptuous living is the path from anxiety to joy and peace.

MATTHEW 7:1–5: MONDAY WEEK 12

In chapter 6, Jesus dealt largely with individual virtues (though the "Our" Father presumes a stance within the community of faith, the Church). Here in chapter 7 he turns for a while to life together in the community of the Church with one's Christian brothers (and by extension, sisters).

Jesus's saying, "Judge not, that you be not judged" (Matt 7:1), is one of the most misinterpreted Bible verses today. In our antinomian, Gnostic age, it gets heard and hurled about in a way that forbids moral judgments absolutely. If someone says some act is wrong, the retort is "Don't judge!" or "Don't judge me!" That's obviously not what Jesus means since he himself laid into people like the Pharisees and scribes, and since he himself in verse 6 will suggest certain people are "dogs" and "swine." The well-formed Christian conscience must make judgments about the quality of moral acts all the time.

But we need not be jerks about it. Judgmentalism is what's in view here, the attitude of the faultfinder, always seeing the flaws in someone, and never the need or the promise. Further, what's in view is the sort of judgmentalism that leaves no room for mercy, no hope for change, that assumes the one judged is a horrible and hopeless person. Such judgment is intended to be final. That's the spirit of the Pharisee. It's also the spirit of the unforgiving servant (Matt 18:23–35), who, though forgiven, refused to forgive in turn, and so received severe and exemplary punishment. Thus Jesus says, "For with the judgment you pronounce you will be judged, and the measure you give will be the measure you get" (7:2). Switching canons, our attitude should be that of Isabella in Shakespeare's *Measure for Measure*. Informed that her brother is "a forfeit of the law" under condemnation, Isabella pleads:

> Why, all the souls that were were forfeit once;
> And He that might the vantage best have took
> Found out the remedy. How would you be,
> If He, which is the top of judgment, should
> But judge you as you are? O, think on that;
> And mercy then will breathe within your lips,
> Like man new made.[13]

In Matthew's Gospel, the disciple should do as God the heavenly Father does, which means acting with mercy and forgiveness.

Judgmentalism also means acting with hypocrisy (Matt 7:5), as did the unforgiving servant. And so Jesus uses a vivid, comic image to make the point: "Why do you see the speck that is in your brother's eye, but do not notice the log that is in your own eye? Or how can you say to your brother, 'Let me take the speck out of your eye,' when there is the log in your own eye?" (7:3–4). Judgmental faultfinders usually have plenty of their own issues, and so they're eager to find fault with others; deep down they know their own failings and think, subconsciously, that bringing others down will raise them up—as we say, it takes one to know one.

But Jesus doesn't simply want his disciples to leave each other be in their faults. Rather, the point of life in the community of the Church is holiness. We help each other grow in

---

[13] Shakespeare, *Measure for Measure*, II.2.

Christian virtue that we might attain heaven. And so Jesus ultimately wants us to remove the logs from our own eyes so that we might then, from a position of strength, help others with their own specks, their failings and shortcomings (Matt 7:5).

MATTHEW 7:6, 12–14: TUESDAY WEEK 12

As we turn to the next section, Jesus says something rather judgmental: "Do not give dogs what is holy; and do not throw your pearls before swine, lest they trample them under foot and turn to attack you" (Matt 7:6). The lectionary might have done well to include it with the prior reading, for it continues the theme in a third move. The first was not judging a brother; the second was helping him with his faults from a position of strength; and now the third is a warning that some people will not be helped and are not worthy of help.

Jews did not esteem dogs at all; it would be odd for practicing Jews to have had them for pets. Dogs ran wild in the streets, threatening people and consuming all manner of trash and offal. As such, the term "dog" became an epithet for pagans, and Jesus will indeed imply the Canaanite woman with the demonized daughter is a "dog" in Matthew 15:26. Pigs, too, were detested, especially since they were declared unclean. Here Jesus might be restricting his mission to Israel (as he does in Matt 10:5–6), telling his disciples not to bother evangelizing pagans. More likely in this context, though, he's suggesting that some Christian brothers with specks in their eyes will not receive constructive, redemptive admonishment, much like the situation in Matthew 18:15–17, in which Jesus provides the process for dealing with a brother who sins against you. If after several attempts he will not listen even to the Church, he is to be treated as a pagan and tax collector (18:17). So too here: "what is sacred" might refer to the sacraments, which the unrepentant should not receive, and "pearls" might be wisdom and admonishment meant to move the sinner to repentance.

The lectionary now moves straight to verse 12: "So whatever you wish that men would do to you, do so to them; for this is the law and the prophets." Jesus now sums up his teaching on how one should treat one's brother with a general rule. Known as the "Golden Rule," his words here are not necessarily original, as other religions and philosophies present its substance in negative form. It's also found in Tobit 4:15: "And what you hate, do not do to any one." And so Jesus might be alluding to a deuterocanonical text, contrary to claims that the New Testament never quotes or alludes to such texts.

Further, his summation here isn't merely a good bit of moral teaching or practical advice; for Jesus it's an organizing principle for interpreting what we call the Old Testament ("for this is the law and the prophets"). Indeed, four times in Matthew's Gospel Jesus speaks of the Law and the Prophets as a unity (5:17, 7:12, 11:13, 22:40). The significance is that Jesus sees the Old Testament as a real unity, and that all its parts, not just the prophets, point forward to their fulfillment in the new dispensation that comes with his advent. Matthew is indeed a Gospel of fulfillment.

Finally, Jesus's words about the narrow gate are meant to introduce the closing section of the Sermon on the Mount, which consists of apocalyptic teachings adjuring disciples to be ready for the end of the world. Here Matthew's Gospel presents the ancient idea of the Two Ways, such as one finds in the *Didache*, the so-called "Teaching of the Twelve Apostles," which dates to AD 70–100. It begins, "There are two ways, one of life and one of death; but a great difference between the two ways" (1.1).[14] Then the *Didache* quotes Matthew's Gospel in giving the principle of the way of life: "The way of life is this: 'First, you shalt love the God who made thee, secondly, thy neighbor as thyself [see Matt 22:34–40]; and whatsoever thou wouldst not have done to thyself, do not thou to another' [see Matt 7:12]" (*Didache* 1.2).[15]

For Jesus, the narrow gate is virtuous Christian life in the Church, while the wide gate and easy way is a sinful life outside of that. Though it may be a hard saying, Jesus here affirms that few find it. All the more reason for those who have had the opportunity to receive Jesus and abide in the Church to hold fast and maintain the course that leads to life eternal.

Many have noticed in Matthew's Gospel a seeming contradiction between Jesus's words here and those like them that teach heaven is hard to achieve, and others that seem to imply the Christian way of discipleship is easy, such as Matthew 11:29–30: "Take my yoke upon you, and learn from me; for I am gentle and lowly in heart, and you will find rest for your souls. For my yoke is easy, and my burden is light." The solution is the grace provided by Jesus's presence with his disciples (1:23, 28:20): Jesus with us, which is God's very presence, enables us to do the things he expects and commands. Just as the last will become first and the first last, what seems hard becomes easy in light of God's empowering grace (and is in any event easier to bear than the pains of hell), whereas what seems easy—indulgence, pleasure, and sin—leads to bondage and misery in this life and the next.

---

[14] *Didache* 1.1 (ANF 7:377).
[15] *Didache* 1.2 (ANF 3:377).

MATTHEW 7:7–12: THURSDAY OF THE FIRST WEEK OF LENT

Jesus returns explicitly to the implicit theme of the Sermon on the Mount and indeed the entirety of the Gospel of Matthew: God as our heavenly Father. The emphasis is on persistence in asking, seeking, and knocking, that one might receive, find, and walk through open doors (Matt 7:7–8). Such persistence is rewarded precisely because the heavenly Father is there to give, be found, and open doors. An implicit contrast with pagan religion is thus present as well: the true God gives to his children because he loves and cares for them, whereas pagans receive nothing in spite of their empty phrases of many words (6:7).

On one hand, it is too easy to domesticate biblical faith and find ways to interpret Jesus's radical promises, subjecting them to the death of a thousand cuts of interpretation. On the other hand, what Jesus promises in prayer here and elsewhere isn't meant to be absurd, as if God is obliged to deliver whatever earthly goodies we desire. The question, then, is what are we to ask for? What are we to seek? Which doors should we knock upon? The answer was already given in Matthew 6:33: we are to seek first God's kingdom and righteousness, and then God provides for our daily needs. Similarly, we pray that God's will be done on earth as it is in heaven (6:10), so whatever we ask for ought to be in accord with God's heavenly will.

Jesus now employs another preposterous image to make a point: "Or what man of you, if his son asks him for bread, will give him a stone? Or if he asks for a fish, will give him a serpent?" (Matt 7:9–10). Not even horribly wicked men would do such to their children. And once again Jesus employs the *qal wahomer / a fortiori* argument: "If you then, who are evil, know how to give good gifts to your children, how much more will your Father who is in heaven give good things to those who ask him!" (7:11).

The section closes with Jesus's summary of the Old Testament, discussed above: "So whatever you wish that men would do to you, do so to them; for this is the law and the prophets" (Matt 7:12). In immediate context, Jesus now turns from our relationship to God to our relationship with men, rooting the latter in the former. As God treats us, so we should treat others. In doing so, we fulfill not just the Law but also the Prophets, and (an important subtext here) exceed the righteousness of the scribes and the Pharisees (see 5:20).

MATTHEW 7:15–20: WEDNESDAY WEEK 12

There is nothing new under the sun. As today, in the times of the earliest Church there were those who used the Christian religion for purposes other than Christ's: for self-aggrandizement, self-enrichment, and self-promotion. And so in the New Testament we see a concern for false prophets. In Acts 20:29, Paul remarks, "I know that after my departure fierce wolves will come in among you, not sparing the flock." In 2 Peter 2:1, St. Peter warns his audience, "But false prophets also arose among the people, just as there will be false teachers among you, who will secretly bring in destructive heresies, even denying the Master who bought them, bringing upon themselves swift destruction." And in 1 John 4:1, St. John advises his audience, "[D]o not believe every spirit, but test the spirits to see whether they are of God; for many false prophets have gone out into the world."

So too in the Gospel of Matthew. In his apocalyptic discourse, Jesus warns, "And many false prophets will arise and lead many astray" (Matt 24:11), and, "For false Christs and false prophets will arise and show great signs and wonders, so as to lead astray, if possible, even the elect" (24:24). There Jesus advises his disciples to ignore them, for when the Christ returns, it will be obvious, and not a rumor subject to interpretation: "For as the lightning comes from the east and shines as far as the west, so will be the coming of the Son of man" (24:27).

In the present passage of Matthew 7:15–20, Jesus is not speaking about the end times but about the ongoing situation of the Church prior to the end. "Beware of false prophets, who come to you in sheep's clothing but inwardly are ravenous wolves" (7:15), Jesus says, and the simple way to determine them is "by their fruits," for grapes are not gathered from thorns, nor figs from thistles (24:16). Good trees bear good fruit and bad trees bad, and the one cannot bear the fruit of the other (24:17–18). Here we see Jesus's insistence that the expression of a thing or person is rooted in what it or he is. The outer will reveal the inner, for all proceeds from the heart. And in point of fact, those who are false prophets, then or now, are discernible. At some point, the mask slips, even from the most charismatic. And following Jesus's advice here also presumes we know what is truly good and truly bad. Holiness and purity are good, whereas flash, charisma, and energy, while sometimes good, should not be mistaken for holiness and purity.

MATTHEW 7:21–27: NINTH SUNDAY IN ORDINARY TIME / THURSDAY OF THE FIRST WEEK OF ADVENT WEEK (1:21, 24–27) / THURSDAY WEEK 12 (7:21–29)

The Sermon on the Mount concludes with two apocalyptic

warnings: first through some direct teaching and then in the famous Parable of the Wise and Foolish Builders. Two general comments must be made. First, as discussed at length in the introduction, the Sermon on the Mount is not a presentation of general ethics for middle-class people based on pure reason. Rather, it's an ecclesial ethic, Jewish in ethos, brought by the Jewish Christ Jesus, and it's apocalyptic through and through, geared for the final age of the Church. Second, it does not stand on its own as timeless teaching rooted in naked reason but rests on Jesus Christ's authority. He is its source and point of reference. Jesus here is not some prophet speaking the words of the Lord but the Lord himself come to earth speaking his own divine, dominical words directly.

In Matthew 7:21–23 Jesus declares that he is the Judge who shall determine who enters the kingdom of heaven at the end of time. He reveals that some who claim him as Lord will not make it. Rather, one must also do "the will of my Father who is in heaven" (v. 21). What is that? Following Jesus, surely, but that means doing what Jesus commands, for that is what God wills for us. Even the charismatic works of prophecy, exorcism, and wonders (v. 22) will mean nothing if one has not done the will of God (v. 23).

Of course we might think of many people in our own day who seem to (and not just seem to) exercise real spiritual gifts—gifted speakers, trusted counselors, real exorcists, and those who have worked miracles—but, whether known or unknown, who fail severely in their Christian life. A simple example: a priest in mortal sin still confects a valid Eucharist. And some of the most famous televangelists, I think, do exercise real gifts and even do real healings, but are also heretical or dissolute or both.

A particular we should not neglect is that Jesus says to the condemned in this passage, "I never knew you" (Matt 7:23).[16] The direction is important: Jesus needs to know us; he does not say, "You never knew me." So the question is, what does it mean for the Lord to know us? When we know someone, it means we recognize them. How do we recognize someone? They appear and sound as they should. They look like themselves. They are not wearing disguises, or disguising their voice, or playing some sort of role (or "putting on a front" to act like someone they're not, as we used to say). That means, then, if we live a life of Christian integrity doing God's will, we appear and sound as we should. We're recognizable. Those who are condemned will have been wearing their Christianity as a sort of costume. But come the end, all masks are off, all costumes cast aside as we stand naked before the Lord for judgment. He will recognize us as we truly are—God willing, as Christians who have cultivated genuine virtue by doing God's will, people who have truly become who we are to be. Finally, knowledge of a person involves intimacy. The way to have Jesus know us is for him to come into us intimately, and the way Catholics do that is by participating in the sacraments, especially the Eucharist, in which we take him into our very selves.

Finally, it should be obvious that the present passage complicates simple claims that salvation is by faith alone. Matthew's Gospel is read best using the lenses of second-temple Judaism and Catholicism, both religions that saw faith not as mere belief or even trust but as fundamental fidelity (from *fides* in Latin, which is the word in that language for "faith" but which is better captured by "fidelity," since that involves not just belief but action) from which issued obedience and

---

16 I appeared on the Deep In Scripture podcast with Marcus Grodi to discuss this passage. The link is at https://chnetwork.org/deep-in-scripture/i-never-knew-you-matthew-721-23-marcus-grodi-and-dr-leroy-huizenga/.

thus good works as a matter of course.

The parable that follows drives home the point and draws again on the Two Ways. It also draws on Proverbs 12:7b, "the house of the righteous will stand," and Proverbs 14:11, "the tent of the upright will flourish." There, and here, the idea isn't that living a good life in obedience to God means one will have it easy on earth, even though that's often how the Parable of the Wise and Foolish Builders is taught. Fidelity to God in both Testaments always involves denial and discipline, often suffering, and sometimes martyrdom. Rather, there in Proverbs and here in Matthew's Gospel, the end is in view. The storms that test the houses of the wise and foolish builders are the apocalyptic storms of the end of time and indeed the final judgment.

The Sermon on the Mount then closes with comments from the narrator emphasizing Jesus's authority: "And when Jesus finished these sayings, the crowds were astonished at his teaching, for he taught them as one who had authority, and not as their scribes" (Matt 7:28–29). Again, the Gospel of Matthew, and indeed the entire New Testament, presents Jesus as God on earth and so stresses his sovereignty; his authority to interpret the Old Law and bring the New Law is not derivative but original, rooted in his divine person. In the Sermon on the Mount, Jesus has asserted himself as the ultimate lawgiver, superior to Moses and certainly superior to the tradents of Jewish tradition such as the scribes (". . . but I say to you . . ."), and even declared himself the one who will judge all men and women at the end of time.

Finally, the Sermon on the Mount opened with Jesus addressing his disciples (Matt 5:1–2: "his disciples came to him . . ."). But here we are informed "the crowds were astonished . . . for he taught them . . ." (7:29). The apparent change of audience is deliberate. While the Sermon on the Mount is for disciples of Jesus in the Church, Christian teaching is public (unlike Gnostic teaching), and so outsiders may draw close, listen in, and join the disciples in the Church on the way that leads to life in the kingdom of heaven.

✝

THE MISSION OF HEALING

MATTHEW 8:1–4: FRIDAY WEEK 12

HAVING ASCENDED THE MOUNTAIN like Moses of old to give the New Messianic Law to the Church (Matt 5:1), Jesus now descends the mountain like Moses of old, followed by crowds who are eligible to constitute the new Israel (8:1; see Exod 34:29), to begin his itinerant ministry of messianic wonder-working. We now encounter two chapters consisting largely of healings, with some exorcisms and some teachings, as well as the call of St. Matthew himself. There is a pattern: three miracles (8:1–17), an exchange about discipleship (8:18–22), three more miracles (8:23–9:8), the call of Matthew and teaching in response to probing questions (9:9–17), and then four miracles (9:18–34), followed by a summary statement of Jesus's activity and his call to pray for more laborers (9:35–38). St. Matthew will often organize material by grouping similar stories in a triad.

In the first miracle, Jesus encounters a leper requesting cleansing. Jesus can heal simply by saying a word, even remotely (as the following story of the healing of the centurion's servant will make clear), but here he touches the leper. This is radical; it is not merely that Jesus could contract the physical disease but that by touching someone unclean, under normal Jewish understanding, Jesus would become ritually unclean himself. In the Gospels, however, Jesus does not contract disease and uncleanness, but rather power flows forth from him to cure disease and cleanse ritual uncleanness. Jesus touching the leper is not just a touching gesture but also indicates the blessing of Jesus's physical presence, such as in the matter of the Eucharist. It points subtly to the sacramentality of Christian faith: God works through matter, even the matter of Jesus's very body.

Jesus bids the leper depart and commands him to "say nothing to any one; but go, show yourself to the priest, and offer the gift that Moses commanded, for a proof to the people" (Matt 8:4). Matthew's Gospel is taking up the theme of secrecy found in the Gospel of Mark, where it functions in service of the idea that the ultimate truth about Jesus is reserved for insiders who would press in to be around him as his disciples: the truth that Jesus, the Christ as God come to earth, must suffer and die. St. Mark wants his audience of insiders to know that one cannot have Jesus as Christ and Son of God apart from understanding him as Christ crucified.

In Matthew's Gospel the situation is different: Jesus's messianic identity is meant to be disclosed gradually and subtly to the public so as not to invite confusion or to arouse opposition too soon. Further, it may be that Jesus retains some optimism about the success of his mission among Jews and indeed the Jewish leadership; Jesus meets no serious questions until chapter 9 and no serious opposition until chapter 12. That may be why he sends the man to the priest to do what Leviticus 13–14 requires, to announce to the cultic authorities that he, Jesus, has arrived to bring the messianic age. On the other hand, Jesus fled after John the Baptist's arrest (Matt 4:12), and in the broader world of Matthew's story, we have seen the narrator sketching opposition to Jesus, from his birth in the flight to Egypt under Herod the Great (chapter 2) to John the Baptist's hostile words toward the Sadducees and Pharisees (chapter 3). Perhaps Jesus's command here is a challenge to the Jewish leadership, then, a throwing down of the gauntlet. Such a reading would be confirmed by the following story, in which an officer in the Roman army seeks help from Jesus and receives the highest of praise; the juxtaposition of the stories suggests the pattern found throughout Matthew's Gospel and the greater New Testament: Jewish opposition to Jesus leads to Gentile inclusion.

Finally, we see the phenomenon of miracles as signs. Certainly many, many people needed healing and exorcism in Jesus's day, and even resurrection, as death stalked humanity on a scale we in the post-industrial West can scarcely fathom. And yet Jesus does not set up a mobile clinic in a tent and zap everyone who can get there. When he works miracles from simple healings to raisings of the dead, the miracles are signs of the end-time *shalom*—the peace and health present in heaven in the kingdom of God. Miracles signify the reality of the kingdom of heaven that will one day be made a reality for those on earth.

MATTHEW 8:5–17: SATURDAY WEEK 12 / MONDAY OF THE FIRST WEEK OF ADVENT (8:5–11) / MONDAY WEEK 6 (8:11–13)

In the next story, a Roman officer, a centurion in charge of a century of men and thus roughly equivalent to a first lieutenant, approaches Jesus in hope of his paralyzed servant being healed (Matt 8:5). Though some believe so, it is not true that Israel was under direct occupation, as if there were Roman legionaries on every corner in a situation of martial law. The nearest full legion was stationed north, in Syria. The temple in Jerusalem did have a detachment of Roman soldiers (about two hundred) in the Antonia fortress, and Roman soldiers and officers would be present in the Holy Land. Yet Rome did control Judea, as it was a formal Roman province by Jesus's day, and many Jews longed for independence.

And so a Roman officer approaching Jesus is plausible, especially in Capernaum, northern Galilee. The man is desperate, and a good number of pagans were philosemites, esteeming the monotheism and morals of Judaism, even following Jewish belief and practicing Jewish prayers, though not undergoing formal conversion; such was Cornelius the centurion in Acts 10. What's radical, then, is not so much the centurion approaching Jesus but Jesus's willingness to go directly to the man's home (Matt 8:7), for Jews did not mix with Gentiles as a rule (see Acts 10:28), beyond what was necessary for mutual coexistence and commerce (perhaps an analogy is the relationship of Amish communities to dominant populations surrounding them today).

But the centurion insists that Jesus coming is not necessary: "Lord, I am not worthy to have you come under my roof; but only say the word, and my servant will be healed. For I am a man under authority, with soldiers under me; and I say to one, 'Go,' and he goes, and to another, 'Come,' and he comes, and to my slave, 'Do this,' and he does it" (Matt 8:8–10). The centurion recognizes Jesus's radical authority over the elements of the cosmos and, on a more mundane level, he might be concerned his servant will die while Jesus is *en route*. Jesus will speak the word and the servant will be healed immediately by that word (8:13). Note the contrast with the prior healing: there Jesus used touch, here he does not. The effect on the reader is to increase wonder at the power of Jesus's ability to heal using a variety of methods.

The passage forecasts Gentile inclusion in the Church and thus the Matthean theme of reversal and inversion in which Jewish resistance to Jesus leads to Gentile inclusion. Jesus says to his followers, "Truly, I say to you, not even in Israel have I found such faith" (Matt 8:10). And the inversion is radical in what's next: "I tell you, many will come from east and west and sit at table with Abraham, Isaac, and Jacob in the kingdom of heaven, while the sons of the kingdom will be thrown into the outer darkness; there men will weep and gnash their teeth" (8:11–12). In fact, Jesus "marveled" (8:10) at the centurion's profound faith, itself a radical statement which the staid English ("marveled") mutes. Jesus is here amazed, bewildered, shocked. In Matthew's Gospel Jesus does not desire to engage in ministry to Gentiles (see 10:5 and 15:21–28), though the narrator provides quotes from Isaiah promising Gentile inclusion (see 4:12–16 and 12:17–21). Here the centurion's faith provokes Jesus's exclamation about many coming from east and west to dine in the kingdom, while its sons will be cast out (8:11–12). The exclamation is an inversion of Jewish expectation, for the understanding was that faithful Israelites would be gathered in from all over at the end of time, while Gentiles would be excluded. Here Jesus overturns that expectation by suggesting it will be Gentiles from east and west who will dine in the kingdom, while many Israelites will not. The pattern is much like the narrator's inversion of Israel and Egypt in the reverse exodus of chapter 2.

Jesus now arrives at his destination in Capernaum, Peter's house. Peter's mother-in-law is sick with fever (Matt 8:14). In ages prior to penicillin, even simple, low-grade fevers were a mortal threat, and infection was a daily danger given the lack of knowledge of germs and often unsanitary conditions (though in places under Roman rule, sanitation was better, and Jews suffered lower rates of infection thanks to the hygienic effects of ritual handwashing and bathing). Jesus touches the mother's hand, and the fever goes away (8:15). What's said next is suggestive and symbolic: "she rose and served him" (8:15). We have here a sign of the resurrection of believers; Jesus's touch can restore those dead or near death (again, a fever puts one at death's door), and the effect is to be at the service of the Lord, on earth when one is resuscitated and in heaven forever when one is raised.

St. Matthew concludes this triad of healings with a summary statement that Jesus exorcised and healed many in Capernaum, which fulfilled a prophecy from Isaiah 53:4: "This was to fulfil what was spoken by the prophet Isaiah, 'He took our infirmities and bore our diseases'" (Matt 8:17). Now St. Matthew does not employ the Hebrew version of the Old Testament underlying most modern English translations. He seems to use various Greek versions and perhaps some Aramaic versions ("targums," loose paraphrases of the Hebrew used in Jewish worship), and he may be doing his own translations and paraphrases. The modern English translation of the Hebrew of Isaiah 53:4 reads, "Surely he has borne our griefs and carried our sorrows." But Matthew 8:17 mentions "infirmities" and "diseases." Whether St. Matthew used a translation that had those words or uses them himself, the effect is that the reader focuses on Jesus's healing ability, not his sharing in our existential griefs and sorrows. Further, the concept of the "suffering servant" of Isaiah and thus of vicarious atonement is likely not in view at this point, especially as the Greek version of Isaiah (which St. Matthew was most likely using) does not present an anonymous suffering servant; instead he identifies the servant as Israel and, further, does not have the servant suffer but rather rewrites the passages to have Israel's enemies suffer.[1] Surely Jesus dies a redemptive death in Matthew's Gospel, but that is not yet in view here in chapter 8.

MATTHEW 8:18–22: MONDAY WEEK 13

Jesus now enters the region of the Decapolis by virtue of crossing the Sea of Galilee to "the other side" (Matt 8:18). Dominated by Gentiles, it seems the centurion's faith in the prior story has motivated Jesus to cast his missionary net a bit wider. Matthew's Gospel presents two would-be followers encountering Jesus in order to provide dominical teaching about discipleship. The first, a scribe, promises radical commitment: "Teacher, I will follow you wherever you go" (8:19). Jesus's response is an enigmatic challenge: "Foxes have holes, and birds of the air have nests; but the Son of man has nowhere to lay his head" (8:20). In essence, Jesus is asking him if he has really counted the cost and is willing to engage in the demands of itinerant ministry. Back then, most rabbis and teachers (such as Greco-Roman sophists and philosophers) stayed put; they did not drag their disciple-students from place to place.

The way of Jesus is different, as he's got a message to spread while he forms disciples. Another reason is that his journey must end at Jerusalem in sacrifice, and his disciples are to follow him to those points as well, though Matthew's Gospel hasn't made that clear yet. Further, the scribe might not be as willing as he puts forth; "scribe" is almost always negative in Matthew's Gospel, and the scribe addresses Jesus not as "Lord" as the noble centurion did (8:6, 8) but as "teacher" (8:19). "Teacher" is at best a neutral in Matthew's Gospel. Jesus uses

---

[1] See Huizenga, *The New Isaac: Tradition and Intertextuality in the Gospel of Matthew*, Supplements to Novum Testamentum 131 (repr. 2012; Leiden, Netherlands: E. J. Brill, 2009), 79–82.

the term (10:24–25, "a disciple is not above his teacher . . . it is enough for the disciple to be like his teacher"), while later reminding his disciples they have one teacher, him, the Christ (23:8), and calls himself teacher in having the disciples secure a room for the Passover (26:18). On the other hand, opponents of Jesus, often hostile, call Jesus "teacher" (12:38, 17:24, 22:16, 22:24), as does a would-be disciple who failed to commit, the rich young man (19:16). The implication is that this scribe is not really ready to commit to discipleship.

Another man, this one called a "disciple," tells Jesus, "Lord, let me first go and bury my father" (Matt 8:21). Does he do so in reply to Jesus's words to the scribe, realizing their radical import regarding the imperative of immediate discipleship? It is likely, and so here, too, the response is one of hesitant deferral. Burial of the dead was a major duty in ancient Judaism, as it remains today, as seen in the story of Tobit, the righteous Jew who buried corpses under pain of death during Babylonian oppression (Tobit 1:16–20). The disciple here probably means that he wants to fulfill the Commandment "Honor your father and your mother" (Exod 20:12), which in practice meant caring for them in their old age until they died. And so he is saying he cannot follow Jesus right now, thanks to his commitment to the Ten Commandments, to the Old Law. But Jesus has brought the New Law, which the man should know since he's named as a disciple, and so Jesus replies, "Follow me, and leave the dead to bury their own dead" (8:22). These words of Jesus are revolutionary; he is essentially throwing a major Commandment overboard.[2] For the reader of Mat-

---

[2] For this reason those who engage in historical Jesus research believe this saying is authentic, for it's so radical nothing similar is found in Judaism, and not much is done with it in the early Church save for its preservation. Therefore it must have come from Jesus, the thinking goes, and not created by the author or early Church.

thew's Gospel, however, the revolutionary import of the saying is not so surprising, since Jesus has presented himself as the one with the radical authority to interpret and change and abolish the Old Law in service of the New Law he brings.

MATTHEW 8:23–27: TUESDAY WEEK 13

Jesus and the disciples find themselves in trouble on the Sea of Galilee. A large freshwater lake, it measures roughly seven by eleven miles and is surrounded by gentle green hills. It's big enough that boating can be dangerous. During my first visit to Galilee, I stood on top of our hotel, high above the sea, in thirty-mile-an-hour winds and watched massive waves swelling, thinking that Jesus and the disciples would have endured similar storms in the Gospel stories.

The storm that is swamping the boat is a *seismos megas*, a great seismic shaking, a "great earthquake" beyond even a severe storm (Matt 8:24). This suggests something deeper, something spiritual, something apocalyptic is going on. The disciples rouse Jesus, for he's sleeping, and cry out for him to save them (8:25). He addresses them as "men of little faith," asking them why they are afraid (8:26). They should not fear because they should know who Jesus is, for they have been his disciples now for a while and have seen his mighty works; would the one who has shown himself master of infirmity and illness let himself be drowned unaware? In the context of Jesus's words about the lilies of the field in the Sermon on the Mount, Jesus had addressed them as men of little faith (6:30), suggesting they lacked solid confidence in God their heavenly Father. Here they lack confidence in him, which subtly suggests Jesus, the Son, and God, the Father, are to be identified together in some way.

Then Jesus "rose" and "rebuked the winds and the sea," and suddenly where there had been a *seismos megas*, a "great earthquake," now by contrast there is a *galēnē megalē*, a "great calm" (Matt 8:26). The story shows Jesus's radical power over creation, a power reserved to the creator in the Old Testament. It's also possible, indeed likely, that given the nature of the storm—not just a major squall but a seismic event—the cause is ultimately demonic. The word "rebuke" is the word used to describe Jesus's exorcism of a boy in 17:18. Indeed, upon landing the boat in the following scene, Jesus will be challenged by two demoniacs. Might not the seismic storm be a satanic preemptive strike meant to prevent Jesus from liberating the territory of the Decapolis from its demonic bondage? Demons are territorial, after all.

The disciples now are not named disciples but merely "men" (8:27), a subtle suggestion that they are not acting like disciples with solid faith but as men of little faith. And they say, "What sort of man is this, that even winds and sea obey him?" (8:27). The question reveals the disciples's ignorance, but it is also meant to provoke the reader to consider more deeply Jesus's ultimate identity, which is God come to earth (see 1:23).

Matthew's Gospel is often presented as a document chiefly concerned with Jesus's teaching, and that teaching is often understood to be merely moral or ethical. But we misread Matthew's Gospel if we miss its radical apocalyptic features. Jesus came not merely to teach but also to make holy war on Sin, Death, Hell, and the Devil, to restore a rebellious cosmos to peace with its Creator.

MATTHEW 8:28–34: WEDNESDAY WEEK 13

In the next scene, the theme of divine victory in apocalyptic holy war continues. Upon landing, Jesus is approached by two demoniacs.[3] The entire scene is unclean: Jesus has brought his disciples to an unclean pagan land with pagans possessed by unclean spirits, to a graveyard (unclean, thanks to the corpses) near a herd of swine (unclean animals; Matt 8:28). We will see here Jesus establishing the territory of the kingdom of God by making the men clean and, by extension, the land clean, particularly through his presence and actions and the destruction of the swine. The pattern is similar to the situation with the healing of the leper in 8:1–4, but now it is Gentiles and Gentile territory being cleansed, not simply a Jewish individual.

When Jesus encounters the demoniacs, they address Jesus as Son of God—the first humans in Matthew's Gospel to do so, though perhaps it is the demons in them revealing the truth about Jesus. The demons know they stand condemned come the end, when the Devil and his angels will be cast into the "eternal fire" (Matt 25:41), but are concerned that Jesus not "torment [them] before the time" (8:29). It's as if they're surprised to see Jesus so early; however, one must keep in mind that in the Gospel of Matthew, the kingdom of God (the end times) actually begins with Jesus's coming and involves a long historical horizon before the final consummation occurs. Thus, their absolute end is not upon them yet.

---

[3] In each of four stories, St. Matthew presents two individuals where Mark's Gospel has one: the two demoniacs in Matthew 8:28 (Mark 5:1–20); the first story of two blind men in Matthew 9:27–31 (perhaps parallel to Mark 8:22–26, though there are great differences); the second story of two blind men in Matthew 20:29–34 (Mark 10:46–52); and St. Matthew's version of the Triumphal Entry in Matthew 21:1–11 (Mark 11:7), which presents both an ass and a colt instead of Mark's single beast of burden. Why? One possibility is that St. Matthew has two creatures in these stories for the sake of effect, to make the miracles all the more impressive. Another solution is that the two in each instance are meant to be taken as witnesses, as Deuteronomy 19:15 requires two witnesses to establish a matter. The ultimate answer is not obvious, however.

So they beg to be cast into the swine feeding nearby (Matt 8:31), and Jesus permits them to do so (8:32). Demons are territorial, looking for people, animals, and even things to inhabit (exorcists will tell us that smart phones are often riddled with demons, given the occasion for sin that they are). Then the swine rush into the sea and drown (8:32); perhaps the implication is that Jesus himself sent the demons to hell in drowning the swine, since the sea was sometimes understood as a gate to the underworld deep below. The cleansing of the land from the unclean swine doesn't mean that Christians can't eat pork, as Jesus makes clear elsewhere that all foods are now clean (15:10–20). It does symbolize cleansing, however. Furthermore it reminds a reader of the drowning of the Egyptian army in the Red Sea (Exod 14:26–29), and it's thus interesting that the symbol of the nearest Roman military regiment (*Legio X Fretensis* in Syria) was the wild boar, a species of swine. The passage thus suggests that Jesus will conquer all, even imperial Rome.

The spectacle terrifies the herdsmen, who flee to the city and tell all that happened (Matt 8:33). They become unwitting evangelists, for all from the city come to meet Jesus but beg him to leave (8:34). Jesus is ready to cleanse pagans, but they are not ready. Perhaps in the world of the story, their rejection of Jesus leads Jesus to restrict his mission to Israel in 10:5.

MATTHEW 9:1–8: THURSDAY WEEK 13

Jesus now sails the Sea of Galilee and arrives at "his own city" (Matt 9:1), which is Capernaum. Some people bring Jesus "a paralytic, lying on his bed" (9:2a). Note the posture: the man is helpless, defeated, prone. Jesus sees "their faith" and declares the man's sins forgiven (9:2b). Of note is the corporate nature of faith: it is the faith of those bringing the paralytic to Jesus that secures forgiveness. For this reason the passage is historically one of the texts supporting infant baptism; the parents's faith functions as the infant's faith. Also of note is that Jesus forgives the man's sins, when the man and those bringing him are simply seeking physical healing. Here Jesus's action points to the root of the matter, the most important thing: forgiveness of sins (which is the stated point of the chalice at the Lord's Supper, the blood of which is "poured out for many for the forgiveness of sins" (26:28).

Some scribes present murmur among themselves that Jesus is blaspheming (Matt 9:3); they perceive in Jesus's words pretensions to divine authority and thus divinity. Jesus perceives what they are murmuring (9:4) and asks the rhetorical question of 9:5, concerning whether it's easier to say, "Your sins are forgiven," or, "Rise and walk." The former is obviously easier to say because the latter is hard to do. And so in 9:6a Jesus states that they will know that "the Son of man has authority on earth to forgive sins." The Son of man is a divine figure in Daniel 7, and the scribes have perceived a claim to divinity in Jesus's pronouncement of forgiveness. In effect, Jesus says, and demonstrates, that they are right in one respect: that it is a divine action to forgive sins.

But they're wrong in another: Jesus is not blaspheming, for he really is God come to reclaim his wayward people. Jesus says to the paralytic, "Rise, take up your bed and go home" (Matt 9:6b), and the man "rose and went home" (9:7). We observe the symbolic pattern pointing to resurrection: the man was brought "lying on his bed" (9:2a), as a corpse might lie on a bier, and now he rises and (in a phrase hinting at the kingdom of heaven) goes "home" (9:7).

In sum, the passage shows that God has come to earth in Jesus to provide for the forgiveness of sins, the healing of disease, and the resurrection into the kingdom of God. The crowd has a mixed reaction: on one hand, they are "afraid"; on the other, they glorify God (Matt 9:8). Interesting to note are the last words of 9:8, with the plural "men": "who had given such authority to men." Either the crowds fail to perceive Jesus's divinity clearly, certainly a possibility, or these words hint at the corporate nature of the Faith, that the "men" who have authority to forgive sins and heal include the clergy of the Church and the members of the Church more broadly.

MATTHEW 9:9–13: TENTH SUNDAY IN ORDINARY TIME / FRIDAY WEEK 13

Now Jesus encounters Matthew, who will become an apostle. At present he is a tax collector. Notorious for their rapacity in collecting taxes for Rome, Jewish tax collectors would also use intimidation and violence to collect more than what was owed so that they could pocket the difference. Therefore they were viewed by other Jews as the lowest of traitors. It's scandalous, then, that Jesus calls Matthew to follow him (Matt 9:9) and that Jesus also goes to dine with him in Matthew's house (9:10). Eating is perhaps the second most intimate thing one can do with another; it suggests fraternity, friendship, and fellowship. Although in our day we have casual dining and see meals as a way to consume calories, eating with someone was far from casual in the ancient Near East.

The scandal increases as "many tax collectors and sinners came and sat down with Jesus and his disciples" (Matt 9:10). "Sinners" would be people who have effectively given up their practice of Judaism and lived licentious, dissolute lives. So Jesus is dining with the dregs of society. Thus the Pharisees ask Jesus's disciples, "Why does your teacher eat with tax collectors and sinners?" (9:11). For them, Jesus's fellowship with such people implies Jesus himself is a bad person—bad company corrupts good morals, after all, and you can judge a man by the company he keeps.

Having heard of it, Jesus responds, "Those who are well have no need of a physician, but those who are sick. Go and learn what this means, 'I desire mercy, and not sacrifice.' For I came not to call the righteous, but sinners" (9:12–13). Jesus's words about the sick needing a physician mean that he has come to reclaim the lost for God's kingdom. In embracing people where they are at, they may encounter mercy and understanding, and so turn and be forgiven. To spend time with a sinner is in no way to condone sin but to encourage their repentance. In today's Church there are actually precious few Pharisees, if Matthew's Pharisees be the model. For even among those Catholics who are most concerned with keeping the Church's laws and discipline one would be hard pressed to find someone who would be dismayed at a repentant lapsed Catholic coming back to the sacraments.

Jesus's quotation of Hosea 6:6—"I desire mercy, and not sacrifice" (Matt 9:13)—isn't meant to deny the important of sacrifice as such, either in Judaism or Christianity. He institutes the sacrifice of the Eucharist, after all (26:26–29), and has already spoken of being reconciled with one's brother and then offering one's gift at the altar (5:23–24). It has been common in Protestant scholarship to pit prophets against priests and side with the prophets, but the prophets themselves generally kept the sacrifices of their day. When the prophets seem to denigrate sacrifice, they're usually inveighing against exterior ritual gestures made empty by a fundamental lack of interior piety and failure to do justice to one's fellow man and woman. The pattern, then, is the same as we see in Matthew 5:23–24: sacrifices should be offered, but one ought to have one's heart and relationships rightly ordered prior to ritual.

In closing, Jesus states he has come "not to call the righteous, but sinners" (Matt 9:13). Now, it's true we are all sinners to one extent or another, and so Protestant interpretation in particular has seen Jesus's words here as ironic: that is, only those who realize they are sinners will want to come to Jesus; and everyone's a sinner, no one is righteous. There may be a grain of truth here, if we envision Jesus speaking with a certain sardonicism to the Pharisees, as if he were saying, "You think you're already righteous, so of course you don't have any real interest in hearing me and following me. Only once you recognize you're a sinner would you hear and follow me."

Yet, in a Gospel such as Matthew's, with its conservative Jewish character, it might be that Jesus thinks that there really are Jews who are fundamentally righteous, who have ordered hearts and relationships and who practice the Jewish faith. Again, Matthew's Gospel is a Gospel of continuity with Judaism, even as Jesus transforms it in bringing the New Law. Of note here is Jesus's response to a Pharisee many chapters later when asked about the greatest Commandment; Jesus responds by quoting from Leviticus and Deuteronomy, affirming that there's actually two, love of God and love of neighbor (Matt 22:34–40). If a Jew is keeping those Commandments rightly, then he is righteous, and all that is needed is for him to follow Jesus as well, for he's already practicing his Judaism on Jesus's terms.

MATTHEW 9:14–15: FRIDAY AFTER ASH WEDNESDAY / SATURDAY WEEK 13 (9:14–17)

Now comes a question from the disciples of John the Baptist, Jesus's forerunner and indeed the very man who baptized Jesus himself. They, too, seem to have a problem with Jesus eating with tax collectors and sinners, for such meals would be something short of a feast, while they (and the Pharisees) fast (Matt 9:14). Instead of challenging Jesus directly, they soften it by asking why Jesus's disciples do not fast. The difference is the presence of Jesus himself. As the kingdom of God is like a wedding banquet, as a later parable makes clear (22:1–14), Jesus is the bridegroom with them, now (9:15a). Then Jesus hints at his Passion, the first real words from Jesus on the subject in the Gospel: "The days will come, when the bridegroom is taken away from them, and then they will fast" (9:15b). After the crucifixion there will be appropriate times for fasting, but not now.

In defense of his feasting with tax collectors and sinners, for which he'll be accused of being a glutton and a drunkard (Matt 11:19), Jesus points to the newness he brings: "And no one puts a piece of unshrunk cloth on an old garment, for the patch tears away from the garment, and a worse tear is made. Neither is new wine put into old wineskins; if it is, the skins burst, and the wine is spilled, and the skins are destroyed; but new wine is put into fresh wineskins, and so both are preserved" (9:16–17). The newness he bestows with his very presence means it is not time to fast but feast.

MATTHEW 9:18–26: MONDAY WEEK 14

We now enter another triad of miracle stories, with the first story being a combination of two healings. Jesus is approached by a ruler (identified as Jairus, a synagogue official, in the parallels in Mark and Luke) whose daughter has just died, begging Jesus to come raise her from the dead (Matt 9:18). Jesus departs, but he's interrupted by a woman suffering from a longstanding, chronic hemorrhage (9:19), in all likelihood a menstrual hemorrhage. The woman, having bled for twelve years, is ritually unclean, and

Leviticus 15:19–33 makes clear anyone who has contact with someone suffering from a hemorrhage also becomes unclean. But the woman approaches Jesus and touches the "fringes" of his garment (Matt 9:20). These "fringes" are the tassels prescribed in Numbers 15:37–39 and Deuteronomy 22:12 to indicate one's adherence to the Law. Jesus is presented, then, as Torah-observant, while the woman is willing to make him unclean; in essence, she's compromising his obedience to the Law. Yet Jesus does not scold her; as we have seen, he is not the one who becomes unclean but the one who makes clean. He says, "Take heart, daughter; your faith has made you well" (9:22).

Following this encounter, Jesus arrives at the ruler's home, where professional mourners and the crowd are lamenting the death of his daughter (Matt 9:23). He commands them to leave and informs them that "the girl is not dead but sleeping," which arouses their mockery (9:24). Now in Christianity, sleep became a metaphor for death (see Eph 5:14 and 1 Cor 15:51), since death was not the end; as people rose from sleep, they would rise from death. And so in nature we find a hint of the resurrection: every night we fall asleep as a little death, and every morning wake in a little resurrection.

After putting the crowd outside (Matt 9:25a), he takes the girl by the hand, touching her as he did the leper of 8:1–4, and the girl rises from the dead (9:25b). As Jesus encountered menstrual impurity in the case of the hemorrhaging woman, here he encounters corpse impurity, but touches the girl nonetheless. And there is of course a progression in the two stories, as St. Matthew raises the ante for the reader: Jesus can heal a hemorrhage, but can he raise the dead? The answer is yes.

MATTHEW 9:27–31: FRIDAY OF THE FIRST WEEK OF ADVENT

Two blind men now follow Jesus while crying out, "Have mercy on us, Son of David" (Matt 9:27). "Son of David" was more or less a title for the Christ in Jesus's day, as most Jews believed the Christ would be King David's ultimate descendant, thus fulfilling the prophecy of 2 Samuel 7:13–14a ("He shall build a house for my name, and I will establish the throne of his kingdom for ever. I will be his father, and he shall be my son"). At this point in the story, then, people are beginning to suspect Jesus is the Christ. Jesus takes them into the house (Peter's house in Capernaum), and he asks them if they believe he can "do this," that is, restore their sight. They reply affirmatively (Matt 9:28). Jesus again employs touch and ties their healing to their demonstrated faith: "According to your faith be it done to you" (9:29). Their eyes having been opened, Jesus commands them, "See that no one knows it" (9:30).

Now secrecy is a major theme in Mark's Gospel, but not Matthew's. In a narrative perspective, then, we might suggest that the reader here would find the rationale for Jesus's command tied to their acclaiming him "son of David," that is, the Christ. Given that most Jews believed the Christ would be a conquering warrior, Jesus here is concerned that he not be misunderstood by premature disclosure of his messianic identity. Nevertheless, "they went away and spread his fame through all that district" (9:31). Nothing comes of their disregard for Jesus's words in the Gospel of Matthew; the summary statement serves to imply that Jesus is becoming ever more widely known. But that fame means that Jesus will need to put together a missionary team to harvest the souls now prepared to receive and follow him, which Jesus will do in the next scene.

MATTHEW 9:32–38: TUESDAY WEEK 14

We come to the concluding miracle of the series of ten. Jesus now heals a mute demoniac by exorcism (Matt 9:32–33a). St. Matthew is here less interested in the miracle, as evidenced by the few words he devotes to it; he is much more interested in the response of the crowd, who marvels and says, "Never was anything like this seen in Israel" (9:33b), and the response of the Pharisees, who say, "He casts out demons by the prince of demons" (9:34). In the progression of the story, St. Matthew is showing the people siding with Jesus and being separated from the influence of the Pharisees. Ultimately, however, the people will turn on Jesus in Pilate's courtyard (27:15–23). The Pharisees, for their part, will again charge Jesus with possession by the prince of demons, Beelzebul, the Lord of the Flies (12:22–32).

With Matthew 9:35 we encounter a summary transition statement nearly identical to 4:23, indicating that Jesus's first missionary tour of Galilee is ending: Jesus went about "teaching in their synagogues and preaching the gospel of the kingdom, and healing every disease and every infirmity" is common to both verses. The Pharisees's hostility now moves Jesus to concentrate on his disciples, and he will shortly pick twelve to be the leadership of his new Israel, as Israel had twelve tribes (10:1–4).

New and more leadership is needed because the crowds are responding favorably to Jesus and he is just one man. Jesus sees the crowds and feels compassion toward them, for the stated reason that "they were harassed and helpless, like sheep without a shepherd" (Matt 9:36). The theme of the people of God being sheep lacking good shepherds is found frequently in the Old Testament (see Num 27:17; 1 Kgs 22:17; Jdt 11:19; Jer 23:1, 50:6), but it finds its fullest expression throughout chapter 34 of the Book of the Prophet Ezekiel. In Ezekiel 34:1–10, the Lord God laments that Israel's leaders, who should be the people's shepherds, have left them alone as sheep without a shepherd. Then the Lord God promises that he himself will become their shepherd:

> For thus says the Lord GOD: Behold, I, I myself will search for my sheep, and will seek them out. As a shepherd seeks out his flock when some of his sheep have been scattered abroad, so will I seek out my sheep; and I will rescue them from all places where they have been scattered on a day of clouds and thick darkness. And I will bring them out from the peoples, and gather them from the countries, and will bring them into their own land; and I will feed them on the mountains of Israel, by the fountains, and in all the inhabited places of the country. I will feed them with good pasture, and upon the mountain heights of Israel shall be their pasture; there they shall lie down in good grazing land, and on fat pasture they shall feed on the mountains of Israel. I myself will be the shepherd of my sheep, and I will make them lie down, says the Lord GOD. I will seek the lost, and I will bring back the strayed, and I will bind up the crippled, and I will strengthen the weak, and the fat and the strong I will watch over; I will feed them in justice. (Ezek 34:11–16)

This is what is happening in Matthew's Gospel: In Jesus, God has come to earth to be the true shepherd of his people. The prophecy of Ezekiel 34:11–16 is being fulfilled.

And so Jesus now turns to his disciples, saying, "The harvest is plentiful, but the laborers are few; pray therefore

the Lord of the harvest to send out laborers into his harvest"
(Matt 9:37–38). Many people have marveled at Jesus's mighty
works, and his fame has spread abroad, thanks at least to the
two blind men (see 9:31), so the time is ripe for reaping a
missionary harvest.

CHAPTER 9

✠

The Missionary Discourse

Matthew 9:36–10:8: Eleventh Sunday
in Ordinary Time / St. Francis Xavier,
Priest (December 3; 9:35–10:1) / Saturday of the First Week of Advent
(9:35–10:1, 5a, 6–8) / Wednesday Week 14
(10:1–7) / Thursday Week 14 (10:7–15)

Given the missionary impulse of the Church in this
age of the new evangelization, the lectionary provides parts of
Matthew 9:35–10:15 on multiple occasions. Simplicity commends treating the lengthy passage here as a whole. Matthew
9:36–38 has been treated immediately above.

Matthew 9:35–10:8 forms a unit concerning the authority and mission of the Twelve Apostles. In fact, while the
Gospel of Matthew itself might not be one grand chiasm, this
particular section is chiastic in structure.

A   Jesus *proclaimed* the gospel of the *kingdom* and *cured* every disease and illness (9:35)

  B   the crowds were like *sheep* without a shepherd (9:36)

    C   ask the master of the harvest to *send out* laborers (9:38)

      D   he summoned his twelve disciples (10:1)

        E   Jesus "gave them authority" (10:1)

      D'   the names of the twelve (10:2)

    C'   *he sent out*[1] these twelve (10:5)

  B'   "Go rather to *the lost sheep* of the house of Israel" (10:6)

A'   make this *proclamation*: "*the kingdom* of heaven is at hand." "*Cure* the sick, raise the dead."[2]

That Jesus "gave them authority" (10:1) is crucial. The Twelve will now do what Jesus himself has been doing, by himself, as he shares with them his authority to teach, preach, exorcise, and heal. Indeed, they are to proclaim, "The kingdom of heaven is at hand" (10:7), as John the Baptist did in 3:2 and Jesus himself did in 4:17. Here we see the identity of Jesus connected with the Church.[3] Ultimately the Church is Christ's body, doing what he does.

And so Jesus is now launching a mission, given that his fame has spread and it is time for an initial harvest. But the mission here is restricted to Israel (Matt 10:5–6), as Jesus

---

[1]   Curtis Mitch and Edward Sri (*The Gospel of Matthew*, Catholic Commentary on Sacred Scripture 2 [Grand Rapids, MI: Baker Academic, 2010], 141) observe two different Greek words are employed (*ekballō* in 9:38 and *apostellō* in 10:5), noting that they can be synonyms.

[2]   See Mitch and Sri, *The Gospel of Matthew*, 141. I'm quoting their presentation of the chiasm nearly verbatim; emphases are original.

[3]   The ancient doctrine of *Christus Totus*, rooted in Ephesians 5:21–31, articulated by St. Augustine and Tradition, and drawn upon by the Second Vatican Council, is relevant here. See CCC 795 and above.

instructs the disciples to go nowhere among the pagans or the Samaritans (whom Jews regarded as unclean half-breeds, descended from the northern tribes who were conquered by Assyria in 721 BC; they intermarried and interbred in Assyria and repopulated the old north along with wholesale pagans). It's unsettling to modern readers who assume Jesus's message is universal. Ultimately his message is, but here in this moment of the story, Jesus is focused first on Israel, which fits the biblical pattern. In the Gospels Jesus moves from Jews to Gentiles; in Acts the earliest Church does likewise, and Paul emphasizes that the gospel message comes first to the Jew and then to the Gentile (see Rom 1:16).

So here with the emphasis on Israel alone, the number of the Apostles, twelve, does not merely signify Jesus is launching a new Israel, given that Israel had twelve tribes, but more particularly that Jesus is a new Moses, as Moses was aided by a leader of each of the twelve tribes during the Israelites's time in the wilderness (see Num 1:1–16).

Often observed is the diversity of the Twelve. The first four called (Matt 4:18–22) and named (10:2) were fishermen. Matthew was a tax collector (10:3). Philip and Andrew (10:2–3) have Greek names, indicating their families were at some distance from conservative Judaism and more comfortable with Greco-Roman Hellenism. Simon the "Cananaean," by contrast, was zealous for the Law, for "Cananaean" is derived from the Aramaic for "zeal."[4] In St. Luke's works he's identified as Simon "the Zealot" (*zēlōtēs*; Luke 6:15, Acts 1:13), which would make him a member of a violent revolutionary group often involved in assassination and insurrection. One wonders if Jesus left him and Matthew the tax collector alone together! St. Matthew probably calls him the "Cananaean"

---

4 Mitch and Sri, *The Gospel of Matthew*, 142.

instead of "Zealot" to distance him (and those having a copy of the Gospel and Christianity as such) from revolutionary associations. And finally is mentioned Judas Iscariot, "who betrayed him" (10:4). St. Matthew here foreshadows a major plot point, and Judas's inclusion in the Twelve (as is the case with Peter's denial of Jesus) points to the Church, and the clergy in particular, as a *corpus permixtum*, a mixed body of saints (who sometimes sin) and sinners.

Jesus sends the Twelve out with nothing: "You received without pay, give without pay. Take no gold, nor silver, nor copper in your belts, no bag for your journey, nor two tunics, nor sandals, nor a staff; for the laborer deserves his food" (10:8b–10). They take nothing, not even shoes; it is a sign of radical dependence on their heavenly Father, in line with Jesus's teaching on the Sermon on the Mount, particularly in chapter 6. They are to presume, then, others's hospitality ("And whatever town or village you enter, find out who is worthy in it, and stay with him until you depart," 10:11), an important virtue in the ancient world. That is how the heavenly Father will provide, and it also puts the Apostles in direct and personal contact with people.

But even then they might encounter rejection and get tossed out of someone's house, or not be received in the first place (Matt 10:12–14). When rejected, the Apostles are to "shake off the dust from your feet as you leave that house or town" (10:14b), a common ritual custom symbolizing rejection of a home, locale, or land. Such houses and towns will receive serious apocalyptic punishment on judgment day: "Truly, I say to you, it shall be more tolerable on the day of judgment for the land of Sodom and Gomor'rah than for that town" (10:15). In rejecting the Apostles and their message, they reject Jesus, and that seldom ends well.

MATTHEW 10:16–23: FRIDAY WEEK 14 / SAINT STEPHEN, THE FIRST MARTYR (DECEMBER 26; 10:17–22)

Having told the Apostles how to go about their mission (as poor itinerants in absolute simplicity in dependence on their heavenly Father) and having suggested to them not all will receive them, Jesus now warns them of the hardships and persecutions coming their way.

The passage also steps out of narrative time and has an enduring application to the Church's missionary endeavors throughout the ages. For on one hand, Jesus forbade the Apostles from going to the pagans and Samaritans (Matt 10:5–6), but here he speaks to them of bearing testimony before governors and kings (who would be Gentiles) and Gentiles as such (10:18). The Gospels aren't simple records of what happened regarding Jesus of Nazareth some two thousand years ago; as Scripture, they're like visual icons, pointing not so much back in time but rather pointing to perpetual and heavenly realities.[5] As far as possible, then, one should read the Gospels as if they speak into every time and place in the Church's history, including today, and passages like the present reveal how helpful and necessary such an approach is.

Missionary work means encountering opposition, hostility, and persecution. Jesus sends these budding shepherds out now like "sheep in the midst of wolves," so they are to "be wise as serpents and innocent as doves" (Matt 10:16). One must keep a pure heart and live a life of Christian virtue, but that does not mean being naïve about the way the world works.

In the next verse, Jesus says, "Beware of men; for they will deliver you up to councils, and flog you in their synagogues"

---

[5] See Huizenga, *Loosing the Lion*, 35–40.

(Matt 10:17). Here, of course, the Jewish world is in view, the councils being elders running synagogue affairs in particular locales, and the punishment they will mete out for testimony to Jesus is flogging. Then Jesus turns to the Gentile world: ". . . and you will be dragged before governors and kings for my sake, to bear testimony before them and the Gentiles" (10:18). The Jews of Jesus's day did not have their own governors (like Pontius Pilate, the "governor" before whom Jesus will be dragged, 27:1–2) or sovereign kings, although Herod the Great (who was ruling the Holy Land when Jesus was born, Matthew 2) was a client king ruling at Rome's behest, as was Agrippa I, who had the Apostle James, son of Zebedee. beheaded and the Apostle Peter arrested, according to Acts 12.

So the pattern here holds: first to the Jew, then to the Gentile. And whether among Jews or Gentiles, mission work involves persecution. In that situation, Jesus advises against anxiety: "do not be anxious how you are to speak or what you are to say; for what you are to say will be given to you in that hour; for it is not you who speak, but the Spirit of your Father speaking through you" (Matt 10:19–20). These words call to mind Jesus's teaching on anxiety in the Sermon on the Mount (6:25–33), in which Jesus three times instructs his hearers not to worry because their heavenly Father cares for them. Here, too, in the situation of persecution: God is there with his providential love. What's more, Jesus's words imply the Trinity: the Spirit of the Father speaks through those being tried as they testify to Jesus the Son.

Jesus's next words are intense and apocalyptic: brothers will betray each other, as well as parents and children, and have each other put to death (Matt 10:21); and everyone will hate the Apostles and later missionaries "for my name's sake" (10:22a). Yet there is salvation after persecution and execution: "But he who endures to the end will be saved" (10:22b).

Just as Jesus will suffer, die, and be raised, so too will faithful witnesses suffer, die, and be raised, for the call to follow Jesus is a call to take up one's own cross and follow him on the way of the Passion (16:24).

The passage now seems to return to narrative time, with the focus on the Apostles's immediate mission, and yet the conclusion is eschatological: "When they persecute you in one town, flee to the next; for truly, I say to you, you will not have gone through all the towns of Israel, before the Son of man comes" (Matt 10:23). The question is what is meant by the coming of the Son of man. One possibility is that the reference is to Jesus's arrival at the temple to cleanse it (21:12-17): the Son of man in Daniel 7 is a divine figure, and in the Triumphal Entry and the temple action in chapter 21, we have the Lord God suddenly come to his temple, as prophesied in Malachi 3:1. Another possibility is Jesus's trial, where he identifies himself as the Son of man (Matt 26:64). In any event, the temple action is what finally gets Jesus arrested, tried, and killed, and as a result of his murder, mission is opened up to Gentiles ("Go therefore and make disciples of all nations," 28:19).

MATTHEW 10:24–33: SATURDAY WEEK 14 / TWELFTH SUNDAY IN ORDINARY TIME (10:26–33)

Having spoken of persecution and death, Jesus now provides encouragement, in terms of both carrot and stick (as we say). He begins by tying their endurance of persecution and martyrdom subtly to his, for no disciple is above his teacher, nor a slave above his master (Matt 10:24); it suffices for the lower to become like the higher (10:25a). The implication is that if Jesus is to suffer and die, so will they. To follow a teacher in the ancient world—whether a Jewish rabbi or a pagan philosopher—was not merely learning content but a way of life that demanded sacrifice and conformity to the teacher's way of life.[6]

Jesus then brings up Beelzebul, the prince of demons (identified as "prince of demons" not here but by the Pharisees back in Matt 9:34): "If they have called the master of the house Be-el'zebul, how much more will they malign those of his household" (10:25b). Not only have the Pharisees asserted that Jesus is possessed by Beelzebul in 9:34, in the context of the healing of the paralytic, but will do so again in 12:24, in the context of claiming Jesus's power to exorcise is diabolical, having already conspired to kill Jesus (12:14). That's the lowest insult one can level, and leveled at Jesus Christ it is precisely backward: Jesus is not Beelzebul incarnate, but God incarnate (1:23). That's why in the Beelzebul controversy Jesus will level the charge of blasphemy of the third person of the Trinity, the Holy Spirit, against those who attribute Jesus's works to the demonic (12:31). Jesus does his works by the power of the Holy Spirit, which came upon him at the baptism (3:13–17), not by the power of Satan.

In any event, the Apostles and other missionaries and witnesses can thus expect the same treatment, to be not just hated but esteemed diabolical. Yet Jesus counsels them not to fear those who would accuse and persecute them so (Matt 10:26a). Rather they are all the more to openly proclaim what is hidden, and bring what is taught in the dark into the daylight, shouting Jesus's whispers from the rooftops (10:26b). Ultimately these persecutors can only kill the body, not the soul (10:28). St. Matthew may not have been an Augustinian or a Thomist, but

---

6 See Pierre Hadot, *What Is Ancient Philosophy?* trans. Michael Chase (Cambridge, MA: Belknap Press, 2004).

their body–soul and earth–heaven dualisms are fundamentally biblical, and we find it here in Matthew's Gospel. Instead of fearing men, then, they are to fear the One "who can destroy both soul and body in hell" (10:28). That One, their heavenly Father, knows when a sparrow falls and has numbered the hairs on their head, and so there is no cause whatsoever for fear (10:29–31). We note here with the language of birds and hair and "heavenly Father" that the themes of the Sermon on the Mount in chapter 6 are again brought to bear; the Sermon is not just an ethic but a manual for training in the sort of rigorous Christian virtue that endures to the end.

So fear not, Jesus says—if you endure in fidelity to him to the end: "So every one who acknowledges me before men, I also will acknowledge before my Father who is in heaven; but whoever denies me before men, I also will deny before my Father who is in heaven" (Matt 10:32–33). Warnings are a negative form of encouragement, and here, as elsewhere (see, for instance, the Parable of the Unforgiving Servant in 18:23–35), we observe that believers—even Apostles—stand under the threat of judgment. For Matthew's Gospel, then, one can "lose one's salvation," although that's a poor way to phrase it, for no one is ultimately saved until they behold God, body and soul, in the Beatific Vision. Matthew's Gospel here presents a deeply Catholic doctrine of salvation. We suffer like Christ and with him; he does not suffer for us apart from us (as doctrines of vicarious plenary atonement suggest), and our salvation is conditional on our real righteousness, not any alien righteousness[7] with which God would regard us as righteous even when we're not. We must become like our Teacher and Master (10:25).

---

[7] The phrase is Luther's, *fremde Gerechtigkeit* in his original German.

MATTHEW 10:34–11:1: MONDAY WEEK 15 /
THIRTEENTH SUNDAY IN ORDINARY TIME
(10:37–42)

Jesus has already mentioned betrayals within families (Matt 10:21); here he returns to the idea, as he came not to bring peace but a sword (10:34). And so he says, "I have come to set a man against his father, and a daughter against her mother, and a daughter-in-law against her mother-in-law; and a man's foes will be those of his own household" (10:35–36). On one hand, the family is a natural society, instituted by God, and Jesus himself will forbid divorce and raise marriage to the level of a sacrament in Matthew's very Gospel (see 5:31–32 and 19:3–9). On the other hand, Jesus teaches, "He who loves father or mother more than me is not worthy of me; and he who loves son or daughter more than me is not worthy of me" (10:37). Allegiance to Jesus takes precedence over all other relationships, which means that a follower of Jesus might find himself or herself persecuted by closest kin. Indeed, Jesus will later define true family: "'Who is my mother, and who are my brethren?' And stretching out his hand toward his disciples, he said, 'Here are my mother and my brethren! For whoever does the will of my Father in heaven is my brother, and sister, and mother'" (12:48b–50).

Returning to the theme of Christian disciples becoming like their Teacher and Master, Jesus now states clearly, "[H]e who does not take his cross and follow me is not worthy of me" (10:38); it follows naturally in that opposition from one's family is a major metaphorical cross to bear. But the reference is first literal: we have here the first explicit mention of Jesus going the way of the Cross in Matthew's Gospel, and it brings the rising intensity of Matthew 10 to a crescendo, as everyone would know what taking a cross meant, since the

Romans (and sometimes Jewish rulers[8]) crucified people routinely. But again, after warnings of persecution, to the point of the most brutal execution conceivable, Jesus offers encouragement: "He who finds his life will lose it, and he who loses his life for my sake will find it" (10:39).

And yet the Church's missionary work isn't all persecution and crucifixion; there will be success, for those who receive missionaries and their message receives Jesus, and in doing so the One who sent Jesus (Matt 10:40). Ambassadors, such as the Apostles and other missionaries are, come and speak with the full authority of those sending them,[9] and so acceptance of the missionary message is reception of Jesus Christ as well as God his heavenly Father.

Further, Jesus mentions "prophets" and "righteous" men: "He who receives a prophet because he is a prophet shall receive a prophet's reward, and he who receives a righteous man because he is a righteous man shall receive a righteous man's reward" (Matt 10:41). Both prophets and righteousness loom large in Matthew's Gospel (on prophets, see 5:12 and 23:34, and on righteousness, see 3:16, 5:6, 5:10, 5:20, 6:33, 21:32). Both prophets and righteous men merit rewards, for they are often persecuted for their fidelity, as Isaiah was persecuted (he was sawed in two upside down according to tradition) and as Jesus mentions those righteous people persecuted for righteousness's sake (5:10). So those who receive Christian prophets and Christian righteous men and women share in them and thus merit their rewards too.

---

[8]   The Jewish Hasmonean king Alexander Jannaeus once crucified 800 Pharisees as entertainment at a party because they had crossed him politically (Josephus, *Ant.* 13.380).

[9]   *M. Berakhot* states, "A man's emissary . . . is like the man himself" (cited by Mitch and Sri, *The Gospel of Matthew*, 149, following Donald A. Hagner, *Matthew 1–13*, Word Biblical Commentary 33a [Grand Rapids, MI: Zondervan Academic, 2015], 295).

And yet the status of Christian is not only for those who are prophets or adults capable of righteousness, but also for children: "And whoever gives to one of these little ones even a cup of cold water because he is a disciple, truly, I say to you, he shall not lose his reward" (10:42). That is, doing good to a Christian merits a reward. For in treating Christian prophets, righteous men and women, and children well, one is actually treating Jesus well. The same principle operates in the Parable of the Sheep and the Goats (25:31–46), where one's treatment of Christian brothers and sisters (Jesus does not have all humanity in view, but Christians in the community of the Church) is ultimately one's treatment of Jesus: "Truly, I say to you, as you did it to one of the least of these my brethren, you did it to me" (25:40; see 25:45).

The passage closes with Matthew 11:1: "And when Jesus had finished instructing his twelve disciples, he went on from there to teach and preach in their cities." Having instructed the Apostles and having sent them out, Jesus now resumes his own missionary endeavors. It is not clear if the disciples are present with Jesus in chapter 11; but they are with him in chapter 12 (see 12:1, where they are mentioned explicitly). It is likely that they are absent in chapter 11, getting on with missionary work left unrecorded.

CHAPTER 10

✝

THE WIDENING CHASM BETWEEN JESUS AND HIS FELLOW JEWS

MATTHEW 11:2–11: THIRD SUNDAY OF ADVENT

ST. MATTHEW'S STORY NOW RETURNS to the figure of John the Baptist, whose arrest and imprisonment were recorded in Matthew 4:12. Since then, Jesus launched and engaged in his own ministry of teaching, healing, and exorcising, and prepared and sent out his Apostles as missionaries, extending his own mission.

John the Baptist "heard in prison about the deeds of the Christ" (Matt 11:2); Matthew's Gospel believes that Jesus is the Christ, and the mighty works he is doing are those of the promised Christ—hence the absolute statement here. Yet John himself is not sure; he sends a delegation asking, "Are you he who is to come, or shall we look for another?" (11:2b–3). "He who is to come" uses the same Greek words as John used in 3:11: "he who is coming after me is mightier than I," and it is almost a title with messianic currency in Jesus's day (i.e., the Coming One). Indeed, the Acts of the Apostles records that disciples of John the Baptist persisted deep into the time of the earliest Church. Apollos has only been baptized by John (Acts 18:25); he has not been baptized in the proper Christian rite. St. Paul encounters a group of disciples of Jesus in Ephesus who likewise were baptized by John (Acts 19:1–7); as Ephesus is relatively far from the Jordan River, on the western coast of Asia Minor, present-day Turkey, they traveled far to see John and be baptized.

So why would John doubt? Like the Pharisees who were scandalized by Jesus eating with tax collectors and sinners (Matt 9:11), so too is John confused by the difference between what John promised of the Coming One and what Jesus is actually doing. (We also note this isn't the first time John appears to have questions about Jesus's actions; John's disciples have already questioned Jesus about his disciples's lack of fasting in 9:14.) John's prophecies in Matthew 3 are apocalyptic, with a strong sense of immediacy. "Who warned you to flee from the wrath to come?" (3:7) he screams at the Pharisees and Sadducees. "Even now the axe is laid to the root of the trees; every tree therefore that does not bear good fruit is cut down and thrown into the fire" (3:10), he warns. The Coming One "will baptize you with the Holy Spirit and with fire" (3:11b), he proclaims. And he closes his words with a dire, apocalyptic, end-time promise and threat: "His winnowing fork is in his hand, and he will clear his threshing floor and gather his wheat into the granary, but the chaff he will burn with unquenchable fire" (3:12).

Thus it seems John the Baptist was expecting the Coming One to usher in the final judgment very soon, even immediately, and to cast the evildoers into the eternal fire while saving the elect. Yet Jesus does not do that: he proclaims the kingdom of heaven, with mercy; he heals, he exorcises, he raises the dead; he even sets up an organization, an incipient Church as a new Israel, to go around, eventually even to pagans. Jesus is setting up a regime of mercy for the long haul, not damning the damned now. And so John sends his delegation.

Jesus sends them back with a cryptic but comprehensible message: "Go and tell John what you hear and see: the blind receive their sight and the lame walk, lepers are cleansed and the deaf hear, and the dead are raised up, and the poor have good news preached to them. And blessed is he who takes no offense at me" (Matt 11:4b–6). Using subtle allusions, Jesus is reminding John of messianic prophecies from the Old Testament (see, for instance, Isa 26:19, 29:18, 35:6, and 61:1). He is doing the works of the Christ, telling the delegates so, and subtly suggesting to them that one should not be scandalized if Jesus does not fit one's prior messianic expectations. Jesus himself gets to be the Christ and define the role.[10]

John's delegation asked a question about the identity of Jesus; now Jesus askes the crowds about the identity of John (Mathew 11:7–15). Jesus in effect reminds them that John was destined for suffering; he was not a "reed shaken by the wind" (11:7b), who would be tossed and turned by circumstances or flattery, nor one "clothed in soft raiment" (11:8b) in palaces, presumably living a soft life of indulgence. No,

---

[10] Here, too, we see the tension between the idea of an imminent kingdom and an immanent kingdom—that is, the expectation that some thought the coming of the kingdom meant an end to time, with the immediate end of the world, while much of the New Testament suggests the kingdom is more about Jesus's presence with his people in his Church, and while history has in fact persisted. John, like many Christians and scholars, was wrong to think that Jesus and the earliest Christians expected the End immediately, or at least in their lifetimes. With regard to the kingdom of heaven on Matthew, see above on 4:12–23.

John the Baptist is hardcore, immovable, fixed on his purpose. By extension, as one who also submitted to John's baptism, Jesus is suggesting to his audience that he, too, is hardcore, immovable, fixed on his purpose. And they have the same purpose, the same mission—even if it's not always apparent.

Above all, John is a prophet (Matt 11:9), and prophets suffer. Again, one thinks of Jeremiah, the prophet of lament and woe, or Elijah, persecuted by Ahab and Jezebel, or Isaiah, sawn in two. Matthew's Gospel makes much of this in chapter 23:

> Woe to you, scribes and Pharisees, hypocrites! for you build the tombs of the prophets and adorn the monuments of the righteous, saying, "If we had lived in the days of our fathers, we would not have taken part with them in shedding the blood of the prophets." Thus you witness against yourselves, that you are sons of those who murdered the prophets. Fill up, then, the measure of your fathers. You serpents, you brood of vipers, how are you to escape being sentenced to hell? Therefore I send you prophets and wise men and scribes, some of whom you will kill and crucify, and some you will scourge in your synagogues and persecute from town to town, that upon you may come all the righteous blood shed on earth, from the blood of innocent Abel to the blood of Zechari'ah the son of Barachi'ah, whom you murdered between the sanctuary and the altar. Truly, I say to you, all this will come upon this generation. (23:29–36)

So it's natural for John to suffer, as that's in the job description of a prophet, and Jesus in chapter 23 also points out that Christian prophets will suffer (23:34).

John is also "more than a prophet" (Matt 11:9b); he is the

one who fulfills the prophecy that Elijah will come before the day of the Lord: "This is he of whom it is written, 'Behold, I send my messenger before your face, who shall prepare your way before you" (11:10). The first part ("Behold . . .") comes from the Greek version of Exodus 23:20, while the second ("who shall . . .") comes from Malachi 3:1. The first is in the context of the Lord's promise that the people will be led to Canaan, to conquer it, and so Matthew's Gospel suggests John himself, positioned at the Jordan, the gateway to the Promised Land, was leading a sort of spiritual entrance into the heavenly Promised Land. And the second, then, which concerns the coming of Elijah before the great and terrible day of the Lord, fits and follows naturally: if John is preparing the people for entry into the spiritual kingdom at the end, Elijah must come, as Malachi prophesied (Mal 4:5). Jesus, in fact, will shortly make explicit that John is Elijah (Matt 11:14). And so John fulfills the last major prediction of the Old Testament prophetic writings and is himself the last of the prophets of the old covenant, who in his baptism of Jesus the Christ inaugurates the new covenant. That is why "among those born of women there has risen no one greater than John the Baptist" (11:11a), and yet "he who is least in the kingdom of heaven is greater than he" (11:11b). The old is great, yet the new is greater.

MATTHEW 11:11–15: THURSDAY OF THE SECOND WEEK OF ADVENT

So John is the greatest prophet of the old age, and yet because the kingdom of heaven is the inbreaking of the new age and the ultimate destiny of the entire created order, even whoever is very least in the kingdom is greater than John (Matt 11:11; see immediately prior). Jesus is saying that the new age is so much greater than the old age that even the greatest man of the old age is least in the new age, in the kingdom of heaven.

Now Jesus utters a confusing statement that has occasioned much speculation: "From the days of John the Baptist until now the kingdom of heaven has suffered violence, and men of violence take it by force" (Matt 11:12). The first part of the statement seems to indicate that in the short time the kingdom has been proclaimed and present in Jesus, the kingdom has endured opposition and persecution, as witnessed by John's very arrest and certain occasions of questioning in chapter 9. The second part either continues this line of thought, that violent men use force to oppress the people of the peaceable kingdom, or there's something more cryptic afoot. Indeed, longstanding tradition holds that Jesus here is saying something ironic: while our enemies in their fury might use violence to oppress us, we ought to act with the same sort of fury to seize our place in the kingdom. In the *Catena Aurea*, St. Thomas Aquinas's collection of the sayings of the Church Fathers on the Gospels, St. Jerome is quoted as saying:

> Because John the Baptist was the first who preached repentance to the people, saying, "Repent ye, for the kingdom of heaven is at hand"; rightly therefore from that day forth it may be said, that "the kingdom of heaven suffereth violence, and the violent take it by force." For great indeed is the violence, when we who are born of earth, seek an abode in heaven, and obtain by excellence what we have not by nature.[11]

---

[11] St. Jerome, in St. Thomas Aquinas, *Catena Aurea: Commentary on the Four Gospels*, vol. 1, *St. Matthew*, trans. William Whiston (London: J. G. F. and J. Rivington, 1842), caput 11, lectio 5, https://dhspriory.org/thomas/CAMatthew.htm#11.

If that is the case, then perhaps the first part of the saying (that the kingdom suffers violence) also refers to our endeavors to secure our place in it.

Jesus now makes a distinction in salvation history: "For all the prophets and the law prophesied until John" (Matt 11:13). "Until" in Greek can be inclusive and not indicate anything about a change in state after (unlike in English)—as when Matthew's Gospel states St. Joseph did not know Mary "until" she bore Jesus (Matt 1:25), or when it has Jesus state he will be with the disciples always, even until the end of the age (28:20). It's not as if Jesus is with us until the end of time but then not with the saints in heaven after. So it's not clear here if John is to be placed cleanly on one side of the divide of the old and new age or the other, though much academic ink has been spilled addressing the question. He is the figure who provides the transition between old and new; he is the last of the old covenant prophets but also the one who first proclaims the kingdom, which is the new age.

As such, he is "Eli'jah who is to come" (Matt 11:14). So is fulfilled Malachi 4:5, which prophesied Elijah (who had been taken up to heaven without dying, 2 Kgs 2:1–12) would return before the day of the Lord. But there's more here: now Jesus says John himself was actually the Coming One: "he is Elijah *who is to come.*" John apparently didn't realize it, but he himself was the original Coming One. John and Jesus work in tandem, each coming to play their role in inaugurating the kingdom of heaven.

MATTHEW 11:16–19: FRIDAY OF THE SECOND WEEK OF ADVENT

Following this comparison to Elijah, Jesus plays on the apparent contrast between John the Baptist and himself. John, the extreme ascetic, is derided as a demoniac (Matt 11:18), while Jesus, the Son of man, enjoys feasting with tax collectors and sinners and is called a glutton and drunkard (11:19). There's no making some people happy, and so Jesus declares that his generation "is like children sitting in the market places and calling to their playmates, 'We piped to you, and you did not dance; we wailed, and you did not mourn'" (11:16–17).

Apparently this sort of thing happened: groups of children would engage in a game with each other, one emulating revelers at a wedding, the other professional mourners at a wake, and try to earn the admiration (and coin!) of the crowds in the market square over the other group. But the revelry and the mourning were an act, and so when Jesus accuses his generation of acting like such children, he's suggesting they're not taking the claims of John or Jesus himself seriously but simply carping to get themselves off the hook. And so Jesus has challenged them about why they went out to see John the Baptist while he was still free and active at the Jordan in the first place: You repented then, but discount us now, Jesus is saying. Unlike John, who is hardcore, immovable, fixed in his purpose, Jesus's generation is like a reed shaken by the wind, concerned with finery (see Matt 11:7–8) instead of the kingdom simplicity proclaimed in the Sermon on the Mount (see 6:25–34).

Nevertheless, "wisdom is justified by her deeds" (Matt 11:19b). Jesus's invocation of "wisdom" is cryptic, and arrests the reader. What might he mean? One simple and true meaning is that John and Jesus are justified by the fruit of their works; they're right, and the results prove it. For in the Bible, it is the wise man who does the works of God, who observes God's law, who concerns himself with the good of his neighbor. John and Jesus are wise in this sense. But another meaning is latent here. Jesus might be pointing to himself as

Wisdom incarnate; we may have here a wisdom Christology. In Proverbs 8:22–35, Wisdom personified is presented as the agent of creation, in a way similar to how the Word (*logos*) is presented as the agent of creation in John 1:1–3. The Word in John 1 has come to be understood as the Son, the second person of the Trinity, and in a similar way the Christian tradition, particularly in the East, has seen Wisdom as the second person of the Trinity.

And so St. Jerome (as cited by St. Thomas Aquinas in the *Catena Aurea*) writes, "'Wisdom is justified of her children'— in other words, the dispensation or doctrine of God, or Christ himself who is the power and wisdom of God, is proved by the Apostles, who are his children, to have done righteously."[12]

Similarly, St. Hilary of Poitiers (again as cited by St. Thomas in the *Catena*) writes,

> He is wisdom itself not by His acts, but by His nature. Many indeed evade that saying of the Apostle's, "Christ is the wisdom and power of God," [1 Cor 1:24] by saying, that truly in creating Him of a Virgin the Wisdom and Power of God were shewn mightily. Therefore that this might not be so explained, He calls Himself the Wisdom of God, shewing that it was verily He, and not the deeds relating to Him, of whom this was meant. For the power itself, and the effect of that power, are not the same thing; the efficient is known from the act.[13]

So when Jesus says "wisdom is justified by her deeds," he may be pointing to himself as Wisdom incarnate, whose works

---

[12] St. Jerome, in Aquinas, *Catena Aurea*, caput 11, lectio 6.
[13] St. Hilary of Poitiers, in Aquinas, *Catena Aurea*, caput 11, lectio 6.

among his generation vindicate his claims and person.

MATTHEW 11:20–24: TUESDAY WEEK 15

Having reprimanded the crowds for their inconstancy, Jesus now delivers woes against the cities "where most of his mighty works had been done, because they did not repent" (Matt 11:20). Jesus mentions Chorazin and Bethsaida for the first time in Matthew's Gospel, which has not recorded any miracles in either location, so it must be presumed that in the world of the story, miracles were performed there. Indeed, it's likely that it was the Apostles who would have done miracles there recently, as they appear to be away from Jesus in chapter 11, rejoining him in 12:1. And so we see the connection between Jesus and the Church, as his Apostles do his works in his name.

Chorazin and Bethsaida will have it even worse than Tyre and Sidon, cities in ancient Canaanite territory that already stand under judgment in the Old Testament (see especially Ezek 26–28), for, Jesus says, Tyre and Sidon would have repented "long ago in sackcloth and ashes" (Matt 11:21b). And so Tyre and Sidon will have it better on the Day of Judgment (11:22). Capernaum also comes in for condemnation, which was where Jesus did most of his miracles in Matthew 8–9. Capernaum has it worse than Tyre and Sidon, for it is compared to Sodom, which, Jesus states, would have remained unpunished had it witnessed Jesus's mighty works (11:23). As such, Capernaum "shall be brought down to Hades" (11:23), and Sodom will fare better on the final day of judgment (11:24).

The non-committal, inconstant crowds, then, have failed to repent at Jesus's coming. His mighty works failed to move them, and so they stand condemned. The lesson is that repentance is the positive response to the presence and works of the kingdom in Jesus.

MATTHEW 11:25–30: FOURTEENTH SUNDAY IN ORDINARY TIME / FRIDAY WEEK 11 (11:25–27) / WEDNESDAY WEEK 15 (11:25–27) / SAINT AMBROSE, BISHOP AND DOCTOR OF THE CHURCH (DECEMBER 7; 11:28–30) / THURSDAY WEEK 15 (11:28–30) / WEDNESDAY OF THE SECOND WEEK OF ADVENT (11:28–30) / MOST SACRED HEART OF JESUS (11:25–30)

In prayer, Jesus now addresses God his Father directly, and St. Matthew makes it so we are privileged to listen in; as readers of his Gospel, we are counted among the "babes" to whom the Father has revealed "these things" about Jesus and his works (Matt 11:25).

To this point in the Gospel, Jesus has spoken frequently of "your (heavenly) Father" and "Our Father" in chapter 6 and again in chapter 10. He has spoken of "my Father" only three times (7:21, 10:32, 10:33), all in the apocalyptic context of warnings concerning the final judgment ("'Not every one who says to me, 'Lord, Lord,' shall enter the kingdom of heaven, but he who does the will of my Father who is in heaven," 7:21; "So every one who acknowledges me before men, I also will acknowledge before my Father who is in heaven; but whoever denies me before men, I also will deny before my Father who is in heaven," 10:32–33). Now we are privileged to peer deeper into the Fatherhood of God and his relationship to Jesus his Son.

Jesus thanks not "my" Father nor "your" nor "our" Father, but simply "Father": "I thank you, Father, Lord of heaven and earth . . ." (Matt 11:25). "My" is implied because Jesus is addressing God the Father directly in prayer, but the lack of a possessive pronoun emphasizes the absolute nature of God as Father, who is also the Creator, the "Lord of heaven and earth" (11:25). Jesus thanks him for hiding "these things" (Jesus's identity, authority, works, and teaching) from "the wise and understanding," instead revealing them to "babes" (11:25).

Here we have the typical pattern of reversal found throughout the New Testament; the last will be first, and the first last, the younger sons eclipse the elder, and salvation comes through a teenaged Virgin girl in the backwaters of Bethlehem. One thinks here, too, of St. Paul's words in 1 Corinthians 1:18–25: "Where is the wise man? Where is the scribe? Where is the debater of this age? Has not God made foolish the wisdom of the world? . . . For the foolishness of God is wiser than men, and the weakness of God is stronger than men" (1:20, 25).

Indeed, "babes" here in Matthew 11:25 means infant; the Greek is *nēpios*, and St. Matthew will often use *pais* or *teknon* for "child, children." So here "babes" is not a poetic, sentimental translation, even if it is a bit antiquated. Rather Jesus is emphasizing the lowly nature of the ones privileged to receive Divine Revelation through and about Jesus the Son and his relationship to the Father.

In Matthew 11:27, we have what is known as the "Johannine Thunderbolt," because the verse is like lighting thrown from John's Gospel into Matthew's: "All things have been delivered to me by my Father; and no one knows the Son except the Father, and no one knows the Father except the Son and any one to whom the Son chooses to reveal him." In John's Gospel Jesus speaks frequently of how the Son relates to the Father (see John 3:35, 5:19–26, 8:28, 14:13), especially with regard to how the Son reveals the Father, because they are inseparable but not identical ("I and the Father are one," 10:30). Here, then, we encounter the same: Jesus is the divine Son of God who alone knows the Father and who reveals him to whomever he chooses. In this point of the story, the idea that Divine Revelation is something privileged is meant to explain why some have accepted and others rejected Jesus's call to discipleship after him in the Church on the way to (and indeed already in) the kingdom of heaven.

As Johannine as the words may be, we also have here the typical Matthean emphasis on Jesus's authority: "All things have been delivered to me by my Father" (Matt 11:27a). Jesus's authority stuns the crowds, as we have already seen (7:29, 9:8). And the Gospel will end emphasizing the risen Jesus's enduring authority: "All authority in heaven and on earth has been given to me" (28:18).

Now Jesus issues a renewed call to discipleship: "Come to me, all who labor and are heavy laden, and I will give you rest. Take my yoke upon you, and learn from me; for I am gentle and lowly in heart, and you will find rest for your souls. For my yoke is easy, and my burden is light" (Matt 11:28–30). The target here is the Pharisees, scribes, and leadership of Israel, who have laden the people with heavy labors either by giving them unnecessary laws upon laws (Jesus will later damn the scribes and Pharisees for binding heavy burdens on men's shoulders without moving a finger to help bear them, 23:4) or by effectively abandoning them, leaving the people as sheep without a shepherd (9:36).

By contrast, Jesus promises rest. God rested the seventh day after the six days's labor of creation (Gen 2:2). That becomes the ground for the Fourth Commandment, having the people rest on the Sabbath (which means "seventh" day) (Exod 20:11). This in turn became a figure for the heavenly rest promised to the saints who endure to the end of time (see

Heb 3:7–4:11). So Jesus here is promising those who follow him rest now and rest later, a Sabbath rest for his people that endures to eternity. Life on earth is marked by toil and labor, while heaven is rest in God. Thus Jesus is promising not simply an easier way than that of the scribes and Pharisees here on earth, but enduring, eternal rest: "you will find rest for your *souls*" (Matt 11:29b, emphasis mine).

Furthermore, Jesus says his yoke is easy and his burden light (Matt 11:30). Disciples would "yoke" themselves to teachers, implying not just that they learn what is taught but that they walk and live as the teacher. Yokes are also not nothing; they do burden the shoulders. Yet Jesus's yoke is easy. How can that be? Following the theme in Matthew's Gospel, Jesus demands what seems impossible, from being perfect to forgiving from the heart to refraining from remarriage in the wake of separation. As stated before, the answer is Jesus himself, present with his people, empowering them to do the very things he commands. As we are yoked to him, any burdens placed on us are borne also by him. In fact, the yoke resembles a cross when looked at from above, with a stronger animal on one side aiding and training a weaker animal on the other. Jesus doesn't place a yoke on us; he shares a yoke with us and takes the lead in helping us bear the efforts of discipleship.

MATTHEW 12:1–8: FRIDAY WEEK 15

With his disciples once again, Jesus now resumes his itinerant ways. Chapter 12 opens with a controversy with the Pharisees, and will continue with rising tension, even to the point of the Pharisees conspiring to murder Jesus (Matt 12:14), later accusing him of being in league with Beelzebul, the prince of demons (12:24). Having disclosed his intimate relationship as the Son to the Father in the quiet prayer of 11:25–30, Jesus now more publicly but obliquely suggests the high stature of his identity, by turns suggesting that he is superior to King David (12:3–4), the priesthood (12:4b), the Sabbath (12:5, 8), the temple (12:6), Jonah (12:41), and King Solomon (12:42).

In Matthew 12:1–8, Jesus's disciples are plucking grain for a snack on the Sabbath (12:1), and the Pharisees accuse them of breaking the law (12:2); Exodus 34:21 forbids harvesting on the Sabbath, and of course the Jewish tradition sought to "fence the Torah" by constructing rules and practices that kept one far from transgressing any explicit scriptural boundary.

With his authority to interpret the Old Law and teach the New, rooted in his identity, Jesus here does not engage in a legal debate but simply, if subtly, asserts his authority. In Matthew 12:3–4 he recalls the story of David and his companions eating the bread of the presence when on the run from King Saul, noting only priests could consume it (1 Sam 21:1–9; this bread was lawful only for priests to eat according to Lev 24:8–9). Like David and his companions, Jesus and his disciples are being pursued by enemies, in this case the Pharisees. He further mentions that the priests who do the required rituals in the temple on the Sabbath thereby break the Sabbath without guilt (Matt 12:5), much like Sundays are not days of real rest for our Catholic priests. He then says, "I tell you, something greater than the temple is here" (12:6).

Jesus's words do not work as strict legal arguments; he's not debating the Pharisees on their terms. Jesus's rejoinders work, however, if he is suggesting he has the same standing and authority as King David and as priests. And yet that standing is also superior, for again something greater than the temple is there. In short, Jesus is engaging in the typical *qal wahomer / a fortiori* argument, from the lesser to the greater; if David and the priests could conduct themselves as they did, how much more can Jesus, the ultimate Son of David and ultimate priest, act as they did.

Then Jesus tells the Pharisees, "And if you had known what this means, 'I desire mercy, and not sacrifice,' you would not have condemned the guiltless" (Matt 12:7). Here narrative dynamics are in play; in 9:13 Jesus had told the Pharisees, "Go and learn what this means, 'I desire mercy, and not sacrifice.'" The implication is that they have failed to do so in the meantime, and so show up again condemning the guiltless, Jesus and his disciples. The Pharisees are concerned about minutiae, while they neglect what Jesus will later call "the weightier matters of the law, justice and mercy and faith" (23:23). They're simply not open to hearing Jesus and his message because they can't get beyond their offense at how Jesus and his disciples are apparent Sabbath-breakers.

Jesus then plays his trump card, making his biggest claim yet: "For the Son of man is lord of the sabbath" (Matt 12:8). Jesus, the Son of man, is now effectively claiming to be divine, for who could be Lord of the Sabbath except the one who instituted it?

Excursus: Matthew 12:9–14

The story of the healing of the man with a withered hand (Matt 12:9–14) is not in the lectionary, but it is important for understanding the development of the plot of the story. It is also key for understanding the very next section (12:15–21), in which Jesus "withdraws" in light of the Pharisees's conspiracy to murder him and in which St. Matthew as narrator provides a quotation from Isaiah promising good things to pagans.

Jesus has just responded to the Pharisees with a rhetorical *tour de force*, declaring himself superior to David, the priesthood, and the temple, and closes by declaring himself lord of the Sabbath (Matt 12:8). Now he enters "their" synagogue (12:9), and "they" ask him whether it is lawful to perform a healing on the Sabbath day (12:10). The antecedents of the pronouns "their" and "they" must be the Pharisees from the prior story. That they have asked about the lawfulness of Sabbath healing indicates they reject everything Jesus has just asserted about himself; they're still focused on the issue of legal interpretation, not the real issue of Jesus's identity and authority. Further, they ask their question about healing on the Sabbath "so that they might accuse him" (12:10b); it's not asked in good faith but rather as an opportunity for confrontation.

And so the Lord of the Sabbath engages them on the turf of their terms, and bests them there. Employing the familiar *qal wahomer / a fortiori* maneuver of arguing from the lesser to the greater, Jesus moves to livestock: "What man of you, if he has one sheep and it falls into a pit on the sabbath, will not lay hold of it and lift it out?" (Matt 12:11). Then he employs the principle of lesser to greater—"Of how much more value is a man than a sheep!" (12:12a)—and finally draws the conclusion: "So it is lawful to do good on the sabbath" (12:12b).

Then Jesus heals the man, who in response to Jesus's command to do so stretches out his hand and finds it restored just like the other (Matt 12:13). Now this story is subtly tied to the healing of the paralytic in 9:1–7. There, any opposition was muted as the scribes said "to themselves" that Jesus was blaspheming (9:3); here there is already open hostility as the Pharisees ask their question looking for a confrontation (12:10b). There the response was holy, awesome fear and the glorification of God (9:7); here the response is a murderous conspiracy: "But the Pharisees went out and took counsel against him, how to destroy him" (12:14).

Above all in this passage and the one before it, we find two views of the Sabbath set in diametric opposition. For the Pharisees, the Sabbath is something belonging to this world, established by God, who gave laws for its keeping. They're living in the old age. For Jesus, the Lord of the Sabbath, the Sabbath is a sign of the new age, something belonging to heaven, indeed the inbreaking of the kingdom of heaven on earth, from which all sickness and sorrow is banished.

MATTHEW 12:14–21: SATURDAY WEEK 15

In response to Jesus's healing of the man with the withered hand, the Pharisees conspire to murder Jesus (Matt 12:14). Now in this passage (12:15–21) we encounter the typical pattern of Jewish rejection of Jesus leading to Gentile inclusion.

Jesus is "aware" of the conspiracy and so withdraws (Matt 12:15). The word here for "withdrawal" in Greek is *anachōreō*, and it has been employed before, in 4:12, when Jesus withdraws in the wake of the arrest of John the Baptist. Jesus now heals all the many who followed him (12:15); in Matthew's Gospel, Jesus provides healings for those who have faith, who press in to be with him, as here. But given that things have come to the point that he's facing a murderous conspiracy, he now adjures them to silence, telling them "not to make him known" (12:16).

Then follows a prophecy from a version of Isaiah 42:1–4 (perhaps a lost Greek version, or St. Matthew's own paraphrase), promising good things to pagans: "Behold, my servant whom I have chosen, my beloved with whom my soul is well pleased. I will put my Spirit upon him, and he shall proclaim justice to the Gentiles" (Matt 12:18). Jesus here is identified as the "servant" of Isaiah, a figure who appears in

Isaiah 42, 49, 50, and 52–53. In the dominant Greek version of Isaiah, the Septuagint, the servant is identified specifically as Israel (or Jacob, Israel's given name). And so here when St. Matthew applies this prophecy to Jesus, it's not simply that Jesus is fulfilling some anonymous figure prophesied by Isaiah, but rather that Jesus is Israel incarnate. We have already seen this in the escape from Herod (chapter 2), which was a reverse exodus, and in the Temptation Narrative, in which Jesus recapitulates Israel's experience in the desert (chapter 4:1–11). So here the Pharisees think they're the ones who interpret God's law rightly, but St. Matthew trumps that by suggesting Jesus is Israel herself.

The middle of the citation justifies Jesus's withdrawal (Matt 12:15) and his adjuration of the healed to silence (12:16) ("He will not wrangle or cry aloud, nor will any one hear his voice in the streets," 12:19) and emphasizes Jesus's mercy ("he will not break a bruised reed or quench a smoldering wick," 12:20) until the eschaton ("until he brings justice to victory," 12:20).

This citation from Isaiah closes with words promising good things to pagans: "and in his name will the Gentiles hope" (Matt 12:21). Jewish rejection leads to Gentile inclusion. The pattern here is the same as one finds in 4:12–16: threat (the arrest of John, the Pharisaic conspiracy), withdrawal (*anachōreō*), and quotation from Isaiah promising good things to the Gentiles.

EXCURSUS: MATTHEW 12:22–37

While not in the lectionary, Matthew 12:22–37 continues the themes of chapter twelve, particularly Jesus's conflict with the Pharisees. It begins with Jesus healing a blind, dumb, demonized man (12:22). The people are "amazed" and ask if

Jesus could be the Son of David, that is, the Christ (12:23), but the Pharisees accuse him of casting out demons by the power of the prince of demons, Beelzebul (12:24). Jesus "know[s] their thoughts" (12:25a) and points out that any divided kingdom, city, or house cannot stand (12:25), so it makes no sense for Satan to cast out Satan (12:26)—it's essentially punching oneself in the face. The charge is also hypocritical: the Pharisees have their own exorcists, but how do they know their exorcisms aren't powered by Satan (12:27)?

Jesus then speaks about what he is actually doing, what is actually going on in his ministry of exorcism. He casts out demons by the Spirit of God, which means "the kingdom of God has come upon you" (Matt 12:28b). The world, it seems, is occupied territory dominated by the satanic usurper, and Jesus leads the invasion to liberate it and reclaim it for God, making it the kingdom of heaven.

Thus Jesus speaks of binding the "strong man" (Matt 12:29), Satan, so that he may plunder his "house." Satan's house isn't divided (12:25–26); rather, Jesus is laying it waste, and whoever is not with him gathering—like the Pharisees—scatters (12:30). Given the truth of the situation, Jesus says, "[B]lasphemy against the Spirit will not be forgiven" (12:31b). Speaking against the Son of man will be forgiven, but not speaking against the Holy Spirit, not now, not ever (12:32). It's one thing to reject Jesus's teaching, even in the face of his mighty works; but it is beyond the pale to look at the liberation of a man from physical infirmity and demonic possession (12:22) and attribute to Satan the man's restoration to physical and psychic sanity, when in fact it's the Spirit who powers Jesus's ministry of miracles.

And so Jesus accuses them of hypocrisy; a good tree bears good fruit and a bad tree bad, but what the Pharisees suggest is like thinking a good tree could bear bad fruit or vice versa

(Matt 12:33). Echoing John the Baptist's words in 3:7, Jesus calls the Pharisees a "brood of vipers" who cannot "speak good" because they are "evil" (12:34). Like trees, good men generate good, and evil men generate evil (12:35). And what is in someone is revealed by his or her words, so one's words will be the warrant for one's justification or condemnation (12:36–37).

MATTHEW 12:38-42: MONDAY WEEK 16

In response to Jesus's fiery words against them, some scribes and Pharisees request a sign from Jesus, addressing him as "Teacher" (Matt 12:38). Only Jesus's enemies call him "Teacher" in Matthew's Gospel (as we have seen in 8:19 and 9:11), although Jesus will call himself a teacher (as we have seen in 10:24–25). So their request is likely not sincere, and in any event Jesus has already performed myriad signs and wonders, and has just been accused of being Satan for the most recent sign.

To their request Jesus responds, "An evil and adulterous generation seeks for a sign; but no sign shall be given to it except the sign of the prophet Jonah" (Matt 12:39). As is common in Matthew's Gospel, Jesus is comparing his contemporary generation with a generation of Israelites prior—namely, the wilderness generation, described as "evil" in Deuteronomy 1:35. (The quotation of Isaiah 7:14 in Matthew 1:23 concerning "Emmanuel" functions to compare Jesus's generation with the generation facing the Assyrian threat, while Jesus's quotation of Jeremiah 7:11 in Matthew 21:13 ["den of robbers"] functions to compare Jesus's generation with those who suffered the Babylonian destruction of Jerusalem and its temple in 586 BC.)

The sign of Jonah is the resurrection, as Jonah's time in

the belly of the whale foreshadows the Son of man's coming time in the belly of the earth (Matt 12:40). Jonah's preaching produced penitence among the pagan Ninevites, who will rise at the final judgment and condemn "this generation" (12:41). So too will the "queen of the South," the queen of Sheba, who traveled to hear Solomon's wisdom (see 1 Kgs 10:1–13; Matt 12:42). The point: Jews like the Pharisees are rejecting Jesus while pagans are receiving him (such as the centurion, 8:5–13), even though something greater than Jonah and greater than Solomon has arrived with Jesus's coming.

EXCURSUS: MATTHEW 12:43–45

Although the lectionary omits it, Jesus closes his speech to the Pharisees with a final word of judgment. He describes how unclean spirits attempt to return to the "house" they had departed and find it clean and orderly (Matt 12:43–44). The unclean spirit brings friends—"seven other spirits more evil than himself" (12:45a)—with the result that "the last state of that man becomes worse than the first" (12:45b). So the orderly house is a metaphor for a possessed man, and it's important to remember this whole exchange with the Pharisees began with the exorcism of a demonized blind and mute man (12:22). With Jesus's declaration—"So shall it be also with this evil generation" (12:45b)—he is comparing his generation with a possessed man. He, Jesus, has come to cleanse Israel from its evil, from its demonic oppression, signified and made real by his healing and exorcising ministry, and yet he is being rejected by those who hold forth as teachers of Israel. The implication is that Jesus's work among his fellow Jews will do no ultimate good for Israel as a whole; the demons Jesus has worked to exorcise will return and wreak havoc sevenfold, letting slip the dogs of war that will forty years later destroy

Jerusalem and its temple, as Jesus will predict in Matthew 24. Israel's house will be laid waste by the Romans.

MATTHEW 12:46–50: TUESDAY WEEK 16

Chapter 12 has had a dark tone up to this point, filled with conflict and dire apocalyptic warnings. Now it turns brighter, as St. Matthew provides positive teaching on discipleship in contrast to the Pharisees's rejection of Jesus.

Matthew 12:46–50 can be awkward for Catholics (and Orthodox Christians, for that matter), for it seems to use Mary as a counterexample and also mentions his brothers. We are told "his mother and his brethren stood outside, asking to speak to him" (12:46). "Outside" marks them as being at some remove from Jesus. In response to their inquiry for him, Jesus stretches out his hand toward his disciples and says, "Here are my mother and my brethren! For whoever does the will of my Father in heaven is my brother, and sister, and mother" (12:49–50).

Now the passage's concern is to emphasize the nature of discipleship: disciples are those who are with Jesus and who do the will of his heavenly Father, and as such they constitute the true Christian family. And yet it raises questions for traditional beliefs about Mary—namely (and broadly), her exalted status and particularly her perpetual virginity (something which Protestants held for a couple centuries, as witnessed by their confessional statements,[14] until the rise of modernist

---

[14] The later Lutheran Confessions contain the perpetual virginity of Mary. The Solid Declaration of the Formula of Concord (1577) declares, "On account of this personal union and communion of the natures, Mary, the most blessed virgin, did not conceive a mere, ordinary human being, but a human being who is truly the Son of the most high God, as the angel testifies. He demonstrates his divine majesty even in his mother's womb in that he was born of a virgin without violating her virginity. Therefore she

biblical studies—instigated by Protestant scholars, largely in Germany, coupled with genteel but real anti-Catholicism—cast critical acid upon everything Christians had held dear, from Mary to the Trinity to the divinity of Christ).

Here Catholics will reply that Mary herself provides the model of discipleship Jesus calls for in submitting to the will of God and being near Jesus. However, it must be conceded that Matthew's Gospel is less interested in the figure of Mary and thus the Marian dimensions of the Faith than are St. Luke (of course, Luke 1–2) and St. John (John 2:1–11, the wedding at Cana, and 19:26–27, where Jesus on the Cross gives the Apostle John and Mary to each other as son and mother).

As far as the perpetual virginity of Mary is concerned, the question about Jesus's "brothers" was answered definitively in the early Church by St. Jerome in his *Against Helvidius*, explaining that Jesus's "brothers" were the sons of Cleopas's (or Clopas's) wife Mary (likely the two disciples who encounter the risen Jesus on the road to Emmaus, Luke 24:13–35). Two of Jesus's "brothers" mentioned in Matthew 13:55 (James and Joseph) are the sons of a different Mary in 27:56: "Mary the mother of James and Joseph" are among the women disciples witnessing Jesus's death from afar (27:55). Further, the word for brothers, *adelphos*, often means simply kinsman (or relative, if one prefers) in the Old Testament. Anglo-Saxon cultures and many European cultures developed complex nomenclatures for the precise delineation of family relationships (I, for one, still cannot grasp the concept of a second

---

is truly the mother of God and yet remained a virgin [*und gleichwohl eine Jungfrau geblieben ist*]." See article VIII in Theodore G. Tappert, trans. and ed., *The Book of Concord: The Confessions of the Evangelical Lutheran Church* (Philadelphia: Fortress, 1959), 595. A generation earlier the Latin, but not German, version of the *Smalcald Articles* (1537) declared the same: "[The Son] was born of the pure, holy, and virgin Mary [Latin: *semper Virgo*, "ever virgin"]." See Tappert, *Book of Concord*, 291–292.

cousin twice removed, even when shown on a chart). Ancient Israelites and Jews, whether speaking Hebrew, Aramaic, or Greek, did not do this. So *adelphos* covered a multitude of relationships. For instance, Lot is described as Abraham's brother (*adelphos*) in Genesis 13:8 and 14:14–16, although Lot is in fact Abraham's nephew; and Laban and Jacob are called brothers (*adelphoi*) in Genesis 29:15, even though Laban is in fact Jacob's uncle.

Mariology is a reflex of Christology; what we believe about Mary is determined by what we believe about Jesus. For instance, she is "Mother of God" because from conception Jesus was divine, against the teaching of Nestorianism, which tends to separate the human and divine natures of Christ. It's similar with the perpetual virginity: because Mary's womb bore God incarnate, it is not fitting that she would have had other children, much like we would never use a chalice used in Holy Mass for the drinking of table wine, or (switching contexts) using our nation's flag as fabric for some other purpose. Discipleship to Jesus Christ, presented as he is in St. Matthew's Gospel as true God and true man, means honoring the one who willingly bore him and gave him his human flesh.

CHAPTER 11

THE PARABLES OF THE KINGDOM

MATTHEW 13:1–23 (OR 13:1–9): FIFTEENTH
SUNDAY IN ORDINARY TIME / WEDNESDAY
WEEK 16 (13:1–9) / THURSDAY WEEK 16
(13:10–17) / FRIDAY WEEK 16 (13:18–23)

WE NOW ENCOUNTER the third great discourse in Matthew's Gospel, the chapter on the parables of the kingdom. It is situated in the storyline after the increasing opposition and rejection of Jesus, shown in chapters 11–12, and is directly tied to what has just happened in the prior chapters: "That same day Jesus went out of the house and sat beside the sea" (Matt 13:1). Thus, many of the parables reflect the division between those who follow Jesus on the kingdom-way and those who refuse, explaining why some follow Jesus and others don't, along with the very nature of the kingdom. The chapter will culminate with another decisive rejection of Jesus, this time in his hometown of Nazareth, not only by religious leaders and the common people but even those of his "own country" and "own house" (13:53–58).

Some comments on the interpretation of parables in general is in order. Older parable scholarship, rooted in Enlightenment notions of simplicity and clarity with a touch of sentimentality about premodern agrarianism, taught that parables explained one simple ethical point, easy for all to grasp. It also imparted that parables were absolutely not allegorical. For those reasons, the explanation attached to the Parable of the Sower (Mark 4:13–20, with the parallel in Matt 13:18–23) was regarded as an invention of the early Church, not something Jesus really said. Nor, when originally taught by Jesus, were they apocalyptic, concerned with the end of the world; the early Church either corrupted or invented parables such as the Weeds among the Wheat (Matt 13:24–30).

More recent scholarship rightly recognizes that the parables are complex and dynamic, and that they're also figurative (if not allegorical in a strict sense). And with the recognition of an apocalyptic Jesus, it is also recognized they can be apocalyptic. As such, they are not always easy to understand. Above all, the shocking nature of many of the details in the parables is recognized. Jesus's characters, usually anonymous, often behave in bizarre and shocking ways.[1] No oriental father would run down the road to greet his wayward son and welcome him back to the family as if nothing happened, as in the Parable of the Prodigal and Elder Sons (Luke 15:11–32). No landowner would pay someone working an hour a full days's wage, as in the Parable of the Workers in the Vineyard (Matt 20:1–16). No king would simply cancel a servant's outsize debt, as in the Parable of the Unmerciful Servant (Matt 18:23–35). And no responsible sower would simply toss seed everywhere, including the path, as seed is expensive (Matt 13:1–9).

---

[1] See Norman A. Huffman, "Atypical Features in the Parables of Jesus," *Journal of Biblical Literature* 97 (1978): 207–220.

Jesus assumes the posture of an ancient teacher in sitting next to the sea (Matt 13:1b, 2b; see on 5:1) while great crowds gather on the seashore to hear him (5:2). Jesus tells them "many things in parables" (5:3a). Then follows the Parable of the Sower. Given it proceeds from that general statement, its preeminence in the chapter, and permitting the occasion to provide teaching about the purpose of parables in general (13:10–17), the Parable of the Sower is the key for understanding all Jesus's parables.

In the parable, the sower sows, and scatters seed everywhere: along the path, where the birds devour it (Matt 13:4); on rocky ground, where it takes no root and the sprouts wither in the sun (13:5–6); and among thorns, which choke it (13:7). Yet some falls on good soil and yields a bumper crop, beyond any possible human expectation (13:8).

Inviting listening, Jesus says, "He who has ears, let him hear" (Matt 13:9). The statement bids hearers to go deeper, to penetrate the mystery. And mystery this parable is. Imagine being a member of the crowd, and hearing merely the parable itself, for the first time. There's not much to it. Some guy tosses seed everywhere, and as one would expect, most of it fails to produce. The seed that does produce rooted itself in good soil. "Of course," a first-century Galilean peasant might say. "So what's the point?"

The point (or points) isn't given to the crowd but to the disciples, privately, alone, when the disciples ask Jesus about why he speaks to the crowds in parables (Matt 13:10). Jesus's answer suggests the purpose of the parables is not to reveal things clearly in simple points, but to conceal, to hide, to obscure: "To you it has been given to know the secrets ["mysteries" is a better reflection of the Greek] of the kingdom of heaven, but to them it has not been given" (13:11). It sounds harsh, and therefore many scholars have said Jesus never taught such a thing. But in the world of the story of Matthew's Gospel, it makes good sense. Jesus had been teaching, healing, and exorcizing publicly from 4:17, and the result was indifference, opposition, and a murderous conspiracy. So now he turns inward to focus on those who are determined to learn from him, to be his disciples, and the contrast between how openly Jesus taught in the Sermon on the Mount (chapters 5–7) and how cryptically he teaches here in the parables chapter could not be more stark.

"This is why I speak to them in parables," says Jesus, "because seeing they do not see, and hearing they do not hear, nor do they understand" (13:13). The language is from Isaiah 6, in which Isaiah receives his commissioning of hardening; he is to preach destruction to a hardened people so that they become ever more hardened. And St. Matthew is happy to provide a formula quotation from Jesus: "With them indeed is fulfilled the prophecy of Isaiah which says: 'You shall indeed hear but never understand, and you shall indeed see but never perceive. For this people's heart has grown dull, and their ears are heavy of hearing, and their eyes they have closed, lest they should perceive with their eyes, and hear with their ears, and understand with their heart, and turn for me to heal them'" (Matt 13:14–15; see Isa 6:9–10). As so often in Matthew's Gospel, here Jesus's faithless generation is compared with a prior faithless generation.

But the disciples are in a different category: "But blessed are your eyes, for they see, and your ears, for they hear. Truly, I say to you, many prophets and righteous men longed to see what you see, and did not see it, and to hear what you hear, and did not hear it" (Matt 13:16–17). Jesus's coming is the decisive moment in salvation history, and the disciples are privileged to learn directly from him the mysteries of the kingdom.

And so Jesus then privately explains to the disciples the

meaning of the parable. It's about reaction to Jesus and his message, the "word of the kingdom" (Matt 13:19). The seed is that word, and the soils are types of people who encounter it. The path is symbolic of people who simply don't understand the word (13:19). Rocky soil is symbolic of those who respond with initial joy but fall away, thanks to "tribulation or persecution" (13:20–21). Thorns symbolize those who fail to respond fully due to the lure of the things of the world, like anxiety and riches (13:22). Good soil symbolizes those who hear the word, understand it, and bear fruit (13:23).

Too often the Parable of the Sower is taught in a moralistic way, as if Jesus was saying, "Be good soil!" That would be shocking, and maybe it's possible, but as farmers and gardeners know, soil is impersonal. People and animals (and some think even plants) respond to commands, but soil does not. A grumpy old man might shout at kids to get off his lawn, but we'd regard him as having lost it if he starts shouting at the lawn itself. Soil can be amended, but it cannot change itself. It is what it is. So in context, the point of the parable is more about explaining the differing responses to Jesus. Some people are bad soil, and in any case, Isaiah did predict rejection of God's word, as the people did in his own day.

Tying particular types of soil to characters in Matthew's Gospel is also difficult. Perhaps the crowds are those who do not understand and so fit the type of the path; perhaps the rich young man of Matthew 19:16–22 fits the thorny soil; and perhaps Peter, whose name means "rock," fits the rocky soil. And yet it does not seem that throughout his Gospel St. Matthew endeavored to present definitive characters who would fit neatly into the four categories here.

In understanding and teaching the parable, then, it's better to address congregants as insiders, as disciples, as those privileged to know Jesus and the mysteries of the kingdom, rather than telling them simply to be good soil. That said, certainly the crowds, the rich young man, and the disciples in their failures are counterexamples of discipleship.

Matthew 13:24–43 (or 24–30): Sixteenth Sunday in Ordinary Time / Monday Week 17 (13:31–35) / Tuesday Week 17 (13:36–43)

The next three parables are given to the crowds, as is apparent not so much from Matthew 13:24 but rather 13:34 ("All this Jesus said to the crowds in parables"). Jesus will then retreat inside a house with the disciples and give them the explanation of the Parable of the Weeds among the Wheat, along with three other short parables (13:36–52), before returning to Nazareth, where he will be rejected (13:53–58).

Older scholarship liked these so-called "parables of growth," in which seeds grow into plants or trees, because parables of growth suggested that the kingdom of heaven was not a violent, end-times, apocalyptic event that Jesus and the early Church expected to arrive at in their own day, but rather a gradual extension of God's reign through time and space over the centuries. It fit with the anti-apocalyptic desires of Enlightenment scholarship and saved Jesus and the early Church from being mistaken about the time of the end. This is one thing older scholarship got fundamentally right, for the parables of growth do suggest that the kingdom stretches out over a long period of time. For Catholics, it also fits with the traditional linkage of the kingdom of heaven with the Church, which many Protestants refused to countenance ("Jesus proclaimed the kingdom, but what we got was the Church," was the snide remark often made). It also helps us get interpretive leverage over difficult sayings where Jesus seems to suggest the arrival of the end is imminent, such as in Matthew 16:28: "Truly I say to you, there are some standing here who will not taste death before they see the Son of man coming in his kingdom," If we are right about the parables of growth indicating the kingdom extending gradually for a long time, we can see this verse as fulfilled in the very next event, the Transfiguration, in 17:1–8.

Jesus first tells the Parable of the Weeds among the Wheat (Matt 13:24–30). A man sows good seed, but an enemy sows weeds while he sleeps. Weeds and wheat appear together, and the householder directs the servants to let both grow to the harvest, when the reapers will gather and burn the weeds while gathering the wheat into his barn. The explanation later given (13:36–43) is both apocalyptic and allegorical (which again is why many scholars of an older generation decided Jesus himself couldn't have given it), and it is given only to the disciples. The sower of the good seed is the Son of man (Jesus himself), the field the world, and the good seed the "sons of the kingdom" (13:38a). So Jesus is talking about Christian disciples that he and his Apostles and other missionaries are making; therefore the passage need not be read as if Jesus were teaching predestination of sinners and saints before the creation of the world.

The weeds are "the sons of the evil one" (Matt 13:38b) sown by the enemy, the Devil (13:39a). Obviously in Matthew's Gospel that would include the scribes, Pharisees, and religious leadership, but here the emphasis is generic; the sons of the evil one are broader than those opposing Jesus in Matthew's Gospel. The harvest is "the close of the age" (13:39a), and the reapers are the angels sent by the Son of man, who will cleanse the kingdom of sin and evildoers and cast them into the fiery furnace (hell). But the sons of the kingdom, "the righteous," will "shine like the sun in the kingdom of their Father" (13:43).

This passage has historically been taken to teach that hell will be a reality for some, and that it does not end; the damned will "weep and gnash their teeth" (Matt 13:42b). Attempts to claim hell might be empty, or that it does not endure, generally do not deal convincingly with this passage, for it is Our Lord's words and it says what it says. Fortunately, Jesus himself has provided knowledge of the means of salvation through this very Gospel: discipleship to him within the Church he founds. The end for the righteous: they will "shine like the sun in the kingdom." Daniel 12:3 says the wise and righteous saints will shine like the stars forever, and Jesus's face shines "like the sun" at his Transfiguration (Matt 17:2, indicating that it is a prior disclosure of what resurrection looks like in heaven at the end of time).

The parable is dualistic because it is apocalyptic. It does not fit our age of Moral Therapeutic Deism, but then, MTD is not Christianity. C. S. Lewis observed that Christianity

goes much nearer to Dualism than people think. One of the things that surprised me when I first read the New Testament seriously was that it talked so much about a Dark Power in the universe—a mighty evil spirit who was held to be the Power behind death and disease, and sin. The difference is that Christianity thinks this Dark Power was created by God, and was good when he was created, and went wrong. Christianity agrees with Dualism that this universe is at war. But it does not think this is a war between independent powers. It thinks it is a civil war, a rebellion, and that we are living in a part of the universe occupied by the rebel.[2]

---

[2] Lewis, *Mere Christianity*, 45.

So the parables of growth may imply that the kingdom extends itself slowly through time and space, but there is an end; just as plants and trees are either harvested or simply wither at the end of the season, so too will the kingdom culminate in the harvest at the apocalypse.

Now comes the Parable of the Mustard Seed. It's not actually "the smallest of all seeds" (Matt 13:32a), as botanists observe, but Jesus here is using the hyperbolic function of the superlative adjective, "smallest" here meaning "really, really tiny." And it does grow into an impressive plant, over time. The cryptic part is the saying about the "birds of the air" coming to "make nests in its branches" (13:32b). In view are passages like Ezekiel 17:22–24 and 31:1–9, which seem to suggest that Gentiles will be gathered in with Israel under God's reign like the birds of the air gathering in the branches of a tree. Another possibility is that the "birds of the air" are hostile enemies of the kingdom, as birds devour the seed that falls on the path in the Parable of the Sower (Matt 13:4), which, given that the Parable of the Sower is in the immediate context, may be the better, if darker, option. This interpretation also fits with the Parable of the Weeds among the Wheat, which teaches that until the end the kingdom will suffer from the sons of the evil one within it.

The Parable of the Yeast (Matt 13:33) is interesting, in that "yeast" or "leaven" is usually used negatively as a metaphor in the biblical tradition. In Matthew 16:5–12, Jesus warns the disciples against the yeast of the Pharisees and Sadducees. In 1 Corinthians 5:6–7, St. Paul reminds the wayward Corinthians that a little leaven corrupts the whole lump of dough and adjures them to "[C]leanse out the old leaven that you may be a new lump, as you really are unleavened." A positive reading of this short parable—"The kingdom of heaven is like leaven which a woman took and hid in three measures of meal, till it was all leavened" (Matt 13:33)—would involve seeing the yeast as equivalent to leaven, and perhaps the dough like the world, and so the kingdom permeates the world as it works toward the world's redemption. This line of interpretation would be in line with the idea that Jesus is privately revealing the mysteries of the kingdom to the disciples in the midst of intense opposition to him (and them) as a way of encouraging them (and us as readers). Yet the negative reading is also quite possible, given the negative valence of yeast in the Bible, its negative use in Matthew's Gospel elsewhere (16:5–12), and the context of the Parable of the Weeds among the Wheat in this very chapter, which suggests that the kingdom will strive with evil until the end.

Jesus having delivered these parables, St. Matthew takes the opportunity to remind readers that Jesus's teaching in parables is a fulfillment of prophecy: "I will open my mouth in parables, I will utter what has been hidden since the foundation of the world" (Matt 13:35b, quoting a version of Ps 78:2). St. Matthew sees everything in the Old Testament as prophetic in some way; Jesus fulfills all the law, the prophets, and the figures and stories. So it's natural for him to see the Psalms as prophetic, as did the early Christians. David, author of most of the Psalms, was the original Christ, so it stood to reason that his Psalms would ultimately point to his ultimate descendant, the end-time Christ.

Matthew 13:44–46: Wednesday Week 17

Jesus now delivers a triad of parables (which the lectionary breaks up). The emphasis turns to the urgency of the kingdom given its absolute, ultimate importance, superior to any earthly concern. As such, operating in the background is the typical Christian binary relationships of eternity and time, heaven and earth, invisible and visible, permanent and transitory. The final parable of this triad (discussed in the next lectionary section) and indeed the entire chapter involves the apocalyptic end, and so functions to hammer the urgency of the kingdom home.

The Parable of the Treasure Hidden in the Field, for which a man sells everything he has (Matt 13:44), suggests that the kingdom might be something to keep from others. This fits with the theme of this chapter on parables, that outsiders get cryptic teaching in parables while true disciples of Jesus receive the mysteries of the kingdom revealed to them. It also tracks with Jesus's words earlier in the Sermon on the Mount about not casting one's pearls before swine, nor giving dogs what is sacred (7:6).

The Parable of the Pearl of Great Price (Matt 13:45–46) simply proposes that the kingdom is worth more than anything one could have this side of heaven; it fits well with Jesus's coming teaching that one ought to sacrifice even one's life on a cross for Jesus's sake, that he or she might ultimately stand in the kingdom (16:24–28).

MATTHEW 13:47–53: THURSDAY WEEK 17

The final parable of the triad draws on fishing techniques on the Sea of Galilee. Being a large lake, fishermen would pull nets between boats or heave them from shore and drag them in, and then separate the fish into species (Matt 13:47–38). So too the final consummation at the kingdom of heaven at the close of the age, when the angels will "separate the evil from the righteous" and cast the evil into the fiery furnace, where the damned will "weep and gnash their teeth" (13:49–50). Thus concludes the chapter on an apocalyptic note; the Jesus of Matthew's Gospel is no mere ethical teacher (such things existed in Greco-Roman society, but not in Judaism, which did not separate religion and ethics, as pagans did), but an apocalyptic prophet come to proclaim the arrival and coming of the kingdom of heaven.

Concluding, Jesus asks the disciples, "Have you understood all this?" (Matt 13:51). They reply in the affirmative with a simple "Yes," acting as Jesus commanded in the Sermon on the Mount, letting their yes be yes (5:37). Here we see the division between the crowds outside and disciples inside, as it were, with Jesus: the disciples understand, whereas the crowds do not (13:10–17). Jesus then says, "Therefore every scribe who has been trained for the kingdom of heaven is like a householder who brings out of his treasure what is new and what is old" (13:52). Here we see the theme of continuity: as much as Jesus rails against the scribes in Matthew's Gospel, Christian disciples are themselves to be scribes, experts in Jesus's New Law, trained by him in his teaching, particularly in their peering into the mysteries of the kingdom of heaven through the vehicle of the parables. And they bring out not only what is new, but also what is old—again, continuity—as the old remains relevant but transformed in its interpretation and application by Jesus himself.

MATTHEW 13:54–58: FRIDAY WEEK 17 / MONDAY IN THE THIRD WEEK OF EASTER

Thus closes the third great discourse of Matthew's Gospel (13:52). Jesus then goes to his "own country" to teach in "their" synagogue (13:54a). That's Nazareth. "Their" synagogue suggests some distance between Jesus and the synagogue, as elsewhere in Matthew's Gospel (see 10:17, 12:9, 13:54). And it is of a piece with their rejection of him: "Where did this man get this wisdom and these mighty works? Is not this the carpenter's son? Is not his mother called Mary? And are not his brethren James and Joseph and Simon and Judas? And are not all his sisters with us? Where then did this man get all this?" (13:54b–56). Whenever someone rises to prominence, there are always family and friends who knew him or her back before he or she became famous, and so remain unimpressed. Jesus therefore replies to their offense at him by saying, "A prophet is not without honor except in his own country and in his own house" (13:57). He refuses to do any miraculous wonders there precisely because of their unbelief in him (13:58). In Matthew's Gospel and in general in all the Gospels, miracles are given to those who believe and trust; they are not signs meant to convince outsiders (see the Pharisees's demand for a sign in 12:38).

CHAPTER 12

✝

RISING OPPOSITION TO
JESUS THE CHRIST

MATTHEW 14:1–12: SATURDAY WEEK 17

IF MATTHEW 11–12 INTRODUCED the theme of opposition
to Jesus in his public ministry, Matthew 14–15 ramp up the
tension. In these chapters we will learn that Jesus's forerunner
John the Baptist has been executed, the Pharisees castigate
Jesus over ritual handwashing and Jesus in turn upbraids
them, the disciples worship Jesus, and a pagan woman wins
exorcism for her daughter. There is an ever-increasing chasm
between those who follow and those who oppose Jesus—the
disciples and pagans, on one hand, and the would-be teachers
of Israel, on the other—which will culminate in Jesus's founding of the Church as a new Israel, a remnant from within
Israel, in chapter 16.

Herod the Tetrarch (which means "ruler of a fourth part")
is Herod Antipas, who reigned over Galilee and Perea from the
death of his father Herod the Great sometime between 4 and

1 BC[1] to AD 39. Colloquially called "King Herod" (see Matt 14:9), though he lacked that formal title which the Romans had granted his father, he "heard about the fame of Jesus" (14:1) and opined that Jesus was really John the Baptist resurrected (14:2). One has to be dead first to be raised from the dead, and so the reader abruptly learns of the Baptist's death, which St. Matthew then records as a flashback. Apparently the execution has happened somewhere in chapters 11–13, as the beginning of chapter 11 records the messengers of John the Baptist coming to Jesus.

Herod had divorced his wife and Herodias her husband to marry each other. The marriage was illicit, given that Herodias was his sister-in-law, as she was the wife of Herod's half-brother Herod Philip (not to be confused with Herod Philip the Tetrarch, who ruled the regions northeast of the sea of Galilee). It was illicit for a second reason: Herodias was also Herod Antipas's niece, as Herod Antipas and Herodias's father (Aristobulus IV) were half-brothers, both sons of King Herod the Great (Herod Antipas being the son of King Herod's wife Malthace the Samaritan; and Aristobulus IV being the son of King Herod's wife Princess Mariamne).

The marriage, then, is not only scandalous but illicit, lawless. One can marry one's brother's wife only upon his death (Deut 25:5–10, the practice of "Levirate marriage," where one raises up children with his late brother's widow), not while he is alive, as Leviticus forbids it (Lev 18:16: "You shall not uncover the nakedness of your brother's wife; she is your brother's nakedness"; and 20:21: "If a man takes his brother's wife, it is impurity; he has uncovered his brother's nakedness, they shall be childless").

---

[1] See Andrew E. Steinmann, "When Did Herod the Great Reign?" *Novum Testamentum* 51 (2009): 1–29.

One can imagine, then, that John the Baptist might condemn such an arrangement, and St. Matthew records that he in fact did; Herod Antipas had John imprisoned (Matt 14:3) because John said, "It is not lawful for you to have her" (14:4). He refrains from having John killed for fear of the people, who regarded John as a prophet (14:5). Yet fear of shame overpowers fear of uprising at a banquet at which Herod Antipas made a rash offer to Salome, daughter of Herodias by her prior marriage, who pleased the elite company of revelers with a dance (14:6–7). As they say, revenge is a dish best served cold, and Herodias and Salome are ice: the daughter, at Herodias's direction, demands "the head of John the Baptist here on a platter" (14:8). The Greek is more emphatic, as it places the ultimate desire last: "Give me here, on a platter, the head of John the Baptist." Herod Antipas fulfills her request with regret (14:9–11), while John's disciples (who still abide) bury the body and inform Jesus (14:12).

The story is straightforward, once one knows a bit about the Herodian family tree (truly a tangled mess of branches) and Jewish law, as well as human nature. Disordered desire leads to flight from God's law and ever-deeper sin, as adultery gives way to persecution, wrath, and murder, especially among elites who are used to exercising power to get their way. Yet this recollection of John the Baptist's execution is tied to at least two other passages in Matthew's Gospel. First, there are parallels to Jesus's execution: both John and Jesus are executed by craven governors ruling at Rome's behest who give in to fear of the mob (Pilate fearing that a riot was imminent, Matt 27:24), and both are mourned and buried by disciples. Second, the request of James's and John's mother to have her sons reign in glory at Jesus's right and left (20:20–28) refers obliquely to the situation surrounding the death of John the Baptist. Jesus says to the disciples, "You know that the rulers of the Gentiles lord it over them, and their great men exercise authority over them" (20:25). Herod Antipas is such a ruler, and his guests such great men. Jesus will tell his disciples that in contrast to ruling by power, they are to serve in humility (20:26–27), even as the Son of man abased himself in becoming a "ransom for many" (20:28).

MATTHEW 14:13–21: EIGHTEENTH SUNDAY
IN ORDINARY TIME / MONDAY WEEK 18

So John the Baptist's death has been recounted for the reader. Jesus now hears about it and "withdraws" (*anachōreō*, Matt 14:13a), exactly as he did upon hearing of John's arrest in 4:12. Jesus has taken a boat for the sake of getting far away as quickly as possible (14:13b). But the crowds find him on foot, having walked around the Sea of Galilee. Jesus has had some rest, then, but the people of the crowds will have expended themselves a great degree. Jesus comes ashore and sees them as a "great throng," and in his compassion he heals the sick among them (Matt 4:14).

There are five thousand "men," males (Greek *anēr*), "besides women and children" (Matt 14:21). Five thousand hungry men is an army. In fact, it's roughly the size of a Roman legion (though these would be Jews). Why do they pursue Jesus? Not to be fed, for presumably they become hungry on the journey. Perhaps raw interest in Jesus, given his fame, or in search of healing and exorcism. But the number five thousand and the placement of the passage in the story of Matthew's Gospel suggests otherwise. Coming as it does right after the report of John the Baptist's execution and given that we've been told Herod Antipas feared the people because they regarded John as a prophet (14:5), it's likely this crowd is coming to Jesus hoping, as Jesus is John's successor, that Jesus will lead them in an uprising against Herod Antipas and the powers that be. (John's Gospel makes the violent intentions of the crowd clearer, stating the people wanted to make Jesus a king "by force" in John 6:15.)

Jesus's kingdom is heavenly, not earthly, even though earth will be made ever more subject to the kingdom, the more the Father's will is done on earth as it is in heaven (Matt 6:10b). And so Jesus works a miracle to feed the crowds and in doing so gives them a sign of the heavenly kingdom, the Eucharist. Jesus takes the five loaves and two fish and then multiplies them in a way foreshadowing the Eucharist: he "blessed" and "broke" them, and "gave" the loaves to the disciples, who in turn give the bounty to the crowds (6:19). This matches the language used at the Last Supper for the institution of the Eucharist: "Jesus took bread, and blessed, and broke it, and gave it to the disciples" (Matt 26:26).

Thus the crowds receive a Eucharistic sign of the heavenly kingdom. But why five loaves and two fish? This miracle of loaves recalls but surpasses Elisha's smaller miracle in 2 Kings 4:42-44, in which twenty barley loaves fed a century of men. The same pattern of protest born of incredulity obtains in each story: Elisha's servant wonders how so few loaves can feed so many, just as Jesus's disciples wonder how so many can be fed with so little (Matt 14:17). Elisha was also Elijah's successor, just as Jesus was the successor of John the Baptist, Elijah-come-again (identified as such by allusion in 3:4 and expressly in 17:9-13). Further, the five loaves represent the Mosaic Torah of five books, an interpretation with deep roots in Christian tradition.[2] As such, Jesus's teaching isn't merely

---

[2] St. Anthony of Padua writes, "The five loaves represent the five books of Moses, in which we find five refreshments for the soul." From his *Sermons for Sundays and Festivals*, vol. 1, trans. Paul Spilsbury (Padua: Edizioni Messaggero Padova, 2007), 180-181.

conceptual but sacramental, reaching body and soul not merely through the intellect but through the physicality of the sacrament, which is the divine Jesus Christ himself.

Put differently, Christianity is not a religion of the book, as Judaism and Islam are. Although Catholics revere the Scriptures, the Catechism teaches:

> Still, the Christian faith is not a "religion of the book." Christianity is the religion of the "Word" of God, a word which is "not a written and mute word, but the Word is incarnate and living" [St. Bernard, *S. missus est hom.* 4,11:PL 183,86]. If the Scriptures are not to remain a dead letter, Christ, the eternal Word of the living God, must, through the Holy Spirit, "open [our] minds to understand the Scriptures" [Cf. *Lk* 24:45]. (108)

So the five books of Moses represented by the five loaves are fulfilled by Jesus himself, the incarnate Word of God, who then gives himself to us not chiefly in the texts of the Gospels but primarily in the Eucharist.

The two fish might point to Jews and Gentiles, and it's even possible that the two fish point to Jesus himself, Savior of both Jew and Gentile, in his two natures, God and man. The fish as a symbol for Jesus (the Greek *IXΘΥΣ*, *ichthus*, functioning as an acrostic for "[I]Jesus [X]Christ [Θ]God's [Υ]Son [Σ] Savior") goes way back in Christian tradition. By the time of St. Clement of Alexandria (AD 150–215)[3] and Tertullian (ca. AD 155–225), it is assumed as a commonplace.[4] It is also found

---

[3] St. Clement of Alexandria writes, "And let our seals be . . . a fish" (*Paedagogus* 3.11 [ANF 2:285]).

[4] Tertullian writes, "But we, little fishes, after the image of our IXΘΥΣ Jesus Christ, are born in water, nor have we safety in any other way than by

in Priscilla's catacombs in Rome, in a manner tying it to the miracle of the feeding of the five thousand. It could very well be that the fish as a symbol for Jesus is even from the apostolic age, generated perhaps by this very miracle witnessed by the apostles, since neither St. Clement of Alexandria nor Tertullian nor the art in the catacombs describe the symbol but rather simply assume its currency, as if it were already well-known.

Furthermore, the feeding of the five thousand recalls God feeding the Israelites manna in the wilderness (1 Kgs 17:8–16), which the later Psalmist calls "food in abundance" (Ps 78:25). Jesus, God on earth, gives the crowds a plethora of bread, more than they can possibly consume, satisfying all, with twelve baskets left over (Matt 14:20). The twelve baskets suggest the superabundance of super-substantial Eucharistic bread (see the Lord's Prayer at 6:11b, where "our daily bread" is literally *ton arton hēmōn ton epiousion*, and the Greek compound word *epi-ousion* would come into English through Latin as "super-substantial" (that is, beyond normal substance); thus the Lord's Prayer, too, might hint at the Eucharist). Note also that Jesus gives the multiplied loaves to the disciples who in turn distribute it to the crowds, just as in the Church today the priestly and episcopal successors to those apostolic disciples, the first bishops and priests, make possible the provision of the Eucharist to us today.

MATTHEW 14:22–33: NINETEENTH SUNDAY IN ORDINARY TIME / TUESDAY OF WEEK 18 IN ORDINARY TIME (14:22–36)[5]

After they are filled, Jesus dismisses the crowds and sends

---

permanently abiding in water" (*On Baptism* 1 [ANF 3:669]).

[5] See immediately following for the alternative Gospel reading for Tuesday of the Eighteenth Week in Ordinary Time.

the disciples in a boat across the Sea of Galilee. He "made the disciples get into the boat" (Matt 14:22), indicating that he's setting them up for something. Jesus goes to pray to his Father, alone in the hills, emulating what he earlier taught in the Sermon on the Mount about praying to one's Father in secret (6:6). Jesus is preparing himself for a theophany, a revealing of God's glory in himself to the disciples.

The boat is far away and bouncing in the waves (Matt 14:24); the Sea of Galilee is a large lake that can suffer severe winds and generate large swells, and one can imagine the disciples felt they were in danger of swamping. In the small hours of the night, the "fourth watch" in Roman time, about 3:00–6:00 AM, Jesus "came to them, walking on the sea" (14:25). The disciples see the miracle of Jesus walking on the water, but they are "terrified," mistaking Jesus for a "ghost," and cry out in fear (14:26). Jesus responds, "Take heart, it is I; have no fear" (14:27). "It is I" is *egō eimi*, literally "I am," and the very Name of God in the Greek Old Testament at Exodus 3:14, where the Lord God reveals himself to Moses in the burning bush. Of course it is also how one would say, "Hey, it's me!" but given what readers know of Jesus in the Gospel of Matthew, there are overtones here of God's Name; the passage subtly identifies Jesus as God.[6]

Peter now asks to be made able to walk on the water to Jesus if he is in fact who he says he is (Matt 14:28). Jesus bids him so and he does (14:29), but Peter becomes afraid in the face of the winds and begins to sink, crying out, "Lord, save me" (14:30). Peter began to focus on the threats instead of Jesus, and so he sank. The lesson is obvious: in the face of

---

[6] The version in Mark's Gospel (6:45–52) makes this clearer, as there's a direct allusion to Job 9:8 and 11, in which God is said to tread the waves of the sea and to pass Job by, and Job does not perceive him, just as the disciples do not perceive Jesus (or God in Jesus) and mistake him for a phantasm.

life's storms, one should keep one's focus on Jesus. But there's also the lesson that even those of "little faith," who doubt like Peter, can still cry out to Jesus and be saved, as Jesus reached out and pulled Peter back above the waves of the wine-dark, wind-swept sea.

As Jesus enters the boat with Peter, the wind ceases (Matt 14:32), which precipitates worship as the disciples acclaim Jesus, saying, "Truly you are the Son of God" (14:33). Having recognized Jesus and having witnessed the radical miracle of the immediate stilling of a storm by his very presence, the disciples now perceive who he ultimately is: the divine Son of God. Looking forward, Peter will soon confess him as such when asked, "Who do you say that I am?" at Caesarea Philippi (16:15–16).

St. Matthew then provides another summary transition. The boat lands at Gennesaret (Matt 14:34), and when the men there recognize Jesus, they bring all the sick for healing (14:35). Simply by touching the mere "fringe of his garment," they are made well (14:36). Often overlooked, such descriptions support the Catholic idea of relics and sacramentals, that God's grace and healing power can be transmitted by objects associated with Our Lord and the saints.

MATTHEW 15:1–2, 10–14: TUESDAY WEEK 18 (ALTERNATIVE GOSPEL)

We now turn to another controversy with the Pharisees and scribes, this time concerning handwashing. The legal argumentation in Matthew 15:3–9 is omitted by the lectionary, as are Jesus's words in 15:15–20 explaining how ritual purity is secondary to the state of one's heart. Either the composers of the lectionary thought the legal argumentation was too hard, or that the passage is too hard on the scribes and Pharisees, or that Jesus sounds uncomfortably like a Protestant in this passage upon a superficial reading.

The Pharisees and scribes in question have come all the way from Jerusalem to investigate the disciples's failure to perform ritual handwashing before meals. (Matt 15:1). Now the Old Testament prescribes ritual washing in the temple before offering sacrifices (Exod 30:17–21), but the Pharisees attempted to extend priestly temple sanctity to everyone insofar as possible.[7] So the disciples aren't violating Scripture, but rather an interpretation thereof, the "tradition of the elders" (15:2). Many Jews believed that Moses set in motion a chain of oral tradition through the ages, as reflected in the Mishnah: "At Sinai Moses received the Torah and handed it over to Joshua who handed it over to the elders who handed it over to the prophets who in turn handed it over to the men of the Great Assembly. The latter said three things: Be deliberate in judgment, raise up many disciples, and make a fence around the Torah."[8] In that chain, the Pharisees believed, were found the practices they advocated.

But Jesus has a ready retort: "And why do you transgress the commandment of God for the sake of your tradition?" (Matt 15:3). In Jesus's view, the Pharisees's understanding of tradition involved contravening the clear commands of Scripture. For example, the Pharisees taught that one could take resources meant for the support of one's elderly parents as fulfillment of the Fourth Commandment to honor one's father and mother (Exod 20:12) and be given over to the temple as an act of piety toward God (Matt 15:5); but this voids the

---

[7] See Jacob Neusner, *From Politics to Piety: The Emergence of Pharisaic Judaism* (repr. ed., Eugene, OR: Wipf and Stock, 2003).

[8] *Pirke Avot* 1.1, in *Pirke Avot: A Modern Commentary on Jewish Ethics*, trans. and ed. Leonard Kravitz and Kerry M. Olitzky (New York: UAHC Press, 1993), 1.

word of God for the sake of tradition (15:6). Jesus calls this hypocrisy (15:7) and finds it foretold in Isaiah: "You hypocrites! Well did Isaiah prophesy of you, when he said: 'This people honors me with their lips, but their heart is far from me; in vain do they worship me, teaching as doctrines the precepts of men'" (15:7–9, quoting a Greek version of Isa 29:13).

So the Pharisees have a concept of tradition that (according to Jesus here) stands in *discontinuity* with Scripture. For those who think this passage supports a Protestant opposition of Scripture versus Tradition, a reply might be that for Catholics, Tradition stands in *continuity* with Scripture, as both come from and rightly interpret Jesus Christ (see CCC 80–83).

That said, Jesus's rejection of the tradition of the elders (even if it's just the Pharisees's particular interpretation of it, that was a widely accepted interpretation) is radical for a first-century Jew. And what he says next is similarly radical. He calls not just his disciples but "the people" to him (Matt 15:10a) and says, "Hear and understand: not what goes into the mouth defiles a man, but what comes out of the mouth, this defiles a man" (15:10b–11). Jesus will later explain to the disciples that what comes out of the mouth is ultimately found in the heart: "Do you not see that whatever goes into the mouth passes into the stomach, and so passes on? But what comes out of the mouth proceeds from the heart, and this defiles a man" (15:17–18). Such things that come out are "evil thoughts, murder, adultery, fornication, theft, false witness, slander" (15:19).

As for the Pharisees taking offense at Jesus's teaching (Matt 15:12), Jesus condemns them: "Every plant which my heavenly Father has not planted will be rooted up" (15:13), and those who follow them will fall into the same pit, as they are blind guides (15:14).

Matthew 15:21–28: Twentieth Sunday in Ordinary Time / Wednesday Week 18

Now Jesus travels to Tyre and Sidon (Matt 15:21), pagan territory; the movement from a Jewish area, where he encounters opposition from the scribes and Pharisees, to a Gentile area is no accident. And yet when he meets a Gentile, a pagan woman desperately seeking his help, he at first refuses to aid her before relenting after repeated inquiries. Two major interpretive possibilities are common: either Jesus means to help her all along and his refusals are meant to tease faith out of her, or Jesus does not mean to help her but she bests him in debate and so he concedes. The former attempts to save Jesus from looking like an exclusivist who would reject pagans and women in favor of showing him to be a universalist. The latter is faithful to the surface sense of the passage but leaves us with a Jesus who does not seem at this point aware of his mission to the Gentiles, and Christian faith has always been deeply uncomfortable with Jesus having limited knowledge.

St. Matthew uses the term "Canaanite" for the woman (Matt 15:22). By his time the term is archaic, as the Canaanites were the enemies of ancient Israel. So the term suggests that she is descended from the ancient enemies of Israel. And Jesus seems to treat her as an enemy. She addresses him politely as *kurios*, either "Sir" or "Lord," and even Son of David, indicating she's not as pagan as one might first suspect (15:22). Jesus simply doesn't answer, and the disciples tell Jesus to dismiss her because her crying after them is annoying (15:23). As in 10:5–6, Jesus then indicates that his mission is for Israel alone: "I was sent only to the lost sheep of the house of Israel" (15:24). He means, apparently, to do what the disciples asked and dismiss her.

But she now kneels before him, saying, "Lord, help me"

(Matt 15:25). Jesus's response seems less than edifying: "It is not fair to take the children's bread and throw it to the dogs" (15:26). As stated before, "dog" was a common Jewish epithet for pagans, as dogs were generally regarded as unclean animals. Jesus may not be insulting her here, but at the very least he is subordinating Gentiles (the "dogs") to Jews (the "children"). Her response is brilliant, as it accepts the subordination inherent in Jesus's saying while finding room in it for what she desires: "Yes, Lord, yet even the dogs eat the crumbs that fall from their master's table" (15:27). Jesus's response: "O woman, great is your faith! Be it done for you as you desire" (15:28). Her daughter is healed remotely and immediately.

The pattern here is similar to that of the centurion in Matthew 8:5–13: a desperate Gentile calls Jesus "Sir" or "Lord" and exercises great faith ("Truly, I say to you, not even in Israel have I found such faith," 8:10b). So it is to persistent, demonstrated faith in him that Jesus responds. Both passages, then, show that the way of the kingdom is open to Gentiles.

More difficult (for us moderns, at least) is Jesus's seeming resistance to the woman. On one hand, a reader can see a pattern in Matthew's Gospel in which Jesus seems uninterested in Gentiles until after the crucifixion and resurrection; he states his mission is for Israel in 10:5–6 and 15:24, but then after "all the people" (27:25) call for his crucifixion in Pilate's courtyard, the situation turns: "Go therefore and make disciples of all nations" (28:19a). Again, Jewish rejection leads to Gentile inclusion. One can see Jesus essentially learning through the events of the story that his mission extends to Gentiles so that his perspective at the end of the Gospel finally matches the eternal perspective, which envisioned Gentile inclusion all along, as shown by the Isaianic prophecies promising good things to Gentiles (referenced in

Matthew 4 and 12). Beyond that, in the world of Matthew's Gospel, Jesus in his humanity is a first-century Palestinian male Jew, and such men had little use or time for pagans and especially pagan women.

On the other hand, Matthew's Gospel as a story does not operate with a simple understanding of narrative time, in which events simply unfold in chronological sequence. Of especial interest is Jesus's prior remark in chapter 10 about bearing testimony before the Gentiles (10:18) and, indeed, his immediate readiness to help the centurion upon his request: "I will come and heal him" (8:7). The Gospel of Matthew is a story, but it's a story that's more like an icon, revealing multiple dynamic dimensions through a relatively static picture.

As far as Jesus's knowledge of his mission goes, then, it's not clear whether Jesus understands that his mission will include the Gentiles. On one hand, Jesus says things that indicate his ignorance of the scope of his mission (see Matt 10:6 and 15:24, where he restricts it to "the lost sheep of the house of Israel"), but on the other hand, the theological tradition has wanted to claim Jesus had full knowledge of his mission and indeed all things since he is divine. One enduring suggestion is that Jesus is feigning ignorance for pedagogical or pastoral purposes, yet that runs the risk of involving Jesus in deceit. The Catechism provides the way forward, even as it doesn't fully resolve the tension regarding Jesus's divine identity and seemingly limited knowledge:

> This human soul that the Son of God assumed is endowed with a true human knowledge. As such, this knowledge could not in itself be unlimited: it was exercised in the historical conditions of his existence in space and time. This is why the Son of God could, when he became man, "increase in wisdom and in

stature, and in favor with God and man" [*Lk* 2:52], and would even have to inquire for himself about what one in the human condition can learn only from experience [Cf. *Mk* 6:38; 8:27; *Jn* 11:34; etc.]. This corresponded to the reality of his voluntary emptying of himself, taking "the form of a slave" [*Phil* 2:7].

But at the same time, this truly human knowledge of God's Son expressed the divine life of his person [Cf. St. Gregory the Great, *"Sicut aqua" ad Eulogium, Epist. Lib.* 10, 39 PL 77, 1097A ff.; DS 475]. "The human nature of God's Son, not by itself but by its union with the Word, knew and showed forth in itself everything that pertains to God" [St. Maximus the Confessor, *Qu. et dub.* 66: PG 90, 840A]. Such is first of all the case with the intimate and immediate knowledge that the Son of God made man has of his Father [Cf. *Mk* 14:36; *Mt* 11:27; *Jn* 1:18; 8:55; etc.]. The Son in his human knowledge also showed the divine penetration he had into the secret thoughts of human hearts [Cf. *Mk* 2:8; *Jn* 2:25; 6:61; etc.].

By its union to the divine wisdom in the person of the Word incarnate, Christ enjoyed in his human knowledge the fullness of understanding of the eternal plans he had come to reveal [Cf. *Mk* 8:31; 9:31; 10:33–34; 14:18–20, 26–30]. What he admitted to not knowing in this area, he elsewhere declared himself not sent to reveal [Cf. *Mk* 13:32, *Acts* 1:7]. (CCC 472–474)

MATTHEW 15:29–37: WEDNESDAY OF THE FIRST WEEK OF ADVENT

Having helped a pagan woman by exorcising her daughter,

Jesus now helps other Gentiles. Matthew 15:29–31 is another summary of Jesus's wonder-working, such as reported most recently in 14:34–36. And yet it's more than a simple summary; in its description of what Jesus is doing it goes beyond the other summaries in both poetry and substance. The crowds bring "the lame, the maimed, the blind, the dumb, and many others" (15:30). Jesus heals them, and the crowd "wonders," or marvels, "when they [see] the dumb speaking, the maimed whole, the lame walking, and the blind seeing" (15:31a). Most importantly, "they glorif[y] the God of Israel" (15:31b). That the deity in question is specified as "the God of Israel" suggests these people are pagans, Gentiles. So St. Matthew's story of Jesus has moved from a single desperate "Canaanite" woman to a multitude of desperate Gentiles.

So too with the feeding of the four thousand: clues abound that this second feeding of a multitude involves Gentiles. In its structure and significance, this feeding matches the prior feeding of the five thousand (Matt 14:13–21); where Jesus gave the Jews there a Eucharistic sign, now Jesus gives Gentiles the same Eucharistic sign.

Thus the structure and substance are the same, and one can apply what was said in general before about the feeding of the five thousand directly here to the feeding of the four thousand. But there are significant differences in the details. In this feeding, Jesus takes the initiative, telling the disciples he has "compassion" toward the crowd and is concerned they are hungry (Matt 15:32), whereas in the prior feeding the disciples had come to Jesus (14:15). Jesus also mentions the crowd being with him now "three days" (15:32) with nothing to eat, which suggests the three symbolic days Jesus will be in the tomb, as he has already hinted at in his words about the sign of the prophet Jonah (12:40). And it is after those three days that Jesus is raised from the dead and then tells his eleven

Apostles to "make disciples of all nations" (28:19).

Further, instead of five loaves (which suggested the five books of Moses) there are seven loaves in this feeding (Matt 15:36) and seven baskets left over (15:37). Commentators routinely and rightly suggest these symbolize the seven nations that Deuteronomy 7:1 describes as the inhabitants of the Promised Land, just as the twelve baskets in the prior feeding indicated the twelve tribes of Israel. Indeed, the number four thousand (15:38) may indicate Gentiles, for the number four was recognized as a number of universality in the ancient world, given the four points of the compass, the four seasons, the four winds, and so forth.

EXCURSUS: MATTHEW 16:1–12

This next section (Matt 16:1–12) is not in the lectionary, but will be treated here since it moves St. Matthew's story forward. Jesus has now returned to Jewish territory (15:39). Now he is approached by Pharisees and also Sadducees, indicating the Jerusalem authorities are becoming interested in Jesus, as the Sadducees dominated Jerusalem and its temple; reports of his doings in Galilee have apparently filtered south to Judea (16:1). They demand a "sign from heaven" to "test" him (16:1). "Testing" is hostile, as is the demand for a sign, especially when Jesus has performed multiple signs in the Pharisees's presence. Jesus tells them they can interpret the turnings of the weather, natural signs, but that they cannot interpret the "signs of the times" (16:3), which would require supernatural insight, which they lack, being "blind guides" (15:14). He also reminds them that an "evil and adulterous generation seeks for a sign" and that they'll receive only the sign of Jonah (16:4), which Jesus has detailed for them already in 12:38–42.

Jesus leaves them, and he and the disciples traverse the Sea of Galilee again. They lack literal bread, but Jesus tells them something allegorical: "Take heed and beware of the leaven of the Pharisees and Sad´ducees" (Matt 16:6). Bound by St. Augustine's "wretched slavery of the spirit"[9] to the mere letter of Scripture, they mistake mere signs for the real things they signify, and so miss the spiritual, allegorical import of Jesus's words: they say, "We brought no bread" (16:7). Jesus lays into them calling them "men of little faith" (16:8) and applying to them the language of Isaiah 6:9–10, asking them, "Do you not yet perceive?" (16:9). He reminds them of the results of the two feedings of the multitudes (16:9b–10), which were spiritual, allegorical signs, and repeats his warning about the leaven of the Pharisees and Sadducees (16:11). St. Matthew then makes the point plain, and the disciples realize the leaven concerns their teaching (16:12).

This conflict with the Pharisees and Sadducees is a final straw for Jesus, as it sets the stage for the next story, the founding of the Church as a remnant community from within Israel meant to carry on Israel's mission to the world: to be a light to the Gentiles.

MATTHEW 16:13–20: TWENTY-FIRST SUNDAY IN ORDINARY TIME / THE CHAIR OF SAINT PETER THE APOSTLE (16:13–19) / SAINTS PETER AND PAUL, APOSTLES (JUNE 29; 16:13–23) / THURSDAY WEEK 18

We come now to the heart of Matthew's Gospel: Peter's confession of Jesus as the Christ and Son of God, and Jesus's

---

[9] *De doctrina Christiana* 3.5.9, in *Teaching Christianity*, trans. Edmund Hill, OP, The Works of St. Augustine: A Translation for the 21st Century (Hyde Park, NY: New City Press, 1996), 173.

founding the Church in turn on Peter. Jesus and the disciples are now in the region of Caesarea Philippi (Matt 16:13), a pagan area in the north with long associations to the god Pan. The location for Peter's and Jesus's respective declarations suggests that the Church's mission will conquer the world.

Jesus asks the disciples a leading question: "Who do men say that the Son of man is?" (Matt 16:13). They respond with a variety of answers, including Jeremiah (16:14), known as the "weeping prophet," who lamented the destruction of Jerusalem in 586 BC, as Jesus later laments the coming destruction of Jerusalem in Matthew 24; St. Matthew records the mention of Jeremiah because he is drawing parallels between the coming destruction of the temple of Jesus's day to the destruction of the temple of Jeremiah's day. Jesus then asks them directly, and the two questions suggest that Jesus is asking them whether they'll side with the popular opinions of the crowds or with the truth: "But who do you say that I am?" (16:15).

Simon Peter gives the reply: "You are the Christ, the Son of the living God" (Matt 16:16). To be Christ means to inherit the kingdom of David, the original Christ, and to deliver the people as David once did. (Again, St. Matthew's story shows how the common expectations of doing so by violence are upset, as Jesus does so not by killing but by dying for his people.) "Son of God" is not new in the Gospel, as the disciples worshipped Jesus with that title in 14:33, but "living" is new here. In biblical and Jewish tradition, the God of Israel was the true God, supreme over all other "gods" (whether it was thought they existed in some way, or not). The pagan gods were derided as mute, deaf, dumb, fashioned of wood or stone, whereas the God of Israel was the living God who really existed.[10] Thus in this pagan territory, dominated by the god

---

[10] The contrast is perhaps best seen in 1 Kings 18, Elijah's contest on Mount

Pan, Peter declares his faith in the living God of Israel and Jesus's Sonship to him.

Peter's insight is a result of Divine Revelation: "Blessed are you, Simon Bar-Jona! For flesh and blood has not revealed this to you, but my Father who is in heaven" (Matt 16:17). Peter's insight is a gift, as is his papacy: "And I tell you, you are Peter, and on this rock I will build my church" (16:18a). Peter has been called Peter throughout the Gospel, but his given name is Simon. Here we have a story in which Jesus gives Simon his new second name of Peter. Name changes in the Bible happen when a significant figure experiences significant revelation. Abram becomes Abraham in Genesis 17 when God declares Abram will become the father of many nations (*Av*, father; *am*, peoples). In the same chapter Sarai becomes Sarah (which probably means "princess"). Jacob becomes Israel when he wrestles with God in Genesis 32:22–32 (Israel meaning "a man [*Is*] who has striven and overcome [*ra*] with God [*El*]," and so Genesis 32:28 explains, "[F]or you have striven with God and with men, and have prevailed").

So the new given name has great significance. "Peter" is not a common name prior to this event at Caesarea Philippi. In the Greek of Matthew's Gospel, it is *Petros*, a masculine form of the common Greek word *petra*, rock. Thus Jesus's naming of Simon as "Peter" indicates that Peter himself is the "rock" on which the Church is built. Some may counter that the rock should actually be the content of Peter's confession—"You are the Christ, the Son of the living God"—but that would sever what is here connected, the person of Peter and his confession. Catholic Faith is never merely content apart from the people, as if it were a pure abstract system of doctrines, but content which comes through and to people in the Church.

Carmel with the pagan prophets of Ba'al.

Jesus says this is "my church" (Matt 16:18a), his assembly (*ekklēsia*); in his authority he reigns over the new assembly of the new Israel, as Moses ruled over the old assembly (*ekklēsia*) of Israel (Deut 9:10, in the Greek). And Jesus promises that the gates of Hades "shall not prevail against it" (Matt 16:18b). Hell (the concept of which grew out of Hades) is not on the offensive, but the defensive; gates are stationary entry points to a walled city, and so when Jesus says the gates of Hades shall not prevail against the Church, it means that the Church is engaged in an assault and siege of hell, to which hell must one day succumb.

Then Jesus gives Peter the "keys of the kingdom of heaven," promising him, "[W]hatever you bind on earth shall be bound in heaven, and whatever you loose on earth shall be loosed in heaven" (Matt 16:19). While the other disciples also receive the power of the keys in 18:18, here the singular "you" is employed; Peter alone is given the keys here. The power of the keys involves three dimensions. First, in accord with Jewish usage of the concepts of "binding" and "loosing," it refers to the power to teach. Second, it has to do with the power of excommunication (which is clearer in the context of Matt 18). Third, it concerns the forgiveness of sins, as "loose" in Greek (*luō* or *apoluō*) is often the word translated as "forgive."[11]

So Peter's person is invested with real authority, the authority even of Jesus himself. And the passage also implies Peter will have successors. For in Isaiah 22:22 "the key of the house of David" transfers from Shebna to Eliakim, stewards of the royal Davidic dynasty.[12] If the kingdom of heaven Jesus brings with the Church is the ultimate fulfillment of the

---

[11] Mitch and Sri, *The Gospel of Matthew*, 210.
[12] Mitch and Sri, *The Gospel of Matthew*, 209.

Davidic promises of an end-time Christ, it stands to reason, then, that that kingdom and Church will be ruled in service by Jesus Christ through a vicar in Jesus Christ's absence from earth, which we have come to call the Pope (after *papa*, "father").

There are good scriptural grounds, then, for seeing in this passage the foundation of the papacy as Catholics understand it. And the early Church simply accepted the apostolic succession of bishops. In the later first century, as early as AD 70 and no later than AD 100, St. Clement (a priest and then the fourth bishop, and thus Pope, of Rome) wrote:

> The apostles have preached the Gospel to us from the Lord Jesus Christ; Jesus Christ [has done so] from God. Christ therefore was sent forth by God, the apostles by Christ. Both these appointments, then, were made in an orderly way, according to the will of God. Having therefore received their orders, and being fully assured by the resurrection of our Lord Jesus Christ, and established in the word of God, with full assurance of the Holy Ghost, they went forth proclaiming that the kingdom of God was at hand. And thus preaching through countries and cities, they appointed the first fruits [of their labours], having first proved them by the Spirit, to be bishops and deacons of those who should afterwards believe. Nor was this any new thing, since indeed many ages before it was written concerning bishops and deacons. For thus says the Scripture in a certain place, I will appoint their bishops in righteousness, and their deacons in faith [Isa 60:17, Greek alt.].[13]

---

[13] St. Clement, *1 Clement* 42.1–5 (ANF 1:16).

Around AD 180 St. Irenaeus wrote the following:

> It is within the power of all, therefore, in every Church, who may wish to see the truth, to contemplate clearly the tradition of the apostles manifested throughout the whole world; and we are in a position to reckon up those who were by the apostles instituted bishops in the churches, and [to demonstrate] the succession of these men to our own times; those who neither taught nor knew of anything like what these [heretics] rave about. . . . Since, however, it would be very tedious, in such a volume as this, to reckon up the successions of all the Churches, we do put to confusion all those who, in whatever manner, whether by an evil self-pleasing, by vainglory, or by blindness and perverse opinion, assemble in unauthorized meetings; [we do this, I say,] by indicating that tradition derived from the apostles, of the very great, the very ancient, and universally known Church founded and organized at Rome by the two most glorious apostles, Peter and Paul; as also [by pointing out] the faith preached to men, which comes down to our time by means of the successions of the bishops. For it is a matter of necessity that every Church should agree with this Church, on account of its preeminent authority.[14]

St. Irenaeus's own clerical lineage ran from Jesus Christ through St. John through Polycarp to himself, as his line of ordination makes him the spiritual great-grandchild of Jesus himself. Although the time of Jesus's death and resurrection to the writing of *Against Heresies*, roughly 150 years, sounds

---

[14] St. Irenaeus, *Adversus haereses* 3.3.1–2 (ANF 1:415).

like a long time, it's not. To put it in perspective, two of President John Tyler's grandsons are alive in early 2019 as of this writing; Tyler was born in 1790 and assumed the presidency in 1841. We might imagine that those grandsons have kept many Tyler family memories, and likewise we might imagine that St. Irenaeus, St. John the Apostle's spiritual grandson, would have kept many memories of the family of the Church and her Tradition from the ages.

As a younger man St. Clement of Rome knew Peter and Paul before their martyrdoms in Rome in the 60s of the first century. Tertullian (died ca. AD 228) writes that Clement was ordained by St. Peter himself,[15] as does St. Hegesippus (died AD 180), suggested by St. Epiphanius.[16] St. Irenaeus, for his part, writes about Pope St. Clement: "This man, as he had seen the blessed apostles, and had been conversant with them, might be said to have the preaching of the apostles still echoing [in his ears], and their traditions before his eyes. Nor was he alone [in this], for there were many still remaining who had received instructions from the apostles."[17]

Not only, then, does the passage in St. Matthew's Gospel imply Peter will have successors (the allusion to Isa 22:22), but also the early Church believed in apostolic succession, stationed St. Peter in Rome, and even asserted that St. Clement was ordained a priest by St. Peter himself.[18] Tradition develops over time, as St. John Henry Newman explained, like newborn creatures growing into the mature creatures they

---

[15] Tertullian, *De praescriptione haereticorum* 32 (ANF 3:258).

[16] St. Epiphanius, *Adversus haereses* 27.6. See the entry on Pope St. Clement in the old Catholic Encyclopedia at http://www.newadvent.org/cathen/04012c.htm.

[17] St. Irenaeus, *Adversus haereses* 3.3.3 (ANF 1:416).

[18] St. Jerome in the fifth century writes that most of the western Church affirmed St. Peter had ordained St. Clement (*Illustrious Men* 15).

inherently are.[19] The acorn of the immovable, enduring oak of the papacy, then, is found in Matthew 16:13–21.

---

[19] John Henry Newman, *An Essay on the Development of Christian Doctrine* (London: Longmans, Green and Co., 1909), 207–247.

PART III

THE PASSION OF JESUS THE CHRIST

CHAPTER 13

✝

THE PASSION AND THE GLORY

MATTHEW 16:21–27: TWENTY-SECOND SUNDAY IN ORDINARY TIME / FRIDAY WEEK 18 (16:24–28)

AFTER PETER IS GIVEN the "keys of the kingdom" (Matt 16:19), Jesus "strictly charge[s] the disciples to tell no one that he was the Christ" (16:20) for the moment, for that would raise the wrong expectations. Jesus is a dying Christ, not a conquering warrior (until the end), and so he immediately explains to his disciples that he must suffer and die in this passage, his first Passion prediction.

Thus we begin the third and final major section of St. Matthew's story, as Jesus concludes his Galilean ministry and begins his final, fateful journey to Jerusalem. And that journey is marked by teaching about cruciform discipleship, the necessity of the Cross for Jesus and those who would follow him as disciples. "From that time Jesus began to show his disciples that he must go to Jerusalem and suffer many things from the elders and chief priests and scribes, and be killed, and on the third day be raised" (Matt 16:21). "Must" is key; Jesus's ultimate mission is to give his life for the forgiveness of sins (26:28), the very reason he came. Here also we see the basic pattern found throughout the New Testament of death and resurrection. The hope of the latter gives the believer endurance to face the former, whether a death as dramatic as martyrdom or the normal death all of us must endure someday. It also functions as a basis for Christian ethics, as we see in Philippians 2:1–12, in which St. Paul states that Jesus Christ was "in the form of God" (2:6) but "emptied himself" (2:7) of the prerogatives of divinity to be found in human form and suffer death on the Cross; St. Paul tells the Philippians they should have the same attitude of humility and service displayed in the divine Christ's humiliation and servant death. We see the same in St. Matthew's own Gospel in response to the request of the mother of James and John in 20:20–28.

While Jesus is talking about suffering and dying, Peter is not having it; he "rebukes" Jesus and says, "God forbid, Lord! This shall never happen to you" (Matt 16:22). The contrast with his confession of Jesus as Christ and Son of God in the passage immediately above is striking, as Peter goes from right to dead wrong. But we ought to cut Peter some slack, perhaps, or at least understand why he would react in such a way. There was no concept of a suffering Christ in Judaism prior to Christianity whatsoever. The Christ was to conquer the Jews's pagan enemies and erect an everlasting kingdom like David's of old. That's why the proclamation of a crucified Christ in Jesus was scandalous, as St. Paul says: "[W]e preach Christ crucified, a stumbling block (*skandalon*) to Jews and folly to Gentiles" (1 Cor 1:23). Jesus has shown himself the Christ by his miracles and authoritative teaching, but he has not yet presented any clear teaching on his necessary death to this point. So Peter is understandably jarred by Jesus's words.

But Jesus is not having it either: he tells Peter, "Get behind me, Satan! You are a hindrance (*skandalon*) to me; for you are not on the side of God, but of men" (Matt 16:23). So the Cross for the Christ might appear to be a scandal, but Jesus says the real scandal is attempting to downplay the Cross. In St. Paul's words, for us Christians, "to those who are called, . . . Christ [crucified is] the power of God and the wisdom of God" (1 Cor 1:24). And so Peter needs to realize that what Jesus says, goes. He's already presented some rather radical teachings in his Galilean ministry, and now he tells the disciples to trust him a stretch further.

Jesus then gives his famous teaching about the cross to his disciples:

> If any man would come after me, let him deny himself and take up his cross and follow me. For whoever would save his life will lose it, and whoever loses his life for my sake will find it. For what will it profit a man, if he gains the whole world and forfeits his life? Or what shall a man give in return for his life? (Matt 16:24–26)

To follow Jesus, then, means taking up one's own cross. In the world of the story, it's a call to real crucifixion, and the disciples would have heard it as such. Jesus has just said he's on his way to Jerusalem to suffer and die. And everyone in the ancient world knew what crucifixion was. The Romans routinely crucified people, and so did Jews at points; in the early first century BC, Alexander Jannaeus, the Jewish Hasmonean king, crucified eight hundred Pharisees at a garden party as entertainment for his guests, also having their families killed.[1]

---

[1] Josephus, *Ant.* 13.380, in *The Jewish Antiquities, Books 12–13*, trans.

And crucifixion was so horrible, Cicero writes, that good Romans shouldn't even mention it.[2]

Of course, most Christians haven't and won't experience martyrdom, and fewer still actual crucifixion. And so what's literal in the story becomes also metaphorical, allegorical: we must bear crosses that come our way in patient hope, and cooperate with God in crucifying our flesh, our old Adam, the sin that remains in us even after baptism.

And we must do so, for judgment is coming. Jesus tells the disciples, "For the Son of man is to come with his angels in the glory of his Father, and then he will repay every man for what he has done" (Matt 16:27). So Jesus offers both carrot and stick, the promise of reward but also the threat of punishment. In any event, it's important here to remember that Jesus in Matthew's Gospel does not simply give commands that we try to fulfill with our own power, either succeeding or failing, but that Jesus is God with his people helping them to fulfill what he commands, even taking up the cross.

Jesus then closes on a note of promise: "Truly, I say to you, there are some standing here who will not taste death before they see the Son of man coming in his kingdom" (Matt 16:28). This passage may trouble those who think Jesus is referring to the end of the world, for it didn't happen before the last of the Apostles died. But its fulfillment is found in the very next passage, the Transfiguration. "And after six days" Jesus took Peter, James, and John up a mountain to witness the Transfiguration (17:1), which is a display of Jesus's resur-

---

Ralph Marcus, LCL 365 (Cambridge, MA: Harvard University Press, 1943), 5:417.

[2] Cicero, *Pro Rabirio Perduellionis Reo* 5.16, in *Pro Lege Manilia. Pro Caecina. Pro Cluentio. Pro Rabirio Perduellionis Reo*, trans. H. Grose Hodge, LCL 198 (Cambridge, MA: Harvard University Press, 1927), 466–467.

rection glory and thus shows the Son of man in his kingdom. It also reveals to the disciples that after the cross comes the promise of resurrection, compared to which even the agonies of crucifixion are a light and momentary trouble.

MATTHEW 17:1–9: SECOND SUNDAY OF LENT / THE TRANSFIGURATION OF THE LORD

The Transfiguration reveals Jesus's end-time resurrection glory and so fulfills his promise in Matthew 16:28 that some there would see the Son of man coming in his kingdom. "After six days" (17:1) suggests the six days of creation, with the Transfiguration coming on the seventh day, evocative of the Sabbath rest, which is a figure of the final Sabbath rest of God's people in heaven. So the Transfiguration on the seventh day is a revelation of the glory of the resurrection in the kingdom of heaven.

Jesus's face "shone like the sun" and his "garments became white as light" (Matt 17:2). Jesus has already spoken of the righteous "shin[ing] like the sun in the kingdom of their Father" at the end of the world (13:43). Dazzling white garments are also suggestive of the end of the world; for instance, in the Book of Revelation, the saints from all the nations wear white robes before the throne of God in heaven (Rev 7:9–17).

Moses and Elijah appear and speak with Jesus (Matt 17:3), and they will disappear (17:8), which suggests that Jesus fulfills the Law and the Prophets, Moses being the great lawgiver and Elijah being the great prophet. Peter, overwhelmed with glory, then speaks, suggesting he construct three booths for the three of them, Jesus, Moses, and Elijah (17:4). The correction of Peter's statement by the heavenly voice (17:5) and the disappearance of Moses and Elijah likely indicate Jesus's supremacy over the Law and the Prophets; he not only fulfills them but interprets them and declares parts obsolete in his sovereign authority.

The cloud is the very glory of God, the *shekinah* (see Exod 24:15–18, where it appears on a mountain; 1 Kgs 8:11, when it appears at the dedication of Solomon's temple; and Ezek 43:1–5, which looks forward to its appearance at the end of time), and a voice comes from the cloud, addressing Peter: "This is my beloved Son, with whom I am well pleased; listen to him" (Matt 17:5). "Beloved Son" alludes to Genesis 22:2, 12, and 16, and thus Isaac, the original sacrifice on which all later sacrifices depend. The voice tells Peter to "listen to him"; the most recent thing Jesus has said has concerned his Passion and the necessity of taking up the cross to follow him. Peter denied the necessity of the Cross in the prior passage, and Jesus taught him and the other disciples about its very necessity for himself and for them.

Here the same pattern is found. Peter is enamored by glory in the moment, but the voice reminds him of the Cross, the only possible route to glory. Triumph will come in resurrection, but only through the crucifixion. Jesus signals that resurrection subtly when he touches the three disciples and tells them in spite of their "awe" to "rise" (Matt 17:6–7); the glory Jesus displays shall be theirs at their resurrection. In lifting up their eyes and seeing Jesus alone (17:8), we have a hint of the Beatific Vision, when *coram Deo*, face to face with God, we will behold God and the Lamb for all eternity.

MATTHEW 17:9A, 10–13: SATURDAY OF THE SECOND WEEK OF ADVENT

Following this revelation, Jesus and the disciples descend the mountain. In doing so they move from glory to Cross, just as the Transfiguration was followed by the heavenly voice adverting their attention to Jesus's sacrificial mission as a new Isaac, as Jesus now hints at the suffering of John the Baptist and his own suffering as Son of man (Matt 17:12).

Jesus and the triad having returned to the larger group of disciples, he forbids them from mentioning the vision until after the resurrection (Matt 17:9; the lectionary omits the relevant part of this verse). The reason lies in the dangers inherent in a theology of glory: reports of the splendorous vision might negate the awareness of the necessity of the Cross. The disciples then ask why the scribes teach that Elijah must come first. The scriptural answer is found in Malachi 4:5–6 (English; in the Hebrew Old Testament it is 3:23–24): the Lord God promises that Elijah (who was taken up to heaven without dying) would return "before the great and terrible day of the LORD."

So it's not surprising that the scribes would teach that Elijah must return first. What is surprising is that Jesus teaches that Elijah has already in fact come, but "they did not know him, but did to him whatever they pleased" (Matt 17:12a). The disciples come to understand then that Jesus "was speaking to them of John the Baptist" (Matt 17:13); Elijah has come in the person of John the Baptist (Matt 3:4 alludes to 2 Kings 1:8, presenting John dressed very much like Elijah). John of course suffered imprisonment and summary execution at the whim of a craven ruler in power, thanks to Rome; so too will Jesus, and so Jesus mentions that "also the Son of man will suffer at their hands" (Matt 17:12b). Jesus's forerunner John endured the utmost for his witness, as will Jesus, and unstated but implied given the context (think of the teaching on the Cross in 16:21–18 and the subtle reminder in 17:5) is that followers of Jesus must suffer too.

MATTHEW 17:14–20: SATURDAY WEEK 18

As the action descends from the mountain, with its revelation of divine glory in the Transfiguration, more characters come into view. The Transfiguration was witnessed only by the inner triad of Peter, James, and John, and then Jesus's teaching about John the Baptist being the coming of Elijah was given to all the disciples, and now the action returns to the crowds (Matt 17:14a).

A man comes to Jesus and kneels low before him, and begs for help for his epileptic son, who often falls into fire and water (Matt 17:14–15); the disciples couldn't heal the boy (17:16). Jesus now speaks of the disciples in terms of the faithless Israelites in the wilderness: "O faithless and perverse generation, how long am I to be with you? How long am I to bear with you?" (17:17; see Deut 32:5, 20). Just as Moses descended the mountain to find the faithless people engaging in the perversity of worshipping the golden calf (see Exod 32), Jesus has descended the mountain to find his disciples failing in their fundamental mission.

Jesus bids the boy be brought to him (Matt 17:17b), and casts the demon out of the boy (17:18). The disciples ask why they could not perform the exorcism (17:19), and Jesus informs them it is because of their "little faith" (17:20a), a phrase already applied to them in 8:26, 14:31, and 16:8. Their failure here provides opportunity for positive teaching: Jesus says to them, "For truly, I say to you, if you have faith as a grain of mustard seed, you will say to this mountain, 'Move from hence to yonder place,' and it will move; and nothing will be impossible to you" (17:20). Just as the mustard seed grows into a great tree (see 13:31–32), so too will faith the size of a mustard seed do great things.

Now in Matthew's Gospel faith does not automatically

work wonders (Mark's Gospel is much more suggestive on that point, even seeming to restrict Jesus's power to do wonders if people lack faith; see Mark 6:5–6). The power to do wonders is a gift of God, delegated to those who have faith, but at all times subject to God's will. So we ought to be careful of thinking that someone is failing in faith if they pray and no good result is seen. (One also ought to notice here that it's Jesus's disciples who are failing here, the Apostles, who are supposed to go and work wonders for the sake of mission; what applies to the disciples in Matthew's Gospel does not necessarily apply to all Christians, an obvious example being that the keys given to Peter simply aren't given to all Christians.) On the other hand, in the West, at least, many of us live lives of comfort with a domesticated faith, and that sort of faith does not move mountains. We would do well to beg God for a supernatural infusion of faith, so that in our love our prayers might be effective for others, that they might come to hope.

Further, Matthew 17:21—"But this kind never comes out except by prayer and fasting"—isn't found in many major manuscripts, and so English translations generally relegate it to mention in a footnote, but it merits consideration. First, the verse has been part of many versions of Matthew's Gospel the Church has used over the long ages. Second, it accords with the general scriptural witness; in Matthew's Gospel, Jesus assumes his followers *will* fast (6:16–18, even if the disciples are not fasting because Jesus is with them, 9:14–15), and Jesus himself fasted forty days and nights before his struggle with Satan in the wilderness (4:2). Third, the experiences of the spiritually mature through the ages demonstrate that effective prayer is powered by fasting. In our own day in *Evangelium Vitae*, Pope St. John Paul II wrote:

Jesus himself has shown us by his own example that prayer and fasting are the first and most effective weapons against the forces of evil (cf. Mt 4:1–11). As he taught his disciples, some demons cannot be driven out except in this way (cf. Mk 9:29). Let us therefore discover anew the humility and the courage to pray and fast so that power from on high will break down the walls of lies and deceit: the walls which conceal from the sight of so many of our brothers and sisters the evil of practices and laws which are hostile to life. May this same power turn their hearts to resolutions and goals inspired by the civilization of life and love.[3]

The demons of the culture of death, powered in our age by Gnostic ideology, come out only by prayer and fasting.

MATTHEW 17:22–27: MONDAY WEEK 19

In very terse language, Jesus now delivers a second Passion prediction: "The Son of man is to be delivered into the hands of men, and they will kill him, and he will be raised on the third day" (Matt 17:22–23a). There are no details here about scribes, Pharisees, elders, chief priests, or Gentiles, just the bare facts of Jesus's coming Passion. We're told that the disciples "were greatly distressed" (17:23b). On one hand, that's understandable, given that Jesus has said twice now that he is to die. On the other hand, the Passion prediction ends not in death but in resurrection, and the passage seems to imply that Jesus's closing line about the resurrection didn't register with

---

[3] Pope St. John Paul II, Encyclical Letter on the Value and Inviolability of Human Life *Evangelium Vitae* (March 25, 1995), §100, http:// w2.vatican.va/content/john-paul-ii/en/encyclicals/documents/hf_jp-ii_ enc_25031995_evangelium-vitae.html.

them. In prior passages, Peter and the disciples are at risk of bypassing the Cross and going straight to glory. Here it's the opposite: all they hear is the word of the Cross, missing that after crucifixion comes resurrection.

This Passion prediction is followed immediately by a passage concerning whether Jesus pays the "temple tax." The juxtaposition is deliberate: Jesus will be killed, finally, for shutting down the temple temporarily (Mathew 21:12–17), and so the temple finds mention now, but the story will also show Jesus to be an obedient and loyal Jew.

The temple tax is rooted in Exodus 30:11–16, in which the Lord through Moses required every male over twenty years of age to pay a half-shekel when a census occurred for the maintenance of the temple. By Jesus's day that seems to have become an annual requirement (a practice that seems to have started after the return from the Babylonian Exile in the late sixth century BC; see Neh 10:32–33). It would have been collected at pilgrimage festivals, but how often Jews far away in the Diaspora (in, say, Italy) would have paid is unclear. Depending on the era, the half-shekel tax (equivalent to a Greek *didrachma*, the very word Matthew's Gospel uses in 17:24b) was somewhere between a half-day and two days's wages for a laborer.

So the collectors of the tax approach Peter and ask him if his "teacher" pays the tax (Matt 17:24). Remember, "teacher" in Matthew's Gospel is often used by those hostile to Jesus (see 9:11, 22:16, 22:24), though Jesus uses it of himself as well (23:8, 26:18). The question, then, is likely not innocent. Peter, without really knowing, it seems, simply replies, "Yes" (17:25a).

Jesus somehow knows about this exchange already: "And when he came home, Jesus spoke to [Peter] *first*" (17:25b, emphasis mine) and poses a question to him, calling him

THE PASSION AND THE GLORY

Simon: "What do you think, Simon? From whom do kings of the earth take toll or tribute? From their sons or from others?" (17:25b). Simon Peter gives the obvious response: "From others" (17:26a), and Jesus draws the moral: "Then the sons are free" (17:26b). For now, until the tearing of the veil signifying the departure of the deity from the sanctuary (27:51a), the temple remains the dwelling place of God the Father. Jesus is his ultimate Son, and Simon Peter and the other disciples are also sons. They should therefore be exempt from paying the temple tax, for royal fathers do not tax their sons.

But Jesus, to avoid scandal, instructs Simon Peter to pay the tax, which he'll obtain not from Jesus's or the disciples's funds but through a miracle: "[G]o to the sea and cast a hook, and take the first fish that comes up, and when you open its mouth you will find a shekel; take that and give it to them for me and for yourself" (Matt 17:27). So in point of fact, neither Jesus nor Simon Peter actually pays the tax; God the Father provides a coin for them (a *statēr*, equivalent to a shekel or to two *didrachma*), demonstrating that the sons truly are exempt from the strictures of the Old Law and its interpretation under the reign of the messianic New Law brought by God's Son, Jesus the Christ.

CHAPTER 14

✝

THE CHURCH DISCIPLINE
DISCOURSE

MATTHEW 18:1–5, 10, 12–14: TUESDAY OF
WEEK 19 IN ORDINARY TIME / TUESDAY OF
THE SECOND WEEK OF ADVENT (18:12–14) /
HOLY GUARDIAN ANGELS (OCTOBER 2; 18:1,
5–10)

WE NOW COME TO THE FOURTH OF THE FIVE great
dominical discourses in Matthew's Gospel, which in this
instance is tied to what has come before: "At that time," we
are told—just after the passage about the temple tax—the disciples ask, "Who is the greatest in the kingdom of heaven?"
(Matt 18:1). Perhaps the dominance of Peter in the prior two
chapters provoked the question, as Simon Peter received the
keys to the kingdom of heaven and as he was the one involved
in the question about the temple tax; certainly the disciples
were prone to jealousy and conflict and the seeking of glory,
honor, and position (see 20:20–28, the request of James and

John, delivered by their mother, to sit at Jesus's right and left side in glory).

Jesus has already delivered teaching on this question once, at the outset of the Sermon on the Mount: "Whoever then relaxes one of the least of these commandments and teaches men so, shall be called least in the kingdom of heaven; but he who does them and teaches them shall be called great in the kingdom of heaven" (Matt 5:19). To be great, then, means obeying Jesus and teaching others to do likewise.

And Jesus teaches humility. Humility is not groveling, nor regarding oneself as worthless, nor cultivating inappropriate feelings of shame; that's humiliation. Rather, humility is knowing exactly where one stands in relationship to God and neighbor. We stand as creatures made in the image of God, fallen but redeemable, as Christians, as sons and daughters of God. Jesus now provides an example of that humility in the figure of the child: "Truly, I say to you, unless you turn and become like children, you will never enter the kingdom of heaven. Whoever humbles himself like this child, he is the greatest in the kingdom of heaven" (Matt 18:3–4).

Many will say that the child in antiquity was a figure of no account, that the concept of childhood is a recent invention.[1] Children were seen as relatively cheap labor in agrarian societies, needing to be housed and fed but not paid, since they were members of the family. Certainly high infant mortality (usually well north of fifty percent until recently) also could

---

[1] Philippe Ariès published *L'Enfant et la vie familiale sous l'ancien régime* in 1960 (English: *Centuries of Childhood: A Social History of the Family* [New York: Random House, 1962]). The book has been overly influential, and its influence was reinforced through its appropriation in Edward Shorter's *The Making of the Modern Family* (New York: Basic Books, 1977). Ariès argued that modernity's advances in medicine, industrialization, and education led to the invention of childhood in the seventeenth century, though many now are skeptical of Ariès's work.

have led to an attitude of detachment. But history witnesses that premodern children were loved.[2]

In fact, childhood and the esteem of children likely owes itself to Judeo-Christian faith. The Old Testament bears witness to children as a blessing,[3] and Gospel passages such as this one here in Matthew's Gospel use children as positive examples. Given antiquity's seeming disdain for children and childhood, the Christian esteem for children was nothing short of a revolution.[4] So with regard to the present passage, one might contrast the pagan view of children with the Judeo-Christian view; it is not true that Jews and Christians did not value children in antiquity. Jesus here is drawing on, not contradicting, the Jewish view of children.

For Jesus, then, children are symbols of humility and receptivity, in contrast to the disciples's concern for honor and position. Jesus then says, "Whoever receives one such child in my name receives me" (Matt 18:5). So on one hand, Jesus's words bolster the child: it's not just that he's used a child as an example, but now children are imbued with the presence of Jesus himself. On the other hand, if the child is

---

[2] Martin Luther lost a daughter, Magdalena, aged thirteen years; for an account, see James M. Kittelson, *Luther the Reformer: The Story of the Man and His Career*, 2nd ed. (Minneapolis: Fortress, 2016), 237. Shakespeare's lines from *King John*, Act III, Scene IV, composed not long after Shakespeare's only son Hamnet died in 1596 at eleven years old, also bear witness to love for children in an age of high infant and child mortality: "Grief fills the room up of my empty child / Lies in his bed, walks up and down with me / Puts on his pretty looks, repeats his words / Remembers me of all his gracious parts / Stuffs out his vacant garments with his form."

[3] See, Rachel and Leah's competitive desire for children in Genesis 29–30 and Israel's lament for his sons, thought lost, in Genesis 37:3, 42:36, and 43:14; see also Psalm 37:26, 103:13, 113:9, 128:3, and especially 127:3–5.

[4] See O. M. Bakke, When Children Became People: The Birth of Childhood in Early Christianity (Minneapolis: Augsburg Fortress, 2005); and Marcia Bunge, ed., *The Child in Christian Thought* (Grand Rapids, MI: Eerdmans, 2001).

a picture of a disciple, Jesus's words here mean that receiving a disciple of Jesus is receiving Jesus himself. Jesus is truly present in his disciples.

The lectionary unconscionably omits here Jesus's hard words of judgment (Matt 18:6–9), which is unfortunate; they fit with the theme of the "two ways" in Matthew's Gospel, introduced in the Sermon on the Mount in the teaching about the narrow gate and wide path (7:13–14). Because Jesus is present in disciples, whoever leads one of the "little ones who believe in me to sin" deserves drowning by a donkey's large millstone (18:6), and those leading others into temptations receive Jesus's cry of woe (18:7). Jesus takes the opportunity to reiterate his hyperbolic teaching on dealing with sin as radically, such as necessary by (rhetorically) blinding and maiming oneself to avoid Gehenna (18:8–9; see 5:29–30).

So Jesus advises his disciples to "not despise one of these little ones" (Matt 18:10), and now introduces another reason: their guardian angels who "always behold the face of my Father who is in heaven" (18:10) watch over them. Threat is implied; to lead someone into sin risks a visit from their guardian angel. Yet there is hope for the sinner, either leading or led into temptation. Jesus now speaks of shepherds finding lost sheep, even one out of a hundred who go astray. The restoration of even one involves great rejoicing (Matt 18:12–13), for it is "not the will of my Father who is in heaven that one of these little ones should perish" (18:14).

MATTHEW 18:15–20: TWENTY-THIRD SUNDAY IN ORDINARY TIME / WEDNESDAY WEEK 19

Now we come to the matter of discipline in the community of the Church. Jesus has just spoken words of hope regarding the restoration of sinners, and now he provides the process. If someone sins against you, you are to reveal to him his fault, privately (Matt 18:15a). The attitude is not confrontational, but redemptive. Maybe he'll listen, and if so, the sinner is restored (18:15b). If not, then the situation becomes more public, as now two or three witnesses (following the model of Deut 19:15) are to be brought into the conversation (Matt 18:16). If that fails, then the whole (local) Church is to be informed (18:17a)—still in hopes of restoration—and if this third step fails, "let him be to you as a Gentile and a tax collector" (18:17b). That sounds like stiff judgment, but in the world of Matthew's Gospel, Gentiles and tax collectors are the objects of mission. And so even now, after the seeming failure of the process, the sinner still remains an object of redemption, with Jesus and the community hoping for his reconciliation.

Following this, Jesus repeats his words about binding and loosing (Matt 18:18). The first time Jesus spoke them to Peter alone, using the singular "you" (16:19). Now Jesus employs the plural "you," and so the words are directed to all the Apostles. In this context, binding and loosing refer to excommunication, and the restoration of the excommunicated. Jesus's next words, about the Father doing whatever two on earth request together, likely concern that restoration; even after someone is excommunicated, the Church ought to pray earnestly for their repentance and reestablishment. And such prayers are powered by Jesus, for "where two or three are gathered in my name, there am I in the midst of them" (18:20).

EXCURSUS: DISCIPLINE IN TODAY'S CHURCH

Jesus's teaching in this prior passage (Matt 18:15–20) demands we discuss Church discipline at some length, for discipline is in short supply in the postmodern West, outside but also inside the Church, as the Church has imbibed the spirits of the age.

Prosperity has led to a period of indulgence, in which technological fixes substitute for virtue, fake remedies for the wages of vice. We take a pound of pills instead of the ounce of cure of discipline. We indulge immoderately in food, drink, and sex, and expect pills to save us. And where a sort of discipline is exercised, it's exercised punitively: those in charge wish to show others that they are "taking matters seriously." The late Francis Cardinal George pegged our problem when he on many occasions pointed out that our culture permits everything but forgives nothing, while God and the Church forgive everything but don't permit everything.

And so we let everything go until it is made public that someone has transgressed some new boundary du jour, while our ongoing cultural revolutions, like mythical Saturn eating his sons, devour ever more of their children, and ours. But medicine is no substitute for virtue, and policy is no substitute for discipline. Pills may arrest disease, and policies may channel outcomes, but we remain human, and only the real disciplining of body, mind, and spirit will make us ever more so, truly free to live as we ought under God.

Living tokens of discipline do abide. Every athlete is only free to excel because she has disciplined her body in years of training. Every musician is only free to excel at his instrument because he has disciplined himself in years of practice. Demosthenes was only free to be a great orator because he practiced speaking over the roar of the ocean waves with pebbles on his tongue. What's true for individuals goes for groups as well: crack military units and famous sports teams excel in battle and match because they have practiced corporate discipline.

These examples illustrate the fundamental if forgotten truth about freedom: it depends on discipline. But we in the

West have been convincing ourselves for hundreds of years that freedom is libertinism, the license to break any and all constraints—the constraints of law, tradition, nature, even the constraints of our own bodies. John Stuart Mill famously called for "experiments of living," just like scientists conducted experiments of nature. Today, the coupling of our hyper-powered science (especially in the area of biotechnology) with our fascination with ever more radical experiments of living has resulted in slavery to the spirit of the age, to the fulfillment of raw desire. If we're to have true freedom, then, in which our lives are lived in harmony with nature as ordered by God, we desperately need a recovery of virtue developed through discipline.

This is true of the Church as well as of the individual and of society. Turning from St. Matthew to St. Paul, we find in him the "Apostle of freedom," having famously written in Galatians, "For freedom Christ has set us free" (5:1). But anticipating antinomian misreadings of his letter, he later continues, "[O]nly do not use your freedom as an opportunity for the flesh" (Gal 5:13). Rather, for Paul the end (being "in Christ Jesus") is pursued by "faith working through love" (5:6). Thus, for him, Christian freedom is not freedom from constraints but freedom for virtue, indeed the highest theological virtue of *agapē*, of *caritas*, of love in the community that is the very body of Christ, the Church.

Love in Christian community requires discipline, both to keep individual members on the path of virtue and, conversely, to keep the community living in the purity of love. An unavoidable reciprocity obtains between body and members, sustained by charity on the way to glory. And so ultimately, discipline in the Church is meant to be remedial, salvific, to keep and bring everyone deeper in Christ on the pilgrim way of salvation. Conversely, the laxity of indiscipline has its obvious results: damage to Christian life and witness, and ultimately the loss of souls. However, the exercise of discipline is difficult and has its dangers. Just as a coach or parent can misread a situation and misapply discipline, so too can ecclesiastical authorities. Discipline is messy, and mistakes are made.

In fact, some of the greatest saints and even doctors of the Church have suffered under errant discipline. St. Hildegard of Bingen, now a Doctor of the Church, was placed under interdict along with her convent for a time in the final year of her life, having permitted an excommunicated man to be buried on the grounds of her convent (for she had believed him to have repented and have received the sacraments before his death). St. Mary MacKillop found herself the victim of intrigue, perhaps involving the scandal of sexual abuse, enduring excommunication for about six months when she declined to agree with her bishop's request to revise the constitution of her order, the Josephites. (He had her excommunication lifted while on his deathbed.) St. Padre Pio was forbidden from public celebration of the Mass and from hearing confessions, as well as responding to correspondence for some years, until Pius XI began to restore his faculties in 1933; Pius XII later worked to rehabilitate his reputation. Whole nations and city-states have been put under the ban for political reasons, and at one point during the Great Western Schism in the context of the Avignon papacies, it can be argued that all of Europe was excommunicated, given differing loyalties to different popes and (as judged later) antipopes. In many dioceses there were even competing sets of clergy loyal to different papal claimants.

And a thought arises: What if Luther hadn't been excommunicated so roughly, but dealt with gently in a longer attempt to keep him formally in the fold? Luther's fiery, uncompromising temperament would have kept the prospect of ultimate success unlikely—short of Rome affirming his theology—but dropping the hammer of *Exsurge Domine* (the papal bull of excommunication) on him most certainly made reconciliation impossible. In retrospect, the last chance to head off the Reformation was for the pious Charles V to have had him burned at the Diet of Worms, but Charles was too honest and charitable a soul to engage in that drastic solution, and so he gave Luther several days's safe passage to escape. Thus the Reformation as we know it launched like a rocket, with Luther safely hidden in the Wartburg and later finding enduring protection in Wittenberg while he wrote and taught freely.

Discipline is thus risky, and hindsight reveals instances in history in which it's been poorly and wrongly applied. Nevertheless, there are also instances in which it proved effective. St. Ambrose excommunicated Theodosius I—the very emperor who had made Nicene Christianity the official religion of the Roman Empire—after the latter engaged in a brutal reprisal, having seven thousand Thessalonians killed for the murder of the military garrison's commander; and the emperor repented. Also, during the intrigues of the Investiture Controversy, Pope Gregory VII managed to have the Holy Roman Emperor Henry IV excommunicated, which was lifted after Henry spent three days in penitence in the snow at Canossa. Closer to our own day, during the difficult days of desegregation in the South, New Orleans's Archbishop Joseph Rummel planned to integrate the Catholic schools, and when segregationist Catholics in government and their supporters began considering a state law barring racial integration in Catholic schools, Rummel dropped the hammer of excommunication to great effect. *Abusus non tollit usum*; abuse does not prohibit use, which is an ancient, Latin way of saying we shouldn't throw out the baby with the bathwater.

Today we sometimes seem to have the problem of exercising discipline according to the world's standards. Priests who appear "intolerant" or "divisive" by teaching and exercising discipline according to the words of the Catechism and canon law—say, refusing sacraments where good warrant exists to do so—can find themselves removed from their ministerial assignments, while others who make statements in support of certain progressive agendas at odds with Catholic teaching persist in peace.

The aftermath of the Second Vatican Council left the Church in a situation of crisis regarding practice and belief, as myriad surveys and statistics reveal.[5] Well before the post-conciliar period, Blessed John Henry Cardinal Newman prophesied a coming age of apostasy, thanks to the tide of modern liberalism sweeping even into the Church:

> For thirty, forty, fifty years, I have resisted to the best of my powers the spirit of Liberalism in religion. Never did Holy Church need champions against it more sorely than now, when, alas! it is an error over-spreading, as a snare, the whole earth. . . . Liberalism in religion is the doctrine that there is no positive truth in religion, but that one creed is as good as another, and this is the teaching which is gaining

---

[5] For a statistical picture of the collapse of American Catholicism since the Second Vatican Council, see Christian Smith, *Young Catholic America: Emerging Adults In, Out Of, and Gone From the Church* (New York: Oxford University Press, 2014), https://www.pewresearch.org/fact-tank/2019/08/05/transubstantiation-eucharist-u-s-catholics/. A very recent Pew survey revealed only 31% of Catholics believe that "during Catholic Mass, the bread and wine actually become the body and blood of Jesus"; the other 69% believe the Eucharist a mere symbol. The statistics for regular mass-goers within the broader category of self-identified Catholics are better, as 63% of them affirm the Church's teaching on the Eucharist, and yet that statistic itself is cause for concern, not celebration.

substance and force daily. It is inconsistent with any recognition of any religion as true. It teaches that all are to be tolerated, for all are matters of opinion. Revealed religion is not a truth, but a sentiment and a taste; not an objective fact, not miraculous; and it is the right of each individual to make it say just what strikes his fancy. . . . There never was a device of the Enemy so cleverly framed and with such promise of success. And already it has answered to the expectations which have been formed of it. It is sweeping into its own ranks great numbers of able, earnest, virtuous men, elderly men of approved antecedents, young men with a career before them.[6]

And it has arrived in our day with full force, as Catholics prominent and obscure reject the Church's express, humane teaching on the nature of the human person. Catholic Ireland's Eighth Amendment, which served to give unborn persons the protection of law, was repealed by a lopsided margin in the 2018 referendum; life was routed. And in our own United States the situation is no better. Former Vice President Joe Biden—a regular mass-goer who once famously asserted his piety by saying, "The next Republican that tells me I'm not religious, I'm going to shove my rosary beads down their throat"[7]—officiated a same-sex wedding in the waning months of his tenure as Vice President. House Minority

---

[6] The speech was made upon the announcement of his being named a Cardinal and delivered May 12, 1879: John Henry Newman, "Biglietto Speech, Rome," in *Addresses to Cardinal Newman with His Replies*, ed. W. P. Neville (London: Longmans, Green and Co., 1905), 61–70, at 64, 67–69.

[7] Kathryn Jean Lopez, "Biden Goes for the Jugular," National Review, May 1, 2007, 2:59 p.m. EDT, https://www.nationalreview.com/corner/biden-goes-jugular-kathryn-jean-lopez/.

Leader Nancy Pelosi, mother of five children and a practicing Catholic, routinely presents herself as a committed Catholic but does all in her political power to advance a proabortion and antifamily agenda.

It's easy to sit in our armchairs and wish we were the ones calling the plays. But none of us laity should want the real burdens borne by bishops (and the best of the clergy do not seek such burdens either but simply obey the Holy Father if he appoints them). Nevertheless, given that discipline is necessary for any individual or group or society to function to its fullest, it's worth considering whether the crisis of our present moment invites reconsideration of the value of the practice of redemptive discipline, as Jesus has called for in our last passage. All renewal in the Church is sparked by and grounded in the sources of Scripture and Tradition, and the source of Scripture itself provides warrant and witness for the exercise of discipline.

Practicing Christians find themselves struck by just how perennial Scripture is, as we today belong to the same Church founded by Jesus and led by his chosen Apostles. St. Paul was also an apostle, chosen by the risen Jesus, and I've often thought that his first letter to the Corinthians might as well have been written to the Americans. Like us, the Corinthians engaged in the sort of theological liberalism Newman decried; instead of using the gospel of Jesus's death and resurrection as the lens to understand and judge their Greco-Roman thinking and behavior, they tried to adapt the Christian message to their own commitments to their culture. Like us today, they needed a conversion of their imagination. And so St. Paul writes to them, teaching them the necessity of discipline and instructing them to exercise it in a way that matches the material substance of what Jesus prescribes in Matthew's Gospel.

The Corinthians's problems were not simply similar to

ours formally, but also materially. Like us, they suffered confusion about the human person, specifically about the body. Good Greco-Romans (even the Jews among them, having imbibed the spirit of Hellenism) thought the body was a problem and weren't sure what to do with it. And so some of them engaged in sexual immorality and drunkenness and even went so far as to deny the resurrection of the dead, even that of Jesus himself. But Paul wrote to them to remind them that purity of doctrine and body are requisite for real peace and unity in the body of the Church.

For St. Paul, the Church is simply one. In 1 Corinthians 3:16–17, he uses an image of the Church as a spiritual temple, undoubtedly calling to mind the temple in Jerusalem as an integral structure dedicated to holiness and sacrifice:

> Do you not know that you all are God's temple and that God's Spirit dwells in the midst of all of you? If any one destroys God's temple, God will destroy him. For God's temple is holy, and that temple you all together are.

I've adjusted the RSV (Second Catholic Edition) translation to make clear the plural "you" in the Greek. Paul is saying that the corporate body of the Church has the Holy Spirit in its midst, and destruction of that holy temple invites condemnation.

Two things threaten the Church's unity: dissent and sin. Addressing the first, St. Paul appeals to the Corinthians, demanding that "all of you agree and that there be no dissensions among you, but that you be united in the same mind and the same judgment" (1 Cor 1:10). Doctrinal disagreement involves factionalism, and the Corinthians divided into groups, rallying themselves around the figures of Paul,

Apollos, Cephas (Peter), and Christ (1:12). Paul reminds them then that there is no other to rally round than Christ and that it's the fact of his cruciform death that puts an end to all human speculation (1:18–25). In essence, Paul is saying that the Corinthians are to accept the Gospel and see everything through it, not contort it, twist it, adapt it in accord with the Greco-Roman spirit of their age.

Addressing the second threat (sin), St. Paul later confronts a horrifying instance of sexual sin. "It is actually reported that there is immorality among you, and of a kind that is not found even among pagans; for a man is living with his father's wife" (1 Cor 5:1; perhaps his stepmother, perhaps his biological mother). Like incipient antinomian Gnostics, they are boasting about their freedom in Christ from the law (5:2, 6). Paul, however, insists on redemptive discipline: "When you are assembled, and my spirit is present, with the power of our Lord Jesus, you are to deliver this man to Satan for the destruction of the flesh, that his spirit may be saved in the day of the Lord Jesus" (5:4–5). The Church is to be pure, so Paul insists the man be excommunicated from the Church—that's what delivering him to Satan means: putting him outside the body of the Church, where Satan has his domain. But it's redemptive: Paul insists on this discipline so that the man might ultimately be saved, not damned.

The passage also presents overtones of the Eucharist, which Jewish ritual sacrifice prefigured: "Cleanse out the old leaven that you may be a new lump, as you really are unleavened. For Christ, our paschal lamb, has been sacrificed" (1 Cor 5:7). It's no accident that later on St. Paul will credit disunity and sin with causing certain Corinthian Christians to suffer illness and death because they're taking the Eucharist unworthily (see 1 Cor 11:17–34). Factions and drunkenness have made a mockery of the Cross of Christ that the Eucharist presents, and some are paying the price. For St. Paul, as for Jesus and St. Matthew, discipline involves receiving the Eucharist worthily—in a state of grace—and so here, too, the Corinthians are to discipline themselves lest the Lord Jesus discipline them further. Even then, as it is in Matthew 18, the Lord's discipline is redemptive: "when we are judged by the Lord, we are chastened so that we may not be condemned along with the world" (1 Cor 11:32).

Unity and purity are necessary for the Church to be fully herself, and St. Paul, among other scriptural witnesses, teaches that discipline is necessary for the Church to achieve that unity and purity. Unity nowadays often appears as an exercise in false concord, however, a unity of appearance, a papering of differences, letting sins and crimes slide while trying to hide them. True unity and purity require the virtue of courage, that we might dare to discipline, from the parish to the Vatican. Then the Church will be more fully herself, holy and pure, a radiant bride without spot or blemish (see Eph 5:27).

MATTHEW 18:21–35: TWENTY-FOURTH SUNDAY IN ORDINARY TIME / TUESDAY OF THE THIRD WEEK OF LENT / THURSDAY WEEK 19 (18:21–19:1)

The theme of forgiveness for the sinner continues as Peter asks Jesus how often he is supposed to forgive his brother. Peter suggests seven times (Matt 18:21), the number of perfection, as it happens, and in any event a large number; most of us have a hard time forgiving someone twice, much less seven times. Jesus responds by upping Peter's number: "I do not say to you seven times, but seventy times seven" (18:22), or, possibly, seventy-seven times. In either case, Jesus's number is hyperbolic, meaning that forgiveness should have no limits, because God's forgiveness is limitless; as God forgives, we are to go and do likewise.

The Parable of the Unforgiving Servant makes that point by way of threat. Jesus tells of a king looking to settle accounts with his servants (Matt 18:23). One owes the king ten thousand talents, presumably of gold (18:24), and a talent was worth six thousand denarii, the denarius being roughly a days's wage for a laborer. A laborer might have 15,000–18,000 working days in a lifetime, so the total amount is in the neighborhood of sixty million denarii. Jesus here is using hyperbole in a shocking way, as he often does in his parables: no king would ever let one of his ministers become so indebted, and it's hard to imagine what one man would do with so much money, short of buying a Roman province on the order of Egypt.

The king orders the man and his family sold into slavery (Matt 18:25), which was not uncommon (see Neh 5:4–5). But the man "fell on his knees," begging to be spared and promising to pay the debt (Matt 18:26). The king relents and forgives the debt, even though the man did not ask for that (18:27). Clearly we have a picture here of God the Father, who forgives without limit, who doesn't expect us to repay what we owe him, for we never could; what could the creature repay the Creator, to whom the creature owes his very existence, or the sinner the Savior, to whom he owes his redemption, purchased on the gibbet of the Cross?

But the servant does not go and do likewise. He finds a fellow servant who owed him one hundred denarii, a manageable if large sum, and seizes him "by the throat," demanding what he is owed (Matt 18:28). This servant falls on his knees, just like the first servant did before the king, and begs for time to pay the debt (18:29). Unlike the king, the first servant refuses and has the second servant imprisoned "till he should pay the debt" (18:30). It's not clear from history whether "debtor's prisons" existed as they did later in (say) England and France, where one could work off a debt without incurring more debt (usually debtors keep running up debts, borrowing from Peter to pay Paul, as it were). It may also be that the line is ironic: the man will never get out, for debts cannot be paid from prison, as one can't work.

Other servants report the matter to the king, their "lord" (the usage of "lord" suggests God is ultimately in view), for they were distressed (Matt 18:31). The king then calls for the first servant and lays into him: "You wicked servant! I forgave you all that debt because you besought me; and should not you have had mercy on your fellow servant, as I had mercy on you?" (18:32–33). The king then has this first wicked servant jailed "till he should pay all his debt" (18:34); whether or not one could pay one's debts off in prison, this amounts to a life sentence, for the figure of sixty million denarii is astronomical. The man is effectively condemned.

And so the point of the parable is a warning of final condemnation: "So also my heavenly Father will do to every one of you, if you do not forgive your brother from your heart" (Matt 18:35). Jesus here reinforces his teaching on forgiveness delivered in the Sermon on the Mount as the didactic coda to the Lord's Prayer: "For if you forgive men their trespasses, your heavenly Father also will forgive you; but if you do not forgive men their trespasses, neither will your Father forgive your trespasses" (6:14–15). We are to be perfect as our heavenly Father is perfect (5:48), and that means forgiving as God forgives, which the Lord Jesus himself makes possible as we share his yoke (11:28–30).

CHAPTER 15

✟

JESUS THE CHRIST COMES
TO JERUSALEM

MATTHEW 19:3–12: FRIDAY WEEK 19

JESUS HAS "FINISHED THESE SAYINGS" (Matt 19:1a), indicating the fourth great block of teaching has come to conclusion. Jesus now departs Galilee and begins making his final journey to Jerusalem by way of the "region of Judea beyond the Jordan" (19:1b) which puts him east so as to avoid Samaria, as many Jews did when walking to Jerusalem. On this journey Jesus will encounter opposition and also provide teaching on discipleship, often as a pattern in which an encounter leads to a question from the disciples; such is in the present passage, in which the Pharisees pose a question to Jesus, and in the story of the rich young man (19:16–30).

Jesus is approached by Pharisees who "test" him by asking him, "Is it lawful to divorce one's wife for any cause?" (Matt 19:3) The question is hostile, as it comes from the Pharisees, who already have conspired to kill Jesus (12:14) and who

323

want to put him to the test, as Satan did (4:1). Jewish teachers had a range of opinion on when divorce was permissible, as Moses seemed to permit divorce in Deuteronomy 24:1–4. In that passage Moses assumes divorce is for some "indecency" and simply forbids remarrying a spouse if she has been remarried in the interim.

Rabbinic interpretation focused on what counted as "indecency" and thus on which grounds one could divorce his wife.[1] Two major schools of thought centered on the great rabbis Hillel and Shammai. Hillel, the liberal, was known for broad interpretations, and he taught a man could divorce his wife simply for making a bad meal. This became the common position in Judaism. Shammai, the conservative, taught that a man could divorce his wife only for sexual transgression, which would include of course adultery but also being found a non-virgin on the wedding night. And a later rabbi, Akiba, who would hail Bar Kochba the messiah in the final, fateful revolt against Rome (AD 132–135) and wind up crucified for it, taught that a man could divorce his wife if he simply found some other woman fairer.

Jesus's answer goes straight back to Genesis 1–2 and thus leapfrogs not only Deuteronomy 24 but also Genesis 3, with radical implications. Jesus alludes to Genesis 1:27 ("male and female he created them") and quotes Genesis 2:24 ("Therefore a man leaves his father and his mother and cleaves to his wife, and they become one flesh"): "Have you not read that he who made them from the beginning made them male and female, and said, 'For this reason a man shall leave his father and mother and be joined to his wife, and the two shall become one'?" (Matt 19:4–5).[2] Jesus draws the moral: "So they are no

---

[1] See *m. Gitah* 9:10, and also *Yer. Soṭah* 1.1.16b.

[2] There are no quotation marks in ancient manuscripts; those were invented in the fifteenth century with the rise of the printing press. Modern transla-

longer two but one. What therefore God has joined together, let not man put asunder" (19:6). Thus, Jesus gives a resounding "no" to the Pharisees's hostile question: God joins man and woman in marriage, and so man may not dissolve marriage.

The Pharisees ask the obvious follow-up question: Why did Moses then permit divorce (Matt 19:7)? Jesus's answer is brutal: "For your hardness of heart Moses allowed you to divorce your wives, but from the beginning it was not so" (19:8). Jesus suggests Deuteronomy is a devolution from the abiding standard in Genesis.

It's important here to see that Deuteronomy is indeed a second law (*deutero*, "second"; *nomos*, "law"). We ought to divide the Torah into two: The first part consists of positive law meant to make the people righteous, to love God and neighbor truly. But after the wilderness generation shows themselves recalcitrant, engaging in everything sinful from idolatry to rebellion, God decides to give them a lesser law, a negative law, a law of restraint, codified in Deuteronomy[3] after the idolatry and exogamy (marrying of pagan women) in Numbers 25.[4] Instead of making the people good, the law now

---

tors and editors of the New Testament thus have to decide whether a string of words matching something from the Old Testament is an allusion, or a more obvious quotation. The determination is made on the basis of how many words are shared, with fewer suggesting an allusion and more a quotation, as well as obvious verbal markers, like mention of a source—an example being the formula quotations, such as "This happened to fulfill what was said by Isaiah the prophet . . ." It's possible, then, that in Matthew 19:4 Jesus is not only alluding to but quoting from Genesis 1:27: God "made them male and female."

[3] When St. Paul is most critical of the Law, it's usually Deuteronomy he has in view. And in general he suggests the Law was not in fact given to make the people righteous: "if a law had been given which could make alive, then righteousness would indeed be by the law" (Gal 3:21).

[4] See Hahn and Bergsma, "What Laws Were 'Not Good,'" who employ the twofold division of the Torah to explain what Ezekiel meant when the Lord said, "I gave them laws that were not good" (Ezek 20:25).

will prevent the people from falling headlong into sin.

So for a people suffering from hardness of heart (the worst condition one can come into, according to the Bible; it was Pharaoh's chronic malady) with men seeking to escape their marriages, if there's no mechanism for divorce, then women are at risk of being murdered or simply tossed into the street. With a mechanism for divorce, under the conditions of sin, women would be spared the worst, and retain some legal status (a *divorcée* having a certificate) and the hope of remarriage.[5]

This being part of the Old Law, Jesus in his authority lays down the New Law: "And I say to you: whoever divorces his wife, except for unchastity [Greek, *porneia*], and marries another, commits adultery; and he who marries a divorced woman, commits adultery" (Matt 19:9). Going back to the time of the early Church, this has been understood to forbid remarriage in the case of regrettable separation, what used to be known nearer our own day as "separation of bed and board," in situations where husband and wife simply couldn't be under the same roof for grave reasons. That remarriage amounts to adultery involves the assumption that marriage, once contracted, is indissoluble, in accord with Jesus's words, "What therefore God has joined together, let not man put asunder" (19:6). Separation is a possibility, but divorce a metaphysical, sacramental impossibility.

The exception clause has merited much discussion, of course. Why does Jesus here, as in Matthew 5:32, seem to provide an exception to his bracing, definitive, clear teaching

---

[5] Protestants permit divorce because they generally have had a pessimistic view of human nature, similar to that envisioned under the second law: if it is hard for people to change, then troubled marriages have little hope of improving, and thus (so the logic goes) it is better for people to divorce than be miserable.

that marriage is indissoluble? The best answer is that *porneia* in the exception clause refers to the forbidden degrees of consanguinity in Leviticus 18 and 20—that is, Jesus is referring to supposed marriages to close relatives, which sometimes happened among pagans. So if someone is "married" in pagan understanding to, say, one's sibling or one's aunt or uncle, it simply couldn't have been a true marriage in the first place; it was invalid from the outset. In that case, then, one can "divorce" one's partner according to pagan law (Greco-Roman, for all practical purposes) since there never was an indissoluble bond. The same would, and does, obtain even today in mission territories with regard to polygamy.

Reading the exception clause this way has the advantage of seeing consistency in Jesus's words; he does not provide such a stark, ironclad teaching only to break it a few sentences later. Had he done so—that is, if the word *porneia* in the exception clause referred merely to adultery, for instance—Jesus would simply be echoing the position of Shammai. If this were the case, the Pharisees likely wouldn't have had too much of a problem with him, and in which case his radical references to Genesis 1–2 would not make sense; he ought simply to have explained his position vis-a-vis other interpreters of Deuteronomy 24.

So Jesus leapfrogs Deuteronomy 24, and in his authority declares a definitive understanding of marriage in accord with Genesis 1–2. In doing so, however, he also leapfrogs Genesis 3, the account of the Fall of humanity, upon which Western Christians have developed their concept of Original Sin. And so we're confronted with the question of just how much Original Sin affects us, especially as regards our married lives. In going straight to Genesis 1–2, Jesus effectively teaches that marriage can be lived according to its original structure and intent in Eden, even after the Fall. And again, as with perfection (Matt 5:38) and forgiveness (18:35), one can do what seems impossible—here, staying married to a wife with which one's fallen out of love—because we are yoked to Jesus who carries our burdens with us. And so marriage now becomes sacramental, because Jesus is involved, giving us the power to live the graces of the sacrament.[6]

The disciples respond to him by saying, "If such is the case of a man with his wife, it is not expedient to marry" (Matt 19:10). The rather flat translation of the RSV doesn't convey the note of cynicism in the disciples's response. It is as if they are saying that if divorce is an impossibility, they'd rather not marry in the first place; they'd be stuck with someone. Jesus takes their cynicism and turns it into a teaching moment: "Not all men can receive this precept, but only those to whom it is given" (19:11); remaining unmarried is now raised to the level of a "precept," a teaching, as marriage has been raised to a sacrament.

Jesus now gives a metaphorical rationale, drawing on the familiar figure of the eunuch (a man who has had his testicles removed; Matt 19:12). Some men are born eunuchs, due to a congenital defect, and others are made so by men, either for reasons of punishment or vengeance or for reasons of serving as a minister to a high official, nobility, or royalty (men lacking their testicles were thought no threat to reign or harem). But Jesus is interested in those "who have made themselves eunuchs for the sake of the kingdom of heaven" (19:12). Here Jesus uses a shocking image in a hyperbolic way to teach that some of his followers will renounce sexual relationships for the sake of the kingdom. The passage thus becomes the scriptural basis for historic Christian teaching on celibacy for those practicing continence, such as priests,

---

6 See CCC 1641–1642.

religious, and other consecrated persons.[7]

One detects a slight tension between the opening and closing of this passage. On one hand, Jesus says, "Not all men can receive this precept, but only those to whom it is given" (Matt 19:11). So celibacy for the sake of the kingdom of heaven is a gift, given by God. On the other hand, Jesus closes his words by saying, "He who is able to receive this, let him receive it" (19:12), suggesting that it's something one should aim for if at all possible. For this reason, many ascetics in the early Church (such as St. Jerome) taught that continence should be the norm for all Christians, that in the new age Christians should reproduce spiritually by making converts, not by physical generation of offspring.[8] And yet Jesus's final words also carry the suggestion of gift; his teaching is something to be "receive[d]" as a gift, not something merely chosen as a decision taken. And here, too, against charges that continence and celibacy are unnatural, or too difficult today, it must be replied that Jesus himself provides the graces necessary, if we would but cooperate with them, as he does in regard to marriage. He is God with us (1:23) who has promised to be with us to the end of the age (28:20).

---

[7] Continence is refraining from sexual relations, something all unmarried Christians (such as teenagers) are called to practice. Celibacy is the formal relinquishment of marriage (and thus sexual relations) for the sake of a particular vocation.

[8] Many Church Fathers, including luminaries like St. Augustine (*De bono coniugali* 9–10, 17; *De Genesi ad litteram* 9.7; *De nuptiis et concupiscentia ad Valerium comitem* 1.14) and St. Jerome (*Adversus Helvidium* 20–21), and before them Tertullian (*De anima* 30), argue that procreation belonged to the time of the old covenant, but under the new covenant it was no longer necessary nor desirable; Christians should make spiritual, not literal, children, by making converts and disciples. See Philip Lyndon Reynolds, *Marriage in the Western Church: The Christianization of Marriage During the Patristic and Early Medieval Periods* (Leiden: Brill, 2001), 266–274.

Excursus: Jesus and Homosexuality

In debates over gay marriage, many will observe that Jesus had no express opinion on homosexuality. For instance, Catholic comedian Stephen Colbert once remarked, "I would like to read to you what *the* Jesus said about homosexuality. I would like to, but he never said anything about it."[9]

Colbert's claim is common, and it's effective because it's true: Jesus did not directly address the matter. But it does not follow that Jesus's words and example have no relevance for marriage, sex, and family, nor that modern Christians should approve of gay marriage. A few observations:

First, *Jesus was a Jew who inherited Jewish Scripture and tradition.* Jesus did not drop out of the sky to bring a brand-new set of moral teachings de novo, as if he were some Enlightenment figure like Immanuel Kant attempting to ground a moral system from scratch. If he did, perhaps his apparent lack of attention to sex and sexuality would be striking. But the Jesus of the Gospels—especially Matthew, the First Gospel—is a conservative Jew, as was the so-called historical Jesus behind the Gospels. And whether we're talking about the historical Jesus or the Jesus of the Gospels, Jesus stands well within the breadth of Jewish tradition. Thus, it's not true that things Jesus doesn't spend an inordinate amount of time on or doesn't mention are unimportant. Rather, we should assume that those things in Jewish tradition which Jesus doesn't overturn or reinterpret are assumed. Jesus doesn't outright forbid homosexual practices in the Gospels, but he doesn't have to, because his Judaism did.

---

[9] Meredith Blake, "Late Night: Jesus never said anything about gays, Colbert says," *Los Angeles Times*, May 11, 2012, 8:25 a.m. PDT, https://latimesblogs.latimes.com/showtracker/2012/05/late-night-stephen-colbert-jesus-bible-gay-marriage.html.

Assuming that religion is a matter of prohibitions, in debates over sexuality people often assume that Jesus came simply to forbid certain behaviors, and if he didn't forbid something, it's therefore permitted. The principle would be "Scripture permits anything not expressly forbidden." But why assume that hermeneutical posture? One could also assume that if Jesus didn't positively affirm something, it ought not be done, in which case the principle would be "Scripture forbids anything not expressly enjoined." The fundamental problem consists in assuming that Jesus came simply, or chiefly, to condemn or approve of certain behaviors, as if he were a mere moral teacher and as if the Gospels could be reduced to a mere rulebook for life, a code of ethics. Thinking this way rips the richness of the Gospels to shreds and leaves us with a boring middleclass Jesus, easily exploited by western bourgeois liberals. We'd do better to read Kant on the metaphysics of morals and have more fun enduring his difficult German than to consider such a tedious Jesus.

Second, relative to other positions ancient and modern, Jesus maintains a radical position on marriage, rooting his view in the male-female complementarity of creation. In his teaching on marriage in Matthew 19, as we have seen, Jesus ups the ante over his Jewish contemporaries. Jesus's teaching is rooted in creation, a category incumbent upon us all, lest we wish to be Gnostics. Jesus alludes to Genesis 1 and quotes from Genesis 2, and when the Pharisees then ask him to explain just what Moses meant in Deuteronomy 24 when he commanded one to give a wife a certificate of divorce when putting her away, Jesus doubles down on Genesis: "from the beginning it was not so." In adverting to the creation accounts in Genesis, Jesus affirms marriage is a matter of male–female complementarity.

Third, in adverting to the creation accounts of Genesis

1–2, Jesus intends marriage to be fecund. In alluding to Genesis 1:27 and quoting Genesis 2:24, is Jesus evoking all of Genesis 1–2? Many biblical scholars now see biblical allusions and quotations as exercises in metalepsis.[10] Metalepsis basically means that when the reader of Scripture encounters a New Testament allusion to or quotation of the Old Testament, the reader should call to mind not only what is mentioned by the source text but indeed the whole background context of a quotation or allusion.

So, when Jesus adverts to Genesis 1:27 and 2:24, he's likely adverting to the entirety of Genesis 1–2 as pertains to marriage. And in doing so he's adverting to the very first command in Scripture, "Be fruitful and multiply" (Gen 1:28). Marriage, then, isn't merely a moral union of compatible soulmates but a real union meant to be fecund, meant ideally to issue forth issue—that is, children. This Jesus affirms. And thus the sort of sexuality same-sex marriage supporters support misses Jesus's mark.

Fourth, interpretation isn't arithmetic. One cannot simply count up verses wherein topics X and Y are mentioned, find X mentioned more often, and dismiss Y. Many claim that marriage, sex, and family are relatively minor themes in Jesus's teaching. Even were that true, it wouldn't mean that Jesus's teaching on the matter could be ignored. His instruction is a symphony of truth, and in any complex and beautiful musical composition, every single note from every single instrument matters, from first violin to the triangle. The parts make up the whole.

---

[10] Metalepsis is a term employed by literary critic John Hollander in *The Figure of Echo* and adopted and adapted for biblical studies by Richard Hays in *Echoes of Scripture in the Letters of Paul*. See Hollander, *The Figure of Echo: A Mode of Allusion in Milton and After* (Berkeley: University of California Press, 1981); and Hays, *Echoes of Scripture in the Letters of Paul* (New Haven: Yale University Press, 1989).

But in point of fact, sex isn't a mere minor theme in Jesus's teaching. Interpretation is not the arithmetic of verses on a given topic. In any event, verses are artificial; the system most modern Bibles use wasn't employed until 1560 in the Geneva Bible. Further, such calculation must necessarily ignore the nuances of Jesus's words on a given subject in a given context. Indeed, interpretation by arithmetic is not interpretation at all.

Positively, good interpretation involves paying attention not to quantity but to quality, as it were. One must know how something fits into the scriptural narrative and have a sense of its gravity. Now, Jesus gives his teaching in Matthew, the First Gospel. Whatever one makes of the modern solution to the synoptic problem (how the Gospels are related in literary terms as sources for one another), the Church has held that Matthew is the "First Gospel," not merely because it was traditionally thought to have been written first but because it is considered the richest Gospel in many ways. As a Gospel of fulfillment, it is fitting that Matthew begins the New Testament, which fulfills the Old Testament. Further, it presents Jesus's teaching clearly and substantively; the Church has found it readily useful in teaching and preaching. Moreover, all the major elements of Christian belief are found there—the Incarnation to the Virgin Birth, Jesus's sacrificial crucifixion, the resurrection. For these and other reasons, Matthew has been reckoned the First Gospel in importance by most Christians in most times and places, whether Catholic or Mennonite. Thus it is no little thing that Jesus addresses marriage in Matthew in particular. There are no minor themes in the Church's First Gospel.

In the same way, Jesus here goes straight to Genesis 1–2, weighty chapters opening the grand biblical narrative, which deal with anthropology: what human beings fundamentally are as male and female and what marriage is. This is creation, and the most important and defining fact about the true living God of the Bible is that he is the Creator upon whom all creation depends.

Now Jesus's coming means that much of the Old Testament is no longer of direct relevance to Christians; thanks to Jesus, Paul, and James (the latter two apostles attending the Council of Jerusalem in Acts 15), bacon double cheeseburgers with milkshakes are on the menu for us. The early Christians (under the aegis of the Holy Spirit, Scripture, Tradition, and Jesus's own revelation) may have decided that things of the Mosaic Law that separated Jew and Gentile—kosher eating, Sabbath keeping, circumcision—were no longer binding and indeed inappropriate since the Church is one body with Jew and Gentile;[11] but Jesus and the early Church didn't overturn traditional Jewish sexual morality.

We've seen how Jesus intensifies it in Matthew 19, vis-a-vis other Jewish teachers. Consider also Acts 15, where the question of whether Gentile Christians are obliged to keep the Law of Moses comes to a head: the early Church under the leadership of St. James decides Gentile Christians do not need to obey the Mosaic Law in its entirety, but they are indeed required to avoid four things:

> Therefore my [St. James's] judgment is that we should not trouble those of the Gentiles who turn to God, but should write to them to abstain from the pollutions of idols and from unchastity and from what is strangled and from blood. (Acts 15:19–20)

---

[11] See Ephesians 2:14–15: "For he himself is our peace, who has made us both [Jew and Gentile] one and has broken down in his flesh the dividing wall of hostility by abolishing the law of commandments expressed in ordinances, that he might create in himself one new man in place of the two."

Jesus and the early Christians double down on traditional Jewish sexual morality. The rest of the Mosaic Law is not binding on Christians—think of how radical that would be for Jews, such as the Apostles were!—but the prohibition on "sexual immorality" remains. (Interesting here, too, is the link between idolatry and sexual immorality, the precise link Paul makes in Rom 1.) Revisionist hermeneutics notwithstanding, the prohibition on "sexual immorality" precludes the sort of sexuality some are selling as somehow compatible with following Jesus.

Bottom line: Much of the Old Testament is no longer directly applicable for Christians; we read it through the lens of Jesus and the New Testament. But Jesus affirms Genesis 1–2 in a way more radical than his contemporaries, which excludes the possibility of revising Catholic teaching on human sexuality.

MATTHEW 19:13–15: SATURDAY WEEK 19

Now Jesus again uses children as an example, and given that Jesus has just quoted from Genesis 1–2, which assumes and commands fecundity, the present passage is suggesting that marriage involves the welcoming of children.

In Matthew 19 Jesus has encountered crowds (19:2), representative of laypeople, and then addresses marriage, celibacy, children, and possessions, in that order, and the order is suggestive. Laymen and laywomen either marry according to Jesus's teaching (19:3–9) or receive the call to celibacy (19:10–12), and if they marry they ought to have and welcome children as Jesus himself welcomed them (19:13–15). Economic life (19:16–30) comes last, because it is secondary to marriage and family life and must serve them. This contrasts with the situation today, in which many put career first, reject children, and engage in a sort of serial monogamy, within repeated (civil) marriages or otherwise.

Children are brought to Jesus that he might bless them, but the disciples rebuke the children (Matt 19:13b). "Rebuke" is a strong word; Jesus rebukes the chaotic storm (8:26) and rebukes a demon (17:18). But instead of rebuking, Jesus speaks his famous words: "Let the children come to me, and do not hinder them; for to such belongs the kingdom of heaven" (19:14).

So here again children serve as a model of discipleship and also a model of how one ought to receive Christians, who are like little children (see Matt 18:5). Theologically, the tradition has found in the passage not only a subtle suggestion that marriage involves the reception of children, but also a warrant for the practice of infant baptism.

MATTHEW 19:16–22: MONDAY WEEK 20

Now Jesus is approached by "one" (Matt 19:16) whom we learn is wealthy (19:22), and so he's known to us as the Rich Young Man (or Ruler, owing to St. Luke's description in the parallel passage at Luke 18:18). He addresses Jesus as "Teacher" (Matt 19:16), which is our first hint that something will go amiss. He asks Jesus, "Teacher, what good deed must I do, to have eternal life?" (19:16). He asks about deeds; Jesus will ultimately suggest the man needs to move beyond deeds into relationship with Jesus himself: ". . . and come, follow me" (10:21b).

The man's focus is first on deeds, but even before that Jesus's focus is on the nature of goodness. Jesus responds, "Why do you ask me about what is good? One there is who is good" (Matt 19:17). St. Matthew isn't presenting Jesus here as denying his own goodness, which would contradict everything else St. Matthew is trying to show us about Jesus. Rather, the question reorients the focus on the nature of goodness and indeed the One who is Goodness itself, God. (And given Jesus's identity as Emmanuel in 1:23, the question invites the man and us to consider Jesus's divine identity.)

Jesus, a good Jew, then directs the man to the Torah: "If you would enter life, keep the commandments" (Matt 19:17b). In good Jewish fashion where a student asks his rabbi to clarify, the man asks which Commandments in particular (19:18a). Jesus lists five that concern human relationships, love of neighbor, though out of the order presented in Exodus 20: "You shall not kill, You shall not commit adultery, You shall not steal, You shall not bear false witness, Honor your father and mother, and, You shall love your neighbor as yourself" (19:18b–19). Omitted is the Commandment about coveting and all the Commandments concerning love of God, and Jesus then provides Leviticus 19:18—"You shall love your neighbor as yourself"—as a good summary of the Commandments he just quoted.

Either Jesus mentions these because the young man is failing them or because he is fulfilling them. It seems the omissions are more significant: Jesus has already directed the man to God's own goodness; Jesus does not challenge the man's statement "All these I have observed" (Matt 19:20); and the omission of the Commandment concerning coveting might suggest the young man's problem is covetousness, a possibility confirmed by Jesus telling the man to sell his possessions and give to the poor (19:21a). That's what it would take for the man to store up "treasure in heaven" (19:21b, see 5:20) and be "perfect" (19:21a), fulfilling Jesus's command in the Sermon on the Mount to be perfect, like the heavenly Father (5:48).

But the young man can't, or won't; "he went away sorrowful; for he had great possessions" (Matt 19:22). The man lacked love for God, and loved things instead; that's the likely significance of the omissions of the Commandments concerning love of God and coveting. In Augustinian terms, instead of loving God and neighbor and using things, he loved things and was willing to use God for the sake of obtaining the ultimate possession, eternal life (19:16), apart from a relationship with God. Heaven might be our aim, but we ought to seek the kingdom of heaven not for our own sake, for the sake of eternal self-preservation, but for God's own sake. God is to be loved above all else, and heaven exists to make it possible for us to love him for all eternity.

MATTHEW 19:23–30: TUESDAY WEEK 20

In the wake of this encounter, the story turns to the disciples. Jesus says to them, "Truly, I say to you, it will be hard for a rich man to enter the kingdom of heaven. Again I tell you, it is easier for a camel to go through the eye of a needle than for a rich man to enter the kingdom of God" (Matt 19:23–24). "Camel" and "eye of a needle" is a play on words in Aramaic, aurally pleasing as well as imaginatively shocking.

And shocked the disciples are: "Who then can be saved?" (Matt 19:25). Why would they ask this? It's likely that in accord with a dominant strand of Old Testament theology, especially in Deuteronomy (and continued in our day in the heretical health-and-wealth version of the gospel), material blessing was seen as a sign of God's favor. Jesus replies, "With men this is impossible, but with God all things are possible" (19:26). Jesus isn't saying that the rich can be saved in spite of covetousness and hoarding, as if repentance wasn't necessary, but that God can move the rich to generosity and, if one is called, divestment and poverty for the sake of the kingdom.

Peter, who as a fisherman was never rich, informs Jesus,

"Lo, we have left everything and followed you," and asks, "What then shall we have?" (Matt 19:27). Peter should know the rough answer to his own question, but Jesus gives him particulars: "Truly, I say to you, in the new world, when the Son of man shall sit on his glorious throne, you who have followed me will also sit on twelve thrones, judging the twelve tribes of Israel" (19:28). These men, the Apostles, reign over the Church, not only on earth but also in heaven. "Israel" here is not only literal Israel, but given what the Church is in Matthew's Gospel, Israel here is also the Church triumphant.

And the promise holds not only for formal Apostles but all Christians: "And every one who has left houses or brothers or sisters or father or mother or children or lands, for my name's sake, will receive a hundredfold, and inherit eternal life" (Matt 19:29). On earth we receive a hundredfold—possessing Jesus in the here and now and having brothers and sisters in Christ surpass temporal possessions and even the natural family—as well as in heaven.

Many modern Christians, living when we do, assume that heaven is egalitarian: you're either in or out, but if you're in, there's no distinction of rank among Christians. But the New Testament suggests that there are greater and lesser rewards in heaven, and greater and lesser status in heaven (see Heb 11:35, which speaks of the reward of a "better resurrection," and 1 Cor 3:10–15, in which St. Paul teaches that believers build on the foundation of Christ and that judgment day will reveal the quality of everyone's work, some receiving a reward and others, although ultimately being saved, suffering loss). In Matthew's Gospel Jesus himself has suggested there are ranks in heaven: "Whoever then relaxes one of the least of these commandments and teaches men so, shall be called least in the kingdom of heaven; but he who does them and teaches them shall be called great in the kingdom of heaven" (Matt

5:19). One is either least or great in the kingdom of heaven.

Jesus closes this section with the theme of reversal: "But many that are first will be last, and the last first" (Matt 19:30). The disciples were surprised at Jesus's teaching that it is hard for the rich to be saved, and here Jesus buttresses his teaching by emphasizing reversal is part of the eschatological reality: the saved and the damned will be determined by God's expectations, not human expectations. Jesus will next give a parable illustrating the point, and close with the same words about the first and the last (20:16).

MATTHEW 20:1–16: TWENTY-FIFTH SUNDAY IN ORDINARY TIME / WEDNESDAY WEEK 20

"For" connects this parable with what has just come before—namely, Jesus's teaching about the first being last and the last first. Given the location of this next parable, the point is meant to counter the possibility of pride inherent in the concept of heavenly rank. It's true that there is hierarchy in heaven, as Jesus has taught in the Gospel of Matthew (as well as immediately prior); but it's also true that heaven is heaven and it's a great reward in itself, whatever one's position therein.

This parable, known as the Parable of the Laborers in the Vineyard, again employs a radical image dulled by familiarity. Laborers are hanging out in the *agora* (marketplace in the city square) waiting for work (as happens in history and often today in many locales). A householder recruits laborers for the day, agreeing with them to pay a denarius (Matt 20:2a, the typical days's wage for a laborer). He keeps coming back, recruiting more at the third, sixth, ninth, and eleventh hours. Whether we assume Roman or Jewish conceptions of timekeeping, we're looking at twelve hours (more or less) of daylight, so the third hour would be around 9:00 A.M., the sixth around noon, and so forth. The eleventh hour is as it sounds to our ears: the last possible hour before nightfall. Nightfall—indeed midnight, its darkest expression—is of course an apocalyptic metaphor in Judaism and the New Testament (see Matt 25:1–13, the Parable of the Wise and Foolish Virgins). And certainly in this very parable it is "evening" when the householder repays the laborers, suggestive of God repaying men and women at the end of time.

The shock of the parable comes from its apparent inequity: the householder (God) insists that the steward (Jesus, his Son) pay everyone a denarius, whether he was hired first thing in the morning or at the eleventh hour (Matt 20:8–10), "beginning with the last, up to the first" (20:8). And so those hired first "grumble" (20:11), saying, "These last worked only one hour, and you have made them equal to us who have borne the burden of the day and the scorching heat" (20:12). The householder tells them, "Friend, I am doing you no wrong; did you not agree with me for a denarius? Take what belongs to you, and go; I choose to give to this last as I give to you. Am I not allowed to do what I choose with what belongs to me? Or do you begrudge my generosity?" (20:13–15).

"Friend" is significant; it's a negative term in Matthew's Gospel. In Matthew 22:12 the man without a wedding garment is called "friend" before he is tossed out into the outer darkness. And Judas is called "friend" when he approaches Jesus with the mob in Gethsemane (26:50). So here there's likely a note of hostility; the householder is annoyed by the laborers's grumbling. He makes the point that they were given what they agreed to, and if it's fairer to others that they got the same in spite of working less, well, it's a matter of generosity, not raw equity. "So the last will be first, and the first last" (20:16). Those signified by the grumblers would be saved, as they received their denarius; Jesus's point here is that the

last—those hired later in the day, even at the eleventh hour—
are accounted "first," just as much as those who worked all
day.

Who are the laborers, and who are the grumblers? Good
theological interpretation recognizes that the Bible has many
senses, and parables especially. The laborers could be Jews,
even Pharisees, who might begrudge Gentiles entering the
kingdom of heaven relatively late in the economy of salvation history. And given that Matthew's Gospel is meant to
be reread in light of the death and resurrection of Jesus as a
particularly Christian, Catholic document (see Jesus's words
in Matt 28:16–20 inviting readers to consider again all that
Jesus has commanded), the laborers could also be Catholics
tempted to contempt for those sinners who slip into the Faith
and heaven at the last minute. Again, God's expectations upset
human expectations, and heaven is the ultimate inequity, as
no one ultimately deserves it, even if God has granted that
we might merit it through the merits of Christ and the saints.

MATTHEW 20:17–28: WEDNESDAY OF THE SECOND WEEK OF LENT / ST. JAMES, APOSTLE (JULY 25; 20:20–28)

Jesus now delivers his third Passion prediction as an aside to
the Twelve while approaching Jerusalem. He foretells exactly
what will happen to him, especially being "mocked and
scourged and crucified" (Matt 20:19), all of which find specific mention in the Passion Narrative. And where the prior
Passion prediction was followed by the disciples's expression
of grief, indicating they had missed the final words about
the resurrection, here the reaction is a request for honored
positions in glory, indicating they missed the entire prediction once again. The juxtaposition is jarring. As Peter was

overwhelmed by glory at the Transfiguration and had to be reminded of Jesus's sacrificial mission by the heavenly voice (17:5), so too here: Jesus has just spoken of his suffering, but James and John (through their mother) seek glory. Jesus then has to remind them of his coming death and teach them that it is a model for all.

"Then"—immediately after the Passion prediction—the mother of James and John brings them to Jesus and kneels before him (Matt 20:20). Prompted by Jesus, she asks, "Command that these two sons of mine may sit, one at your right hand and one at your left, in your kingdom" (20:21). Those are the highest positions possible in an ancient oriental court. And the mother's request is ironic but also theologically suggestive: Jesus will achieve his kingdom on the Cross, and those on his right and left are two fellow victims of crucifixion. If James and John wish to reign in glory next to Jesus, they should be prepared to suffer next to him on earth.

And so Jesus informs them that they (the "you" is plural) do not know what they ask, and asks them if they are able to drink the "cup" he is about to drink (Matt 20:22). The "cup" in Scripture is usually the cup of suffering or wrath or both (see, for instance, Ps 11:6, 16:5, 75:8; Isa 51:17–23; Jer 25:15–28, 49:12; Zech 12:2–3; Lam 4:21; and Hab 2:15–16). So too here, and James and John and their mother would have understood the reference. The only way to glory is the way of the Cross. Nevertheless, with bravura bordering on arrogance, the brothers respond that they are indeed able (20:22).

Jesus informs them that they will drink his cup (Matt 20:23), suggesting a strong identity of the Apostles with Jesus, especially in their future martyrdoms (James will be beheaded in AD 44 under Herod Agrippa, while John will suffer torture but ultimately die of old age; the other Apostles, save Judas, will endure martyrdom). But they will not necessarily inherit positions directly next to Jesus in glory, for "to sit at my right hand and at my left is not mine to grant, but it is for those for whom it has been prepared by my Father" (20:23). Jesus as the Son is divine, but he is not the Father, from whom originates the economy of salvation.

The other ten Apostles are hopping mad at the two brothers (Matt 20:24), which provides Jesus with an opportunity for a teaching moment: Jesus's giving of himself on the Cross is an example for all. For reasons of contrast—as he often does in Matthew's Gospel (see 5:47, 6:7, 18:17)—he mentions how power works among pagans ("Gentiles") (20:25). But the Christian way is not the pagan way of power: "It shall not be so among you" (20:26). Those who would be great and first must be servant and slave (20:26b–27), for that is the model of Jesus: "even as the Son of man came not to be served but to serve, and to give his life as a ransom for many" (20:28).

"Ransom" is a concept we're familiar with only within the context of kidnapping, which, while it happens, is rare in western societies. In the ancient world it was much more common, and the concept of ransom (without kidnapping) more common still. Slaves, debtors, and prisoners of war, along with land and possessions that had been forfeited, could be freed or bought back. A synonym more readily comprehensible might be "redemption." In any event, the primary image of salvation the words ransom or redemption imply is *liberation*. That is, the "many" for whom Jesus gives his life as a ransom are held in bondage by someone, and in the story of Matthew's Gospel (and Christian faith more generally) that someone is Satan. Jesus's death on the Cross and his resurrection are a victory over Satan. The model of salvation on offer in Matthew's Gospel, and in the wider New Testament, is largely *Christus Victor*: Christ conquers Sin, Death, Hell, and the Devil for us.

MATTHEW 21:1–11: PALM SUNDAY OF THE PASSION OF THE LORD (PROCESSION)

In Matthew 21, the Lord comes to his temple (Mal 3:1) in the holy city of Jerusalem and proclaims its destruction. Jesus will prophesy, but largely through actions, prophetic enactments. We often think of prophecy as something spoken and written, given the books of the prophets in the Old Testament. Yet when we read those books, as well as the histories in their treatments with the prophets, we find certain prophets engaging in prophetic *actions*. Ezekiel is a great example: in chapter 4, the Lord commands Ezekiel to construct a model of Jerusalem under siege; then he is to lie down on his left side for three hundred and ninety days to symbolize the punishment of the northern kingdom, and then lie on his right side for forty days to symbolize the punishment of the southern kingdom. Another example: Hosea marries a prostitute, Gomer, to symbolize Israel's unfaithfulness.

Jesus, the Apostles, and any fellow travelers reach Bethpage, which means "house of unripe figs" (Matt 21:1); St. Matthew is preparing the reader for what will happen later with the cursing of the fig tree (21:18–22). Bethpage is at the Mount of Olives, overlooking the massive temple complex, and was (and is) thought to be the site where the Christ would return (see Zech 14:4–9). Today it has a large cemetery on it, as faithful Jews have sought burial there so as to have the advantage of being among the first raised when Christ comes again. It is also the site where Jesus delivers his speech detailing the destruction of Jerusalem to his disciples (Matt 24), and the church of *Dominus Flevit* ("The Lord Wept") stands there, marking Jesus's lamentation over the holy city.

Soon Jesus will be acclaimed "son of David" (Matt 21:9)—that is, the Christ—and it is thus instructive that

David withdrew to the Mount of Olives when taking flight from Absalom's rebellion (2 Sam 15:13–31, esp. 30.). The son of David returns to the location and city from which David fled, and in the world of St. Matthew's story, it suggests that payback is coming for the rebels among Israel of Jesus's own day: those who refuse to recognize him as the Christ just as Absalom and his rebels refused to recognize David long ago.

Sequentially, Jesus tells two disciples to go into the village, find a donkey and colt tied there, and to untie them and bring them to Jesus (Matt 21:2). If anyone protests, they are to respond, "The Lord has need of them" (21:3). It's weird—akin to a Jedi mind trick—but Jesus walks on water, opens the eyes of the blind, and raises the dead, among other things, so this is not out of character. St. Matthew is beginning to accentuate a major theme of his Christology: Jesus's authority. His sovereignty has been emphasized throughout, and as we enter the Passion Narrative, we will see that St. Matthew portrays Jesus as having total and ultimate control over all events. So too here: the force of the simple words "The Lord has need of them," buttressed by Jesus's authority, will secure the release of the droids. Whoops. The animals. Further, David of old had two donkeys when on the Mount of Olives (2 Sam 16:1–2), so the very number of donkeys points to Jesus's identity here as the son of David.

As usual for St. Matthew, he finds here the fulfillment of prophecy (Matt 21:4–5, quoting Zech 9:9). The words of the prophecy from Zechariah are privileged to the reader; they're not announced to the people in the world of the story. But the sign is unmistakable, and so the crowds perceive the messianic symbolism and acclaim Jesus the "Son of David" (Matt 21:9)—that is, the Christ, the ultimate son of David. The spreading of cloaks (21:8) is a royal sign, as such was done for Jehu (2 Kgs 9:13), and the crowds cry out, "Hosanna," which means "Save us!" Given popular expectations of the day, the crowds probably presume Jesus is the one who will liberate them from Roman domination. And yet if one reads Zechariah a verse further, one finds a prophecy not of war but of peace:

> [He] will cut off the chariot from E'phraim
>   and the war horse from Jerusalem;
> and the battle bow shall be cut off,
>   and he shall command peace to the nations;
> his dominion shall be from sea to sea,
>   and from the River to the ends of the earth.
> (Zech 9:10)

Jerusalem is "stirred" at Jesus's arrival, asking, "Who is this?" (Matt 21:10). It's not clear whether the crowds acclaiming Jesus the Christ are already in Jerusalem for Passover, or residents of Jerusalem, or both, or, on the other hand, if they have come with Jesus on the way of discipleship as he's made his final journey to Jerusalem. It's likely the former: Jesus brings a crowd of would-be disciples with him on the way of discipleship from Caesarea Philippi, but Jesus finds the residents of Jerusalem unreceptive to him, to say the least. It's Jesus's own followers who are shouting "Hosanna," not the Jerusalemites. Jerusalem and Jesus are opposed in the Gospel of Matthew, an opposition depicted as soon as the story of Herod and the Magi in Matthew 2, as "all Jerusalem" was "troubled" along with Herod when the Magi came seeking the new King of the Jews (2:3–4). And here St. Matthew distances Jesus from Jerusalem further; the crowds respond to the question, "This is the prophet Jesus from Nazareth in Galilee" (21:11). True enough, but not ultimately sufficient; the response is reminiscent of what the disciples say people utter about Jesus's identity in Matthew 16:14: "Some say John the Baptist, others say Eli'jah, and others Jeremiah or one of the prophets." The true response is Simon Peter's: "You are the Christ, the Son of the Living God" (16:16). Yet the response is not far from the mark, as many Jews believed "The Prophet" coming into the world at the end of time would be the Christ.

EXCURSUS: MATTHEW 21:12–22: JESUS'S TEMPLE ACTION AND THE CURSING OF THE FIG TREE

The lectionary does not include Jesus's action in the temple or the cursing of the fig tree, but the sequence is important for understanding Matthew's Gospel, for it is in many ways the fulcrum of a major theme: how the Church with Jesus's Eucharist comes to carry on Israel's mission to the world. That is, the sequence is a major moment in the transition of "his people" (Matt 1:21) moving from Jews to Christians (both Jews and Gentiles who follow Jesus in his Church).

"Cleansing of the Temple" is a misnomer, for Jesus doesn't so much "cleanse" the temple from something polluting, like the exchange of money and sale of animals, both of which were necessary for the temple's sacrifices, so that it can carry on its mission in purity. Rather, Jesus pronounces judgment upon it because of the Jewish leadership's sins and failings.

Two lines of interpretation here are wrong. First, some have said the problem is exchanging money and buying and selling in the temple complex. The anachronistic influence of St. Francis of Assisi is felt here, with his disdain for money, forbidding his brothers even to touch it.[12] But the exchange of

---

[12] A brother once picked up a coin he found and placed it in a church's poor box. St. Francis, who had ordered his brothers never to touch money, forced him to dig a bunch of coins out of a pile of dung with his lips as a form of penance.

money was necessary, for pilgrims would bring pagan coinage from far away that needed to be exchanged into shekels to be kosher. And the sale of animals was necessary, for it was impractical to bring sacrificial animals all the way from (say) the Italian peninsula. Admittedly, this interpretation seems obvious as St. Matthew mentions selling, buying, and money changing expressly (Matt 21:12) and calls out those who have made it a "den of robbers" (21:13b), and St. John's later version does seem to make the incident a matter of trade ("Take these things away; you shall not make my Father's house a house of trade," John 2:16). But the exchange of money and selling of animals was simply necessary for the temple's purpose, which was sacrifice.

A second line of interpretation sees the problem as sacrifice itself. Jesus does say, "My house shall be called a house of prayer," quoting Isaiah 56:7 in Matthew 21:13a, and so some have pitted prayer against sacrifice. But prayer was liturgical in Jewish temple piety, and liturgy was sacrificial. In the ancient world, among Jews, pagans, and Christians, religion simply was sacrifice; religion as a matter of mere ethics is an invention of the Enlightenment. What is more, in the immediate context of what Jesus quotes from Isaiah (in the exact same Isaian verse, immediately prior to that which Jesus quotes), prayer involves sacrifice: "their burnt offerings and their sacrifices will be accepted on my altar; for my house shall be called a house of prayer for all peoples" (Isa 56:7). Seeing sacrifice itself as the problem is the fruit of genteel nineteenth-century antisemitism.

The problem isn't the temple as such, or the trade necessary for sacrifice, which was the very purpose of the temple as ordained by God. The problem, in St. Matthew's story, is the Jewish leadership, the key being "den of robbers" in Matthew 21:13b. It's a partial quotation of Jeremiah 7:11, and the context is Jeremiah's prediction of the first temple's destruction, thanks to the people's grave sins: "Do not trust in these deceptive words: 'This is the temple of the LORD, the temple of the LORD, the temple of the LORD'" (Jer 7:4). Just because it is the temple does not mean that it is inviolable; it can be razed. Jeremiah, speaking the words of the Lord, recommends repentance:

> For if you truly amend your ways and your doings, if you truly execute justice one with another, if you do not oppress the alien, the fatherless or the widow, or shed innocent blood in this place, and if you do not go after other gods to your own hurt, then I will let you dwell in this place, in the land that I gave of old to your fathers for ever. (7:5–7)

But the people will not listen; they sin gravely and think that the temple will protect them:

> Behold, you trust in deceptive words to no avail. Will you steal, murder, commit adultery, swear falsely, burn incense to Ba'al, and go after other gods that you have not known, and then come and stand before me in this house, which is called by my name, and say, "We are delivered!"—only to go on doing all these abominations? (Jer 7:8–10)

And then Jeremiah employs a metaphor: "Has this house, which is called by my name, become a den of robbers in your eyes?" (Jer 7:11a). Robbers were highwaymen who would ambush travelers, kill them, take the spoil, and retreat to caves in the hills. Jeremiah evokes this image. It is as if the people are acting like murderous bandits, sinning gravely and then retreating to the temple, thinking that they are safe there in spite of their transgressions.

Not so. The hammer drops:

> Go now to my place that was in Shiloh, where I made my name dwell at first, and see what I did to it for the wickedness of my people Israel. And now, because you have done all these things, says the LORD, and when I spoke to you persistently you did not listen, and when I called you, you did not answer, therefore I will do to the house which is called by my name, and in which you trust, and to the place which I gave to you and to your fathers, as I did to Shiloh. And I will cast you out of my sight, as I cast out all your kinsmen, all the offspring of E'phraim. (Jer 7:12–15)

Shiloh was the first and major sanctuary in the old northern kingdom; Joshua set up the tabernacle at Shiloh for a time (Josh 18:1), and it became a regular sanctuary (see 1 Sam 1–4), replaced in prominence by Solomon's temple (the first temple). Thanks to the Lord's wrath, Shiloh was destroyed at some point (see Ps 78:60). And so Jeremiah is reminding the Jews (Judahites, Israelites of the southern kingdom of his day) that God's presence is no guarantee of a sanctuary's survival. God abandoned Shiloh; he will abandon Solomon's temple too.

Thus Jesus is prophesying by his action (effectively stopping the temple's sacrificial system) and by quotation that the second temple of his day will be destroyed like Shiloh and like Solomon's temple because of grave sin. The mention of the shedding of "innocent blood" in Jeremiah 7:6 is key, for Jesus's innocent blood (and that of innocents before him) will be the crime for which the temple is destroyed forty years later by the Romans in AD 70. Jesus will also prophesy later all the blood of the innocent righteous will come upon the scribes and Pharisees, from innocent Abel to Zechariah son of Barachiah (Matt 23:34–35). Further, Judas laments that he has shed "innocent blood" in betraying Jesus (27:4).

Finally, the chief priests and scribes complain about children praising Jesus (Matt 21:14–16a). Jesus's response quotes Psalm 8:3: "Out of the mouth of babes and sucklings thou hast brought perfect praise" (Matt 21:16b). The children are praising Jesus, but in the Psalm the praise is directed to God. So here we have another subtle claim to divinity from the lips of Our Lord.

Now we move to the cursing of the fig tree (Matt 21:18–22), which also foretells the destruction of the temple. Jesus, hungry, sees a fig tree but finds no figs, only leaves (21:18–19). In the Old Testament, the fig tree represented both the fidelity of the people of Israel were to exercise (see Jer 24:1–10) and also God's wrath at their failure (see Jer 8:13, "When I would gather them, says the LORD, there are no grapes on the vine, nor figs on the fig tree; even the leaves are withered, and what I gave them has passed away from them"). The suggestion is that the temple has the appearance of life but no longer provides any nourishment. Jesus thus curses the fig tree, and by extension, the temple: "'May no fruit ever come from you again!' And the fig tree withered at once" (21:19). The Church with its Eucharist will abide after the temple with its sacrifices disappears. Then Jesus's disciples ask how the miracles were possible (21:20), and Jesus responds that it's a matter of faith free of doubt (21:21). His words suggest the temple is in view: "[E]ven if you say to this mountain, 'Be taken up and thrown into the sea,' it will be done" (21:21b). The suggestion is that in his pluperfect faith Jesus is effectively commanding the temple (which sits on the temple mount, Mount Zion, the mountain that is to be removed to the sea) to be destroyed.

And the mention of the sea is not mere pictorial poetry; the sea is the gate to destruction, a way to the underworld, the path to perdition for God's enemies, from the ancient Egyptian army (Exod 14–15) to the demons drowning in the swine (Matt 8:28–34). In his words about the fig tree and faith, then, Jesus is actually condemning the temple.

Matthew 21:23–27: Monday of the Third Week in Advent

The Gospel of Matthew has presented Jesus as one having authority, even God's own divine authority. But now the chief priests and elders challenge Jesus on that very question: "By what authority are you doing these things, and who gave you this authority?" (Matt 21:23). Jesus answers with a shrewd question of his own, asking them whether John's baptism was of divine or human origin (21:24–25a). They're stuck, because they didn't believe John (21:25b) but the people did and do (21:26), so they refuse to answer (21:27a). Jesus repays in kind, refusing to answer. Not only is Jesus getting himself out of a tight spot, but he is also withholding revelation from those unworthy of receiving it. Taking his own advice in the Sermon on the Mount, he's not casting his pearls before swine (7:6).

Matthew 21:28–32: Twenty-Sixth Sunday in Ordinary Time / Tuesday of the Third Week in Advent

While Jesus does not answer, he does tell a parable, which introduces the theme of the vineyard (crucial for the next parable as well), the vineyard being an enduring image of Israel (Isa 5:1–7). Like the next parable, this vineyard parable is directed against the Jewish leadership. A father tells his two sons to go work in the vineyard; the first refuses but then later goes, while the second says he will but doesn't (Matt 21:28–30). Jesus asks, "Which of the two did the will of his father?" (21:31a). The obvious answer is the first, which is the response the chief priests and elders give (21:31b). Here we have the contrast between words and action, typical for Matthew's Gospel and indeed moral philosophy as a whole, ancient and modern. It's not what one says but what one does that ultimately matters.

So who do the sons represent? At this point Gentiles are not in view; Jesus tells the chief priests and elders, "Truly I tell you, the tax collectors and the harlots are going into the kingdom of God ahead of you" (Matt 21:31b). They, the tax collectors and prostitutes, the lowest of sinners, are the first son, who refused to follow God's way at first but then get on board and obey his will when John the Baptist and Jesus arrive, restoring them to fellowship with the God of Israel (see 9:10–13); they thus take their place in the vineyard of Israel. Jewish leadership is the second son, full of words of obedience but empty of deeds, who refuse their obligatory work in the vineyard of Israel. The leadership rejected John's way of righteousness, while the worst of sinners accepted it. Thus they will enter the kingdom before the Jewish leadership, who may not enter at all.

Matthew 21:33–43: Twenty-Seventh Sunday in Ordinary Time / Friday of the Second Week of Lent (21:33–43, 45–46)

Now we come to the Parable of the Wicked Tenants. Isaiah's vineyard (Isa 5:1–7) is in view, as Matthew 21:33 contains a direct allusion to Isaiah 5:2 in mentioning "vineyard," "wine press," and "watchtower." So Jesus's vineyard is Isaiah's vineyard, Israel. The landowner departs, leaving tenants in charge (21:33b), and at harvest time sends slaves to the tenants to collect the produce (21:34). But it's not the Parable of the "Wicked Tenants" for nothing; they beat, kill, and stone the slaves sent to them (21:35), and then it's wash, rinse, repeat, as they go again a second time and do likewise to yet more slaves (21:36).

At this point, it's clear what's in view: the Wicked Tenants are the Jewish leadership, and the slaves are the prophets and wise men sent to Israel over the centuries. Jesus, in fact, will shortly condemn the scribes and Pharisees for acting like their murderous forefathers:

> Woe to you, scribes and Pharisees, hypocrites! for you build the tombs of the prophets and adorn the monuments of the righteous, saying, "If we had lived in the days of our fathers, we would not have taken part with them in shedding the blood of the prophets." Thus you witness against yourselves, that you are sons of those who murdered the prophets. Fill up, then, the measure of your fathers. (Matt 23:29–32)

The Parable of the Wicked Tenants suggests they will do exactly that: "Afterward he sent his son to them, saying, 'They will respect my son.' But when the tenants saw the son, they said to themselves, 'This is the heir; come, let us kill him and have his inheritance.' And they took him and cast him out of the vineyard, and killed him" (21:37–39). The son is the Son, obviously Jesus. Not only are they wicked, they are also usurpers. And here we have an allusion to Joseph of the Old Testament: "come, let us kill him" (*deute apokteinōmen auton*) is precisely what the sons of Jacob say about their brother

Joseph (Gen 37:20 LXX). So just as Joseph was persecuted by his brothers, Jesus is persecuted by those Jewish compatriots who should be his brothers. Jesus's life has a pattern in Joseph more broadly as well: Joseph descends just a step north of death, an Egyptian dungeon, and rises to become the effective Lord of the world, reigning over Egypt at its zenith and saving the world thereby through his wisdom (Egypt was the breadbasket of the ancient Mediterranean and Near East, so crop failure in Egypt means famine across the biblical world).

Following the story, Jesus asks the chief priests and scribes what the vineyard owner will do to the tenants (Matt 21:40), and not yet realizing they're the target, they respond, "He will put those wretches to a miserable death, and let out the vineyard to other tenants who will give him the fruits in their seasons" (21:41). Jesus, his voice heavy with sorrow (one might imagine), quotes from Psalm 118:23–24: "Have you never read in the Scriptures: 'The very stone which the builders rejected has become the cornerstone; this was the Lord's doing, and it is marvelous in our eyes'?" (21:42). The Psalm is one of the traditional Passover pilgrimage hymns, and so readers are reminded of the Triumphal Entry, in which Jesus entered the city as the Davidic Christ; he is now to be made the cornerstone of Israel, even though rejected by builders as something, or someone, cast aside.

Jesus then draws the moral in one of the most significant verses for the understanding of Matthew's Gospel: "Therefore I tell you, the kingdom of God will be taken away from you and given to a nation producing the fruits of it" (Matt 21:43). Because of their opposition to Jesus, which will culminate in his quasi-judicial murder, the kingdom of God, which belongs ultimately to God, will be taken from them by God. But to whom is it given? Who is that people? The word is singular, not plural; Jesus is not speaking of Gentiles replacing Jews here. Rather, the singular "people" in possession of the kingdom of God is God's Church, established by his Son, Jesus. And opposition to the Son, the new cornerstone, bears a price: "And he who falls on this stone will be broken to pieces; but when it falls on any one, it will crush him" (21:44).

For now, Jesus escapes: realizing they're the target of the parables, the chief priests and now the Pharisees, who have apparently been listening in, desire to arrest Jesus (Matt 21:45–46), but the crowd's support of Jesus as a prophet means they can't at the moment. They will have to wait till later, under cover of night, when Judas betrays Jesus's location to them among the hundreds of thousands of people camped out for Passover.

MATTHEW 22:1–14: TWENTY-EIGHTH SUNDAY IN ORDINARY TIME / THURSDAY WEEK 20

Even after upsetting the priests and Pharisees, Jesus continues speaking. He is apparently addressing the crowds and Jewish leadership, though the narratorial introduction to the present parable makes it sound more general, as if it's now out of narrative time: "And again Jesus spoke to them in parables" (Matt 22:1). "Parables" is plural, although a single parable follows, the Parable of the Wedding Feast.

In this story, the kingdom of heaven is compared to a king giving a wedding feast for his son (Matt 22:2); the king is God and the son is Jesus. Given those obvious identifications, Jesus may not have salvation history in view, as if the parable dealt with how the old covenant led up to his advent, but rather his own situation in the present and future: the wedding feast is for the son, and Jesus began his public ministry relatively recently. Further, Jesus often speaks in the prophetic present as if the future is in view, as he did in the missionary discourse in Matthew 10:16–23 and as he will do shortly in Matthew 23:34: "Therefore I send you prophets and wise men and scribes, some of whom you will kill and crucify, and some you will scourge in your synagogues and persecute from town to town."

So the invitees are those called to follow Jesus on the way of the kingdom, but they refuse, and refuse twice (Matt 22:3 and then 4: "Again he sent other servants . . ."). The second refusal is when everything has been prepared (22:4). Divine patience is suggested by the two invitations: in spite of the first refusal, a second invitation has been given, even at the latest of hours when the banquet is spread.

The guests's refusal is obstinate and aggravated by the very divine patience shown. Their refusal is also violent: some go about their quotidian business (Matt 22:5), but others "seized his servants, treated them shamefully, and killed them" (22:6). Thinking ahead again to 23:34, and back not only to 10:16–23 but also to Jesus's words in the Sermon on the Mount promising persecutions for righteousness's sake (5:10–12), the servants of the king are the Apostles and other missionary disciples of Jesus.

Justified in his anger, the king "sen[ds] his troops and destroy[s] those murderers and burn[s] their city" (Matt 22:7). In light of Jesus's express words coming in Matthew 24 about the destruction of the temple and the prophetic significance of his prior temple action (21:12–22), this is a rather obvious reference to the coming destruction of Jerusalem. The holy city and its temple will be leveled by the Romans in AD 70, and not to be overlooked is the reference to "his troops"; Jesus is suggesting that the Romans are the agents of God's wrath upon the city and people that persecutes the proclaimers of the kingdom of his Son.[13]

Now the servants are told to go find whoever they can to come to the wedding feast (Matt 22:8–9). Given that the first invitees are most likely the Jewish leadership, this second batch of rag-tag invitees is likely tax collectors and sinners, as well as Gentiles. The servants find "both bad and good" (22:10) to fill the wedding hall. This is a reference to the composition of the Church as a *corpus permixtum* (in St. Augustine's phrase), a mixed body of saints and sinners, of those who will one day be saved and those who will be damned, as the next section of the parable makes clear.

The king reviews the guests, but finds one who is unprepared, lacking a "wedding garment" (Matt 22:11). It's not clear that Jews wore special clothes for wedding festivities, though some have suggested that it was the custom that the groom would provide garments to his guests. In any event, it must be supposed that the man wasn't wearing his best, which would be a great slight to a king. (And the passage should have us thinking about how we dress for Mass, which is the wedding feast of the Lamb on earth.) But in Christian tradition certain garments are associated with saints and salvation, as in Revelation 19:6–8, in which the Church triumphant is "clothed with fine linen, bright and pure," which is "the righteous deeds of the saints" (v. 8). Unclothed, the man is unfit for the kingdom of heaven.

St. Gregory the Great writes that the lack of the wedding garment signifies faith without love:

> What do we think is meant by the wedding garment, dearly beloved? For if we say it is baptism or faith,

---

[13] Josephus also thought the Roman legions were the agents of God's wrath upon Jerusalem and its temple. See footnote 5 in Chapter 17.

is there anyone who has entered this marriage feast without them? A person is outside because he has not yet come to believe. What then we must understand by the wedding garment but love? That person enters the marriage feast, but without wearing a wedding garment, who is present in the holy Church, and has faith, but does not have love. We are correct when we say that love is the wedding garment because this is what our Creator himself possessed when he came to the marriage feast to join the Church to himself.[14]

Revered as the Apostle of faith, St. Paul himself saw love as supreme in at least two instances. In 1 Corinthians 13:13, he writes, "So faith, hope, love abide, these three; but the greatest of these is love." In Galatians 5:6 he writes, "For in Christ Jesus neither circumcision nor uncircumcision is of any avail, but faith working through love." For Catholics, and for St. Matthew (and St. Paul), faith can never be alone. It must involve good works and chiefly love (charity), from which good works flow for God's own sake.

And so the man without a wedding garment is representative of those Christians who will lack the requisite merits to enter the kingdom of heaven at the end, in accord with many other passages in Matthew's Gospel. One thinks of Jesus's words at the end of the Sermon on the Mount, in which not everyone who calls Jesus "Lord" will enter the kingdom, and in which those who do not do Jesus's words will be like the fool who built on sand and sees his house crash (Matt 7:21–27). Or again Jesus's threat to the disciples that they risk suffering the fate of the unforgiving servant if they do not forgive their

---

[14] St. Gregory the Great, *Forty Gospel Homilies*, Cistercian Studies 123 (Collegeville, MN: Cistercian Publications/Liturgical Press, 1990), 347.

brothers from their heart (18:21–35). And yet again Jesus's description of the separation of the sheep and the goats at the end (25:31–46), which teaches that all will be judged not on what they merely believed but on what they actually did in light of their claimed beliefs.

The man is "speechless" (Matt 22:12b). He has nothing to say for himself, for there simply is no excuse; love and deeds are simply requisite. And so the king orders the attendants to "[b]ind him hand and foot, and cast him into the outer darkness; there men will weep and gnash their teeth" (22:13). Including this reference, the phrase "there men will weep and gnash their teeth" occurs six times in Matthew's Gospel (8:12, 13:42, 13:50, 22:13, 24:51, 25:30), all with obvious reference to the pains of hell (e.g., "outer darkness" in 8:12 and 25:30; "furnace of fire" in 13:42 and 50). So the man is damned. Jesus concludes the parable with the point that "many are called, but few are chosen" (22:14), echoing his words about the narrow gate to life, that "those who find it are few" (7:14).

This parable presents a hard teaching, but so does much of Matthew's Gospel and indeed the broader New Testament. The simple fact is that Christian faith involves apocalyptic judgment, however much moderns may wish it away, and so the Church has taught, and does teach, that hell is a possibility for Christians.[15] Rather than deny it, it's best to take steps to avoid it, and again, Matthew's Gospel, like the Catholic Faith, operates with deep grace: God is in Jesus with us, empowering us to do what he commands and thus become the kind of people fit for heaven.

---

[15] See CCC 1021–1022, 1033–1037.

MATTHEW 22:15–21: TWENTY-NINTH
SUNDAY IN ORDINARY TIME

In response to the parables told against them, the Pharisees attempt to entrap Jesus. Tag-teaming with the Herodians (supporters of the Rome-backed family stemming from the late Herod the Great), they send their disciples who address Jesus as "teacher," which we have seen does not indicate things will go well for those addressing Jesus as such. Further, they flatter him as being "true," a man who "teach[es] the way of God truthfully," ignoring the opinions of others (22:16). Those sent then pose a question they think is impossible for Jesus to answer, given the results of both possibilities: "Is it lawful to pay taxes to Caesar, or not?" (22:17). If Jesus says no, then Rome will crush him as a rebel. If Jesus says yes, Jews will discount him as a collaborator.

Most Jews would have resented the imperial tax to Rome, for it was high and was a reminder of the reality of Rome's rule over them. This would have been especially true for certain Pharisees, some of whom were politically calculating and even revolutionary (in spite of the idea popularized by Jacob Neusner that they withdrew from politics). At the very least the Pharisees would have hoped and prayed for the coming of the Christ, which would crush Rome and establish an everlasting and free Jewish kingdom. And so it's hypocritical for the Pharisees to cooperate with the Herodians; the former were pious Jews who longed for God's direct rule free of Rome, while the latter may have practiced Judaism with some degree of piety but who were quite happy with Roman rule, since they were part of it. Politics makes strange bedfellows, however, and it is said the enemy of my enemy is my friend, and so here religion and state, otherwise opposed, team up to crush the Christ whom the Pharisees should want and whom the state should fear.

Thus Jesus calls the Pharisees "hypocrites" for their cooperation with the Herodians (and vice-versa) and shows them all to be such by requesting a coin (Matt 22:18–19a). They produce one (22:19b), implicating them deeper in hypocrisy, for their possession of this pagan token shows them quite willing to pay the tax. Jesus asks, "Whose likeness and inscription is this?" (22:20). The denarius of the day bore Caesar's image, the image namely of Tiberius Caesar (r. AD 14–37), with inscriptions deeming him "High Priest" and "Son of the Divine Augustus." And so they reply, "Caesar's" (22:21a).

Jesus then delivers his famous response: "Render therefore unto Caesar the things which are Caesar's; and unto God the things that are God's" (Matt 22:21b, KJV). On one hand, Jesus has effectively said, Yes, it's fine to pay the imperial tax. On the other hand, in doing so he offers another radical, authoritative teaching rooted in his lessons about detachment from the things of this world, especially mammon, in the Sermon on the Mount (6:19–20, 24–34). Jesus would have his disciples (and everyone on earth should be his disciple) live a higher way of life, detached from the concerns of the world, in simplicity, as much as possible. The kingdom is of heaven, not of earth, though one day it will come to rule earth. It is something God advances, something God sends (as we pray, "Thy kingdom come"), not something to be forced by political action. And so taxes can be paid to Rome without concern; our citizenship is in heaven.

Jesus's answer leaves his interlocutors gobsmacked (a fairly accurate translation for the word rendered "marveled"), and they simply depart (Matt 22:22), with no response possible.

EXCURSUS: MATTHEW 22:23–33: MARRIAGE
AT THE RESURRECTION

Though not treated by the lectionary, the passage concerning controversy with the Sadducees over the question of the resurrection is important for St. Matthew's story for two reasons. First, it shows Jesus besting another Jewish party, so that Jesus is shown in the Gospel routing all major Jewish parties and offices (Pharisees, scribes, Sadducees, elders, chief priests, etc.; minor groups like the sects of the Essenes and Therapeutae do not find mention). Second, it shows Jesus's messianic movement as a doctrine of hope over and against the Sadducees and Jerusalem (the former largely ruling the latter, as they dominated the high priesthood in the holy city), for the Sadducees (and Jerusalem by extension) do not believe in life after death,[16] as our passage expressly mentions that they "say that there is no resurrection" (Matt 22:23).

Because they deny the resurrection, they put Jesus on the spot. They use the example of Levirate marriage from the Torah (which is all they regarded as Sacred Scripture, as they rejected the prophets and writings as canonical). Levirate marriage (see Deut 25:5–6) involved a brother marrying a dead brother's childless widow so that she might conceive and bear, in effect having children raised up for her late husband. The Sadducees put forth a case in which a woman married seven brothers in sequence, each dying in turn, but was left childless, and then she died too (Matt 22:25–27). They ask Jesus, "In the resurrection, therefore, to which of the seven will she be wife? For they all had her" (22:28).

Their challenge trades on the apparent absurdity of polygamy in the eschatological age (although the Torah, the

---

[16] See Acts 23:8, and Josephus, *Ant.* 18.16.

Sadducees's only "bible," certainly presents examples of polygamy, such as Jacob and his two wives, though the practice is never commanded nor explicitly approbated and almost always attended by difficulties). Given that absurdity, they think, resurrection itself is absurd.

Jesus flatly declares them "wrong" since they "know neither the scriptures nor the power of God" (Matt 22:29). Jesus means not only that they don't know the Scriptures they affirm, the Torah proper, but also that they don't have the full Scriptures; they reject the prophets and writings in which the resurrection is sometimes affirmed (see Isa 26:19 and Dan 12, as well as 2 Macc 7, which was "scripture" for most Jews of Jesus's day, though perhaps not for those in Judea and Jerusalem). Further, denying life after death means death is more powerful than the living God, the God of life, and so they also do not know the absolute "power of God," which involves power over death.

Furthermore, Jesus declares their example doesn't work because there is no marriage in the kingdom of heaven (Matt 22:30; see also 19:10–12, in which Jesus teaches some renounce marriage precisely for the sake of the kingdom of heaven). Rather, people are like angels, who do not marry. Then Jesus turns to the Torah, the Sadducees's scripture, and makes an interesting claim: after their deaths, the patriarchs Abraham, Isaac, and Jacob still have God as their God in the present tense: "I am the God of Abraham, and the God of Isaac, and the God of Jacob" (22:32). It does not say "I was the God" but "I am the God" of the patriarchs.

So that implies with some force that the patriarchs are not in fact dead, but living. But neither are they resurrected yet bodily (and resurrection almost always means bodily resurrection[17]). So either Jesus is teaching that resurrection is merely a matter of the soul returning to God apart from any consideration of the body, or (as the Church teaches about the faithful dead) their souls are with God awaiting the resurrection of the body, when body and soul are reunited.[18] The latter fits the Gospel of Matthew better. Jesus's own resurrection is bodily (regardless of how different the resurrection body is from the natural body), and we are told that right after Jesus's death, "the tombs also were opened, and many bodies of the saints who had fallen asleep were raised, and coming out of the tombs after his resurrection they went into the holy city and appeared to many" (Matt 27:52–53).

MATTHEW 22:34–40: THIRTIETH SUNDAY IN ORDINARY TIME / FRIDAY WEEK 20

Now a Pharisaic expert in the Mosaic Law, a "lawyer," poses a question to Jesus to "test" him (Matt 22:35). The question is

---

[17] See N. T. Wright, *The Resurrection of the Son of God*, Christian Origins and the Question of God 3 (Minneapolis: Fortress, 2003), 85–206. One exception is *Jubilees* 23:31, which speaks of the bones of the righteous resting in the earth while their spirits experience joy in heaven.

[18] As regards the middle ages, Dante in *Paradiso*, canto 14, writes:

> When our flesh, made glorious at the Judgment Seat, dresses us once again, then shall our persons become more pleasing in being more complete. . . .

> And "Amen!" cried the souls of either chain with such prompt zeal as to make evident how much they yearned to wear their flesh again;

> perhaps less for themselves than for the love of mothers, fathers, and those each soul held dear before it became an eternal flame above. (14.43–45, 61–66)

In Dante Alighieri, *The Divine Comedy*, trans. John Ciardi [New York: Penguin, 2003], 715.

hostile as it comes from a Pharisee challenging Jesus, and he calls him "Teacher" (22:36a), which in Matthew's Gospel is a deficient title for Jesus. The question, however, isn't a hypothetical functioning as a trap, as other questions posed to Jesus by the Pharisees (such as the question regarding paying taxes to Caesar) or the Sadducees (the question concerning marriage at the resurrection). This question is honest, and many rabbis engaged in asking and answering this question: "[W]hich is the greatest commandment in the law?" (22:36).

Jesus gives a twofold answer, each part taken from the Mosaic Law itself. "You shall love the Lord your God . . ." (Matt 22:37) is Jesus's adaptation of Deuteronomy 6:5, part of the *shema* (coming from the opening word of this verse, which means "hear"), the fundamental Jewish creed and command: "Hear, O Israel: The LORD our God is one LORD; and you shall love the LORD your God with all your heart, and with all your soul, and with all your might" (Deut 6:4–5). So love of God comes first: "This is the first and great commandment" (Matt 22:38). Then in second position comes love of neighbor: "And a second is like it, You shall love your neighbor as yourself" (22:39). This is taken directly from Leviticus 19:18.

In this passage we have the definitive rejection of Marcionism. It is named for the second-century heretic Marcion, a wealthy shipbuilder from the Black Sea who came to Rome's churches with a large financial gift, which the Roman Church immediately returned once Marcion opened his mouth. A sort of Gnostic, Marcion claimed the god of the Old Testament was a lesser god, cruel and vindictive, but the god of the New Testament was the true God, the loving Father of Jesus Christ. Marcion also issued an edition of the New Testament, comprised of the Gospel of Luke and ten letters of Paul, all expurgated of what Marcion regarded as Jewish interpolations.

Many modern Christians are effective Marcionites. Part of the reason is the legacy of liberal Protestantism, made by the Enlightenment's influence, which in our day has become Moral Therapeutic Deism, with Jesus recruited as its mascot. Another part of the reason is that the churches have done a poor job teaching their people how to rightly read the Old Testament as Christian Scripture, which would involve attention to the fourfold sense, to mystagogy, to how Jesus and Paul and the apostolic Church deal with the particulars of the Old Testament.

When I was a teaching assistant at Duke Divinity School, one fellow divinity student once wrote on an exam, "The Old Testament presents a God of wrath. Fortunately we follow Jesus, who taught us to 'love the Lord our God with all our heart, soul, strength, and mind,' and to 'love our neighbor as ourselves.'" Because she had simply absorbed contemporary American Marcionism and apparently didn't know the Old Testament very well, she was oblivious to the fact that Jesus went deep to Deuteronomy and Leviticus in establishing his dual love principle for interpreting the Law.

The point: Jesus's most important teaching, given here, concerning the right way to order interpretation of the Old Testament ("On these two commandments depend all the law and the prophets," Matt 22:40) and thus the essence of Judeo-Christian religion, is rooted in the Old Testament. He doesn't do away with the Old Testament but rather, as the Jewish Christ bringing the New Law, accepts and interprets it. There is continuity, then, between the Old Testament and Jesus and his Church. Indeed, Jesus is likely channeling the two tables of the Law in the Ten Commandments (Exod 20), as the first three Commandments, the first table, concern love of God and the second seven, the second table, love of neighbor.

Western Christianity (including magisterial Protestantism, like Lutheranism) has often described the essence of the Faith in this way, as love of God and love of neighbor, thanks to the legacy of St. Augustine, who made Jesus's teaching on dual love (as well as the three theological virtues, faith, hope, and love, the greatest of which is love) the center of his theological project.

EXCURSUS: MATTHEW 22:41–46: THE IDENTITY OF THE CHRIST

Jesus has given the definitive principles for arranging the materials of the Old Testament, and then here turns around and poses a question to the Pharisees. "What do you think of the Christ? Whose son is he?" (Matt 22:42a). The response is the common one: "The son of David" (22:42b), meaning the ultimate descendant of David, the Christ, who will usher in an everlasting kingdom surpassing David's kingdom.

Jesus then asks how David could call his ultimate messianic descendant "Lord" (Matt 22:43) in his Spirit-inspired Psalm 110: "The Lord [God] said to my Lord [the Christ], Sit at my right hand, till I put your enemies under your feet" (Matt 22:44, quoting Ps 110:1). Forefathers are generally greater than their descendants, but here the descendant of David is greater than David. And so Jesus asks, "If David thus calls him Lord, how is he his son?" (Matt 22:45).

Jesus is not denying his Davidic descent as the Christ but inviting his hearers to consider more deeply the identity of the Christ and thus indeed the identity of Jesus. For David's words are inspired by the Holy Spirit (22:43), as most Jews believed David to have possessed supernatural inspiration, and David called the Christ "Lord." Are Jesus's hearers ready to believe not only that Jesus is the Christ but that the Christ is divine, God himself? The answer is too much for most to bear, and so "no one was able to answer him a word, nor from that day did any one dare to ask him any more questions" (22:46).

CHAPTER 16

✢

JESUS THE CHRIST PRONOUNCES JUDGMENT: WOES, TEMPLE, APOCALYPSE

MATTHEW 23:1–12: THIRTY-FIRST SUNDAY IN ORDINARY TIME / TUESDAY OF THE SECOND WEEK IN LENT / SATURDAY WEEK 20

WE ENTER NOW INTO THE LAST of Jesus's five great discourses in the Gospel of Matthew, parallel in length with the Sermon on the Mount. This last discourse concerns the coming destruction of Jerusalem and its temple and, with the advent of the kingdom of heaven brought by the Christ, the end of the world. The first discourse, the Sermon on the Mount, was the charter for life in the Church as it anticipates the kingdom. This final discourse describes the destruction of Jerusalem (a penalty for not believing Jesus and his kingdom message) and the advent of the kingdom. In chapter 23 Jesus will condemn the scribes and Pharisees, delivering seven prophetic woes against them, and issue a lament over Jerusalem.

In chapter 24 Jesus will predict the destruction of the temple and present it as a sign of (but event distinct from) the end of the world. In chapter 25 Jesus will present two parables and some straightforward teaching about the final judgment.

Having silenced the Pharisees in the prior passage, Jesus now turns to the crowds and his disciples to contrast their way with the way of the new remnant community, the Church. The scribes and the Pharisees, according to Jesus, are marked by pride and striving for rank and honor, whereas his way is the way of unity in fraternity through humility.

Jesus tells them to "practice and observe whatever they [the scribes and the Pharisees] tell you," for they "sit on Moses' seat" (Matt 23:2). On its face, Jesus's words here seem to conflict with much of the rest of his teaching in St. Matthew's Gospel. Not only has Jesus himself brought the New Law and effectively abolished certain parts of the Old Mosaic Law (see, particularly, ch. 5 of this book), but he has also had severe conflicts with the Pharisees over their interpretation of the Law (quite apart from their hypocrisy).

Two paths provide possible ways out of the tension. First, given Jesus's hostility toward the scribes and the Pharisees, which comes to a head in this very chapter, Jesus might here be engaging in sardonic, even sarcastic, irony.[1] It is as if he

---

[1] Many are loath to find passionate rhetoric in the New Testament, for overwrought passion strikes us as somewhere between uncouth and sinful, and one suspects that many have simply assumed the idea that the Bible is a collection of dispassionate doctrines. Yet in places like 1 Corinthians 15:1 we find aggressive irony (Paul wants to "make known" to the Corinthians what they have effectively forgotten, the very gospel, though most translations soften Paul's irony with "remind"). So too in Galatians 5:12, where St. Paul suggests that the Judaizers trying to get Paul's converts to undergo circumcision should go all the way and castrate themselves; it is as if he is saying, "They want your foreskin? They should cut off their own -----." Those are examples from St. Paul; with regard to Jesus, we observe that Our Lord is sometimes angry, and expressions of anger often involve irony and sardonicism.

might be saying, "By all means, follow every jot and tittle of the Law of Moses as they do, to show up their hypocrisy all the more"; this would be to beat them at their own game. Whether Jesus literally means for his followers to do so would remain an open question, and it seems at odds with the positive teaching that soon comes in Matthew 23:8-12.

Second, Jesus could be suggesting something in line with his words in Matthew 15:1-6, where he charges the Pharisees with negating the written word of God by means of their tradition. So perhaps Jesus means his followers ought to heed the Pharisees in so far as they teach the true meaning of Moses's words—hence the reference to "Moses' seat" (23:2), which at the least is symbolic of Moses's authority and which might also refer to the actual stone seat in synagogues where an authorized teacher would read and expound upon the Torah. In any event, we see here Jesus teaching the very Catholic attitude of deference to legitimate authority, even when that authority is unworthy, and in truth both paths are possible at the same time. Jesus could be speaking with angry irony while also teaching obedience to the written word of God and deference to authority.

Easier are Jesus's words on Pharisaic hypocrisy. We as followers of Jesus might do what they teach, but should not do what they do, for they fail to practice what they preach (Matt 23:3). Pharisees lay heavy burdens on others and do not help men with them (23:4), in contrast to Jesus's easy burden and light yoke (see 11:28-30). Once they've finished crushing others, they elevate themselves, Jesus says; "[t]hey do all their deeds to be seen by men" (23:5a), seeking honor through ostentation, loving the adulation and rank their perceived piety brings them (23:5b-7).

The way of Jesus is different: he teaches the crowds and his disciples that they are all on one fraternal plane under

God and his Christ, their teacher, who are on a higher level (Matt 23:8–10). In Jesus's description of the situation with the scribes and Pharisees, God and his Christ are absent, and so all that is left is for men to seek rank over each other. In his Church, God and his Christ reign, and his followers are all brothers (and sisters) equal in dignity, if not office. And so true greatness requires humble service (23:11); those like the scribes and Pharisees who exalt themselves will receive an eschatological humbling (the import of the passive in 23:12a), while the humble will find themselves exalted at the eschaton (23:12b).

So Jesus here is teaching a form of the Two Ways: the way of pride, which leads nowhere good, and the way of humility, which leads to one's final, heavenly exaltation. His point is humility. That explains his hyperbole, his exaggeration for effect in telling them not to be called rabbi (Matt 23:8) nor master (23:10), and above all to call no man "father" on earth (23:9). Certainly Jesus wouldn't deny children the obvious and natural use of "father" to address their own fathers. As far as priests being called "Father" goes, it stems from the reality that priests are spiritual fathers to their parishioners, for the Church is a family; the water of baptism is thicker than blood.

MATTHEW 23:13–22: MONDAY WEEK 21

Next Jesus begins the seven woes of condemnation against the scribes and Pharisees, emulating prophets of old (see, for instance, Isa 5:8–22). Jesus's targets receive condemnation for two reasons: First, because they reject Jesus's kingdom message and hinder others from following him ("you shut the kingdom of heaven against men; for you neither enter yourselves, nor allow those who would enter to go in," Matt 23:13). And second, because following their own casuistic way of interpreting Torah makes them hypocrites, attentive only to the externals of religious observance for the sake of esteem in the eyes of men (see the prior passage on Matt 23:1–12).

Therefore, while Jesus's kingdom-way is the narrow path that fits men and women for heaven, the way of the scribes and Pharisees fits them for hell: "for you traverse sea and land to make a single proselyte, and when he becomes a proselyte, you make him twice as much a child of hell as yourselves" (Matt 23:15). It seems then in Jesus's day, Pharisaic Judaism had a missionary component, reaching out to Gentiles to make them Jews. But Jesus says their missionary endeavors fit converts for hell, given their wrong understanding of God and his Law, in contrast with the Church's mission to Gentiles, which will fit them for heaven (see 28:16–20). And so Jesus continues with the theme of the Two Ways.

Jesus points out their hypocrisy, as they take more seriously the gold of the temple than the temple itself , and the gifts at the altar more seriously than the altar itself (Matt 23:16–19). Where the Pharisees are focusing on human action (the gold and the gifts mentioned being something given by man), Jesus places God in first place, observing that God's heaven, temple, and altar are prior (23:20–22). Pharisaic legalism forgets God, as at its worst it is a tangled net of contradictory casuistic results deduced from the Law, understood as a mere legal code. Jesus, by contrast, places God at the center.

Again, then, one thinks of Jesus's teaching in 23:1–12, wherein Jesus tells his disciples to practice and observe what the Pharisees teach, since they sit on Moses's seat, while not doing what the Pharisees do, as they're hypocrites. The Pharisaic, scribal way forgets God in its emphasis on human compliance with contemporary interpretations of a written code, while Jesus's way orients all to God the heavenly Father and orders all in relation to him. Another way of understanding this is to see Pharisaic (and later rabbinic) Judaism, along with Islam, as religions of the book, with the book (Torah or Koran, respectively) seen as a set of legal codes needing interpretation for their application. Judaism and Islam, it has been observed, do not have theology proper, which would be focused on the very nature of God's divine substance: God is the great lawgiver for them, but consideration of the divine nature doesn't come into play, for Jewish and Islamic conceptions of God are generally voluntarist; that is, God is pure will (*voluntas* in Latin), and nothing else.

Christianity, by contrast, derives its beliefs and practices from theology. The Old Law is interpreted in light of this, for Jesus reveals the fullest revelation of God's nature, and the New Law taught by Jesus in word and deed reflects the divine nature. God is in substance a Trinity of three divine persons possessing together the one divine nature, and the second person of the Trinity became incarnate, Jesus Christ. Divine Revelation for Christian faith, then, is found first in Jesus Christ himself; indeed, it is Jesus himself. Written Scripture is revelation secondary to that and interpreted in light of that.

For these reasons, the Christian Bible, the Jewish Torah, and the Islamic Koran are not equivalent in the system of their respective religions (and no disrespect is intended toward the latter two faiths by virtue of such a statement). If anything, Jesus Christ himself would be the proper parallel for the Torah and Koran; he is in Christian understanding the "Word" of God (John 1:1, 14, 18). And so Christianity is not a "religion of the book." As the Catechism teaches:

> Still, the Christian faith is not a "religion of the book." Christianity is the religion of the "Word" of

God, a word which is "not a written and mute word, but the Word is incarnate and living" [St. Bernard, *S. missus est hom.* 4,11:PL 183,86]. If the Scriptures are not to remain a dead letter, Christ, the eternal Word of the living God, must, through the Holy Spirit, "open [our] minds to understand the Scriptures" [*Lk* 24:45]. (CCC 108)

MATTHEW 23:23–26: TUESDAY WEEK 21

The Pharisees's way of legalism involves disorder, the swapping of majors for minors and minors for majors. Jesus's way provides proper order. So the scribes and Pharisees, in Jesus's view, are quite concerned with tithing (in this case, their herbs) but have "neglected the weightier matters of the law, justice and mercy and faith" (Matt 23:23a). For Jesus, then, right interpretation of the law should flow from general principles rooted in God himself (justice and mercy) and fidelity to him (faith as commitment, not mere belief).

Jesus then says, "[T]hese you ought to have done, without neglecting the others" (Matt 23:23b). This is not to be overlooked. Moderns have presented a Jesus who teaches a religion of the interior, of complete reliance upon emotion (a "feeling of absolute dependence," as nineteenth-century German protestant theologian Friedrich Schleiermacher put it[2]), a Jesus who eschews externals altogether. But Jesus in this verse says "without neglecting the others"; Jesus is telling the Pharisees and scribes that under the situation of the Old Law, they should have indeed kept tithing their herbs but subordinated such relatively minor concerns to the major principles rooted

---

[2] See Friedrich D. E. Schleiermacher, *The Christian Faith*, ed. H. R. Mackintosh and J. S. Stewart (London: T & T Clark, 1999), especially 12–14 and 22–23.

in God ("justice and mercy and faith"). Not only do they not follow Jesus's way, but their own way is disordered.

Therefore these "blind guides" end up breaking the Law they purport to uphold; they strain out a gnat but swallow a camel (Matt 23:24; there's a play on words in Aramaic here: *galma* is gnat, *gamla* is camel.). Both are unclean (see Lev 11:41 and 4, respectively). The former reference involves the practice of filtering one's drinks through a thin mesh to make sure one consumed no unclean insects, and so it's ironic that Jesus's opponents would then turn around and (figuratively) consume a camel; again, majoring in minors is the problem.

Because of this, the scribes and Pharisees are hypocrites: their externals appear in order—they are ritually clean on the outside—but they themselves are in disorder because they are unclean on the inside. "[Y]ou cleanse the outside of the cup and of the plate, but inside they are full of extortion and rapacity. . . . [F]irst cleanse the inside of the cup and of the plate, that the outside also may be clean" (Matt 23:25–26). Here we have Jesus's typical emphasis on the internal, but again that doesn't mean he eschews externals. Integrity is having inside and outside in alignment; hypocrisy is having them out of alignment.

MATTHEW 23:27–32: WEDNESDAY WEEK 21

Jesus continues the theme of the Pharisees's hypocrisy with mention of death. Cemeteries can be beautiful, thinking of (say) Arlington, the American cemetery at Normandy, or the major monuments the wealthy can afford for their beloved dead from antiquity to now. Yet all the peace and beauty and dignity of a cemetery cannot remove the fact that there are rotting corpses everywhere, even in an age of embalming, which merely arrests the corruption of death and delays decay.

Six feet under the noblest tombstone is a lifeless body, slowly corrupting to ashes and dust.

The scribes and Pharisees, Jesus says, are like this: "[Y] ou are like whitewashed tombs, which outwardly appear beautiful, but within they are full of dead men's bones and all uncleanness" (Matt 23:27). Thus their righteousness is a matter of external appearance, but the reality of their interior is that they are "full of hypocrisy and iniquity" (23:28).

Continuing the theme of tombs, though in a different key, Jesus now levels the charge of murder: "you build the tombs of the prophets and adorn the monuments of the righteous, saying, 'If we had lived in the days of our fathers, we would not have taken part with them in shedding the blood of the prophets'" (Matt 23:29–30). But in honoring the prophets and righteous, the scribes and Pharisees condemn themselves, for they concede they are the direct descendants "of those who murdered the prophets" (23:31) and thus bear their ancestors's nature and character, as like begets like. Therefore, Jesus delivers ominous words: they will fill up "the measure of [their] fathers" (23:32). Just as their fathers murdered the prophets and righteous, the scribes and Pharisees will do the same to Jesus and his followers.

Curiously, the lectionary omits Matthew 23:33–36, even while including most of Matthew 23. In these verses Jesus delivers a prophecy as the culmination of his woes: the scribes and Pharisees, "serpents" and a "brood of vipers" (23:33a, echoing John the Baptist's words of condemnation in 3:7), will not escape condemnation to hell (23:33b), for they will "kill and crucify" and "scourge" and "persecute" certain Christian "prophets and wise men and scribes" that Jesus himself will send on mission (23:34). As a result the scribes and Pharisees will endure "all the righteous blood shed on earth, from the blood of innocent Abel to the blood of Zechari'ah the son of Barachi'ah, whom you [in the person of their fathers] murdered between the sanctuary and the altar" (23:35).[3] Jesus then solemnly declares, "Truly, I say to you, all this will come upon this generation" (23:36). This does not mean the entire Jewish race but only that specific temporal generation that will still remain when the Romans level Jerusalem and the temple in AD 70.

Jesus's next words are a prophecy of that destruction: Jerusalem kills prophets and others sent to her, and rejecting the love and mercy of the God who came to earth in Jesus ("How often would I have gathered your children together" in 23:37 implies a longer time frame than Jesus's earthly life) means that her "house is forsaken and desolate" (23:38). Here "house" means both legacy and dynasty, as well as the "house" of the physical temple, Jerusalem's center. And so Jesus will next deliver ever more explicit teaching about the temple's coming destruction.

EXCURSUS: MATTHEW 24: THE DESTRUCTION OF JERUSALEM AND ITS TEMPLE AND THE END OF THE WORLD

The lectionary does not include Matthew 24 entirely, but it matters very much for the Matthean storyline, and so we treat all of it here. Jesus has just issued a public lament over Jerusalem's coming destruction. Now Jesus speaks to his disciples privately in detail about the imminent destruction and the close of the end of the age. What in Matthew 24 pertains to the destruction of Jerusalem and its temple and what to the

---

[3] Zechariah, the biblical prophet, lived in the sixth century BC, and tradition as witnessed by *Tg. Lamentations* 2.20 and *Ecclesiastes Rabbah* 3.16 holds he was murdered in the temple. Another Zechariah is murdered on the temple's most sacred precincts (2 Chr 24:20–22).

end of the age is not clear; put differently, then, how does Jesus relate the destruction of Jerusalem to the close of the age?

On one hand, it seems that Jesus distances the end of the world from the destruction of Jerusalem and its temple, given all sorts of clues in Matthew 24:1–28 that the destruction of Jerusalem does not mean the end of the world. On the other hand, Jesus says in verse 29 that the signs of the end and his coming as Son of man will come "[i]mmediately after the tribulation of those days." One possibility is to understand the Greek word for "immediately" (*eutheos*) as an inferential adverb, with the weaker force of "then," as in Mark 1:21, 23, and 29.[4] Reading it in this way would put the events of the end detailed in Matthew 24:29–31 into the indefinite future, as if Jesus were saying, "So then, sometime after that tribulation . . ." This supposition is reinforced by Jesus's striking concession that not even the Son knows the day or hour of the end (24:26).

The chapter opens with the disciples pointing out the edifices of the temple complex (Matt 24:1), which Herod the Great had refurbished and expanded beginning in 19 BC in an attempt to surpass the glories of Solomon's temple. Jesus then explicitly declares its destruction (24:2). So the occasion of the teaching in this chapter is Jesus's prediction of the destruction of the temple; much, if not most, of the chapter concerns that event, which came to pass in AD 70.

Now the temple was regarded as ground zero of the cosmos, the very place where heaven and earth met, and the high altar was supposed to be situated at the very spot where

---

4 Walter Bauer, F. W. Danker, W. F. Arndt, and F. W. Gingrich, *Greek-English Lexicon of the New Testament and Other Early Christian Literature*, 3rd ed. (Chicago: University of Chicago Press, 1999), accessed electronically on Accordance.

Abraham began to sacrifice Isaac, and thus where God himself appeared to Abraham (Gen 22:14). Thus the disciples naturally ask not only about the time of the destruction of the temple but also about Jesus's coming to bring about the close of the age (Matt 24:3), for in their minds the destruction of the temple can only mean the end is nigh.

Jesus's first move is to tamp down apocalyptic expectations; he warns the disciples against being led astray by false Christs (Matt 24:4–5) and being deceived by wars, famines, and earthquakes (24:6–8). Tribulation, persecution, apostasy, betrayal, and hatred are coming, along with false prophets and an increase in wickedness (24:10–12). Endurance to the end—either the end of one's own life or the very end—will mean salvation (24:13). But the end will not come until the gospel of the kingdom is proclaimed "throughout the whole world, as a testimony to all nations" (24:14a); only then will the end come (24:14b). This implies a long period of missionary activity, but on the other hand, it refers to the Roman world, which Christian missionaries like St. Paul evangelized thoroughly before AD 70, and Paul himself writes in the late 50s that the gospel has been made known to all nations (Rom 16:26).

The next section (Matt 24:15–28) presents all sorts of clues that the destruction of Jerusalem is in view and that there will be a long period of history after that event. The "desolating sacrilege" (24:15) is a reference to the trampling of the sanctuary and even the Holy of Holies by Gentiles, such as happened during the time of the Maccabees when Antiochus IV Epiphanes desecrated the temple by having a sow sacrificed on the high altar. Jesus warns his disciples to take flight at that point: "let those who are in Judea flee to the mountains" (24:16). Flight makes no sense if the end is in view. Rather, Jesus is warning his disciples to avoid getting caught within the Roman siege of Jerusalem. And in Matthew 24:21, Jesus says, "For them there will be great tribulation, such as has not been from the beginning of the world until now, no, and never will be." "Never will be [again]" also implies a period of history after Jerusalem's destruction. So when Jesus talks about those days being "shortened" (24:22), he's talking about God putting a limit on the time the Romans would wage horrible war in Judea.

More warnings against false prophets are given (Matt 24:23–26), which are reasonable to give, as the fall of Jerusalem and its temple would (and did) raise apocalyptic, messianic expectations to a fever pitch. Instead of looking for signs or seeking earthly Christs, the disciples are to look to the heavens, for the coming of the Son of man, Jesus, will be obvious, "as the lightning comes from the east and shines as far as the west" (24:27). So the disciples are to look for heavenly deliverance; Jesus will come to bring the end. They are not to look for earthly deliverance in the person of an earthly warrior sent to break the siege and drive the Romans back.

And Jesus gives a final cryptic signal that he is talking about the Roman siege of Jerusalem: "Wherever the body is, there the eagles will be gathered together" (24:28). Jesus has not had many nice things to say about Jerusalem to this point (and St. Matthew observes Jerusalem aligned itself with Herod in being "troubled" when Jesus was born, 2:3), and so Jerusalem is the body or corpse where the eagles—Romans, with their sacred eagles on their standards—will gather. The Greek for the birds in question is *hoi aetoi*, which can also mean "vultures," so a double meaning is possible, likely intended by Jesus: When the Roman legions with their eagles (*aetoi*) invest, reduce, and destroy Jerusalem, it will be like vultures (*aetoi*) feeding on a corpse.

Now Jesus speaks explicitly about the end. Darkness will

reign as sun, moon, and stars fail (Matt 24:29), and then "the sign of the Son of man" will appear in heaven. All tribes of earth will mourn as they observe "the Son of man coming on the clouds of heaven with power and great glory" (24:30). Jesus's return as Son of man will be obvious and public; there is no need to seek signs or to hope in rumors of a Christ come to relieve the holy city from its Roman siege.

Then Jesus returns to the present issue of the coming destruction of Jerusalem. The fig tree which Jesus cursed as a symbol of the destruction of the temple (Matt 21:18–22) now becomes a reminder to the disciples. They should know when Jerusalem is to be annihilated, and so when they see all the things pertaining to that destruction, they will know "it is near" (not "he," as in many translations, 24:33; my translation), as if the coming of the Son of man at the end were in view. When Jesus says that "this generation will not pass away till all these things take place" (24:34), he means that many living then will be around to endure Jerusalem's passion. When Jesus says, "Heaven and earth will pass away" (24:35a), he's speaking about the temple perishing, since "heaven and earth" was a Jewish circumlocution for the temple, as again it was ground zero of the cosmos, the place where heaven and earth met. The temple will end, but Jesus's disciples, even though Jews, need not fear or lament, for Jesus assures them that "my words will not pass away" (24:35b).

It is clear that Jesus is not teaching that the end of the world follows immediately after the destruction of Jerusalem; Matthew 24:36 says, "But of that day and hour no one knows, not even the angels of heaven, nor the Son, but the Father only." If Jesus here concedes that he as Son does not know "that day or hour" of the end, then he cannot very well be teaching that it will happen within the disciples's lifetimes after Jerusalem's destruction. He can't teach what he does not know.

MATTHEW 24:37–44: FIRST SUNDAY OF ADVENT

The lectionary now picks up the bulk of the second half of Matthew 24. Here Jesus teaches about the uncertainty of the time of the end. He himself declares that not even the Son— Jesus himself, of course—knows when "that day and hour" will come (24:36). By way of illustration, Jesus calls upon the example of Noah (24:37–39): Noah and his family had warning judgment was coming, but they were not given the exact time. They were simply ready when the rains fell and the waters rose, safe in the ark, riding out God's de-creation, as the flood took back the land it had conceded at creation when God gathered the waters into one place (Gen 1:9–10). Then Jesus gives parabolic examples: two men will be in the field, one taken and one left, and two women will be grinding, one taken and one left (24:40–41).

Jesus then makes the point plain: "Watch therefore, for you do not know on what day your Lord is coming" (Matt 24:42). Precisely because both the Son (on earth) and his disciples do not know when the Lord will return, the disciples are to keep perpetual vigil, to be ready at all times, just as Noah and his family were ready, lest they be among those left behind at Christ's coming or lest they be like a homeowner who failed to protect his property in the night (24:43). This passage thus cuts against apocalyptic speculation, which often seizes American Christians like a fever. Given what Jesus says here, it is a form of sloth to expend our energies poring over Ezekiel, Daniel, Revelation, and other apocalyptic passages and texts in attempts to correlate contemporary events with prophecy and discern the time of the end. And Jesus hammers the point once more: "Therefore you also must be ready; for the Son of man is coming at an hour you do not expect" (24:44).

MATTHEW 24:42–51: THURSDAY WEEK 21
(SEE IMMEDIATELY PRIOR FOR VV. 42–44)

Faithful and unfaithful servants is the theme of Jesus's next parabolic teaching. Perpetual vigilance is hard; it is taxing to always be on the watch, in a state of battle readiness not knowing if the call is coming now, or later, or never. But that's what Jesus calls us to. As servants of Christ, we are to live good Christian lives in a state of grace 24/7 (as my students say), loving God and neighbor, and so ready to be found ready at the return of Our Lord: "Blessed is that servant whom his master when he comes will find so doing" (24:46).

Since constant attentiveness is hard, many will flag. For some early Christians it seemed like Christ's promise to come again had failed (see 2 Pet 3), and we today are living almost twenty centuries after Jesus's words. And so Jesus presents the example of the wicked servant who takes the delay of the return of the master as an occasion for misbehavior and dissolution (Matt 24:48–49). The result is the punishment of perdition, as wicked servants will receive their place "with the hypocrites; there men will weep and gnash their teeth" (24:50–51).

As we have seen often in St. Matthew's Gospel, there is a real threat of punishment for disciples, for believers, in accord with the Catholic concept of salvation as free cooperation with divine grace (also held by other Christians, such as Methodists, Pentecostals, Nazarenes, and Wesleyans). Christian beliefs about eternal punishment, though clearly part of the Faith, do not fit well in today's ethos of Gnosticism and Moral Therapeutic Deism. It may be helpful to remember, however, that prior ages before modernity also had great difficulty with such teachings for the same reasons: hell is almost too heavy a concept to bear, and it seems unjust that any might go there. There is nothing new under the sun. The best remedy for hell (and its subtle denial) is a radical reliance on God's grace. As St. Paul says, "[W]here sin increased, grace abounded all the more" (Rom 5:20). In St. Matthew's Gospel, the threats and warnings are real but ought to be overshadowed by Jesus's words about our heavenly Father (e.g., Matthew 6) and his promise of salvation. One man or one woman may be left while the other will be taken. But not to fear: Christ will soon institute the Eucharist to strengthen us in our journey of perpetual vigilance.

MATTHEW 25:1–13: THIRTY-SECOND SUNDAY IN ORDINARY TIME / FRIDAY WEEK 21

Jesus's apocalyptic discourse ends with three parables about the end. The theme of vigilance persists through them all, but it's important to observe that that vigilance isn't simply a matter of keeping oneself unstained by deliberate sin; it is also a matter of positively doing the things Jesus commands. The former, in the world of St. Matthew's Gospel, would be the attitude of the Pharisee. The latter (without neglecting the former) is the way of the Christian.

This Parable of the Ten Maidens (usually known as the Parable of the Ten Virgins) emphasizes vigilance. The five wise maidens were prepared with sufficient oil (pitch, probably) to keep their torches burning until the wedding party should arrive (Matt 25:4; we should envision torches here, not small clay lamps, as the latter wouldn't be sufficient for the sort of illumination envisioned). The foolish maidens did not prepare, and so precisely at the moment of the announcement of the bridegroom's arrival, they need to leave to get more pitch (25:10a). While away, the bridegroom arrives for the wedding feast, and the door is locked (25:10b). When the foolish maidens arrive, they are not granted reentry, even though they cry out, "Lord, lord, open to us" (25:11); the bridegroom replies, "Truly, I say to you, I do not know you" (25:12). And Jesus helpfully makes the point of the parable obvious: "Watch therefore, for you know neither the day nor the hour" (25:13), repeating his express words of 24:42.

The bridegroom is Jesus (see Matt 9:15, where he refers to himself as such obliquely), and the wedding feast is the kingdom of heaven. As Pope St. John Paul II emphasized in his catecheses now known as the Theology of the Body, the Bible employs marital imagery to symbolize God's relationship with his people. Israel is the bride, God the husband, and the idolatry in which Israel all too often engages is spiritual adultery. In the New Covenant, the Church is the bride, and Jesus, God's agent and indeed divine himself, is the bridegroom, the husband. Parables like the present one teach that our relationship to God isn't primarily legal but familial. Salvation, therefore, isn't a matter of merely being acquitted from the guilt of our sins but is the establishment and maintenance of a loving relationship, as committed and intimate as that of husband and wife.

We also notice a parallel with Jesus's teaching in Matthew 7:21–23: "Not every one who says to me, 'Lord, Lord,' shall enter the kingdom of heaven, but he who does the will of my Father who is in heaven" (7:21). Jesus continues, "On that day many will say to me, 'Lord, Lord, did we not prophesy in your name, and cast out demons in your name, and do many mighty works in your name?' And then will I declare to them, 'I never knew you; depart from me, you evildoers'" (7:22–23). In the present parable the foolish maidens also call out, "Lord, Lord," and the bridegroom similarly responds, "I do not know you" (25:11–12). With regard to Matthew 7:21–23, I suggested that Jesus will recognize us if we are true Christians, acting as we should, for at the end, all masks are removed; we are seen for who we really are. If we are hypocrites—and the very term in Greek referred to an actor on stage wearing a mask—we will be seen as such, for "nothing is covered that will not be revealed, or hidden that will not be known" (10:26).

MATTHEW 25:14–30 (OR 14–15, 19–21): THIRTY-THIRD SUNDAY IN ORDINARY TIME / SATURDAY OF WEEK 21 IN ORDINARY TIME

Here Jesus delivers the Parable of the Talents. A man departs on a journey and gives one servant five talents, another two, and another one (Matt 25:14–15). The man is Jesus, and the departure will be his ascension and presence in heaven until his personal return. While the man is gone, the first two servants double what they had been given (25:16–17), but the third simply preserves his one talent by burying it (25:18). The first two are rewarded upon the master's return (25:19–23), as faithful Christians will be rewarded upon Jesus's return. Important here is the phrase "enter into the joy of your master" (25:21b, 23b). That would be a weird thing for a master to say to his servants on a literal level, and so it points to the joy of heaven on a spiritual level.

But the third servant is not rewarded, for he did not earn. He slouches forward and says, "Master, I knew you to be a hard man, reaping where you did not sow, and gathering where you did not winnow; so I was afraid, and I went and hid your talent in the ground. Here you have what is yours" (25:24–25). This servant does not view his master favorably, but sees him as a taskmaster in whose business he has no real share. He describes him as a hard man, taking the labors of others for his own. This represents the would-be follower of Jesus who finds Jesus's teachings simply too difficult and probably does so because he has the attitude of a Pharisee, seeing religion as a matter of legalistic compliance.

The master hoists the servant on his own petard: If the master was so rapacious, then the servant should have had the sense to keep him happy by investing the money with people who knew what they were doing, and thus earn a return (Matt 25:26–27). His one talent is then given to the one with ten talents (25:28), on the principle that "to every one who has will more be given, and he will have abundance; but from him who has not, even what he has will be taken away" (25:29). There is apparently rank and levels of reward in heaven (think of Jesus's words in 5:17–20 about those who are either least or greatest in the kingdom of heaven), even though it's counter-intuitive to us in our egalitarian age; the saying means those who merit rank and reward in heaven will find their reward compounded even more, while those who do not (like the worthless servant) will lose everything and be assigned a place in the "outer darkness" where "men will weep and gnash their teeth" (25:30; the theme of apocalyptic judgment continues: see 24:51 for the same phrase).

MATTHEW 25:31–46: THIRTY-FOURTH SUNDAY IN ORDINARY TIME / MONDAY OF THE FIRST WEEK IN LENT

Jesus closes his apocalyptic discourse with the famous Parable of the Sheep and the Goats, in which Jesus says both to the righteous and the damned that what they did, or didn't do, for the "least of these" (Matt 25:40, 45), they did, or failed to do, to him; Jesus is present in the poor, the prisoners, the naked, the hungry, the stranger, the sick. It's often used in support of social justice efforts, with the apocalyptic judgment stripped out, to make the simple point that we should treat those in need like we would treat Jesus, for he is with them and in them. There's more going on, however. This parable caps off Jesus's repeated admonitions to be vigilant in faith and works while awaiting his return, showing now quite clearly the final rewards and punishments awaiting the just and the unjust, either to eternal punishment or eternal life (25:46), either to "inherit the kingdom prepared for [the blessed] from the foundation of the world" (25:34) or "the eternal fire prepared for the devil and his angels" (25:41); again we see the Two Ways, here their ultimate destination. In fact the passage is less of a parable and more of a straightforward apocalyptic revelation of the very end.

This passage then reveals the great and final judgment of "all the nations" (Matt 25:32a), which it seems are judged and separated as corporate nations (25:33). So on one hand, we have here a vision in which the Gentile nations are being judged on the basis of how they treat Christians, who (as Jesus has prophesied in St. Matthew's Gospel, see especially 5:10–11) will suffer greatly as the message moves into the nations around the world (see 24:9–14). What of non-Christians? There are righteous found among the nations who will not have known Jesus, but Jesus will know them—which, as we have seen with regard to 7:21–23 and 25:11–13, is more important, and Jesus can save people in God's grace and will apart from their knowledge of him (as in the "baptism of desire"). On the other hand, the discourse is directed to the disciples alone (24:3) and fits with the theme of the dire warnings given to those who know and follow Jesus. That is, the judgment of Christians is also in view here; are we taking care of our brothers and sisters in the Lord?

It's true that our corporal works of mercy need to be directed to all in need, regardless of their creed, but the social justice interpretation of the parable runs into difficulty when

Jesus identifies "the least of these" as "my brethren" (Matt 25:40). In the New Testament, "brothers" or "brethren" specifies Christians in particular, as those who believe in God the Father are made siblings in the family of the Church; through divine filiation they are made sons and daughters of God, and Jesus has already identified the disciples as "brethren" (23:8b) in this same apocalyptic discourse. The Gospel of Matthew is first and foremost Scripture for the Church about Jesus's relationship to the Church, not a manual of general ethics, and so we shouldn't be surprised to find Jesus concerned with the treatment of Christians in particular. Indeed, in today's climate we Christians need to stand by and support other Christians as they endure whatever trials—hunger, thirst, a stranger, naked, sick, imprisoned—for no one else is going to.

CHAPTER 17

✝

The Passion of Jesus the Christ

Matthew 26:14–27:66 (Long Form) or 27:11–54 (Short Form): Palm Sunday of the Passion of the Lord

Given the lectionary's adoption of the bulk of Matthew 26–27, we will not treat every passage in detail but examine the distinctives of the Matthean Passion Narrative as a whole.

Jesus's Control of Events

Above all, the Matthean Passion Narrative presents Jesus as the one in control of events. His arrest, torture, and crucifixion do not happen to him; he permits them and even orchestrates them. The opening of Matthew 26 presents a pattern. In 26:1–2, Jesus tells his disciples that he will be crucified two days later at Passover. Only "then" (26:3), after Jesus's prediction, do the chief priests and elders conspire with the high priest, Caiaphas, to arrest Jesus and kill him

(26:3–4). But they decide not to do it during Passover, "lest there be a tumult among the people (26:5).

Of course Jesus will be arrested during the feast, and a tumult does take place among the people in Pilate's courtyard: "So when Pilate saw that he was gaining nothing, but rather that a riot [*thorubos*, the same word translated as "tumult" in Matt 26:5] was beginning, he took water and washed his hands before the crowd" (Matt 27:24). Jesus's words come true, while the conspirators's plot fails in its details. Jesus is in control.

"Then" (Matt 26:3) shows up also in the arrest of Jesus (26:47–56), as part of the familiar two-step pattern in 26:1–5. Thus Judas has arranged a signal: the crowd is to arrest the man whom Judas kisses (26:48). Judas approaches Jesus, greets him, and kisses him (26:49). Now according to Judas's plan, Jesus is supposed to be seized right then and there. But Jesus intervenes, saying, "Friend, now do what you have come for" (26:50a, my own translation of *eph' ho parei*). Jesus gives permission for the plot to proceed, and only "then" (26:50b) is Jesus seized.

Jesus's control of events is also seen in his remark about the "twelve legions of angels" upon whom he could call to save him (Matt 26:53). That's 72,000 angels. But Jesus does not call on them, instead choosing to go the way of the Cross. In the world of the story (and for us who believe), the angels are real. They are there; they could rescue the Christ. But again, for a second time, Jesus refuses angelic aid; the first instance was the Temptation Narrative, where Satan suggested that Jesus cast himself down from the pinnacle of the temple because Scripture (Ps 91:11–12) promises angels would protect him (Matt 4:5–7). As the late and famed Yale scholar Nils Dahl notes, "The hearer of Matthew's story hardly doubts for a moment that twelve legions of angels would have been at the disposal of Jesus the Christ if he had prayed for them. But that was a moral impossibility (26:53; cf. 26:61, *dynamai*, 'I am able')."[1]

So Jesus goes the way of the Cross, and Jesus's control of events is finally seen similarly, if subtly, on the Cross itself. Would nails suffice to hold fast the One who has shown himself master and commander over nature, sickness, death, and demons? His obedience to his sacrificial commission, given him by his Father, is what held him there. As St. Catherine of Siena said, "For nails were not enough to hold God-and-Man nailed and fastened on the Cross had Love not held Him there."[2]

The Betrayal of the Christ (Matthew 26:14–25: Wednesday of Holy Week)

The lectionary includes the betrayal of Jesus by Judas. Judas offers to betray Jesus, who in turn is offered thirty pieces of silver (Matt 26:14–16). In terms of betrayal, Judas probably divulges two things: First, he likely confirms for the chief priests that Jesus did in fact believe himself to be the Christ, which Jesus said not to proclaim. Second, he will betray Jesus's location late at night. Jerusalem would swell during the week of Passover / Unleavened Bread to as many as 100,000 pilgrims (its normal population being perhaps 20,000 or 30,000), with parties camped out all over, surrounding the city. Taking Jesus by stealth (26:4) requires seizing him under the cover of darkness, when most would be sleeping, and doing that requires someone who knows where he is.

---

[1] Nils Dahl, "The Passion Narrative in Matthew," in *The Interpretation of Matthew*, ed. Graham Stanton (Edinburgh: T&T Clark, 1995), 42–55, at 44.

[2] St. Catherine of Siena, *Letters* 38, to Monna Agnese.

The institution of the Eucharist is set in the explicit context of a Passover meal; in Matthew 26:17–19, the word "passover" is mentioned three times, once in each verse. Jesus, ever in control of events in the Matthean Passion Narrative, simply tells the disciples to enter the city, find a certain man, and declare what will be: "The Teacher says, My time is at hand; I will keep the passover at your house with my disciples" (26:18b). This is the Jews's most sacred ritual meal—and Jesus transforms it into his Church's own ritual meal—and so the occasion makes the betrayal all the more striking.

At table, Jesus prophesies that one of his disciples will betray him (Matt 26:21). Each asks if it is he (26:22). Jesus does not identify Judas, but says cryptically, "He who has dipped his hand in the dish with me, will betray me. The Son of man goes as it is written of him, but woe to that man by whom the Son of man is betrayed! It would have been better for that man if he had not been born" (26:23–24). We likely have here an allusion to Psalm 41:9: "Even my bosom friend in whom I trusted, who ate of my bread, has lifted his heel against me." For St. Matthew and the earliest Christians, the Psalms were prophecies written largely by the first christ, King David, so they pointed then to the ultimate Christ, Jesus. Thus we find many allusions to the Psalms in the New Testament, especially in the Passion Narratives.

Of great theological significance is Jesus's statement, "The Son of man goes as it is written of him, but woe to that man by whom the Son of man is betrayed!" On one hand, because Scripture is ironclad, what is written must happen to Jesus, the Son of man. It can be no other way. So Judas is predestined to do what he did. On the other hand, Judas did so freely, of his own will, and so "woe" to him; "It would have been better for that man if he had not been born." Here we see the Catholic conception of providence involving a non-competitive view of the relationship of human will and the divine will. In Catholic understanding, God wills that we exercise our will— that is, we choose—freely. As we're made in the image of God, his will is the very thing that powers (as it were) our will, so even things that God foresees and foreordains are done freely by the agents who do them. Humans have real free will, and it cooperates with God's will; human will does not compete with God's will.

And so Judas then asks, "Is it I, Master?" (Matt 26:25a). Jesus does not answer directly, but cryptically: "You have said so" (26:25b). Judas knows what he is doing, and his question is likely a ruse to keep the other disciples from knowing. So too is Jesus's answer, for he wills to go the way of the Cross in obedience to fulfill his Father's will. But Jesus's answer is also subtly affirmative, in keeping with the indirect Semitic style: Judas has declared himself so simply by asking the question, which includes the very words *ego eimi*; when construed as an indicative, they mean "It is I."

The Institution of the Eucharist

Now we come to one of the weightiest moments in St. Matthew's Gospel, the institution of the Eucharist. Again the setting is the traditional Passover meal, but Jesus takes the ritual and makes it his own, in continuity with it. The customary meal involved the slaughter and consumption of a lamb, slain in the temple by the priests and then taken by a representative of a party of pilgrims back to their campsite. But in Jesus's Eucharistic ritual, no lamb is mentioned. Perhaps they are eating the lamb ("Now as they were eating," Matt 26:26), but the lack of its express mention leads to the implication that St. Matthew intends for us to understand Jesus as the new Passover Lamb, as St. John makes clear in his Gospel (see John 1:29, 36).

So Jesus himself is the new and decisive sacrifice; his blood is "poured out" (*ekchunnō*, Matt 26:28), a technical term in Greek referring to ritual sacrificial slaughter. In St. Matthew's story, Jesus has predicted the destruction of the temple in deed (his prophetic action of "cleansing the temple" in 21:12–17) and in word (Matt 24). That means sacrifices will disappear, for sacrifice can only be conducted in the temple. So Jesus here provides the new and decisive sacrificial ritual for the Church, the new Israel, that will abide after temple sacrifices cease. His Eucharistic ritual offers the blood of the new[3] covenant until the advent of the kingdom (26:29).

That Jesus has provided his Church with a ritual to make present his cruciform sacrifice as long as time abides should put paid to all talk about Jesus founding a non-sacrificial, non-sacramental religion (though many forms of Christianity do in fact hold that). Jesus the Jew is not opposed to ritual, seeing it as something that gets in the way of faith. Rather, as is the case with law, the question concerns not doing away with the Law and ritual but following Jesus's New Law and new ritual.

Finally, the institution of the Eucharist answers for the reader the implicit question of Matthew 1:21: Jesus will save his people (the Church) from their sins, not by killing for them (as his very name Jesus, "Joshua," and his status as the Christ

---

3   Some ancient manuscripts lack "new," other important ones have it. The question is whether St. Matthew originally wrote "new" and a scribe omitted it for some conscious or unconscious, accidental reason, or whether St. Matthew didn't write it, and some scribe added it later in a manuscript to emphasize the distinction between Jesus and Judaism. The text-critical issue should be resolved by including "new" in the text, for while the Faith Jesus delivers stands in continuity with Judaism, by this point in the story the tension between Jesus and the Jewish leadership is at a fever pitch, and so it seems most likely St. Matthew himself would have written "new."

would suggest) but by dying for them. The ironic reversal of expectations is complete.

Here we also find a subtle argument for Jesus's real and true presence in the Eucharist. In Matthew 26:29, he says, "I tell you I shall not drink again of this fruit of the vine until that day when I drink it new with you in my Father's kingdom." Jesus enters his Father's kingdom not at the end of time but at his resurrection and ascension, at the end of Matthew. So one can conclude that when the Apostles celebrate the Lord's Supper, Jesus is there with them, in (say) AD 37. And that might be why we don't have Mass but only communion on Good Friday. "Until that day" runs from the end of the Last Supper to Jesus's resurrection only three days later.

Fulfilling the Figure of Isaac

If Jesus is the decisive sacrifice, he would have to be presented as a new Isaac; the binding of Isaac (Gen 22; the *Akedah*) was thought to be the source of all later sacrifice and to have occurred on what would later be Mount Zion, the temple mount, precisely where the high altar was built. And we find in the Gethsemane sequence (Matt 26:36–56) many allusions and thematic parallels presenting Jesus as Isaac.

Gethsemane presents two allusions to Genesis 22. In Matthew 26:36 Jesus commands his disciples, "Sit here, while I go yonder and pray" (*kathisate autou heōs apelthōn ekei proseuxōmai*). In Genesis 22:5 Abraham says to his servants, "Stay here . . . [we] will go yonder and worship" (*kathisate autou . . . dieleusometha heōs hōde kai proskunēsantes*). Moreover, Jesus tells Peter, James, and John to watch and pray so that they may not enter into temptation (*peirasmon*, Matt 26:41), while Abraham was "tested" (*epeirazen*) by God (Gen 22:1). Both Gethsemane and the *Akedah* are occasions of testing.

The arrest of Our Lord (Matt 26:47–56) also presents allusions to Genesis 22. The words of the phrase "with swords and clubs" (*meta machairōn kai xulōn*) in 26:47 and 55 match the Greek words in Genesis 22:6, 7, 9 and 10, there translated "knife" and "wood." However translated in each passage, both Greek terms denote implements of violent sacrificial death. What is more, in Matthew 26:50, after Judas greets Jesus, the crowd "laid hands on Jesus" (*epebalon tas cheiras epi ton Iēsoun*), while the angel in Genesis 22:12 commands Abraham not to lay his hand on the boy, that is, Isaac (*mē epibalēs tēn cheira sou epi to paidarion*). Finally, in Matthew 26:51 a nameless disciple "stretched out his hand and drew his sword" (*ekteinas tēn cheira apespasen tēn machairan autou*), while Genesis 22:10 says, "Abraham put forth his hand, and took the knife to slay his son," Isaac (*exeteinen Abraam tēn cheira autou labein tēn machairan*).

The allusions are too strong to be coincidental. And they produce thematic parallels. Isaac in Jewish tradition was presented as obedient to his father's will in the matter of his sacrifice, and St. Matthew stresses obedience in general and Jesus's own obedience in particular (see Matt 5:18–20; 7:15–23; 12:33–37; 12:46–50; 21:28–32; 21:43; 25:1–30; 25:31–46; 28:20). In this very passage, Jesus obeys his Father's will that he go the way of the Cross. There is no real struggle in St. Matthew's Gethsemane sequence, no progression of surrender as one finds in St. Mark's Gospel. As Davies and Allison write, "[Jesus's] course is fixed by the will of God, and this overrides whatever beliefs or feelings he has about death, so there is no real resistance. For Jesus the issue is not death but submission to the divine will: 'Thy will be done.'"[4]

---

[4] Davies and Allison, *Saint Matthew*, 3:502. See also Moberly, *The Bible,*

So when the thugs of the crowd come for him, Jesus does not flee but rises to meet them. "Rise, let us be going; see, my betrayer is at hand" (Matt 26:46). He invites the disciples to go with him on the final leg of the way of the Cross. *Agōmen,* the verb here for "let us be going," is a verb of approach and confrontation, not flight (the word for flight would be *anachōreō,* as in 2:12, 13, 14, 22; 4:12; 12:15; 14:13; 15:21; see also 9:24 and 27:5).

The crowd who lays hands upon Jesus to make his sacrifice happen wields "swords and clubs"; Abraham would have laid hands on Isaac to sacrifice him using the sacrificial implements of knife and wood. All events in the world of St. Matthew's story, even those done by God's human and satanic enemies, are under God's control and serve God's purposes. Jesus's death is thus a result both of human conspiracy (see Matt 12:14 and 26:3–4) by those who stand under Satan's rule (12:34) and also of the will of God the Father; St. Matthew's Gospel stresses the necessity of Jesus's Passion and its sacrificial nature in passages such as the Passion predictions (16:21; 17:12, 22–23; 20:17–19; 26:1–2), the ransom saying (20:28), and the words over the cup in the Last Supper (26:28).

In short, God as Father of Jesus, the beloved Son, in effect wields the crowd with its swords and clubs to cause Jesus's sacrificial death in the same way that Abraham as father of Isaac, the beloved son, wielded the "knife" and "wood" to cause Isaac's sacrificial death. We have, then, these parallels:

Theology, and Faith, 211–215.

GENESIS 22	MATTHEW 26: 36–56
Abraham	God
Knife and wood	Crowd with swords and clubs
Isaac	Jesus

Furthermore, Jesus explains the scriptural necessity of his Passion: "But how then should the scriptures be fulfilled, that it must be so?" (Matt 26:54). Jesus's closing words, that "all this has taken place, that the scriptures of the prophets might be fulfilled" (26:56), also mean that his death is necessary. The Scriptures in question here include Genesis 22, making Jesus a type of Isaac.

The Fidelity of Jesus the Christ

In the trial scenes that follow—Jesus is tried by the Sanhedrin and Peter "tried" by a "maid" (Matt 26:69, in all likelihood a slave girl)—Jesus's fidelity is contrasted with Peter's infidelity, and thus all the Apostles and disciples, as Peter, the foremost Apostle, represents them all. Jesus is tried by real men with real power, led by Caiaphas, the Jewish high priest; but there is no real legal recourse, as the trial at night is irregular at best and likely, even under Jewish law, illegal. First Jesus is accused of claiming he could destroy the temple and rebuild it in three days (Matt 26:61), an obvious reference to the resurrection. Here again (as in 12:14 and 21:45–46) Jesus's enemies intend to harm him, but they speak truth, presenting Jesus himself, God incarnate, as the one who is the new temple where God's presence will abide. And in doing so, they play their part in the Passion, bringing about the salvation of the world in the very act of railroading Jesus.

The charge precipitates Caiaphas's decisive question, "I adjure you by the living God, tell us if you are the Christ, the Son of God" (Matt 26:63). Jesus answers affirmatively but obliquely, using the same words he did in responding to Judas: "You have said so" (26:64a). He then seals his fate further by declaring, "But I tell you, hereafter you will see the Son of man seated at the right hand of Power, and coming on the clouds of heaven" (26:64b). They receive this as blasphemy, for they believe Jesus to be lying, or deceived. It would be a bit like someone declaring himself Mohammad-come-again, and Islamic authorities refusing to recognize him. And so Caiaphas rends his garments and solicits the death sentence, which the Sanhedrin delivers (26:65–66).

After this, Jesus is beaten (Matt 26:67) and mocked with the taunt, "Prophesy to us, you Christ! Who is it that struck you?" (26:68). In the very next scene, Peter's denial (26:69–75), the Christ proves himself a true prophet, for St. Matthew reminds his readers that Jesus prophesied Peter's denial: "And Peter remembered the saying of Jesus, 'Before the cock crows, you will deny me three times'" (26:75). And so St. Matthew again shows Jesus's control of events: even in beating and mocking Jesus, even in Peter's denial of Jesus, figures in the drama are playing the parts foreordained for them to bring about the necessary sacrifice of the Christ. Moreover, the contrast between Jesus and Peter comes to its climax: Jesus is faithful, Peter unfaithful.

The Culpability of the People

Caiaphas now has Jesus handed over to Pilate (Matt 27:1–2), since the Jews couldn't carry out their own death sentences without Roman permission (which required Roman legal condemnation as well, Roman law being supreme). Pilate asks Jesus if he is in fact the "King of the Jews" (27:11a), and Jesus now for a third answers with the cryptic affirmative, "You have said so" (27:11b). Jesus was identified as such by the Magi in chapter 2, and here now he subtly affirms the claim. After that he remains silent in the face of thunderous charges from the Jewish leadership (27:12–14).

So now Pilate, sensing Jesus is getting railroaded, tries to get the crowd to send Barabbas to death and to release Jesus (Matt 27:15–23). Barabbas is a true revolutionary, a murderer with real blood on his hands (27:16). In some ancient manuscripts of the Gospel of Matthew, he is twice called "Jesus Barabbas" (27:16–17). I think, on textual grounds, that St. Matthew originally wrote "Jesus Barabbas" but a later scribe who held the Name of Jesus sacred eliminated "Jesus" from before "Barabbas" in the copy of the Gospel he was making, to avoid associating sinless, holy Jesus with a murderer. In fact, it is only recently that Catholics began using "Jesus" regularly; it used to be we would use the circumlocution "Our Lord" to avoid pronouncing the sacred Name of Jesus, in good biblical fashion, just as Jews wouldn't (and won't) pronounce the Name of God as given in Exodus 3:14.

So St. Matthew is setting up a contrast between two different Jesuses: Jesus Barabbas and Jesus Christ. The former's name (Barabbas) actually means "son of the father" in Aramaic, but readers of the Gospel know that Jesus Christ is presented as the true Son of the Father. Thus the crowd has a choice between a false son of the father, and the true Son of the true Father. Of course, tragic as St. Matthew's story is, they will pick the wrong one at the instigation of the chief priests and elders (Matt 27:20):

The governor again said to them, "Which of the two do you want me to release for you?" And they said, "Barab'bas." Pilate said to them, "Then what shall I do with Jesus who is called Christ?" They all said, "Let him be crucified." And he said, "Why, what evil has he done?" But they shouted all the more, "Let him be crucified." (27:21–23)

Pilate relents, and famously washes his hands of the situation, saying, "I am innocent of this righteous man's blood; see to it yourselves" (Matt 27:24). Pilate here speaks truth; Jesus is in fact righteous, which is also the Greek word for innocent (*dikaios*). The crowd responds with fateful words: "His blood be on us and on our children!" (27:25).

In Christian tradition, those words have often been understood as the Jews (as a race) calling down a perpetual curse upon themselves, with deadly consequences in history. But attention to the narrative dynamics of St. Matthew's story offers another fruitful possibility, and in fact two. First, they are praying an unwitting prayer of salvation, asking that the blood of Jesus Christ would cover them, as it does those of us who trust in Christ. Second, the generation of Jews in the courtyard (the younger among them, at least) and their children after them are the two generations who will be around to suffer the siege of Jerusalem and destruction of the temple that Jesus has predicted. That siege and destruction is God's recompense for the murder of his Son. After that, any judgment ends; the Jews are not perpetually cursed.

And of course Pilate is guilty as well; St. Matthew does not exculpate him but rather presents him as a coward, like the Herod who had John the Baptist executed (Matt 14:1–12). Pilate declares Jesus innocent (*dikaios*) but sends him to his excruciating doom anyway. In the matter of the crucifixion of Jesus, Jew and Gentile conspire together to murder the Son of God.

The Sacrificial Death of Jesus

In St. Matthew's Gospel, Jesus dies alone, forsaken by man and God. There is no penitent thief (that's in St. Luke's version, Luke 23:39–43) and no presence of Mary and St. John the Apostle (that's in St. John's version, John 19:25–27). Rather, in St. Matthew's version, everyone mocks Jesus, from the chief priests to the two robbers crucified with him, even though they share the same fate (Matt 27:38–44). And then the sky darkens (27:45), indicating Jesus is being cut off from the heavens and thus God, and Jesus utters his cry of dereliction in the words of Psalm 22:1: "My God, my God, why hast thou forsaken me?" (Matt 27:46). However, Jesus is misunderstood, as the bystanders think the *Eloi* ("My God") is a call for Elijah (27:47–49). It's ironic, for John the Baptist is actually Elijah come again (17:9–13). And so Jesus dies (27:50), alone, cut off from man and God, misunderstood.

But now the cosmos awakes again, as natural and personal apocalyptic phenomena occur: "And behold, the curtain of the temple was torn in two, from top to bottom; and the earth shook, and the rocks were split; the tombs also were opened, and many bodies of the saints who had fallen asleep were raised, and coming out of the tombs after his resurrection they went into the holy city and appeared to many" (27:51–53). Jesus Christ's claims are here vindicated by the One who controls the cosmos, who raises even the dead, God the Father. And so even the execution detail is moved to faith: "When the centurion and those who were with him, keeping watch over Jesus, saw the earthquake and what took place, they were filled with awe, and said, 'Truly this was the Son of God!'" (27:54).

The tearing of the temple curtain is significant. Most understand it to signify that Jesus's death now gives us direct access to God, as if we can now stride into the Holy of Holies, thanks to Jesus's sacrifice, and approach God directly. But in the world of St. Matthew's story, the direction is opposite. God the Father is abandoning the sanctuary in recompense for the murder of his Son. Jesus dies; God flees. And so the temple will be left unprotected when the Romans level it forty years later.[5]

---

[5] Those skeptical of this reading should consider the witness of extrabiblical Jewish texts in circulation in St. Matthew's day. In them, the tearing of the curtain is a sign of the temple's coming destruction. In *2 Baruch* 6:7–9, the earth swallows the temple veil and the sacred vessels before the temple is trampled, and in *Lives of the Prophets* 12.12, the rending of the veil is associated with the temple's destruction. See Catherine Sider Hamilton, "'His Blood Be upon Us': Innocent Blood and the Death of Jesus in Matthew," *Catholic Biblical Quarterly* 70 (2008): 82–100, at 97. The Jewish historian Josephus (who himself fought for the Jews as a commander during the Roman siege of Jerusalem, and then was captured but spared thanks to his significant talents) evinces this idea as well. In *Ant.* 3.202–203, he states that God dwells in the sanctuary of the temple. Josephus also records gruesome violence occurring in the vicinity of the temple and the temple itself in passages such as *War* 4.151 and 4.313. In his view, such actions defiled Jerusalem and her temple:

[T]he whole city was a scene of dejection, and among the moderates there was not one who was not racked with the thought that he would personally have to suffer for the rebels' crime. For, to add to its heinousness, the massacre took place on the sabbath. (*War* 2.455–456 [in *The Jewish War*, LCL 203, at 1:501])

[G]lutted with the wrongs which they [the "brigands"] had done to men, they transferred their insolence to the Deity and with polluted feet invaded the sanctuary. (*War* 4.150 [in *The Jewish War*, LCL 487, at 2:201])
As a result, God abandons the temple and sides with the Romans:

My belief, therefore, is that the Deity has fled from the holy places and taken His stand on the side of those with whom you are now at war. (*War* 5.412 [in *The Jewish War*, LCL 210, at 3:133])

The Meaning of the Cross

What, then, is the meaning of the Cross? It shows not only
God's love for us, in sending himself in the person of his Son
to die for us, but it also shows us the depths of our sin. The
crucifixion was required to solve our problem, and so our
problem must be severe.

If I may be permitted some personal reflections to
examine this concept: Holy Saturday is a difficult day to keep
holy. Some parishes mark it with Morning Prayer from the
Liturgy of the Hours, but most don't do anything, which is
certainly appropriate; Jesus Christ is liturgically dead. And
so I've taken to my own observances. Some years ago after the
Good Friday communion liturgy, my wife and I watched *The
Passion of the Christ*, and on Holy Saturday we kept things
low-key while listening to Bach's *Matthäus-Passion* and
Johannes-Passion, as well as Mozart's and Verdi's Requiems.

But life goes on. Our young kids can't help but play, sometimes cooperating, sometimes protesting in shrill tones about
some grave injustice the other has perpetrated by encroaching
on (say) a Thomas the Tank Engine track layout. My mother

Moreover, at the feast which is called Pentecost, the priests on entering the
inner court of the temple by night, as their custom was in the discharge
of their ministrations, reported that they were conscious, first of a com-
motion and a din, and after that of a voice as of a host, "We are departing
hence." (*War* 6.300 [in *The Jewish War*, LCL 210, at 3:265])

They [the "brigands"] committed these murders not only in other parts
of the city but even in some cases in the temple; for there too they made
bold to slaughter their victims, for they did not regard even this as a des-
ecration. This is the reason why, in my opinion, even God Himself, for
loathing of their impiety, turned away from our city and, because He
deemed the temple to be no longer a clean dwelling place for him, brought
the Romans upon us and purification by fire upon the city. (*Ant.* 20.166,
in *The Jewish Antiquities, Book 20*, trans. Louis H. Feldman, LCL 456
[Cambridge, MA: Harvard University Press, 1965], 9:91)

hosts Easter dinner, and so we prepare some food for that. And for many people, even those who will be in Easter Sunday services, Holy Saturday is another Saturday filled with shopping, yardwork, recreation, and the like.

However, Holy Saturday started to hit me differently a few years ago. I suspect it had to do with three major events occurring within a period of several months. First, I turned 35, which meant my life was half over (as I'd count myself blessed to make it to seventy); I began to feel life was now downhill. Second, our son Hans was born, and as parents know, having children entails epistemological paradigm shifts: we see the world differently. Third, just a few weeks after Hans's birth, I buried my father. And so I came to the existential realization that life was short and moving ever faster and that we play for keeps.

Sensitive now to the fragility of human life and the grave responsibilities laid upon us by God and nature, and newly alive to the joys and terrors of life in this beautiful and horrible world as a member of a glorious and murderous race, Holy Saturday punched me in the gut.

They killed him. They really did.

Many Christians in modernity, I think, have a conception of the crucifixion restricted to a legal version of penal substitutionary atonement: Our problem is the *guilt* of sin, for which God must punish us, but loving us and desiring to forgive us, God punishes Christ in our place.

True enough as far as it goes, perhaps, but when compared to classical conceptions of salvation—whether Orthodox, Catholic, or Protestant—it doesn't go very far. For it leaves the horror of the human condition outside of us, as this model concerns merely our legal status, and thus leaves no remedy for the wretched realities ruining us within. It deals with guilt, but not the root of our guilt, our sin, original and actual.

What about sin as a condition within us, in our very natures? What about the four traditional enemies of Sin, Death, Hell, and the Devil, those hypostasized forces which animate mortal and demonic violence against us, often from within us?

Sin, Death, Hell, and the Devil afflict us from within and without. Our problem isn't only God's posture of wrath toward us, thanks to our guilt, which can seem far away, terrible as it is. Our problem is that we and the World are both fallen and afflicted, evil within, evil without.

The Cross isn't just a component in the economy of our salvation, something God needed to do to Christ to acquit us, to declare us innocent when we are in fact guilty. It also reveals the stance of the human race toward God, which runs from indifference to hatred. They killed him: God comes into the World in Jesus Christ, and Jew and Gentile conspire to cooperate in killing God for reasons of convenience. The World stands guilty of deicide.

And so on Holy Saturday I generally feel sick to my stomach. The one man who could have helped us we hammered to a Cross. This means two things: deep down, I'm capable of murder, and I'm liable to being murdered. I am Cain and I am Abel. We mustn't deceive ourselves about our capacity for sin, and violent sin, and that capacity in others.

Most people have a *theologia gloriae*, a theology of glory in which we bypass the Cross as we affirm ourselves as we are and affirm God for affirming us as if he waits for our approval in a circle of Moral Therapeutic Deist bilge. True theology, as even Martin Luther so rightly and so often stressed, is a *theologia crucis*, a theology of the Cross, in which God's murderers are saved by God through the very instrument of his murder. Our salvation cannot consist of self-improvement; our salvation consists of our own crucifixion by sharing in Christ's.

God doesn't affirm us; God saves us. But not yet, not today, on Holy Saturday. Tomorrow, Easter Sunday. For now, we killed him. *Kyrie eleison.*

MATTHEW 28:1–10: EASTER VIGIL / OPTION FOR EASTER SUNDAY RESURRECTION OF THE LORD

Our culpability in the Cross is not the final word. Forgiveness and new life is, because crucifixion is not the final word; resurrection is. In fact, resurrection completes our salvation, as we need to share in Jesus's risen life if that life is to be given to our mortal bodies (see Rom 8:11).

St. Matthew's version of the discovery of the empty tomb is marked by apocalyptic phenomena, as was his version of the crucifixion. Mary Magdalene and the "other" Mary (probably the mother of James and Joseph, Matt 27:56 and also 61) approach the tomb, but the angel of the Lord has already rolled away the stone by means of an earthquake (28:2). The angel remains, and he is terrifying, described in 28:3 as appearing "like lightning" with "raiment white as snow." This is how beings from heaven are often described. The guards more or less pass out from fear (28:4); but the women are told to have no fear, and the angel then announces to them that the Christ whom they seek is not there but has risen and goes ahead of them to Galilee (28:5–7). Now what is crucial here is the angelic invitation to the women to make sure they tell the disciples that Jesus is in fact risen and will meet them where it all began, in Galilee. These are the same disciples who apostatized in Gethsemane and in the person of Peter denied Jesus. And yet they're invited to begin again, to return to Galilee and once more take up the way of discipleship.

With fear and joy to do so, the women depart, and then

they encounter Jesus himself (Matt 28:9a). They hold his feet and worship (*proskuneō*) him (28:9b), which implies in Greek a posture of kneeling or prostration in reverent worship. They do exactly what the Magi did in 2:11: they kneel or even prostrate in worship when encountering the Risen Lord. There is a lesson for Catholics here, for we, too, encounter the Risen Lord in the Eucharist, and the proper posture would be kneeling.[6] Jesus then repeats the angel's instructions and sends the women to tell "my brethren" to meet him in Galilee (28:10). He is declaring that the disciples are restored in spite of everything.

The resurrection is many things. At the very least, it's the vindication of Jesus. Jew and Gentile condemned him, but God raised him from the dead, overturning their unjust verdict. It is also a bodily phenomenon: it is not Jesus's soul or spirit going to heaven, but his very body risen and transformed. The empty tomb is the Gospel's way of reminding readers that resurrection means bodily resurrection, not the simple Platonic, Gnostic immortality of the soul.

It is furthermore the inbreaking of the new creation: darkness reigned and the heavens shook at the crucifixion, but now it is early the first day of the new week (Sunday) and the sun has risen at dawn (Matt 28:1). Creation has gone from darkness to light; a new age has dawned with the resurrection of the Christ. His body, the body of the second Adam, is made from the material stuff of creation just like the body of the

---

6 Congregation for Divine Worship and the Discipline of the Sacraments, *Redemptionis Sacramentum* (March 25 2004), §§90–92 (issued *in forma specifica* by Francis Cardinal Arinze, then-prefect of the Congregation), guarantees Catholics the right to receive the Eucharist on the tongue while kneeling. See also the *General Institution of the Roman Missal*, 160, which states the norm for reception of the Eucharist in the United States is standing, unless an individual wishes to receive kneeling, and which cites *Redemptionis Sacramentum*, 91.

first Adam (Gen 2:7). And so as we are bodies born in sin and death in Adam, the resurrection of Christ's body is necessary for our salvation, as we need to share in Jesus Christ's risen flesh through faith and sacrament to achieve our own future resurrection, and even experience that resurrection life here and now (see Rom 6).

MATTHEW 28:8–15: MONDAY WITHIN THE OCTAVE OF EASTER

As the women depart and go to tell the disciples what the angel and Jesus himself told them, the tomb remains empty. St. Matthew relates the cover-up for the "scandal" of the empty tomb: the chief priests, we are told, paid the soldiers to spread the lie that the disciples stole the body by night (Matt 28:13). Here too as in the crucifixion Jew and Gentile conspire together, this time to thwart the mission of the Church in spreading its resurrection message. And the reader must note how twisted this little passage presents both the Jewish leadership and the Roman soldiers, representative of Gentiles: both would rather have falsehood reign than concede the truth, the very truth that would set them free.

The idea that the disciples stole the body is thus the most ancient attempt to explain what really happened to Jesus, and it has had its modern defenders. Yet, as Christian apologists point out, the theory is ultimately absurd, because it is a fact of history that the disciples did not profit from their proclamation of the gospel message of Jesus's resurrection but rather suffered and died horrible deaths for it. Conspiracies are hard to maintain, and it is most unlikely that the disciples would have maintained a conspiracy for some decades and then died horrible deaths for the sake of a lie.[7]

MATTHEW 28:16–20: THE ASCENSION OF THE LORD

Now we come to the Great Commission. The eleven remaining disciples will have heeded the women's words, for they go to Galilee and meet Jesus on a mountain (Matt 28:16). The omission of Judas reminds us of the finality of the sin of despair; the other disciples are forgiven, but now no forgiveness for Judas is possible (if it ever were, given the gravity and foreordination of his crime). The disciples worship Jesus as did the women, but they also doubted (the Greek implies all, not just some, doubted: *kai idontes auton prosekunēsan, hoi de edistasan*). I think the sense here isn't straight-up doubt, but rather a sense of joyous disbelief at something obviously so true—there's Jesus himself in the risen flesh—but also something seemingly so impossible. So St. Matthew here isn't denigrating the disciples, but rather reinforcing the wonder provoked by the power of the resurrection.

Jesus then equates himself with God, declaring he has all authority in the cosmos, heaven and earth (Matt 28:18). Because of that, the disciples are compelled to make disciples of "all nations" (28:19a). There is thus a parallel: As the risen Jesus is established as Lord of all heaven and earth, he is Lord of all nations, and now all nations must be made aware of that fact and receive their true Lord as Lord; they will have to lay down their gods and embrace the truth of Jesus the Christ in the community of the Church.

---

[7] For arguments supporting the resurrection as a historical fact with contemporary significance, see N. T. Wright, *Surprised by Hope: Rethinking Heaven, the Resurrection, and the Mission of the Church* (New York: HarperOne, 2018), 53–78.

The disciples are to baptize converts from among the nations in the Trinitarian name (Matt 28:19b), implying again Jesus himself is not only sent by God or come from God but indeed is God himself, as incorporation into Christ incorporates one into the totality of the three-personal God. And important for understanding the import of St. Matthew's particular story is Jesus's command that the disciples are to teach them "to observe all that I have commanded you" (28:20a). First, submitting to baptism means taking on the responsibility of living according to the teaching of the Lord, into which one is baptized. Second, the command concerns Jesus's own teaching, not Moses's; he is the new Moses who brings the New Law, just as Moses brought the Old Law. Third, the command is an invitation to the reader to reread the Gospel again from the beginning, for what Jesus commands is found in the very Gospel of Matthew prior to its ending here. And doing so the reader now reads the Gospel of Matthew through the lens of the death and resurrection of Jesus the Christ, just as Christians read the Old Testament through the lens of the crucified and risen Christ. St. Matthew's Gospel then takes on new meanings once a reader reads it with the end of the story in mind: the altar in the temple becomes the altar of numberless Catholic churches; we become the disciples (in many but not all respects); mentions of bread become foreshadowings of the Eucharist.

Finally, Jesus's closing words now look not backward to the Gospel of Matthew, transformed into a deeper Christian key, but forward to the enduring age of the Church that will close with the end of the world. The "age" Jesus mentions (Matt 28:20b) is the new age of the kingdom of God, proclaimed and made present by the Church in her activities and existence. And the promise of Jesus to be with the disciples and thus the Church "always" (28:20a) is the very thing which makes following his very commands possible, since he is present with us, transforming us, as we cooperate with divine grace.

✠ FINIS ✠

III. Resources for Further Study

The following resources are recommended for those wanting to go deeper into the issues of the cultural situation in contemporary America and into St. Matthew's Gospel. Many of these resources, especially the essays and articles, are technical and academic, though general readers committed to knowing the Gospel more deeply would certainly profit by reading them.

On Gnosticism, Moral Therapeutic Deism, and Therapeutic Culture

Rieff, Phillip. *Triumph of the Therapeutic: Uses of Faith After Freud*. Wilmington, DE: Intercollegiate Studies Institute, 2006.

> *Originally published in 1966, Rieff explains how American culture became "therapeutic"—that is, a society in which feelings and desire reign supreme over reason and tradition.*

Smith, Christian. *Young Catholic America: Emerging Adults In, Out Of, and Gone From the Church*. New York: Oxford University Press, 2014.

> *Catholic sociologist Christian Smith reports on his longitudinal research into the declining involvement of young Catholics in the Church.*

Smith, Christian, and Melissa Lundquist Denton. *Soul Searching: The Religious and Spiritual Lives of American Teenagers*. New York: Oxford University Press, 2005.

Smith and Lundquist Denton examine what young people actually believe and find it to be what they coined as "Moral Therapeutic Deism," in which God is somewhat remote but wants people to be generally good to each other and have us feel happy.

Weaver, Richard M. *Ideas Have Consequences.* Chicago, IL: University of Chicago Press, 2014.

Originally published in 1948, Weaver argues that the relativism rising in the West was causing its deep decline, and that the relativism and therapeutic approach operative in the twentieth century had roots in William of Occam's nominalism of the fourteenth century. Nominalism is the doctrine that there are no real metaphysical, universal Things—like (for example) Man or Woman or Marriage or Horseness or Chairness—but rather that there are only words we use by convention to refer to things in the realm of experience that happen to look like each other. With that, the stage was set for the ability of those who control language to redefine reality, since there is no ultimate reality to which our words truly correspond. The idea of nominalism led to the consequence of relativism.

COMMENTARIES ON ST. MATTHEW'S GOSPEL

Davies, W. D., and Dale C. Allison, Jr. *A Critical and Exegetical Commentary on the Gospel According to Saint Matthew.* 3 vols. International Critical Commentary. Edinburgh: T&T Clark, 1988–1997.

The most important historical-critical commentary in the English language.

Hauerwas, Stanley. *Matthew.* Brazos Theological Commentary on the Bible. Grand Rapids, MI: Brazos, 2006.

Written by the man TIME magazine named "America's Best Theologian" in 2001, Hauerwas provides an efficient book on the storyline of St. Matthew's Gospel, full of theological insights that critical commentaries ignore.

Mitch, Curtis, and Edward Sri. *The Gospel of Matthew.* Catholic Commentary on Sacred Scripture 2. Grand Rapids, MI: Baker Academic, 2010.

Mitch and Sri provide an accessible commentary on St. Matthew's Gospel in full accord with Catholic teaching, which preachers and laypeople would do very well to read.

Wright, N. T. *Matthew for Everyone.* 2 vols. Louisville, KY: Westminster John Knox Press, 2004.

> *Wright is arguably the world's leading English-speaking biblical scholar. An Anglican bishop, Wright's scholarship is quite friendly to Catholic concerns, to the point that some conservative evangelicals are concerned reading Wright's work and accepting his conclusions are a gateway to becoming Catholic. These books are truly popular and yet substantive, and so are great resources for preachers as well as laypeople.*

MONOGRAPHS / BOOKS ON PARTICULAR ISSUES AND THEMES IN ST. MATTHEW'S GOSPEL

Kingsbury, Jack Dean. *Matthew: Structure, Christology, Kingdom.* Minneapolis, MN: Augsburg, 1991.

> *Kingsbury provides an alternative outline of St. Matthew's Gospel focusing on transition points in Matthew 4:17 and 16:21, instead of seeing it ordered around Jesus's five great discourses. He thus divides the Gospel into three main parts, and his outline works best for reading the Gospel as the story it in fact is.*

Longenecker, Fr. Dwight. *Mystery of the Magi: The Quest to Identify the Three Wise Men.* Washington, DC: Regnery History, 2017.

> *Fr. Longenecker dives deep into history and finds that the Magi were indeed real, historical figures (contrary*

to much critical scholarship) and identifies them as Nabatean Arabs who served in the court of the king at ancient Petra (in present-day Jordan).

ESSAYS AND ARTICLES ON PARTICULAR ISSUES AND THEMES IN ST. MATTHEW'S GOSPEL

Dahl, Nils. "The Passion Narrative in Matthew." In *The Interpretation of Matthew*, 42–55. Edited by Graham Stanton. Edinburgh: T&T Clark, 1995.

Dahl presents seminal, unique insights into the narrative dynamics and theology of St. Matthew's account of Jesus's suffering, death, and resurrection.

Fletcher-Louis, Crispin H. T. "The Destruction of the Temple and the Relativization of the Old Covenant: Mark 13:31 and Matthew 5:18." In *Eschatology in Bible & Theology: Evangelical Essays at the Dawn of a New Millennium*, 145–169. Edited by K. Brower and M. Elliot. Downers Grove, IL: InterVarsity, 1997.

Fletcher-Louis finds that Jesus did not so much predict the end of the world in his lifetime (problematic in that we are now almost two thousand years past his lifetime) as he predicted the destruction of the temple a generation after his lifetime.

Donald Senior, "The Lure of the Formula Quotations: Re-Assessing Matthew's Use of the Old Testament with the

Passion Narrative as a Test Case." In *The Scriptures in the Gospels*, 89–115. Edited by Christopher M. Tuckett. Leuven: Leuven University Press, 1997.

Senior expands our horizons to see the multifold, interesting ways St. Matthew appropriates the Old Testament in his Gospel to present Jesus as the fulfillment of many Old Testament figures and stories.